Christ Church

D1631396

FROM
IBRARY

# Socialism, the State and Public Policy in France

Edited by
Philip G. Cerny and Martin A. Schain

Frances Pinter (Publishers), London

© Philip G. Cerny and Martin A. Schain 1985

First published in Great Britain in 1985 by
Frances Pinter (Publishers) Limited
25 Floral Street, London WC2E 9DS

**British Library Cataloguing in Publication Data**
Cerny, Philip G.
    Socialism, the state, and public policy in France.
    1. Socialism—France
    I. Title    II. Schain, Martin A.
    335′.00944    HX266

ISBN 0-86187-384-X  Hb.
       0-86187-547-8   Pbk.

Typeset by Folio Photosetting, Bristol
Printed in Great Britain by SRP Ltd., Exeter

# Contents

List of Contributors                                                                     v

Introduction *Philip G. Cerny and Martin A. Schain*                                      1

## I: POLITICS AND POLICIES OF LEFT PARTIES

1   Socialism, Power and Party Politics *Philip G. Cerny*                                13

2   The French Communist Party: Historic Retard, Historic
    Compromise, Historic Decline — or New Departure?
    *Mark Kesselman*                                                                     42

3   Conditional Support for Communist Local Governments in
    France: Alienation and Coalition-Building *Martin A. Schain*                         60

4   Socialism in One Country: Mitterrand and the Struggle to
    Define a New Economic Policy for France *Peter A. Hall*                              81

5   Defence Policy Under François Mitterrand: Atlanticism,
    Gaullism or 'Nuclear Neutralism'? *Jolyon Howorth*                                  108

## II: THE LEFT AND THE STATE

6   The Socialist Elite, 'les Gros,' and the State *Pierre
    Birnbaum*                                                                           129

7   'L'Alternance' and the Higher Civil Service *Anne Stevens*                          143

8   The Tranquil Revolution at Clochemerle: Socialist
    Decentralization in France *Mark Kesselman*                                         166

9   Decentralizing or Recentralizing the State? Urban Planning
    and Centre–Periphery Relations *Irene B. Wilson*                                    186

## III: STRUCTURAL CONSTRAINTS AND POLICY
##      ARENAS

10  State Capitalism in France and Britain and the International
    Economic Order *Philip G. Cerny*                                                    202

11  Politics and Mass Mobilization: Relations Between the
    CGT and the CFDT *Martin A. Schain*                                                 224

12  Socialism and the Farmers *Sally Sokoloff*                                          245

13  Corporatist Decentralization and Commercial Moderniza-
    tion in France: The Royer Law's Impact on Shopkeepers,
    Supermarkets and the State *John T.S. Keeler*                                       265

Index                                                                                   292

# List of Contributors

MARTIN A. SCHAIN is Associate Professor and Director of Graduate Studies in the Department of Politics, New York University. He is the author of *French Communism and Local Power: Urban Politics and Political Change* (Frances Pinter and St. Martin's Press, 1985) co-author of *European Society and Politics* (West, 2nd edn. 1976) and co-editor of *French Politics and Public Policy* (with Philip G. Cerny) (Frances Pinter, St. Martin's Press and Methuen University Paperbacks, 1980). He is currently writing *Issues in European Politics: The Decline of the Welfare State in Europe* (Prentice-Hall), which was first presented as a 45-part credit course on CBS Television in 1982.

PHILIP G. CERNY is Lecturer in Politics at the University of York (England), and has been a visiting professor at Harvard University and Dartmouth College. He is the author of *The Politics of Grandeur: Ideological Aspects of de Gaulle's Foreign Policy* (Cambridge University Press, 1980; paperback edition, Frances Pinter, 1984), co-editor of *French Politics and Public Policy* (with Martin A. Schain) and *Elites in France: Origins, Reproduction and Power* (with Jolyon Howorth) (Frances Pinter and St. Martin's Press, 1981); and editor of *Social Movements and Protest in France* (Frances Pinter and St. Martin's Press, 1982). He is currently writing *The State: An Introduction to Comparative and International Politics* and editing a collective study of *The French State in the 1980s*.

MARK KESSELMAN is Professor of Political Science at Columbia University. He is the author of *The Ambiguous Consensus: A Study of Local Government in France* (Knopf, 1967) and editor of *The French Workers' Movement* (Allen and Unwin, 1984). He has written extensively on French local politics, the French Communist Party and problems of Marxist ideology and politics in France. He was also a contributor to Cerny and Schain, *French Politics and Public Policy*.

PETER A. HALL is Assistant Professor of Government and Research Associate at the Center for European Studies, Harvard University. He has written extensively on the problems of economic policy planning and the state in France and Britain. His doctoral dissertation on the politics of financial policy in Britain received the Harvard University Samuel Beer award in 1983 and is currently being revised for publication.

JOLYON HOWORTH is Senior Lecturer in French History in the Department of Modern Languages, University of Aston in Birmingham (England). He is the author of *Edouard Vaillant et la création de l'unité socialiste en France*

(EDI/Syros, 1982), and co-editor of *Elites in France: Origins, Reproduction and Power* (with Philip G. Cerny) and *Defence and Dissent in Contemporary France* (Croom Helm, 1984). He is working on a history of the French left since 1870.

PIERRE BIRNBAUM is Professor of Political Science at the University of Paris I (Sorbonne), and has been a visiting professor at Nuffield College, Oxford University, and the New School for Social Research. He has authored many works on political sociology and, in particular, on French elites and the state, including: *The Heights of Power* (University of Chicago Press, 1983), *La Classe dirigeante française* (Presses Universitaires de France, 1978), *Le Peuple et les gros: histoire d'un mythe* (Grasset, 1979) and *La Logique de l'État* (Fayard, 1982).

ANNE STEVENS is Lecturer in Contemporary European Studies (Politics) at the University of Sussex (England). She has written numerous articles on public administration in France and Britain, among which is a contribution to Cerny and Schain, *French Politics and Public Policy*.

IRENE B. WILSON is Senior Lecturer in Town and Regional Planning in the Faculty of Environmental Studies, University of Dundee (Scotland), and is also a professional planner. She is a member of the Royal Town Planning Institute and the International Society of City and Regional Planners, as well as an Associate in BK Parnell and Associates (Chartered Town Planners). She has written extensively on French and British planning, particularly on the development of New Towns.

SALLY SOKOLOFF is Lecturer in Contemporary History and Politics at the University of Salford (England). She has written several articles on French rural history and politics, among which is a contribution to Cerny and Schain, *French Politics and Public Policy*.

JOHN T.S. KEELER is Assistant Professor of Political Science at the University of Washington, where he also chairs the West European Studies Committee at the Henry M. Jackson School of International Studies. His publications include contributions to J. Ambler, ed, *The French Socialist Experiment* (1984); S. Cohen and P. Gourevitch, eds, *France in the Troubled World Economy* (1982); S. Berger, ed, *Organizing Interests in Western Europe* (1981); and W. Andrews and S. Hoffmann, eds, *The Fifth Republic at Twenty* (1981). He is currently completing a book entitled *The Politics of Neo-Corporatism in France: Farmers, the State and Agricultural Policymaking in the Fifth Republic* and undertaking research on 'Supermarkets, Shopkeepers and the State: The Politics of Controlling Commercial Development in France and Britain'.

# Introduction

Just over three years ago, in May 1981, the Socialist and Communist left formed a government for the first time in French history. With a Socialist President, a clear majority in the National Assembly (elected in June), and control of two-thirds of the larger cities in the country, the French left appeared to be in the strongest political position in its long and complex development. Only the marginally important Senate was still controlled by the parties of the right. Now, as we go to press, the Socialist leadership, buffeted by many pressures but determined to continue with its controversial austerity policy) adopted in 1982–3), has formed a government on its own, with the Communist Party refusing to participate, with a new Prime Minister, Laurent Fabius, at 37 the youngest French head of government in the twentieth century, and with President Mitterrand seeking to reaffirm his mandate by calling a national referendum on civil liberties. None the less, with Communists still considering themselves a part of the 'majority' of the left,' and with the Socialists and their close allies still with a clear parliamentary majority for the next two years, the left still controls the decision-making institutions of the French state.

Clearly, this control gave the left an unprecedented opportunity to implement the main lines of a program which it had debated and developed during the more than two decades of opposition to the Gaullist Republic. Although the Common Program of the Left, adopted in 1972, accepted the institutions of the Fifth Republic, it linked strong commitments to social and economic justice with modifications to and the reorganization of state power. In general, the left argued that, as Mark Kesselman points out, it would not merely augment, but also rationalize, state power to make it into a more effective instrument with which to bring about social justice and more efficient economic management (see Chapter 8). The nationalization of certain major industries (and the part of the banking system not already in the public sector) and the decentralization of the state, taken together, were therefore intended to complement each other in a more effective process of economic planning, reinforced by a more just balance of social forces (exemplified by the Auroux Laws and educational reform) which would, in turn, permit a more just distribution of wealth and income.

François Mitterrand has linked the elements of social justice in socialism to the power of the presidency and the rationalization of the state. 'For Valéry Giscard d'Estaing the presidency is a point of arrival,' he wrote in 1974. 'For me it is a point of departure . . . If I am elected, I will change the course of things, and therefore the life of my contemporaries.'[1] The essential problem, Mitterrand wrote in 1976, is the distribution of profits, 'and with it the distribution of power. Neither profit nor power must be reserved for a small number to the detriment of all.' Distribution is a prerogative of the nation using the tools of the state, and the state must use 'democratic planning as the framework within which the industrial apparatus is made to serve the national interest.' It is in this context that nationalization is important. 'For us, nationalization is a tool, and it has no meaning if not taken in conjunction with a definite and coherent industrial policy.'[2] Thus, the rationalized state can use the tools at its command for both economic expansion and a more just distribution of profits and power. The role of the socialist state is to liberate true 'free enterprise' from the constraints of overbearing capitalism:

it is incorrect to maintain that capitalism and free enterprise are identical ... Do you really believe that a small and dynamic firm could grow and survive without eventually becoming dependent on private industrial or banking groups? The barriers to expansion put up by large-scale private interests are insurmountable nowadays.[3]

The promise of socialism, then, is also the promise of the more rational and the more effective state.

The development of the modern state, however, has always been inextricably intertwined with that of the capitalist economy. The state was central to the sweeping away of the web of patrimonial and ascriptive relationships of the feudal economy and the providing of a legal framework based on contract. It often acted as the midwife of economic change through the procurement of war materials, the provision and regulation of infra-structure, communications and transportation, the gaining of access to raw materials, the widening of markets, the protection of infant industries, the provision of direct or indirect subsidies for production, control of the labor supply, and much more — even in its phase of so-called '*laissez-faire.*' And it has also been a producer in its own right, from the state monopolies of seventeenth century *colbertisme*, through a range of defense industries and public works, to the nationalized industries of the twentieth century. As the world economy — and the 'national' economies of the nation-state system — has grown in both size and complexity, so have the tasks, roles and activities of the state.

These tasks, roles and activities have varied enormously from country to country, depending upon differences in economic structure, political leadership and ideology, and upon the rhythm of historical events and longer-term processes of change. Generally speaking, however, 'state intervention in the economy' — something of a misnomer for a complex process of interaction — has sought to pursue, at one and the same time, two potentially contradictory goals. The first has been to favor the creation of national wealth through promotion of and support for private capital and the efficient market allocation of resources. And the second has been to counteract the social imbalances and cyclical crises created by capitalism, by regulating its abuses, smoothing out market imperfections which threaten the maintenance of the system, providing for the production of crucial goods and services which are inherently unprofitable, and establishing a 'welfare safety net' — either out of humanitarianism or out of fear of revolution — for those groups deprived of the system's benefits.[4]

Thus the modern state and the capitalist economy are bound together not merely in terms of their everyday activities, but also in that deeper structure which provides for their legitimacy and links them with the cultural values of 'industrial society.' Nowhere is this clearer than in the political process and public life of the advanced capitalist liberal democracies — the competition of political parties and political elites for the support of the voters for election to formal public office. Indeed, the central political cleavage of capitalist industrial societies, the one which impinges most strongly upon the political consciousness of both the mass of voters and the elites who make up and influence the decision-making processes of the state, is that which turns on the questions of more or less overt 'state intervention in the economy.'[5] At the same time, however, it would seem to be an underlying assumption of capitalist political culture that such state intervention, whether couched in terms of production (economic growth, demand management, supply-side interventionism) or distribution (welfare, social justice) is only partially legitimate. At best it is seen as a potentially disruptive tinkering with 'natural' market forces.[6] At worst, it is denounced as a threat to the economic freedom upon which political freedom (democracy) is alleged to depend.[7] The key political problem of the advanced capitalist democracies, then, is that while state intervention in economic life is broadly accepted for pragmatic reasons, it is generally seen as a *necessary evil*, and there is widespread disagreement about the objects and purposes of intervention. And the denser the pattern of intervention, the greater the paradox appears.

In this context, the winning of power in capitalist democracies by 'socialist' parties has classically raised a number of problems for political analysts. The most obvious is the traditional image of socialism as being an alternative to capitalism, true to its sources in nineteenth-century ideology. Despite the dominance of reformist social democracy among European socialists since the turn of the century, reinforced by the bitter split with Soviet Bolshevism after the Russian Revolution and embodied in Keynesian class collaboration after the Second World War (see Chapter 1), even the French Socialists in the 1970s spoke of an eventual 'rupture' with capitalism. Thus the rhetoric reinforced the impression that state intervention does not support capitalism but attacks it. Secondly, conservative and centrist parties present their policies as either reinforcing the status quo or providing change through the spontaneous mechanisms of the market — as in former French President Valéry Giscard d'Estaing's 1974 campaign slogan, 'change without risk.' Socialist parties generally present programs based on innovative, rather than merely reactive, state intervention. This means that the state must experiment with new, or at least ostensibly new, tasks, roles and activities, and these may require a capacity on the part of the state institutions for creative policy-making, adaptability, and what has been called 'steering' or forward-looking, co-ordination (including economic planning). However, state institutions may not have been designed to carry out these tasks efficiently — and existing patterns and practices of bargaining, decision-making and policy imple-mentation may be disrupted. Thus the structures of the state have to deal with a heavier 'political load,' potentially leading to unintended consequences and opportunity costs as well as a heavier investment of time, energy and resources in changing the state structures themselves rather than channeling that investment directly and efficiently into the economy. Such investment by the French Socialists in 1981–2, in the process of nationalization, blunted the economic thrust of that major innovative measure (see Chapter 4). While conservative parties can often benefit from inertia, socialist parties when they come to power are expected to 'do things' — and their detours, failures and conjunctural *bricolage* are judged by the public (and the opposition) by the standards of their campaign objectives rather than for their pragmatism.

Finally, socialist parties generally owe their election in large part to groups in society which benefit least from the capitalist economy. This is the traditional source of socialist inspiration and the mass base of electoral support. However, not only do such groups often define their own interests and objectives in conflicting ways (skilled vs. unskilled, employed vs. unemployed, blue-collar vs. white-collar, etc.), but they also are not in and of themselves sufficiently large to form an electoral majority in advanced industrial society. The majority comes from either winning the allegiance of new constituencies — e.g., the 'new middle class' — or temporarily attracting 'floating voters' whose main motive is often dissatisfaction with the performance of non-socialist parties in power rather than any belief that the socialist program is particularly good or workable (see Chapter 8). Thus a socialist party in power, in catering to its working-class base, may lose the marginal support on which its majority was put together in the previous election; alternatively, if it caters to its marginal supporters, it may create dissatisfaction among its 'own.' In the former case, it will lose the next election; in the latter case, the result may be strike and protest activity, party splits, and voter abstentionism or desertion. Although it may be thought that poor and working-class voters have 'nowhere to go', working-class support for de Gaulle in the 1960s or for Margaret Thatcher in Britain in 1979 and 1983 was crucial to right-wing electoral victories. The role of the French Communist Party (see Chapter 2) and the workerist and syndicalist traditions of the French trade-union movement (see Chapter 11) are potential constraints. Of course, this problem, easily enough papered over in times of economic growth, becomes crucial in the increasingly 'zero-sum' conditions of economic recession and structural economic conversion (see Chapter 10).

These problems faced by socialist parties in power are cross-cut by the fact, all too often blurred in the public rhetoric of contemporary politics in advanced industrial societies, that different aspects of state intervention in the economy may conflict in ways which can seriously undermine the balancing act which socialist parties attempt to perform. The primary conflict is that between the two ways in which the state interacts with the economy, often referred to as the 'consumption function' and the 'production function' of the state. The first refers to those tasks, roles and activities which concern the distribution, regulation and redistribution of *existing* resources by the state — whether those resources pass through the state directly (transfer payments, etc.) or are distributed according to authoritative actions by the state (minimum wage laws, environmental controls, etc.). The second refers to those tasks, roles and activities of the state which concern the production of *new* resources — whether through distribution/redistribution by the state (subsidies to firms, research and development expenditure, etc.), the authoritative regulation of private productive activities (fiscal and monetary policies, antitrust legislation or support for industrial concentration, trade policy, etc.), or direct state ownership and control of production (nationalized industry, some public services, etc.).

Of course, many public policies may cut across these two categories. Fiscal policy that emphasizes broad tax cuts across the higher tax brackets and selective tax cuts such as investment tax credits are meant to redistribute potentially taxable revenue from the mass of taxpayers (generally middle-class or working-class) to the already wealthier sections of society which are thought to have the greatest surplus income to divert from their private consumption into new investment, thereby increasing production. This is the core of what has been called 'supply-side policy' in the United States in the 1980s. However, that phrase has been criticized as a misnomer, since there is no guarantee that such a surplus will actually go into productive investment rather than into private consumption or money markets, and also since very different policies (state subsidies, nationalization, etc.) can also be referred to as 'supply-side' — *state* supply-side policy as distinct from 'private' or 'market' supply-side policy.

Inversely, the 'welfare state' is often connected with Keynesian 'demand management.' In this case, redistribution of income and resources from the mass of taxpayers to the *worse*-off, by increasing the buying power of the latter, is intended to increase demand for goods sufficiently to ensure a profitable return on investment, thereby attracting a continuing flow of private investment into production to meet that demand — and thereby also maintaining full employment, further maintaining demand. Here, too, however, effects can be counterproductive, especially if demand fuels inflation rather than new production. Historically, the capacity of socialist parties to gain legitimacy as 'parties of government' in the long period of economic growth and prosperity in the West from the late 1940s to 1973 depended upon their ability to strike a Keynesian/welfare-state bargain between the working class and the business community based on continuing economic growth.[8] However, in the 1970s, such Keynesian policies were blamed for inflation and its counterproductive consequences, causing a crisis in many of the European social democratic parties, especially in Britain and West Germany. In France, the situation was somewhat different (see Chapter 1).

As will be obvious from these two examples, the relationship between the production function and the consumption function of state intervention is highly problematic. The first problem is that to have a comprehensive policy approach which effectively integrates the two functions may imply the attaining of a high enough level of overall state control to trigger a number of counterproductive opportunity costs and side-effects already alluded to here. It may stretch the structural capacities of the state to the point where broad structural reforms, with all of their unpredictable consequences, become necessary. It may lead to first building up state capacities and then dismantling them as electoral fortunes change — e.g., the cycle of nationalization, denationalization, and renationalization of industries. Or it may create such resistances from interest groups and socio-economic categories that concessions undermine reforms.

The French Socialists' attempt to reform the structures of the state through decentralization has evoked controversy over the relationship between promise and performance, a controversy which is reflected in Chapters 8 and 9. Party splits within the PS (Parti Socialiste) over the pace and content of economic policy, increasingly vocal threats from the neo-Gaullist and neo-Giscardian right of a reversal of policy if they win the 1986 legislative elections (including pledges of denationalization), and the tension between the PS and their erstwhile coalition partners, the Communists, have all increased political pressure on the Government's attempts to reconcile the two functions (see Chapters 1–4). Social pressure has come from a growing range of groups and socio-economic categories reacting to complex government initiatives: the business community and other elites (see Chapter 6); small business and farmers (Chapters 12 and 13); and, as jobs are increasingly cut back in declining areas of the public sector in 1984, the once-quiescent unions are beginning to raise their voices (Chapter 11). But the Socialist Party's vital control of the presidency and the National Assembly (Chapter 1), its ability to make foreign and defense policy (Chapter 5), and its somewhat more problematic control over the bureaucracy (Chapter 7) and over much of local government despite the disapointing results of the March 1983 local elections

(Chapter 3), provide it with political resources with which to govern at least until the 1986 parliamentary elections, which is as it should be in a democracy.

The second problem concerns the constraints of the economic conjuncture. The easiest way to reconcile production and consumption functions in economic policy is to have an 'expanding pie' — increasing profits for the private sector, rising standards of living for the wage and salary earners, and sufficient tax revenues to finance public services, public sector investment, infrastructure and the welfare state. Economic growth increases crucial state and private resources and permits a variety of policy lines to be pursued simultaneously. But recession reduces the profitability of the private sector, creates unemployment and downward pressure on real wage levels, and causes a 'fiscal crisis of the state.' Thus the state, faced with existing obligations, a stagnant private sector, and international market forces which are very difficult to control, must seek to do more with less. This problem faces conservative regimes as well as socialist ones (see Chapter 10), but it affects the latter more because of the heavier policy 'load' that their programs call for as well as the interrelated questions of gaining and maintaining support.

The third problem concerns the web of ongoing linkages between state and society which characterize the advanced capitalist epoch. The behavioral paradigm of the 'political system' popularized in the 1950s and 1960s — the heyday of consensual Keynesianism — stressed the 'inputs' from society into the state and the policy 'outputs' of the state, but tended to neglect the 'withinputs' of social processes within the state itself. More recent studies which have focused on the welfare state and on 'corporatism' (or 'neo-corporatism')[9] have helped remind analysts that the structure of the state itself is not a neutral factor, not merely a field in which the relative balance of actors' pre-existing resources is weighed and outputs produced, but rather a structured field of action, which gives weight to certain resources and 'selects out' others. The state not only makes, but can often bend and break, its own rules. Around this structured field develop continuing state/society linkages or circuits of power. These circuits can be formal or informal, and can exist at many levels.

Within this context, the politics of the welfare state has tended to involve activities clustered around the state's consumption function. This is because the welfare state has developed by increasingly including in its policy perspective wider and wider categories of social groups that have exerted influence through the electoral process and through widespread protest movements at certain times in history. The advanced capitalist state had developed broad legitimacy by maintaining a certain level of 'fairness' through transfer payments and other forms of redistribution of the fruits of capitalist wealth-creation. Mass political parties have tended to define their public differences in terms of the distribution or redistribution of pre-existing resources created by the private sector or the 'mixed economy' (with the private sector still as the 'locomotive' but the public sector maintaining the tracks.)

At the same time, however, capitalist states have always participated in the production process, generally in an *ad hoc* or reactive fashion, and through an overlapping set of corporatist state/society linkages. Corporatism has tended to emerge on the dark side of the state, out of the public limelight. Its most public manifestation was in the fascist corporatism of Mussolini's Italy,

Franco's Spain, Dollfuss's Austria, prototypes of a range of regimes which were based on repression and which did little to provide the concept with a respectable image. None the less, it did develop a democratic variant (hence Schmitter's use of the term 'neo-corporatism'), based on the 'incorporation', through regular, formalized or semi-formalized, consultative processes between the major 'interests' of capitalist society — big business, finance and labour — and the state itself, along with, to varying degrees, other interests such as agriculture, small business, and even religious and educational bodies which still see themselves as heirs of medieval *corps*.

Although corporatist relations overlap with the consumption function, much as the welfare state overlaps with the production function, they are particularly significant as a structural framework or forum within which decisions which affect production can be negotiated, alternative policy measures canvassed for their acceptability or unacceptability, and bargains struck along lines which would be more problematic in a more public or democratically accountable arena. This was true, for example, for the early French planning process in the middle and late 1940s, when the traditional parliamentary stalemate was being re-established under the Fourth Republic. The Commissariat au Plan worked away in its relatively independent corner of the state, extensively consulting all of the main economic interests, and using its own funds — mainly derived from the Marshall Plan — to escape the stifling oversight of the Finance Ministry. It has been true also in so far as it has led to what Peter Lange has called 'consensual wage regulation', i.e. wage restraint agreed and enforced by the trade unions themselves, in a number of Western countries at times of economic downturn. Finally, it has been true in the development of 'industrial policy' since the end of the long boom in 1973. Through the corporatist process, the state has sought not only policy solutions to pressing problems, but also a stable process of policy development that effectively integrates powerful private groups into public policy-making.

Although socialists have traditionally been concerned with consumption-oriented welfare-state policies, control and coordination of the key instruments of production through the state — nationalization and socialist planning — have become an essential prerequisite for more just consumption policies. Moreover, when capital is scarce, the state, legitimizing its actions through traditional socialist rhetoric, can also use planning and nationalization to redirect capital into productive channels, sometimes even at the expense of certain groups of workers who may be asked to delay or forfeit the rising standard of living which they hoped a socialist electoral victory would bring.

For socialists, as well as for parties of the right, the capacity to pursue a policy mix of this type — what Michel Rocard has called 'socialist rigor' — depends on their ability to maintain control over three kinds of related linkages: state–elite linkages; elite–elite linkages; and elite–mass linkages. Both the left and the right have different capacities to do this. For example, the strongest corporatist links for the right are generally with business and finance, while the left is more strongly linked with trade unions and other mass organizations. Moreover, governments of the left are generally less inclined than governments of the right to act simply as good brokers among powerful private interests, and are more strongly committed to using corporatist linkages as a tool of change and as elements in the planning process. Thus, the key political problem for the right is generally to maintain order among those groups allied with the left, while tilting their policy preferences towards their natural allies; the problem for a government of the left is to maintain a reservoir of support among private producers, without whom economic planning is difficult if not impossible in a capitalist system, while generating sufficient consumption benefits to maintain the support of the mass membership groups with which they are politically allied.

In this context, the chapters in this book indicate that the Government of the left that assumed power in France in 1981 confronted some very special problems. Previous patterns of state–elite relations had virtually excluded trade-union elites, while elites of producer groups either had developed close, collaborative relations (the CNPF or employers' federation) or good working relations (the CGPME and CID–UNATI representing different small and medium business sectors, and the FNSEA, the farmers' union) with the governments of the right during the Fifth Republic (see Chapters 12 and 13). The strong corporatist relations that had grown among these elites during the first twenty-three years of the Fifth Republic had become the established pattern of policy development, and were an important element in the maintenance of public order. Moreover, corporatist collaboration had served to strengthen and institutionalize the links between the leaders of these groups and their mass following.[10]

Socialist policy and policy-making directly disturbed these existing relationships. At the same time, the Socialist Government attempted to reorder and even reconstruct the pattern of corporatist collaboration. Nationalizations and tax policy undermined relations with both big and small business, while the Government made some heavy-handed attempts to reorient privileged relations among agricultural groups. At the same time, the Government collaborated more closely with the large trade-union confederations, and promoted policies that would augment their influence and stability in the labor relations balance. Understandably, the Socialist–Communist coalition Government attempted to develop a pattern of corporatist collaboration that would be different from that of the Government they replaced. They hoped to bring about change by challenging the pattern of collaboration among producer groups, and to maintain support and social order by augmenting the power of groups formerly excluded from the corporatist process.

The rapid breakdown of this experiment is related not only to the constraints of the economic *conjoncture*, which in the end left little room for maneuver, but also to the nature of the groups that the Government challenged and those from which they sought support. Before mid-1983, the Government successively challenged the producer groups that had benefited from the institutionalized strength which they had gained under the previous system. Their organizations were strong, and they were capable of using the politics of the streets to challenge the Government, much as the unions had attempted to do during crucial periods when the right was in power. Thus groups with the strongest links with their mass base have been excluded or alienated from the policy-making process, and have been in deep conflict with the state.

On the other hand, trade-union elites, who have been most closely associated with the Socialist experiment, have always had weak links with their mass base, and these links have been growing progressively weaker since 1976 (se Chapter 11). The shift in government policy to 'socialist rigor' after 1983 has also weakened the links of collaboration between the state and trade-union leaders, and unions, with their leaders hurrying quickly behind them, have also begun to challenge the Government in the streets. Thus, midway through the term of the Government of the left, corporatist collaboration appeared to have broken down almost entirely. The old process could no longer serve as a basis for either policy formulation or the maintenance of public order, while the Government has failed to develop a new process that would serve a similar purpose, at least in the short run.

In the longer run, the Government hoped that 'more democratic' coordination and collaboration would develop through some of the new institutions that had been established during its years in office. Thus, the Auroux Laws have mandated an obligation for employers to bargain collectively, and have reinforced the rights and the role of union organizations in the bargaining process. By strengthening the role of unions, the Government anticipated a more general strengthening of an 'active contractual policy' (Chapter 11). The Auroux Laws were meant to encourage workers, through their unions, 'to become the actors of change in the enterprise,' but also to encourage unions to become important actors in the development of industrial policy and industrial order.

Coordination would also be strengthened by prudent use of nationalized industries as the primary tools of economic and policy planning, as well as the arenas of bargaining and collaboration with unions. As a hub of a system of planning, the role of the nationalized industrial enterprises would be substantially different from their role under governments of the right. Finally, as Mark Kesselman points out, decentralization would strengthen, rather than diminish, the capacity of the state to control and coordinate. By directing a plethora of demands to more powerful and democratic *local* governments, decentralization would permit the state to concentrate 'on the primary challenges of developing overall regulatory mechanisms, arbitrating among social classes, and strengthening France's productive apparatus to compete better in international markets' (Kesselman, Chapter 8). Reforms in the state apparatus of economic planning and regional development have been designed to reinforce these changes.

In the short run, however, democratic coordination and collaboration is not yet a reality. The trade-union movement has found it difficult to exploit its new rights as its mass base (and therefore its ability to coordinate mass action) continues to diminish, and as austerity exacerbates industrial conflict, particularly in the public sector. As Peter Hall notes, planning has not become a guiding force behind economic policy, and the nationalized industries, hindered by heavy losses in the most recent world downturn (especially in 1982), have been used more as funnels for investment than as agents for coordination or arenas of collaboration. Finally, decentralization has not yet freed the state from a plethora of demands or the influence of internal vested interests. As Mark Kesselman has argued, decentralization has actually accentuated the politicization of local government, and, indeed, may actually increase the range of demands for state intervention, while, as Irene Wilson points out, at the same time reducing its capacity to respond efficiently and fairly to those demands.

The net result of the breakdown of the old system of collaboration and coordination established over twenty-three years by the right, and of the left's failure thus far to develop a new pattern of state/society linkage structures, has increased the scope of demands and the range of conflicts in the political arena. Stanley Hoffmann referred to the 'ungodly spectacle' of the politics of the streets in the early years of the Fifth Republic, and we are again experiencing an upsurge of this pattern.[11] In both cases the politics of the streets reflect the difficulty that the French state has in managing socio-economic conflict. In the early period the prime challenge came from groups linked to the left, while more recently the challenge has been from the right. In both cases, however, extraparliamentary activity has provided an outlet for groups that feel that they have been excluded from the normal political processes. In this sense, the National Front of Jean-Marie Le Pen, which had such success in the recent European elections, is as much (and perhaps more) of a challenge to the parliamentary right as it is to the government of the left. Nevertheless, we should not underestimate the resilience of state institutions which have resisted not only the challenges of the early years of the Fifth Republic, but also the Events of May 1968.[12] The powerful executive has created a direct link with the mass electorate which has enabled it to maneuver over the heads of powerful interest and protest groups, and Mitterrand's recent announcement of his intention to hold a referendum on civil liberties is a particularly salient example of this most *gaullien* of characteristics of the French state.

The eruption of protests and demonstrations, the losses of the Socialists (and, even more dramatically, the Communists) in the European Assembly elections of 17 June 1984 (along with Le Pen's unexpectedly strong showing), the increasing severity of the Government's industrial policy in the first half of 1984, and, finally, the recent changes in the Government and the withdrawal of the Communist ministers, have underlined the significance of the more formal institutional arrangements of the Gaullist Republic in maintaining both policy-making and public order. Party discipline in the National Assembly (especially on confidence votes), government control of the parliamentary timetable and other procedural weapons, the significance of the Government's autonomous powers of 'regulation', the heightened role of interministerial councils and committees, the acceptance by ministers of governmental solidarity (ministerial responsibility), and the predominance of the President of the Republic in matters of *arbitrage*, policy leadership and public accountability (highlighted in the recent referendum decision and the appointment of Mitterrand's closest personal adviser for many years, Fabius, as Prime Minister) — all of these constitutional devices have been crucial in confronting the challenges of the past three years. And no doubt they will become even more important in the period leading up to the parliamentary elections of 1986 and the presidential elections of 1988, now that the Communists have left the Government, the trade unions have sharpened their opposition to austerity, the Socialist leadership seeks to make a comeback from a position of widespread unpopularity, and the right, scenting victory in 1986 and wishing to regain those voters who switched to Le Pen, becomes more determined to obstruct the left's policies. Of the *gaullien* repertoire, only Article 16 (emergency powers) remains unused as yet.

Thus for François Mitterrand, the presidency has been neither a point of arrival nor a point of departure. A series of promising first steps have been undermined by the situation of the international economy, the disparate nature of the Socialist Party and the left coalition, and the problems of managing a heavy and complex 'innovative load' on the state apparatus. What sort of new balance the Fabius Government will strike is as yet unclear, although early signs indicate an intensification of the attempts to trade off a highly active industrial policy with fiscal benefits and incentives to both workers and industry (rather than increased transfer payments or 'social gains' such as shorter hours or longer vacations). With the balance of payments moving towards a surplus in 1985, the Social Security system (health, pensions, etc.) back in the black, the nationalized firms in the 'competitive sector' either having become profitable in 1983 or rapidly moving in that direction, those in the 'non-competitive sector' (declining industries like coal, steel and shipbuilding, which have eaten the lion's share of government assistance) being ruthlessly rationalized, and inflation moving steadily downward, the Socialist government is not without advantages. None the less, the dramatic rise in unemployment in 1984, which may reach 3 million in 1985, will hit the left where it hurts the most — in the electorate. No issue has been more important in the elections of 1983 and 1984 in alienating both floating and marginal voters. The fate of the Callaghan Government in Britain in 1979 is indicative of the problems of 'socialist rigor' — with the Labour Party subsequently going through a phase of 'socialist rigor mortis' through the elections of June 1983. The key to the Socialists' success in France will lie in their ability to pursue a sufficiently vigorous industrial policy, to create a revival to rival its austerity. There is a long way to go.

*PHILIP G. CERNY*
*MARTIN A. SCHAIN*
Hanover, N.H., and New York
24 July 1984

NOTES

1.  François Mitterrand, *The Wheat and the Chaff* (New York: Seaver, 1982), p. 128.
2.  Ibid., pp. 209–14.
3.  Ibid., p. 212.
4.  See Theodore J. Lowi, *The End of Liberalism* (New York: Norton, 1969).
5.  The question of covert or *de facto* state intervention is far more complex, but tends to be submerged by the terms of the public debate as generally accepted by both sides. See Jonathan R.T. Hughes, *The Governmental Habit* (New York: Basic Books, 1977).
6.  Traditionally, the forms of state intervention most acceptable to the right might include protection against import penetration, the provision of infrastructure (highways, water, etc.) for the use of private enterprise, currency stabilization, military protection of economic activities (trade routes, colonial undertakings, etc.), export guarantees, subsidies, etc. They are intended to counteract factors which hinder private capital accumulation.
7.  See Friedrich A. Hayek, *The Road to Serfdom* (London: Routledge & Kegan Paul, 1944).
8.  See Michel Beaud, *Le socialisme à l'épreuve de l'histoire, 1800–1981* (Paris: Seuil, 1983).
9.  See Philippe Schmitter and Gerhard Lembruch, eds, *Trends Towards Corporatist Intermediation* (London and Beverly Hills: Sage, 1979), and Douglas E. Ashford, *British Dogmatism and French Pragmatism: Central–Local Policymaking in the Welfare State* (London and Winchester, Mass.: Allen & Unwin, 1982).
10. This argument is quite different from the one developed by Frank Wilson. Wilson has presented a case for French exceptionalism, arguing that France is 'a near classic case of interest group pluralism', where links between the state and interest group elites are extremely weak, and where the state has played the role of the good broker, standing above squabbling of interest group interaction. Clearly, this is not our reading of the role of the state in France, and the relationship between the state and interest group elites. See the

following articles by Frank Wilson: 'Alternative Models of Interest Intermediation: The Case of France', *British Journal of Political Science*, **12** (April 1982); 'Les Groupes d'intérêt sous la Cinquième République: Test de trois modèles théoriques de l'interaction entre groupes et gouvernement', *Revue Française de Science Politique*, **33**, (April 1983); 'French Interest Group Politics: Pluralist or Neocorporatist?' *American Political Science Review*, **77**, No. 4 (December 1983). John Keeler has developed a perspective closer to our own in his forthcoming study, *The Politics of Neocorporatism in France: Farmers, the State and Agricultural Policymaking in the Fifth Republic*.

11. Stanley Hoffmann, 'Paradoxes of the French Political Community', in Hoffmann *et al.*, eds. *In Search of France* (Cambridge, Mass.: Harvard University Press, 1963), p. 94.
12. P.G. Cerny, 'The Fall of Two Presidents and Extraparliamentary Opposition: France and the United States in 1968', *Government and Opposition*, **5**, No. 3 (Summer 1970), pp. 287–306.

# I POLITICS AND POLICIES OF LEFT PARTIES

## 1 Socialism, Power, and Party Politics

*Philip G. Cerny*

The French Socialist Party (PS) came to power in 1981, with its leader, François Mitterrand, winning the second ballot run-off in the race for the Presidency of the Republic on 10 May — he polled 51.75 percent of the votes to incumbent Valéry Giscard d'Estaing's 48.24 — and its parliamentary candidates winning 266 seats, a solid majority in the 491-member National Assembly, in the subsequent legislative elections on 14 and 21 June.[1] Indeed, with the fourteen Left Radicals (MRG) and some others elected in direct alliance with the PS, the Socialist parliamentary group had 285 seats, or just marginally fewer than the Gaullists had won in the landslide election of 1968; and the Communist Party (PCF), although it saw its representation drop from eighty-six seats to forty-four (many of which had been lost to the Socialists), was immediately invited to form a coalition government (with four Communist ministers out of a total of forty-four). Thus the first Government of Socialist Prime Minister Pierre Mauroy could count on the support of 329 Deputies, just over two-thirds of the total. Although a handful of seats have been lost in by-elections since that time, and although the Government has undergone major changes in structure and personnel — most notably the very recent reshuffle of July 1984, in which Laurent Fabius replaced Pierre Mauroy as Prime Minister and the Communists declined to participate (though announcing their intention to remain in the 'majority of the left') — the underlying balance of power has hardly changed in three years. If anything, reshuffles of March 1983 and July 1984 further concentrated control of government policy in the hands of the President and the Prime Minister. And despite growing conflict over policy between the PS and PCF, the parliamentary troops demonstrated their continuity at 2.30 a.m. on the morning of 20 April 1984, when they voted in favor of the last Mauroy Government's 'general declaration of policy' by 329 votes to 156.[2]

This striking continuity of the majority and solidity of the Government appears in sharp contrast to the image of internal dissension, social conflict, and the unpopularity of the Socialist Party and its leaders as measured by opinion polls three years on. Sections of the right have even attempted to deny the legitimacy of the Government. A variety of social groups, some not generally allied with the left, like farmers, doctors, small businessmen, truck drivers and parents of children in Catholic schools, and some representing an anti-left backlash among normally pro-left categories, such as teachers, professors, lower- and middle-ranking civil servants, students and manual workers in declining industries, have taken to the streets in mass demonstrations and engaged in disruptive economic action ranging from the traditional and symbolic one-day general strike to the blockage of many of the country's main highways by truck drivers during a two-week protest which escalated from a relatively tangential grievance in February 1984. Not only did the Communist Party begin strongly to criticize government austerity policies during 1983 and 1984, but the trade unions, especially the Communist-linked *Confédération Générale du Travail* (CGT) — of which the Mauroy Government was long solicitous in its search for neo-corporatist labor discipline — have been at the center of protests over the new wave of unemployment in traditional industries since November 1983. And within the PS itself the return of Jean-Pierre Chevènement and Pierre Joxe to the Government (both are former Ministers of Industry) is an attempt to reduce growing internal dissension within party elites as well as the rank-and-file. After all, their voters did not vote for the left in order that workers should continue to lose their jobs and that they be subjected to increasing austerity.

The *climat politique* and the *climat social*, then, are in marked contrast to the realities of power as shaped by the electoral systems and institutional arrangements of the Fifth Republic.[3] The center of this power structure is, of course, the office of President of the Republic. François Mitterrand has developed a presidential style which has totally submerged his early and strong opposition to the powers of the presidency — seen then as merely the extension of *le pouvoir personnel* of General de Gaulle. Now, he admits, the office suits him very well. And his ability to use national-interest rhetoric and foreign policy symbolism to counteract the domestic *malaise* of the post-honeymoon period has been rather effective,[4] although he is no de Gaulle. More imortant have been, firstly, his ability to construct a majoritarian Socialist Party and a coalition with the Communists *on his own terms* in the 1970s and to see them continue as a party and coalition *of government*, and, secondly, his success at controlling the inner politics of the executive and the policy process, a success which has been growing since the middle of 1982. His personal assumption of political responsibility for the direction of policy — and of the need for sacrifices in the longer-term national interest (specifically in reference to the continuing and sharp contraction in the steel industry) — was never clearer than in his press conference of 4 April 1984.[5] The effectiveness of the Socialist Party as a majoritarian party, and the ability of the President and the Government to control policy, will be the main foci of this article.[6] Whether that cohesion and control will prove sufficient to stave off the defeat which most commentators currently believe to be inevitable in the forthcoming parliamentary elections in June 1986 will be at the core of our concerns, and will be explicitly addressed at the end.

## I. A MAJORITY PARTY AND A PARTY OF GOVERNMENT

The trajectory of the Socialist Party from being a casualty of the demise of the Fourth Republic towards its current position as a stable majority party has been characterized by two main sorts of changes. In the first place, the party has established its strength and credibility as a competitor in the structured field of action which we call a party system; in other words, it has had to become effective in its interaction with the other parties in the system. Here the essential problematic lies in the fact that in countries like France, Italy, Spain, Greece, or Japan, it must compete on two fronts. It must maintain sufficient credibility as a party of the center–left to be able to attract potential 'floating voters' from parties of the center and center–right. At the same time, however, it has had to compete for a different kind of 'floating voter', the one who for a variety of reasons (protest, left-wing idealism, etc.) had been prone to vote for the Communist Party — which throughout the Fourth Republic had been the largest party in France, generally winning about a quarter of the votes — but who was not a die-hard PCF loyalist. One crucial category, cutting across both of these 'fronts,' has been the member of the 'new working class,' possibly from a provincial city or a conservative rural background, newly proletarianized, and employed in the expanding industries of the 'long boom' which France, like the rest of the capitalist world, experienced from around 1950 to the mid-1970s.[7] And in the second place, it had to develop a sufficiently coherent program — especially in the context of the 1970s and 1980s — both to keep the internal factions of the party reasonably united and to make credible its two-front electoral strategy. Here the PS could neither fit the mould of the large social democratic parties of Germany, Britain, Sweden or Austria, nor resign itself (given the Fifth Republic electoral and institutional systems) to the role of a small swing party like the Italian Socialist Party — or even like its forerunner, the SFIO, under the Fourth Republic. The proof of this particular pudding has involved two courses — the rebuilding period (1969–81) and the experience of government since that time. Let us trace the development of the Socialist Party's strength and policy orientation across these years.

## The Socialist Party and the Party System

The Socialist Party as it exists today is in crucial ways the creation of François Mitterrand. The old SFIO (the 'French Section of the Workers' International' — the Second International — founded in 1905, but also known colloquially as the *parti socialiste*) had not been able to mount an effective two-front strategy after the failure of the Popular Front in the 1930s and the deepening of the Cold War in 1947. It clearly chose a centrist strategy — called the Third Force — at the latter date, shunning the PCF (as all the other parties did, too) by refusing to count even the Communists' favorable votes in their coalition calculations. The SFIO fully entered into the game of unstable coalition governments during the Fourth Republic (1946–58), with regular conflicts erupting between its more left-wing rank-and-file and its parliamentary leaders and their tactical priorities[8] — although it was the Socialist Prime Minister, Guy Mollet, who headed the longest-lasting Fourth Republic government through eighteen months in 1956–7 at the height of the Algerian War. The party was divided on the question of whether or not to go along with de Gaulle and support the Fifth Republic constitution. After 1958, however, it became more implacably opposed to both the new republic and its president, leading the '*cartel des non*' in the referendum of October 1962 on the election of the President of the Republic by universal suffrage, and making limited electoral agreements with the PCF in the November parliamentary elections of that year. Electorally, the party wavered between a left-wing, 'popular front' strategy (especially as the PCF was beginning to liberalize as the result of changes in the Soviet line under Khrushchev), and an attempt to ally with the Catholic centrist MRP (Popular Republican Movement). With a presidential election coming up for the first time (the first time by universal suffrage, that is) in late 1965, however, the leaders once again opted for the center alliance with the right-wing Socialist Gaston Defferre as the prospective presidential candidate around whom the coalition would form. But the alliance faltered by late 1964 because of the traditional issues which had always divided the SFIO and the MRP — church schools and the municipalization of building land. With the collapse of the Defferre option, the SFIO seemed without a strategy.

François Mitterrand was not a socialist and not a member of the SFIO. A moderate Catholic intellectual, he came of age politically during the Second World War in the Resistance movement, and in the spirit of the Liberation period, when a new consensus seemed to unite France, bringing together Socialists, Communists, Catholics and liberal-minded conservatives, Mitterrand and the even more moderate Catholic René Pleven founded a new small party, the UDSR (Democratic and Social Union of the Resistance), in the hope of capturing this spirit and preventing the old parties from redividing. The experiment failed, although Mitterrand and Pleven remained in the National Assembly through judicious electoral alliances, and Mitterrand held ministerial posts in the Fourth Republic eleven times. What set him off from the SFIO, however, and from much of the rest of the center–left political class, was his conviction that in the long run the broad left would only be viable in France if it were able somehow to reintegrate the Communist Party into the coalition-building system. When de Gaulle was maneuvring in May 1958 to return to power following the *coup d'état* in Algiers, Mitterrand was maneuvring to find a viable alternative government of the left, based on a coalition agreement between the PCF and the various non-Communist left and center–left parties, both to forestall de Gaulle's return (he later referred to the Fifth Republic as the 'permanent *coup d'état*') and to pursue his own vision of left-wing unity.[9] Nearly seven years later, when the Defferre option failed, Mitterrand was ready to fill the gap.

Mitterrand's success at making himself the 'single candidate of the left' depended upon two crucial factors. In the first place, he was not himself a member of any of the major left or center–left parties. Therefore he did not have to get involved in the internal politics of any of the parties, and neither did the parties *qua* parties need to negotiate with each other. Either they endorsed Mitterrand, or they didn't. And given the failure of the Defferre option and the lack of another alternative, with the election drawing ever closer in mid-1965, neither the SFIO nor the smaller but still influential Radical Party was in a position to quibble. In the second place, the Communist Party, whose candidate had been the only substantial opposition to de Gaulle in the 1958 presidential election (based on an electoral college of parliamentarians and town councillors), was at an even more serious stage in its transition from cold war party to pluralistic competition. Its long-term pro-Soviet leader, Maurice Thorez, had died in 1964, and the party, along with other Western communist parties, was beginning its serious search to revive 'popular front'-type coalitions and to seek greater democratic legitimacy, going beyond parliamentary negativism and toward governmental collabo-ration. The PCF did not wish to present a separate candidate, and went along with Mitterrand all the more easily because he was, as we have already noted, outside the other left-wing parties. The PCF threw its machine enthusias-tically into Mitterrand's campaign, the first step towards its rehabilitation and new respectability.

Mitterrand's further — relative — success in the December election (32 percent of the vote on the first ballot to de Gaulle's 44; 45 percent in the run-off to de Gaulle's 55) seemed to spell the end of the centrist option for the

SFIO. He was now the acknowledged leader of the opposition, although centrist candidate Jean Lecanuet (with 16 percent of the first-ballot vote) tried to revive the badly eroded center group. A *cabinet fantôme* (shadow cabinet) of Socialists, Radicals and other left parties (but not including the Communists) was presented with much fanfare to the press, and the SFIO and Radicals were more formally joined together in the FGDS (Federation of the Democratic and Social Left —'social' being a more moderate catchword, acceptable to much of the center, than 'socialist') with Mitterrand at its head. An electoral alliance was concluded with the PCF for the upcoming 1967 parliamentary elections — the first of a regular series of electoral pacts providing for the withdrawal of all but the best-placed left-wing candidate (in terms of first-ballot votes) in each constituency before the second ballot. Indeed, this alliance succeeded in reducing the combined right-wing majority in the National Assembly (Gaullists plus Giscardian Independent Republicans) from thirty-five seats to just one. In early 1968, a vague but still pathbreaking 'common platform' was agreed upon between the FGDS and the Communists and the future direction seemed clear. A *malaise* was said to be sweeping the country, as the Government of Prime Minister Georges Pompidou pushed through special decree powers to reform (or cut back) the welfare system and the main issue in the National Assembly seemed to be whether the state television monopoly should allow commercial advertising.[10] The parliamentary left was itching to expand, but the next parliamentary and presidential elections seemed far away in 1972.

The *malaise*, however, soon turned into unexpected and uncontainable revolt, and the left was caught up in a whirlwind which it could not ride. The Events of May 1968, starting with a student revolt in Paris and leading to a long general strike, sucked in a reluctant Communist Party to support the movement as the working class joined the strike, and the FGDS creaked at the seams, with Mitterrand himself injudiciously announcing that he would be available to head a transition government. When de Gaulle and Pompidou eventually defeated the strike movement by calling parliamentary elections, the left was swamped in the right-wing backlash despite the strict maintenance of the electoral pact. The FGDS bcame a dead letter, while the SFIO revived the centrist option under the urging of Pierre Mauroy. The main casualty seemed to be Mitterrand and his vision of left-wing unity as the path to power. The decline continued in 1969, as de Gaulle's referendum proposals were defeated in April primarily because of the defection of the center–right (making a centrist strategy seem all the more credible to the left), and as the main opposition to Pompidou in the June presidential election (after de Gaulle's resignation) came from the centrist candidate Alain Poher. On the first ballot, Pompidou duplicated de Gaulle's 44 percent, while Poher received 23 percent, much of it from SFIO voters. The Communists put up a candidate, Jacques Duclos, who received 21 percent, while Defferre, standing as an SFIO candidate, received only 5.5 percent. Mitterrand was not a candidate, and was concentrating on reinforcing his own small power base, a network of moderate socialist clubs called the Convention of Republican Institutions (CIR). After the election, though, the centrist option looked with hindsight to have been self-defeating. With part of the center–right supporting Pompidou, and the Communists abstaining, Poher was easily swept aside in the second ballot (58 percent to 42 percent), clearly showing the limits of even a popular centrist candidate in the French electoral system.

Thus the stage was set for major surgery and a surprisingly rapid recovery. In 1969, the SFIO dissolved itself and re-formed as the PS, generally referred to at the time as the 'New Socialist Party,' led by Alain Savary (recently Mauroy's Minister of Education), and looking for ways to revive the left-unity option. By 1971, at the watershed Épinay Congress, a dominant new alliance had emerged, composed of the new groups and aspiring younger leaders within the PS who had for either strategic or programmatic reasons assimilated Mitterrand's goals in the 1960s, along with outside groups which were merged with the party, including the CIR. Mitterrand was elected First Secretary of the Socialist Party. Within a year, a 'Common Program of Government' had been negotiated with the PCF (and, somewhat more reluctantly, the MRG — the left wing of the now-split Radical Party) with a view to the upcoming 1973 parliamentary elections. In late 1972, opinion polls showed the coalition of the left to be capable of winning a majority. That the left lost that election was due to a number of factors, including the efficient tactical cohesion of the right behind Pompidou's presidential leadership and the fear of some centrist floating voters that the PCF, which was still the largest party in the left coalition (measured by percentage of votes), would dominate a left-wing government. The loss exacerbated tension between the PS and the PCF — the former seeking to attract those very floating voters in the center in order to win an overall majority, and the latter fearful of losing its position as the largest left party and thus its major source of influence on the policy decisions of any government of the left. Pompidou's death in April 1974 and the sudden presidential election in May highlighted several of the trends, both conflicting and converging, which characterized the first few years of the post-de Gaulle party system. The first was the final split of the center between left and right, a split which was solemnized by the relative eclipse of the Gaullists and the victory of their center–right allies behind the new president, Valéry Giscard d'Estaing. The second was the total dominance of Mitterrand as the left's presidential candidate. The second ballot was a classic left–right duel, aimed at the floating voters in the center, and the margin of victory was narrow.

Mitterrand's revived credibility as a presidential candidate demonstrated the dependency of the Communist Party at the level of presidential elections upon the rapidly growing PS. Mitterrand had ignored the PCF's attempts to influence his campaign and program, though welcoming the vital support of the Communist Party organization and voters. The PS further extended its reach at the Pau Congress in 1974, when most of the leadership of the small intellectual–radical Unified Socialist Party (PSU), led by Michel Rocard (currently Fabius's Minister of Agriculture), joined. By the time of the cantonal (county council) elections of 1976, the Socialist Party was by far the largest electoral party in France, with around 30 percent of the votes. But Communist dissatisfaction was rising rapidly, as the party began to wonder if it had not made too many concessions in the name of left-wing unity, Eurocommunism, and *détente*. These discontents were obscured by the sweeping victories of joint left-wing lists, especially in the medium-sized and larger towns and cities, in the municipal elections of March 1977. This new latent majority seemed set to advance to the national level in the upcoming parliamentary elections of March 1978. But the Common Program of the Left, signed in 1972, had only been a five-year pact. The attempt to renew it, in the context of the PCF's relative decline, led to an attempt by the Communists to use the negotiations to ensure greater Communist input into the way a left-wing government would interpret and implement Common Program-based policies. And the breakdown of these negotiations in September 1977, which was a major factor in the left's loss of the 1978 elections, provided a graphic illustration of the sting in the tail of Mitterrand's long-term vision of left-wing unity.

For Mitterrand's embrace of the Communist Party had always had the quality of a bear hug. He regarded the PCF as having prevented the growth of an effective left-wing force in France after its emergence in 1920, and especially during the Fourth Republic. By pulling it into an alliance with a revived and expanding non-Communist left alliance or party, such as the FGDS might have become or the PS had become after 1971, he hoped in the long run both to control it and to reduce it to relative political marginality. With the expansion of the PS in the 1970s, he decided in 1977 that he could afford to resist Communist interpretations and demands at the renegotiating table. And indeed, 1978 may not have seemed so strategically critical. If the left had won, it would have faced constitutionally tricky relations between a left government and President Giscard d'Estaing. Mitterrand was doubtless looking to the 1981 presidential elections, which failure *in* government might have foreclosed. But the 1978 loss merely exacerbated the debate within the PCF, with much of the rank-and-file — who had joined the party in the 1970s in the hopes of furthering left-wing unity — and the intellectual, Euro-communist faction within the party blaming the leadership for the loss. At the same time, the leadership moved to increase its control of the apparatus and to switch at least partially from an 'electoral strategy' to a 'membership strategy,'[11] reaffirming its working-class roots while attempting to attract more white-collar and technical workers.[12] Although the 1978 loss also created tensions within the Socialist Party, with Rocard and Mauroy attempting to outmaneuver Mitterrand at the 1979 Metz Congress and pushing him into a tactical alliance with Chevènement's more left-wing CERES faction (Center for Socialist Studies, Research and Education) and with Rocard hoping to run for president himself, Mitterrand never lost control of either the party apparatus or the center ground within the range of party factions. When he announced his candidacy for president in the autumn of 1980, the Socialist Party united behind him.

The heart of Mitterrand's strategy had long been one of presidentialism. He was aware that the power of the presidency, allied to control of a majority party, could give the bear the strength to keep the PCF in its embrace, and his experiences between 1965 and 1969 had concentrated that understanding. Only under a strong Socialist president could the left strategy finally succeed, for only then would the Communist Party be faced with the stark choice of participating in the Government as a junior partner with little influence on the general direction of policy, on the one hand, or of *not* participating in (or leaving) the Government, and being perceived by its less die-hard supporters as marginal and impotent, withdrawn to a shrinking ghetto, on the other. In the 1981 presidential election, Mitterrand again ran his campaign on his own program — the 110 Propositions — and not on the official party program, the *Projet socialiste*, which had been drawn up in collaboration with CERES in 1979–80. He presented himself as the *force tranquille* — calm strength — in contrast to the increasingly arrogant style of Giscard d'Estaing,[13] the populist campaign of the neo-Gaullist Jacques Chirac (whom Giscard had referred to in April 1979 as *un agité*),[14] and the rather strident justificatory tone of the Communist candidate, PCF Secretary General Georges Marchais (who saw his party's vote drop to 15 percent). Despite the animosity between the PS and the PCF, between Mitterrand and Marchais, the Communists threw their support to Mitterrand on the second ballot, remaining faithful to the electoral formula in force in both parliamentary and presidential elections since the mid-1960s. And the results of both the presidential and parliamentary elections of 1981 demonstrate Mitterrand's success and the Communists' dilemma. The PCF was the main loser in the cantonal elections of 1982 (down to 12 percent of the vote), the 1983 municipal elections and the June 1984 European elections (less significant because they do not involve a shift in power *within* France and are carried out by proportional representation, obviating bipolar coalition-building) in which they received only 11 percent. Once the March 1985 cantonal election results are in, the upcoming parliamentary elections of June 1986 will concentrate the parties' minds wonderfully.

### *The Socialist Party's Approach to Policy Issues and Governing in the 1980s*[15]

Most Western 'socialist' or 'social democratic' parties from the end of the Second World War until the economic crisis of the 1970s had made a set of fundamental choices about their role as parties of government in 'advanced capitalist society.' These had involved extensive acceptance of the framework and principles of capitalism and the rejection of most of the traditional principles and objectives of socialism, both in theory and in rhetoric. The model which they had in common involved three elements. The first was what in the United States would be called 'welfare state liberalism,' based on the Keynesian conjunction of demand management and social expenditure. 'Fine tuning' plus the provision of a welfare safety net would maintain relatively full employment, counteract cyclical downturns, and provide a basic minimum for those who none the less were unable to benefit directly from the resulting long-term economic growth. The second was the mixed economy, in which state ownership of certain 'infrastructural' and public service industries, along with unprofitable 'lame ducks' whose bankruptcy would have negative knock-on effects on other parts of the economy, would not only coexist with, but support the profitability of, the dynamic, growth-oriented private sector. And thirdly, a special consultative role would be given to trade unions, to counterbalance business pressures on the setting of government priorities and plans — incorporating the workers into a cooperative relationship within the capitalist economy, rather than excluding them as pariahs or backing them into a disruptive (even revolutionary) corner. Short-term wage restraint was negotiated in return for some combination of social benefits, job protection, formal consultation and the longer-term prospect of rising wages as the economy expanded. Conservative governments, too, accepted a wider role for the state, altering the balance of influence between capital and labor during their periods of office but respecting the social gains and the institutionalization of capital–labor–government consultative mechanisms as well as the welfare state and the mixed economy.

The key to this 'centripetal politics' or consensualism was the existence of general economic growth in the developed industrial capitalist economies as a whole. The British Labour Party, especially under the leadership of Hugh

Gaitskell in the 1950s, the German Social Democratic Party, in the Bad Godesberg Program of 1959, and other European social democratic parties, shed their socialist rhetoric, developed policy packages which aimed at making advanced capitalism more efficient and more humane through judicious but restrained interventionism, and set out to attract the floating voters of the center to their 'catch-all' parties. In the 1960s, social democracy seemed to be the wave of the future, linked with wider cultural and political changes ranging from *détente* and the (temporary) liberalization within the Soviet bloc to civil rights movements, 'counterculture,' and student activism — despite the failure of the French model in May 1968. It was widely believed that, despite temporary difficulties from time to time, there would, in the long run — as Labour politician Ian Mikardo argued in the 1964 British general election campaign — be plenty of money to go around, to keep private industry happy and to finance new social measures. But Britain, first hit by the recession as the result of long-term factors of structural decline, was, in the 1960s — and even more so in the 1970s — the first state controlled by a social democratic party to try to use the mechanisms developed in the growth phase — in particular its close ties with the trade unions — in order to impose an austerity program through incomes policy.

When the recession became generalized after the 'oil shock' of 1973–4, the social democratic compromise unravelled in the face of stagflation. Social democratic parties in government experimented with monetarism, incomes policies and austerity programs, but their industrial policies remained rooted in *ad hoc* measures, a loss-making public sector, currency and trade problems, and the 'fiscal crisis' of cost inflation and static revenues. 'Stagflation' caused internal party crises and electoral defeats such as that of the British Labour Party in 1979 and the German Social Democratic Party in 1983, although the Austrian Socialist Party has managed to maintain power and the Swedish Social Democrats, defeated in 1976 , returned to power in 1982. Thus the recession has — to a greater extent in some countries than in others, and with differential sectoral impact — drastically reduced the scope for consensual policy-making. And conservative parties are no longer content with just shifting the balance, with monetarism, public expenditure cuts, deregulation, denationalization, and reduced consultation of trade unions stimulating both old left and new left demands. Both the economic conditions of consensus — growth — and the political conditions — being able to pull interest groups, party factions and voters towards the center of the spectrum — have been undermined. European social democracy in general has yet to find a new formula for dealing with the crisis, as the German and British elections of 1983 so clearly showed — with the Green Party in Germany and the Liberal/Social Democratic (breakaway) Alliance in Britain draining large numbers of crucial votes away from an SPD and a Labour Party rent by internal quarrels. But the PS's 'learning curve' has been different.

The trajectory of the French Socialists has been far more mixed and problematic. In the first place, despite the close collaboration of the SFIO in the reforming fervor of the Liberation, neither was it credited with those changes (as was the Labour Party) — most of the credit going to the Provisional Government under de Gaulle before the political scene became mired down in divisive constitutional issues — nor was it in a position to adapt effectively to a stable consensual environment in the 'long boom' (as the German SPD and the Austrian Socialists were able to do). The Fourth

Republic was a frustrating time for the SFIO, drawn first into narrow centrist coalitions to protect the regime against Communists and Gaullists in 1946–51, mainly in opposition from 1951–6 (as a faction of the Radical Party under Pierre Mendès-France came to represent the 'modern' left), and then mired in the Algerian débâcle under the Mollet Government before dividing over the return of de Gaulle in 1958. No consensual party-linked mechanism could be constructed. At the same time, state economic management was broadly carried out in a sub-bureaucratic arena — the planning system and the financial state and parapublic apparatuses — divorced from party control over parliament or executive, as well as in a supra-bureaucratic arena — the European Coal and Steel Community and the negotiations for establishing the European Economic Community — which crossed both party and national boundaries. Keynesian management was itself rudimentary, and the relationship of the SFIO to any ideology of planning highly problematic.[16] Thus neither did corporatist mechanisms draw in the political state (parties and governments), nor was the SFIO constrained to develop a coherent economic strategy during the period of economic growth. The marginal role of trade unions to both relationships — planning and party politics — was reinforced by the isolation of the predominant union 'central,' the Communist-linked CGT, with its attitudes forged in the Cold War. This simply removed another possible linkage mechanism.[17]

In the second place, the long period during which the French left was in opposition, 1958–81, ensured that any attempts to reorient the Socialists towards consensual social democracy took place in a vacuum at several levels. Firstly, the state was closed to them. The ideology of national interest which permeated the Fifth Republic was the property and product for many years of General de Gaulle and his followers. The elective offices were dominated by the Gaullists and Giscardians. And the bureaucratic apparatus of the state was controlled by an administrative elite whose ethos dovetailed with Gaullist perspectives and intentions, whose wider political role dovetailed with the presidential regime and *l'État UDR* — the more direct links between party and bureaucracy — and whose transition to Giscardianism mainly involved a change in the balance of the fractions of capital with special links to the corporatist decision-making processes.[18] Thus, whether the state was going through a 'social' phase, an expansionary cycle, a period of interventionism, reflation or retrenchment, a time of planning or *déplanification*, the Socialists (and, of course, the Communists) were mere spectators whose natural reaction was to declare their opposition — not to define a stance from within the parameters of a social democratic 'party of government.' Thus the disarray of the parties of the left in May 1968.

Other potential linkages with the state were also unavailable or unreliable. The trade unions were divided, working-class support for de Gaulle was high until the late 1960s (mainly because of de Gaulle's 'nationalitarian' appeals), and the state generally succeeded in marginalizing the trade unions further. It either bypassed them in direct offers of 'participation' (favored by de Gaulle) such as the Vallon Amendment on worker shareholding, or bargained directly with them in such a way as to complicate or undermine union–party (and even union–business) relations, as in the 1968 Grenelle Agreements or the 'contractualization' process of Pompidou's Prime Minister, Jacques Chaban-Delmas, and his adviser Jacques Delors (then Mitterrand's Finance Minister). It also firmly confronted the unions when openly challenged, as in the 1963 miners' strike. At another level, it was demonstrated that existing nationalized industry could serve the right as well as the left — and it was under the control of the former. Finally, the Socialists' position, until the mid-1970s, as only the second largest party of the left, meant, as we have noted earlier, that the prospect of a left electoral victory was overshadowed by traditional anti-communism on the center–left as well as the right; this fear played an important role in the 1973 and 1978 legislative elections. Only in the arena of local government were the Socialists (and the Communists) able to carve out a role as a 'party of government,' and despite (or partly because of) the Communists' head start in this area, the municipal councils in particular provided both an important training ground and career ladder for Socialist politicians and a policy basis on which to build a national electoral program.[19]

Therefore the Socialist Party, during its long period in opposition, developed its structure and program in a power vacuum, not unnaturally attempting to construct — for the first time in its history — a majoritarian party capable of winning power in the first place. Had they won power in the 1960s, it is possible that they might have developed a closer fit with the European social democratic model described earlier. However, they were much smaller then, and the Communist Party far too large and unreconstructed for that to have been an easy task. Had they won power in the early 1970s, before the oil crisis, when France was being touted by the Hudson Institute as the future industrial powerhouse of Europe, they might have been able, through 'side-payments' to the unions and the Communists, to embark on the development of a *modèle français* along the lines of the *Modell Deutschland*, and based on appropriately selected extracts from the 1972 Common Program. However, even at that time, the PCF was still marginally larger in terms of electoral support, and despite its gradual integration into the political system, its rejection of the social democratic model was explicit, and its interpretation of the ambiguities of the Common Program owed too much to the 'state monopoly capitalist' perspective for any such prospect to be easy.[20]

Furthermore, after its disastrous showing in the 1969 presidential elections and the restructuring process of 1969–71, the spectrum of opinion was greatly enlarged within the party, requiring the leadership to undertake an ongoing integrating and balancing act in charting a policy orientation. This complexity was increased by the entry of new elites, such as the PSU leadership, the expansion of party membership and militant activity to include many new groups ranging from former participants in May 1968 to single-issue pressure groups,[21] and the broadening of the party's electorate to new categories — progressive Catholics, new members of the working class, white-collar workers in the new service industries, etc. The PS played a cat-and-mouse game with the formerly Catholic trade union CFDT (Confédération Française Démocratique du Travail), which insisted on keeping its organizational and ideological distance as well as maintaining its informal links with one faction of the PS, led by Michel Rocard, the former PSU leader.[22] Meanwhile, relations between the PCF and the CGT vacillated during the period of Eurocommunism,[23] as did those between the CGT and the CFDT.[24] Thus the PS did not develop an organizational trade-union linkage mechanism, and the growing state of poor relations between the Socialists and the Communists further undermined any attempt to fashion the PS into a post-war-style social democratic party.

What did hold the party together was its set of strategic priorities — building an electoral force which could both win power and ensure that the PS was the dominant party within the broad left. The PS was not so much a 'catch-all' party in the sense of being 'voter-directed' — the key element in Otto Kirchheimer's notion of the 'catch-all' party and also the central characteristic of the expansion of other European social democratic parties in the 1950s and 1960s;[25] rather it sought to 'catch' a wide range of existing *factions* — formally integrated into the voting system at PS congresses as *'courants,'* with letters 'A,' 'B,' 'C,' or 'D,' linked with particular faction leaders (evolving over time), and claiming proportional representation on the party's executive organs. Thus to ensure strategic unity, Mitterrand and the party leadership went through a number of tactical maneuvers. The two best known of these were, firstly, the alliance with the Rocardian (ex-PSU) faction — essentially a technocratic faction with a blend of free-market economics and worker self-management — at the Pau Congress in 1974, and, secondly, the switch — after the Rocard/Mauroy challenge to Mitterrand's leadership at the 1979 Metz Congress — to a coalition with the more left-wing and *étatiste* CERES faction. The leadership coalition produced by the latter tactical alliance actually drew up the ambitious *Projet socialiste* in 1980, which, as we have noted, Mitterrand quietly put to one side in preparing the policy package for his presidential campaign in 1981. This factional structure, along with the desire to appeal to floating voters of both the center and the left, left the Mauroy Government with a complex legacy in 1981. It was committed to a policy repertoire which promised new measures right across the board — civil liberties, welfare measures, extensive nationalizations, increased worker participation, greater planning, measures for reforming agricultural markets, support for small business, the restructuring of old industries and expansion of the high-technology sector, tax reform, democratization of civil service training, longer vacations and a shorter work week, trade and export policy to cope with the recession, resolving the 200-year-old dispute with the Roman Catholic Church over private schools, and even overhauling and decentralizing the 300-year-old structure of the French state, something even the French Revolution had failed to do.[26]

Of course, grave tensions existed in such a program. In the first place, it would put a heavy strain on the policy-making capacity of the Government and the policy-implementing capacity of the state. In the second place, certain elements seemed in themselves potentially mutually contradictory — increasing the range and depth of state economic policy while decentralizing the state structure, which has led to the accelerated decline of the Plan, or increasing the viability of the private sector while engaging in extensive nationalizations. In the third place, government economic resources were limited, especially during the recession. As suggested earlier, the ability of the European social democratic parties to pursue the range of objectives included in the model which we have outlined for the 1950s and 1960s in Britain, Germany, Sweden and Austria depended heavily on the factor of the long boom, the postwar expansionary period which saw the economic cake grow quickly enough to ensure many contenders a bigger slice. But the appearance of stagflation meant not only that government tax revenues grew less quickly in real terms but also that expenditures, which through 'entitlement' programs were more inelastic, could only painfully be cut below the rate of inflation. Conservative governments as well as social democratic ones were undermined by this same syndrome, including the 'bourgeois coalition' in Sweden in 1982, the post-Franco UCD-led Governments in Spain, the Fraser Government in Australia, the center–right 'Social Democrats' in Portugal, and, of course, the Giscard/Barre Administration in France. Even large cuts in government spending, as in Britain under the Thatcher Government, have coincided with an increasing weight of such expenditure compared with national output. This percentage growth in state spending as a whole has been particularly salient in France in the 1970s and 1980s, partly because the self-governing schemes for Social Security (basic welfare, health insurance, etc.) and unemployment compensation (UNIDEC) reacted more quickly to such inflationary pressures as rising health costs than to the reduction in the number of their contributors through growing unemployment. Only government bail-outs prevented these schemes from collapsing.

Even before the Socialists came to power, then, the 'pie' had stopped growing, and the Government was unable to prevent the demand for slices from growing even faster than before to compensate for the new hard times. Steadily declining private industrial investment, despite a new growth of government subsidies and tax breaks in the 1970s,[27] undermined Barre's policy of 'industrial redeployment' before it got off the ground. Central to the success of such a wide-ranging program as that of the Socialists, then, was the need for rapid and almost immediate economic growth in order to pay for the range of measures included. It was hoped that the reflationary policies would provide a breathing space of growth to allow time for the other policies to be implemented — leading to an effectively revamped France competing effectively in the world market.[28] A new virtuous circle of growth would replace the vicious circle of stagflation. Given the structural vulnerability of the French economy to international factors, however,[29] the second half of 1981 and most of 1982 turned out to be a most unfavorable period for the Socialist experiment. In particular, the world's leading capitalist economy, the United States, headed into a new period of even more extreme recession (before growth re-emerged in 1983). In France, the expansion of demand fed primarily into import penetration, and had only a very short-term effect on national economic growth. Although inflation did not increase, it did not come down as quickly as it was doing in the United States and Britain, thereby increasing the 'inflation differential' affecting the competitiveness of French goods in the export markets which were vital for future growth. The costs of the Socialist program increased the budget deficit considerably, although at 2.5 percent of Gross National Product in 1982 and just under 3.0 percent in 1983 it was considerably smaller than those in the United States (6 percent), Italy (17 percent), or even West Germany and Japan. Only Britain had a smaller budget deficit among OECD countries. Unanticipated extra costs of nationalization, currency exchange fluctuations, low demand for French exports and other factors caused a shaking out of priorities by the Mauroy Government, leading to the reshuffle of March 1983, the sharp cutbacks in 1984 in certain older industries like steel, coal and shipbuilding, and the more dramatic recent changes at the top. A more austere 'state capitalist' model has emerged, with an interesting potential for creative policy-making,[30] although it will lead to further tensions on the left as 1986 approaches.

## II.  THE SOCIALIST PARTY AND POLITICAL POWER

Thus the development of the Socialist Party into a majority party and a party of government has required a major on-the-job training program over the past three years. Had it not been for the fact that the political institutions of the Fifth Republic in France are capable of carrying a greater innovative load — both in terms of effective decision-making and in the policy instruments in the hands of central decision-makers in the financial and economic sphere[31] — than systems such as that of the United States or of less stable parliamentary systems, then the Mauroy Government might easily have been deadlocked, defeated or decomposed. Central to this equation, of course, is presidential politics, particularly effective presidential supervision of the policy-making activities of the Government. Another important element is party discipline. The Mitterrand presidency marks the first time in the Fifth Republic where something approximating 'party government' has existed: the party predated the capture of power, and that power is in the hands of party leaders, not figures who emerged outside of (or above) the party system, like de Gaulle or Pompidou, or whose party base was a narrow minority in a cobbled-together coalition, like Giscard; and there is a long tradition of rank-and-file politics on the left, which, along with the factional structure of the PS, the coalition with the PCF, and the re-emergence of parliamentary politics, makes the public airing of dirty linen and the need for continual negotiation and compromise more salient. All of these factors make an evaluation of the current political situation — and of the run-up to the 1986 parliamentary elections — more complex, both increasing and constraining the options of the Socialist Party and the Government. Let us look first at the way in which political power has been controlled since May/June 1981, and then consider the range of options in the hands of the Government and the party which might affect the political situation as 1986 approaches.

### Gaining, Maintaining and Exercising Institutional Control

The key to the control of power by the Socialists — in terms of both navigating through the internal power relationships within the PS and imposing their will on the wider political environment — lies in the interaction between Socialist officeholders themselves, and other officeholders, within the 'structured field of action' formed by the institutional framework of the Fifth Republic. Embedded in this framework is a number of more or less manipulable constraints.[32] These provide pitfalls and opportunities for actors, depending upon the range of resources and skills brought to bear. The story of the rise of the PS in the 1960s and 1970s was one of the painful adaptation of the party itself and of its coalition behavior to what seemed like almost insurmountable constraints in organizational and electoral terms and a seemingly dominant position maintained by its adversaries on the right. The 1958 Constitution was seen by many for a long time as not only tailored to fit General de Gaulle but also as inconsistent with Socialist parliamentary traditions and the distaste for strong executive institutions with potential for the abuse of personal power. Given the continuing control of the institutional system by the right, and the problematic relationship with the Communists on the left, only the actual practice of institutional control could finally banish the twin specters of Eastern Europe in 1947 and Chile in 1973.

In fact, the Socialist Party's manner of gaining power ensured that its office-holders would enjoy virtually all of the latent advantages inherent in the constitutional rules of the game, both in terms of their domination of other forces of the right and left and of their capacity to use the levers provided by the institutions themselves. In the run up to the 1978 elections, long-running debates on the potential sources of conflict and stalemate embedded in the institutional structures of the Fifth Republic were aired with a new urgency by academic commentators,[33] scenario-minded journalists,[34] and politicians themselves. The nub of these debates lay in legislative-executive relations, especially in the context of one or both of the following conditions — opposing 'presidential' and 'parliamentary' majorities, and clashes within a majority coalition over the distribution of government posts and/or conflicting public policies. The role of the Prime Minister, in particular his ambiguous position with regard to the President of the Republic — who appoints him and has the capacity (by convention rather than direct constitutional grant) to dismiss him — and the National Assembly — which can reject him and overturn the government — is a critical feature of such potential situations. So is the tendency of both historical and technical factors to emphasize at critical times the partial 'quadripolarity' of the party system, reinforcing secondary divisions between the major allies within the broad coalitions of right and left in addition to the primary bipolar division which has been such a noted innovation during the Fifth Republic. In 1978, the testing of these scenarios was partially avoided by the victory of the right — although divisions within the right-wing coalition deepened and contributed to Giscard d'Estaing's defeat in May 1981. Holding both the presidency and an absolute majority in the National Assembly, the Socialists have the opportunity to make the system work for them despite extraparliamentary pressures, as we have seen at the beginning of this chapter. None the less, the debates of 1978 were themselves revivals of earlier debates and identified one of the critical 'faultlines' of the Fifth Republic. They will recur in 1986 and 1988.

Within this context, however, the Socialist victories did reinforce a number of key features of the Fifth Republic. The first of these is the legitimacy of the institutions themselves. One aspect of this is the basic fact that political legitimacy in a liberal–democratic system is partially tied to the real possibility of the *alternation* of opposing parties in power as well as the formal procedures such as voting, representation, civil liberties, etc. The elections of 1981 made the possibility of alternation self-evident — in contrast to earlier attacks, mainly by the left in the 1960s, on the regime itself as embodying the personal power of de Gaulle, or later, in the 1970s, on the monolithic 'État UDR' of Pompidou as perpetuating a political–bureaucratic elite open to favoritism and corruption (especially during a period of rapid industrial development and financial strength). Another, more complex, aspect is that legitimacy is not simply an attribute of attitude but one of political culture, the evolution of which requires a longer time-span, at least intergenerational. The restabilization of the institutional structure under the Socialists — after the uncertainty of the Giscard years when the largest party in the governing coalition, the neo-Gaullist *Rassemblement pour la République* of Chirac, could significantly hold up the Government's budget proposals, forcing Barre to use the special motion of confidence procedure (passage without an actual vote) — has not only reinforced the acculturation process but extended it.[35]

The role of the opposition, also crucial to alternation and legitimacy, has been more mixed. On the one hand, the successful use of parliamentary devices to extend debate on the nationalization bills in 1981–2 (including an appeal to the Constitutional Council which upheld the Government's general right to expand the public sector but which altered the terms on which it could do so) could be seen as strengthening the parliamentary institution, long considered the weak relative of the Fifth Republic. But ironically, the opposition parties — quite significantly divided among themselves — and in particular the RPR, have accused the Mitterrand Administration of illegitimacy. The lead was taken by Michel Debré, an influential if idiosyncratic 'baron' of Gaullism and de Gaulle's first Prime Minister (1959–62).[36] He, and later others, in different terms and with varying degrees of vehemence, including Chirac, the Gaullist parliamentary leader Claude Labbé, and Giscard's former right-hand man Michel Poniatowski, based their argument on the contention that the Socialists — or, more frequently, the 'socialo-communist' coalition — were not merely another party in power, making decisions with the framework of existing socio-economic structures (particularly with regard to the relation of public and private sectors within the economy). Rather they were undermining the capitalist consensus upon which the Fifth Republic's legitimacy itself rested in their eyes. Whatever its substantive merits — and the relationship of institutional legitimacy to the dominant mode of production is a complex analytical issue — this proposition has found a response neither in public opinion nor in the development of a more coherent political opposition, although it has fanned the flames among certain right-wing pressure groups. Indeed, it has proven to be one of a number of issues dividing the opposition, interacting with the various organizational and personal rivalries, and the ideological divisions patched up or submerged by de Gaulle and Pompidou, which have long characterized the right side of the French political spectrum. It has been seen as partially calling into question the right's own commitment to liberal democracy and as subordinating political stability to social conservatism — a charge reminiscent of the image of certain elements of the traditional French right, such as the Action Française's distinction between the *pays légal* and the *pays réel*. And it has on occasion redounded to the benefit of the Socialists, as President Mitterrand has replied with great effectiveness in a *gaullien* rhetoric of national unity,[37] calling upon the developing reservoir of support for the institutions *per se*, for democracy in general, for France's foreign and defense policies, and for effective symbolic and instrumental presidential leadership in particular. By the Autumn of 1983, opposition rhetoric had cooled on the legitimacy issue, as it became more and more obvious that rhetoric and demonstrations alone would not bring the Government down, but it flared up again in mid-1984 as the right called for a dissolution of the National Assembly. The right's feeling that it is the only legitimate ruling group in France is deep-rooted, and may surface again in the run-up to 1986. Mitterrand's call for a referendum on civil liberties is addressed precisely to this issue.

The second key feature of the regime to be reinforced by Socialist predominance, a feature closely bound up with that of legitimacy, is presidential supremacy. Despite the potential pitfalls of the Fifth Republic's constitutional arrangements, notably the bicephalous executive, presidential supremacy within the executive branch — along with executive supremacy in the policy-making process — has frequently been identified as the most significant innovation in the French political system since 1958. The phenomenon has four major aspects, all of which have more or less dovetailed with the practice of the Mitterrand presidency. Firstly, the famous French bureaucracy, often accused of being a 'state within a state', especially during periods of political instability under previous republics, has generally been more accountable to its political masters. The Socialist practice of power has reinforced this control, both directly, using limited but significant powers of promotion and transfer of officials, and indirectly, through a positive and interventionist policy style requiring greater coordination and supervision of an activist civil service. In general, too, the administration itself has adapted well to its new bosses, with its *colbertiste* traditions minimizing bureaucratic obstruction for the most part. Secondly, the President himself has asserted his dominant position within the executive, both in day-to-day business and longer-term policy-making, through a personal style which is both activist and interventionist yet discreet[38] (maintaining that 'distance' which de Gaulle saw as so essential to prestige and thus to presidential effectiveness), and in reaction to a number of disputes between ministers, between particular ministers and the Prime Minister, or between the Government and the leaders of the Socialist parliamentary party or party organization, over both policies and 'territory'.[39] This has considerably reinforced presidential oversight and control over both the legislative and executive decision-making processes, sometimes as a final arbiter, sometimes through direct intervention, but most often in terms of anticipated reactions. Fabius's appointment as Prime Minister will further strengthen the President's hand.

Thirdly, presidential supremacy continues to provide the focus for the party system. This is as obvious on the left, given the key role of François Mitterrand, as on the right, where the lack of agreement over leadership in the wake of Giscard d'Estaing's defeat and the general dislike of Chirac among the other right-wing parties have prevented the opposition from fully exploiting the Government's weaknesses. The growing strength of the PS in the 1970s, the effectiveness of its alliance with the PCF, and Mitterrand's skilled handling of the presidential campaign, were reinforced exponentially by his decision — and his constitutional power — to dissolve the National Assembly and call immediate legislative elections for the very purpose of underpinning and stabilizing presidential leadership itself — with Socialist candidates elected very much on presidential coat-tails. Since coming to power, the Socialist Party structure has been altered to eliminate (at least on a formal basis) the famous *courants* — indeed, the Bourg-en-Bresse Congress in Autumn 1983 was a remarkably muted affair, despite underlying disagreements on policy — and this change succeeded most effectively in relegating Michel Rocard, Mitterrand's main potential in-house rival in 1981, and Jean-Pierre Chevènement, who has hopes of representing the party's left in 1988, to a back seat (Rocard's within the Government, Chevènement's literally on the back-benches) prior to Chevènement's return in 1984, this time to the Education Ministry. Indeed, the recent governmental changes should greatly solidify the party leadership around the practice of presidential government. And fourthly, Mitterrand's actions and rhetoric as President have reinforced the cultural underpinning of the presidency as the most salient political office, specially charged with protecting the national interest. The style mentioned earlier, the predominance of the President in party matters and over policy, the special responsibility of the President for foreign policy with all its symbolic resonance,[40] the use of prerogatives like the referendum and changing the Prime Minister, and Mitterrand's effective use of the media, have all helped to maintain the aura of the office which de Gaulle wanted to be second nature to the French people and which is crucial to the legitimacy of the regime itself.

A third key feature of the Fifth Republic which is reinforced by Socialist dominance is that of the autonomy of the state within the capitalist social formation, a feature again associated with the policies of financial strength, economic growth and industrial development characteristic of the presidencies of de Gaulle and of Pompidou.[41] However, as later chapters will show in more detail, the path of economic policy has not been smooth. None the less, the attempt by the Mitterrand Administration to strengthen its capacity to act — already strong, compared to the United States and Britain[42] — as what Chalmers Johnson has called (with reference to Japan) a 'developmental state,'[43] has led to a far-reaching state capitalist program which could have significant implications for other developed capitalist democracies.[44]

Thus the Socialist Party has been quite successfully inserted into the institutions of the state. The powers of the state have been reinforced and concentrated by the new majoritarianism, and the exigencies of controlling the state have shaped the ongoing development of the PS.[45] Nevertheless, a number of factors have highlighted the difficulties of the tasks which the PS has set itself. The honeymoon period (or 'state of grace') came to an end during the Winter of 1981–2. Problems have emerged, not only at the level of economic policy *per se*, but also with regard to governmental coordination, intra-party politics, relations with pressure groups, and electoral politics. The Government's internal disputes have the familiar ring of reformist socialist coalitions: disagreements between the Finance Ministry and the spending ministries over the pace of reform; disagreement over the content of policy, and, in particular, the extent to which an activist industrial policy should be compensated by cushioning of declining industries and the maintenance of employment; disagreements over the party and electoral implications of government actions; not to mention clashes of faction and personality. In such situations, a majoritarian party has both the advantage of having to live together, of being able to settle such disputes *en famille*, and the disadvantage that in a context of such ostensible strength the disappointment and frustration of those interests and factions whose hopes had been raised thereby but who find their ambitions stymied in practice will be exacerbated and spill into the public arena. Although the presidential dominance of the Fifth Republic does provide a technically effective way of resolving such disputes, the division of functions between the presidential office and the Government does provide a number of structural loopholes or niches in which disputes can incubate before they become subject to presidential arbitration; it lacks the overall coordinating capacity of, for instance, the practice of collective responsibility in the British system. Prime Minister Pierre Mauroy operated a relatively loose system of overseeing and reconciling such disputes during his first year or so in office,[46] creating a public image of disharmony and perhaps depending too much upon presidential arbitration. With the government reshuffles of June 1982, March 1983, and, of course, July 1984, however, a more closely coordinated style of

management has emerged, leaving the impression of an increasing solidity
which may actually be increased by the Communists' departure and by
Fabius's reputation for firmness and efficiency.

None the less, disputes still exist — within the Government, within the PS,
and within the majority coalition as a whole. These disputes reflect the
particular problems which reformist socialist governments have with
innovative loading. For the most part, conservative and centrist policy-
making tends to be dominated by the management of existing policies and
structures; change tends to be incremental and in response to conjunctural
pressures. Even when conservative programs are more radical, as with the
Thatcher and Reagan Administrations, the emphasis is upon reducing
governmental activities (except in the defense field). Reformist socialist
governments, in contrast, tend to be more concerned — although in widely
varying ways — with the strategic extension of a range of governmental
activities. Now it is a rule of thumb in social science that change is more
problematic than continuity; it engages more resources, and its outcome is
always contingent and its consequences frequently unseen and unintended.
Innovative loading puts strain on institutional capacities, governments, and
organizational relationships. In such contexts, latent conflicts exist along
several dimensions — between leadership or personality factions, between
groups with different ideological or policy priorities, and between groups with
different power bases and structural resources (including rank-and-file party
activists, party organizations, parliamentary groups, related organizations
such as trade unions, and, of course, groups of voters). Such disputes often
become particularly debilitating not during the honeymoon period with its
innovative momentum, but thereafter, when earlier distributive payoffs have
led to financial constraints, when regulatory changes are just moving into
gear and their complexities are becoming obvious, and when redistributive
transfers have already created a disgruntled reservoir of 'losers.' They
highlight persistent differences over both the extent of policy innovation (no
change is ever sufficient in itself, and pause and retrenchment, with greater
attention to conjunctural factors, always remain an alternative course to
dealing with policy problems through further innovation) and the specific
policy priorities which clash over the limited resources (more social services?
which services? more industrial investment? which industries and how? who
is going to pay? etc.).

Conflicts of this kind clearly exist within the Socialist Party, the
Government, the left-wing coalition, and the pressure groups connected with
the coalition. The negative side-effects of the Government's reflationary
policies in 1981 led to pressure, centered in the Finance Ministry, for
retrenchment — the 'stop' phase of a classical 'stop-go' cycle. Reactions were
strong from several quarters, from the somewhat more protectionist
approach of Chevènement to major interest groups who saw their gains
endangered. The emphasis of Mitterrand, former Finance Minister Jacques
Delors, and the current Prime Minister, Laurent Fabius (previously the
Industry Minister), on profitability in industry has been attacked both within
the PS and by the PCF.[47] Symbolic clashes between the Government and the
Socialist parliamentary group have occurred, for example over legislation to
reintegrate into the armed forces reserve the officers (including some
prominent ex-generals) who participated in rebellious acts during the
Algerian War, although major clashes have been avoided in the Assembly.

The trade unions — themselves divided over the issue of job maintenance and wage claims versus industrial restructuring — were relatively quiescent until late 1983, but have exploded (especially the CGT) over the cutbacks in traditional public-sector industries such as steel, shipbuilding and coal, and the PCF line on this within the Government gradually hardened to the extent of bringing about the withdrawal of Communist ministers. And the environmentalist lobby, politically important in the build-up of opposition to Giscard in the late 1970s, has been disappointed by the Government's decision to go ahead with most of the ambitious nuclear power program initiated by previous administrations. That these conflicts have not had a much greater impact, however, is due, firstly, to the size of the Socialist majorities of 1981 with the attendant ramifications for the party system — including a certain amount of disarray among both the Communists and the opposition — and, secondly, to the manner of those victories  and to the capacity of the President of the Republic and the Government to use the resources embedded in the institutional framework of the Fifth Republic to dominate and control the decision-making process. But with legislative elections now only two years away, will these resources be enough to beat back the tide of dissatisfaction in the country? How can the Socialist Party, and President Mitterrand, approach the electoral period if they are to have any hope of maintaining their power?

## The Socialist Party and the Future

The strength of the tide has just been demonstrated, at the time of writing, by the results of the elections to the European Assembly held on 17 June 1984. Given the public's perception of the European Parliament as a relatively inconsequential body, and the fact that these elections were held by nationwide proportional representation with party lists (no personal preference votes), the vote had the air of an occasion to protest against the Government without directly affecting it — the 'off-year election' *par excellence*. The PS attracted only 20.76 percent of the vote, and the PCF had its worst results since the Second World War, 11.28 percent — half of its accustomed electoral support in the 1950s and 1960s. The RPR and the UDF (a confederation of smaller center and right parties put together by Giscard in 1978) presented a unified list headed by Simone Veil, whose UDF list had been the major success of the 1979 European elections; it received 42.88 percent of the vote, and its relative success may be a significant factor in assessing the run-up to the 1986 parliamentary elections, as we shall discuss below. Most of the other lists had very small percentages (although the two lists representing primarily different factions of ecologists received nearly 7 percent between them) — with the outstanding exception of the renascent anti-immigrant, extreme rightist National Front, led by Jean-Marie Le Pen, which garnered an unexpectedly high 11 percent protest vote, the highest such vote since the Poujadist challenge in the parliamentary elections of January 1956![48] The success of the Le Pen list, especially at attracting urban votes in traditional Communist *'bastions'*, creates another challenge which the left must face in 1986.

At the same time, however, such indicators are an insufficient base on which to make longer-term projections. Electoral results in off-year elections are notoriously difficult to use as predictors of major general elections, as American mid-term elections and British local government elections demonstrate, although their complex signals are a vital source of information. An analysis of the March 1983 municipal election results, in which the Socialists did fairly badly but avoided disaster (while the Communists lost votes in key strongholds), concluded that they brought together the four characteristics of an *élection intermédiaire*: stability of the core of party voters; differential abstention, favoring the right on the first ballot but showing a return to the left on the second; a marginal shift of those voters who had switched to Mitterrand in the 1981 presidential election back to the right (the 1981 election having been decided by just such a marginal shift to the left); 'and finally, the potentially reversible character of this broad pattern, since more than one-third (36 percent) of such "disappointed Mitterrandists" said that they wanted the left to win any parliamentary elections.'[49] In the European elections of 1984, the combined UDF/RPR list received virtually the same vote total as the separate UDF and RPR lists had received in the 1979 European poll, similarly just about two years before the next major national elections (the 1981 presidentials, which showed a swing to the left). And about half of the voters who cast their ballots for the National Front indicated that they would not have done so in a major national election.[50]

Furthermore, the mix of voting systems has its own independent effect, especially in France[51] where electoral methods differ so drastically from level to level — from the almost 'pure' proportional representation of the European elections, through the mixed local and regional systems, to the two-ballot parliamentary and presidential elections with their crucial constraints on choice. The cornerstone of the system is, of course, the presidency itself, and the unique interaction between this most salient office — and its holder, along with prominent opponents — at presidential, and parliamentary, election time. It has frequently been pointed out that President Giscard d'Estaing's intervention in the parliamentary elections of 1978 was an important element in the right's overall victory, despite the consistent left lead in prior opinion polls.[52] However, despite Mitterrand's advantages as President, he has, for most of the past year or so, been receiving low popularity ratings in opinion surveys. In a survey conducted by the Sofres organization for *Le Figaro* in April 1984, only 23 percent of respondents were 'satisfied' with his performance as President since May 1981, down from 30 percent in April 1983; those 'disappointed' in his performance over that period had risen to 61 percent from 54 percent a year earlier. Among those who had voted for Mitterrand on the second ballot in 1981, those 'satisfied' and those 'disappointed' were evenly divided with 44 percent each (from 53 percent 'satisfied' and 33 percent 'disapointed' a year earlier).[53] A Gallup poll in *L'Express* (4 May 1984) showed Mitterrand's popularity somewhat higher, 31 percent (down 2 percent on the previous month), and a significantly lower disapproval rating of 45 percent (down 6 percent); the most significant trend, in fact, was the increase of don't know/no reply, up 8 percent to 24 percent. Confidence in the President had declined most among PCF supporters (—11 percent) and PS voters (—9 percent); interestingly, however, his approval rating had improved among the opposition supporters, especially the UDF (+9 percent).

Such swings are probably less important in themselves than in the very fact that they are occurring. What they indicate is an increased volatility among potentially 'floating' voters, a disaggregation on the surface of the electorate, after a long period prior to 1981 in which, unlike Britain and the United

States, major-party voting across the spectrum (RPR, UDF, PS, PCF) and coalition discipline in second-ballot voting had by and large been on the increase under the Fifth Republic. That this trend has stalled or reversed itself is not surprising, for two reasons. In the first place, Giscard d'Estaing during his presidency and in his unsuccessful attempt to reduce the Gaullists to junior partner status in the National Assembly had helped to exacerbate long-standing underlying tensions on the right, while his UDF was itself a loose confederation of small parties; divisions on the right were primarily responsible for his defeat in May 1981. And, secondly, the left has been hurt by the loss not only of floating voters but also of certain elements of hardcore support, especially for the Communists, since their accession to power and their changing economic line. The main lines of support have not altered, as the Sofres poll mentioned above shows. Among the socio-economic categories asked whether the victory of the left in 1981 had been a 'good thing' or a 'bad thing,' the general direction of the results was predictable: workers, civil servants and retired people thought it a 'good thing;' farmers, managers/ executives, professionals and (by the largest margin) shopkeepers thought it a 'bad thing;' and white-collar workers were more or less evenly divided. Most interestingly, however, were the two alternative replies to the question: 'neither good nor bad,' and 'no opinion.' If these two replies are added together, the degree of volatility stands out sharply: workers 27 percent undecided or no opinion; retired people, 34 percent; white-collar workers, 38 percent; civil servants, also 38 percent; managers/executives (*cadres*), 40 percent; shopkeepers 41 percent; professionals, 42 percent; and farmers 49 percent. The leeway is significant.[54]

Thus, although the task ahead of the left in preparing for the 1986 and 1988 elections is huge, the weight of conjunctural factors will be the real decider. One merely has to remember the poor showing of the British Conservative Party in public opinion surveys in early 1982, just before the Anglo-Argentinian War over the Falklands/Malvinas Islands, and then think of the results of the British general elections of June 1983. More to the point, several features of the British situation in 1982–3 are pertinent to the French situation, to wit: the volatility of the electorate between elections; the divisions within the opposition; the unpopularity of a government pursuing a difficult austerity policy; the capacity of the Government to manipulate short-term economic policy in the run-up to the election itself; the unpredictability of international events; the impact of leadership and incumbency; etc. Two years can be a very long time in electoral politics when the situation is as fluid as it has become in many Western democracies; indeed, leaders and incumbent governments are unpopular in many parts of Western Europe today, but their opponents are often fairly unpopular too! What we can do is to identify a number of interrelated variables which will be particularly critical in shaping the developing campaign for, and the results of, the June 1986 elections. We shall briefly outline two longer-term or 'governmental' variables, two medium-term, strategic and tactical 'party/coalition' variables, and two short-term 'conjunctural' variables. Then we will consider some scenarios for 1986.

At the level of the Government — its policy and its credibility — two factors, both of which have been discussed in earlier sections of this chapter, stand out. The first is economic policy, which has, of course, been the focus of most of the dissatisfaction in public opinion, as illustrated by a number of responses to a Sofres poll done for a group of provincial newspapers in late April;[55] only on the issue of maintaining the gains made by the left in the social field did respondents have more confidence in the left than the right, whereas for a wide range of other issues — a healthy economy, the creation of jobs, defense of the franc, maintenance of purchasing power, foreign policy, the unity of the French, security, and even the defense of liberties — the right elicited more confidence than the left. In the earlier Sofres poll in *Le Figaro*, discussed above, responses on economic policy showed a high degree of skepticism and dissatisfaction (with the interesting exception of the recent measures taken in the steel industry), and 63 percent thought that if the left lost the 1986 legislative elections, Mitterrand (who would of course still be President) should 'profoundly' alter existing policies (24 percent against). Fifty-four percent of respondents in the same survey feared the possibility of a new crisis comparable to that of May 1968. Unemployment is rising sharply after two years of being held to around 2 million, affecting the core of left support (as the gains by the National Front have recently shown). And yet, with the balance of trade deficit halved in recent months, and inflation on course for a rise of only 6–7 percent in 1984 — and the economic recovery in the United States finally exerting a pull on French exports — it is not impossible for the recession in France, which has come nearly two years later in France than in Britain or Germany, to 'bottom out' well before June 1986, perhaps even just in time for the elections. With the OECD expecting investment to show a very large increase in 1984,[56] after a long period of decline since the mid-1970s, a general recovery would not be impossible, although any significant fall in unemployment from a predicted peak of near 3 million in 1985 would undoubtedly lag behind.

The second governmental factor is that of the cohesion and capacity of the Government itself to maintain the sort of control over the state apparatus which we have discussed earlier in this chapter. Indeed, there is no reason to think that any serious deterioration will take place. There will be no elections of national significance before 1986, and even the exit of the Communists from the Government will not change the basic relationship of forces deriving from the presidential and parliamentary victories of 1981. In recent months, commentators have even noted that the Government, or at least the Socialist members of it, had, after the March 1983 reshuffle, achieved a smoother working relationship (with the Communists dissenting only in unofficial contexts) and showed greater solidarity and tranquillity than was possible in the first eighteen months, with its multiple policy directions, legislative and bureaucratic hyperactivity, personality clashes and relative inexperience. The changing of the Prime Minister in the run-up to a major election has been the standard practice of the Fifth Republic, although it remains to be seen how Fabius, the youngest Prime Minister (at age 37) in France this century, performs in his critical role. He must not antagonize major sections of the party, but he must at the same time develop greater personal weight and authority, a difficult balancing act. Mitterrand's leadership will be crucial, both within the Government itself and in terms of appealing to the public. His recent successful visits to the United States and the Soviet Union will not have done him any harm. Thus this second longer-term governmental variable, as we foreshadowed in the introduction and described in greater detail earlier in this chapter, represents the Government's main trump card in the pre-electoral period; however, there will be great pressure on the constitutional structure underpinning governmental stability unless some of the other variables are also working in the left's favor.

The rest of the variables are considerably more problematic, although they will probably be broadly dependent upon the first two factors: if government solidarity holds and the economy clearly recovers, the Socialists and the left in general will be in a better position to respond to and even to manipulate medium- and short-term issues; however, if, to take the worst case, the economy continues to 'bump along the bottom' of the recessionary trough, and if, for example, a government reshuffle creates tensions and dysfunctions in the policy process, then the other variables will doubtless exacerbate the situation on the electoral front.

The two medium-term variables concern the strategic and tactical situation of the various parties and coalitions themselves — in short, the state of the left and the state of the opposition. The state of the left, firstly, can be divided into two dominant aspects, the condition of the Socialist Party internally and the condition of the PS/PCF coalition. Within the PS, we have already noted that factional differences have to some extent been muted by the exercise of presidential (and prime ministerial) authority within the Government, by the quiescence of the parliamentary party, and by the submerging of factions at the party congresses. None the less, a number of factors could shake that unity. Disappointed factional leaders, like Chevènement or Rocard, might become more aggressive if the Government's economic and other policies continue to provoke widespread social opposition, especially among the working class; the party congress scheduled for the autumn of 1985 could provide the focus for intra-party conflict even if the parliamentary party remains relatively docile, and such a forum could mobilize a disgruntled rank and file. A government reshuffle that antagonized groups within the party, as we have noted, could play a role in such a development. And, of course, the parliamentary party could revolt, too, although that is less likely given the constitutional supremacy of the executive and a desire to retain power. The recent promotion of the PS parliamentary leader, Pierre Joxe, to a ministerial post, will strengthen the executive's hand. Lower echelons of the party will also have a greater role to play at regional, departmental (county) and municipal level with the coming into effect of the Government's decentralization plans; in protecting their flank against anti-left voting trends, local control and local issues might push local party sections into emphasizing disagreements with the Government as well as with the opposition. Local parties' disagreements with lay-offs and plant closures in the nationalized industries, or dislike of the Government's compromise measures on church schools (which were not radical enough for left-controlled local governments who resent having to pay the costs of private education, which is usually religious and often politically oriented towards the right), could become issues, for example, in the 1985 cantonal elections (to the departmental councils). As for the relationship with the Communist Party, it is certain that the Socialists could govern quite happily until June 1986, as they have an absolute majority in the National Assembly. However, without the support of Communist voters in an electoral pact such as the ones that have been the rule since 1965, the PS probably could not win the 1986 elections alone. If the PCF slips entirely out from Mitterrand's bear hug, then the PS will have to have an eventual alternative coalition — whether at electoral level or in the new National Assembly — in mind. The loss of even a marginalized junior partner could have broad consequences, especially for a weakened Socialist Party.

As for the opposition, there are two main problematic aspects. In the first place, the French right has been characterized by growing interparty squabbles since the death of Georges Pompidou. There has been no love lost between the main factional leaders in the past decade. And none of these leaders has a clear and commanding advantage in popularity over the others. In the Sofres/*Le Figaro* poll quoted earlier,[57] the RPR leader Chirac was the choice of 36 percent of respondents as the best future presidential candidate; Raymond Barre was the choice of 16 percent, Simone Veil of 12 percent, and Valéry Giscard d'Estaing of 11 percent. Although Chirac leads the pack, he arouses strong antagonism as well as support.[58] The presentation of a right-unity list, headed by Mme Veil, in the European elections was something of a surprise. If it presages greater unity on the right over the next two years, then, on recent election returns and poll results, the right would be in a position to mount a majoritarian challenge in 1986; even some disunity is acceptable on the first ballot in the French parliamentary electoral system, providing that right-wing discipline is adhered to on the second ballot. On the other hand, fissures are more likely at parliamentary election time, when various factions and small parties (the UDF being a tenuous compromise organizationally, and alliances with other parties, such as the National Front, being possible at constituency level) are all represented, at least on the first ballot. And these fissures could be exacerbated not only by clashing personalities, but also by strong differences over the issues. Chirac's recent theme of a kind of neo-Reaganism, drastically pruning the public sector, the welfare state, and economic planning, not only goes against the grain of traditional Gaullism, but could also backfire with the smaller center–right parties; it is not for nothing that Chirac deferred to Simone Veil to head the European list, but it remains to be seen whether the right will hold at parliamentary level, and whether the electorate will find their policy prescriptions credible at the time. The PCF's withdrawal from the Government, furthermore, eliminates a major issue which the opposition has tried hard to exploit — the fear of Communism.

There are, finally, two short-term conjunctural variables which can be mentioned, but the effects of which cannot be predicted. The first of these is simple electoral volatility, which we have discussed above and about which little more can be said — except to emphasize that tidal wave movements in 'off-years' are often reversible, and there is some fragmentary survey data to suggest that a swing away from the Socialists might be followed by a swing back by 1986. The second conjunctural variable is more complex, and here we are talking about the capacity of the government of the day, in a pre-electoral period, to manipulate *short-term* economic conditions, whether as one phase of a longer-term economic recovery or as a primitive, even cynical, bid for survival — the 'short-run fixes' which Edward Tufte deploringly analyzes with regard to American electoral politics.[59] Existing studies of the 'political-business cycle' in the Fifth Republic have concluded that it has been at best weak, and often non-existent.[60] However, there is no reason to believe that the potential is not there. If one looks at presidential elections since 1965, two have taken place abruptly ahead of schedule (1969 and 1974) and one involved an incumbent who refused to take short-term expansionary measures on principle (1981); only in 1965 was there the time and the possible intention, but the attention of political leaders was generally elsewhere. Similar comments could be made for most parliamentary elections, and American experience would suggest that the big guns are kept for presidential years. But the extent of control that the Government (and President) has over the economic apparatus of the state in France is large,[61] and there is no reason to think that the Socialists would have a particularly difficult task should they decide to use short-run stimulation in 1986. The Conservative Government in Britain did it to great effect in 1983 (allied to the 'Falklands factor'). Visible increases in direct transfer payments, increased budget deficits, increases in the money supply, tax cuts and wage increases are all part of the potential armory. Such measures, in the short term, require little coordination (they use existing government organizational resources), they can be carried out by executive and administrative agencies with little scrutiny in the short term (and these agencies have organizational vested interests in cooperating), and, perhaps most importantly, their greatest impact is upon the natural electorate of the left — poor, working-class and lower middle-class voters — whose numbers are especially critical. Finally, such measures are also perceived in relatively short-run terms. It is a feeling of being better off, on a rising curve, even if only in comparison to a low point a few months previously, which matters.[62] (Reagan's question in 1980, 'Are you better off now than you were four years ago?', is partly a red herring and partly an exception to the rule.) Combined with electoral volatility, short-run stimulation has the potential to dominate the conjuncture in 1986, *ceteris paribus*.

Let us finally look briefly at two 'polar' scenarios for the 1986 elections. If the economy has not significantly recovered, the Government's grip on the state has weakened, the Socialist Party is squabbling with itself and with the Communists, the opposition is relatively united, the electorate is still disillusioned and inclined towards protest votes, and the Government does *not* undertake short-run stimulative economic measures (whether from disarray or principle), then the outcome of the parliamentary elections will not be far short of the collapse currently being envisaged by the French media for the left. On the other hand, if the economy has bottomed out and recovery has begun (or is seen to have begun), if the Government is still solidly in control of the state apparatus, if the Socialists have pulled together for the electoral battle and the PCF still feel that they have no alternative but to go along by accepting another electoral pact, if the opposition is divided along personality and/or policy as well as party lines, if the electorate is swinging back towards the left in pendulum fashion given the 'national' significance accorded to the elections themselves, and if the Government effectively applies short-term economic stimulation in the classic manner, then the crisis of 1984 will seem very long ago, as does today the atmosphere of certain defeat hanging over the Conservative Party in Britain in early 1982. As we have said before, two years is a long time in politics, especially politics as fascinating and volatile as those of France. Ultimately, however, it is almost certain that neither of these scenarios will apply in its purity, and that the variables which we have outlined will exhibit a more complex and differentiated pattern. But the parameters of change are broad, and the outcome will be critical not only to the left (and the right), but also to the character of the Fifth Republic itself — to the stability of the regime, the democratic character of the political process, the nature and control of the state apparatus, the relationship between the state and the economy, and the social integration of '*les deux France*,' all of which are currently under pressure. There is everything to play for.

NOTES

1. For detailed results and analyses, see André Laurens, ed., *L'Élection présidentielle, 26 avril-10 mai 1981: la victoire de M. Mitterrand* and *Les Élections législatives de juin 1981: la gauche socialiste obtient la majorité absolue* (Paris: Supplements aux dossiers et documents du *Monde*, 1981). A very useful extended survey is Vincent Wright, 'The Change in France,' in Wright, ed., *Continuity and Change in France* (London and Winchester, Mass.: Allen & Unwin, 1984), pp. 1–81. See also David S. Bell, ed., *Contemporary French Political Parties* (London and New York: Croom Helm and St. Martin's Press, 1982).
2. *New York Times*, 20 April 1984.
3. For a detailed treatment of the impact of electoral systems and institutional rules on the French party system, see P.G. Cerny, 'The New Rules of the Game in France,' in P.G. Cerny and M.A. Schain, eds, *French Politics and Public Policy* (London and New York: Frances Pinter, St. Martin's Press and Methuen University Paperbacks, 1980), Ch. 2.
4. See P.G. Cerny, 'Mitterrand's Foreign Policy: Continuity and Vulnerability,' *Politics* (UK), 3, No. 2 (October 1983), pp. 3–8.
5. *Le Monde*, 6 April 1984.
6. Despite the PS's numerical strength in the National Assembly, it can not be argued that the PS is a 'dominant party' analogous to Charlot's analysis of the Gaullists in the late 1960s. See Jean Charlot, *The Gaullist Phenomenon* (London: Allen & Unwin, 1971).
7. See Guy Michelat and Michel Simon, *Classe, religion et comportement politique* (Paris: Presses de la FNSP and Éditions Sociales, 1977).
8. See Duncan MacRae Jr., *Parliament, Parties and Society in France 1946–1958* (New York: St. Martin's Press, 1968).
9. Franz-Olivier Giesbert, *François Mitterrand ou la tentation de l'histoire* (Paris: Ed. du Seuil, 1977).
10. On this period and the 'Events of May' 1968, see P.G. Cerny, 'The Fall of Two Presidents and Extraparliamentary Opposition: France and the United States in 1968,' *Government and Opposition*, 5, No. 3 (Summer 1970), pp. 287–306.
11. For the difference between these strategies, see David Robertson, *A Theory of Party Competition* (London: Wiley, 1976).
12. See Jolyon Howorth, 'The French Communist Party and "Class Alliances": Intellectuals, Workers and the Crisis of Social Ideology,' in D.S. Bell, *Contemporary French Political Parties*, op. cit., Ch. 5.
13. On Giscard's style, see Wright, 'The Change in France,' op. cit., pp. 14–16.
14. On the Gaullist party in this period, see P.G. Cerny, *Gaullism, Advanced Capitalism and the Fifth Republic*, in Bell, *Contemporary French Political Parties*, op. cit., Ch. 2, esp. pp. 40–8.
15. The next two sections draw in part on Cerny, 'Dead Ends and New Possibilities: Mitterrand's Economic Policy Between Socialism and State Capitalism,' *Contemporary French Civilization*, VIII, Nos. 1–2, Special double issue on 'France under Mitterrand' (Fall/Winter 1983–84), Ch. 1, and Cerny, 'Democratic Socialism and the Tests of Power: The Mitterrand Presidency Eighteen Months On,' *West European Politics*, 6, No. 3 (July 1983), pp. 197–215.
16. See Richard F. Kuisel, *Capitalism and the State in Modern France: Renovation and Economic Management in the Twentieth Century* (Cambridge: Cambridge University Press, 1981).
17. Martin A. Schain, 'Corporatism and Industrial Relations in France,' in Cerny and Schain, eds, *French Politics and Public Policy*, op. cit., Ch. 10.
18. Ezra Suleiman, *Politics, Power and Bureaucracy in France: The Administrative Elite* (Princeton, N.J.: Princeton University Press, 1974); Suleiman, *Elites in French Society: The Politics of Survival* (Princeton, N.J.: Princeton University Press, 1978); Francis de Baecque and Jean-Louis Quermonne, eds, *Administration et politique* (Paris: Presses de la FNSP, 1981); Pierre Birnbaum, 'The State in Contemporary France,' in Richard Scase, ed, *The State in Western Europe* (London: Croom Helm, 1980); Birnbaum, 'The Giscardian Politico-Administrative Elite,' in Wright, *Continuity and Change in France*, op. cit., Ch. 3; and Anne Stevens, 'The Higher Civil Service and Economic Policy-Making,' in Cerny and Schain, *French Politics and Public Policy*, op. cit., Ch. 4.
19. Martin A. Schain, *French Communism and Local Power* (London and New York: Frances Pinter and St. Martin's Press, 1985).

20. See Mark Kesselman, 'The Economic Analysis and Program of the French Communist Party: Consistency Underlying Change,' in Cerny and Schain, *French Politics and Public Policy*, op. cit., Ch. 9.
21. See P.G. Cerny, ed, *Social Movements and Protest in France* (London and New York: Frances Pinter and St. Martin's Press, 1982).
22. Richard P. Shryock, 'The CFDT: Beyond Really Attainable French Socialism?,' *Telos*, No. 55 (Spring 1983).
23. See George Ross, *Workers and Communists in France: From the Popular Front to Eurocommunism* (Berkeley, Los Angeles and London: University of California Press, 1982).
24. See Chapter 11.
25. Otto Kirchheimer, 'The Transformation of the Western European Party Systems,' in J. La Palombara and M. Weiner, eds, *Political Parties and Political Development* (Princeton, N.J.: Princeton University Press, 1966).
26. See various chapters in this volume.
27. Diana M. Green with P.G. Cerny, 'Economic Policy and the Governing Coalitions,' in Cerny and Schain, *French Politics and Public Policy*, op. cit., Ch. 8.
28. See Chapter 4, and P.G. Cerny, 'Economic Policy: Crisis Management, Structural Reform and Socialist Politics,' in Stuart Williams, ed, *Socialism in France: From Jaurès to Mitterrand* (London and New York: Frances Pinter and St. Martin's Press for the Association for the Study of Modern and Contemporary France, 1983), Ch. 9.
29. See Chapter 10.
30. See Chapters 4 and 10, and also Cerny, 'Dead Ends and New Possibilities,' op. cit.
31. On financial policy instruments, see John Zysman, *Governments, Markets and Growth* (Ithaca, N.Y.: Cornell University Press, 1983), Ch. 3, and Peter Hall, 'Patterns of Economic Policy: an Organizational Approach,' in S. Bornstein, D. Held and J. Krieger, eds, *The State in Capitalist Europe* (London and Winchester, Mass.: Allen & Unwin, 1984, Ch. 2.
32. Cerny, 'The New Rules of the Game in France,' op. cit.
33. For example, Léo Hamon, *Une République présidentielle? Institutions et vie politique dans la France actuelle*, 2 vols. (Paris: Bordas, 1975 and 1977), or, a little later, Maurice Duverger, *Échec au roi* (Paris: Albin Michel, 1978).
34. E.g., Philippe de Commines, *Les 180 jours de Mitterrand* (Paris: P. Belfond, 1977) was perhaps the best-known 'scenario' work.
35. For a consideration of these issues, including a comparison (in advance) of various scenarios for the outcome of the 1981 elections, see P.G. Cerny, 'The Problem of Legitimacy in the Fifth French Republic,' paper presented to the Workshop on Normative and Empirical Dimensions of Legitimacy, Joint Meetings of Workshops, European Consortium for Political Research, University of Lancaster, April 1981.
36. The seminal piece in this campaign was Michel Debré, 'Ce gouvernement est légal. Est-il légitime?' *Le Figaro Magazine*, 9 April 1982, p. 69. See also the reply of Lionel Jospin, First Secretary of the Socialist Party, 'De curieux légitimistes . . . ,' *Le Monde*, 4 May 1982. Debré has been repeating his charges in the wake of the European elections.
37. Compare, for example, Mitterrand's speeches during a tour of Limousin, when both the opposition's attacks on the Government's lack of legitimacy and the pressure on the currency and on economic policy generally had been rising, *Le Monde*, 5 May 1982; and during his tour of the Midi-Pyrénées, when again opposition polemics coincided with a serious run on the franc, *Le Monde*, 28 and 29 September 1982.
38. See the fascinating journalistic study of presidential networks and working methods by Maurice Szafran and Sammy Ketz, *Les Familles du Président* (Paris: Grasset, 1982).
39. Discord within the Government was particularly salient in the Spring of 1982 (see the article by André Laurens in *Le Monde*, 22 April 1982) and in early 1983, when the wages and prices freeze had ended and future policies were still under discussion; the municipal elections of March 1983, followed by the resignations of Chevènement and Jobert and an extensive reshuffle, displaced internal opposition to the backbenches.
40. See Cerny, 'Mitterrand's Foreign Policy,' op. cit., and *The Politics of Grandeur: Ideological Aspects of de Gaulle's Foreign Policy* (Cambridge: Cambridge University Press, 1980). The special relationship of the President and foreign policy was highlighted by Mitterrand's major televised interview on the program 'L'heure de vérité,' 16 November 1983, followed by a significant (if temporary) rise in his popularity ratings.
41. See Birnbaum, 'The State in Contemporary France,' op. cit. Cf. P.G. Cerny, 'Frankrijk: bestuurlijke democratie en de grenzen van de legitimiteit,' in Uriel Rosenthal, ed, *Politieke stelsels: Stabiliteit en verandering* (Alphen aan den Rijn and Brussels: Samsom, 1982), Ch. 6.

42. Zysman, *Governments, Markets and Growth*, op. cit., *passim*.
43. Chalmers Johnson, *MITI and the Japanese Miracle: The Growth of Industrial Policy, 1925–1975* (Stanford, Calif.: Stanford University Press, 1982), Ch. 1.
44. See Chapter 10.
45. Cf. Ezra Suleiman, 'Toward the Disciplining of Parties and Legislators: The French Parliamentarian in the Fifth Republic,' in Ezra Suleiman, ed, *Parliaments and Parliamentarians* (forthcoming), and Julian Petrie, 'The French Deputy as a Member of the Elite,' in Jolyon Howorth and P.G. Cerny, eds, *Elites in France: Origins, Reproduction and Power* (London and New York: Frances Pinter and St. Martin's Press for the Association for the Study of Modern and Contemporary France, 1981), Ch. 11.
46. See Mauroy's own comments on the virtues of openness in government, 'Gouverner autrement,' *Le Monde*, 20 April 1982; also the chapter on Mauroy's methods and networks in Szafran and Ketz, *Les familles du Président*, op. cit., pp. 119–38.
47. For the PCF, see Chapter 2; also see Patrick Jarreau, 'Les limites du débat communiste,' *Le Monde*, 27 June 1984.
48. Although the more traditional Poujadists ran their own list, headed by Gérard Nicoud and Pierre Poujade himself, it only received 0.7 percent of the vote. Traditional Poujadism was mainly a provincial phenomenon, appealing to the lower-middle class left behind by advanced industrial society, and its earlier organizations had long since been 'incorporated' into the Fifth Republic: cf. Keeler's analysis in Chapter 13, and Roger Eatwell, 'Poujadism and Neo-Poujadism: From Revolt to Reconciliation,' in Cerny, *Social Movements and Protest in France*, op. cit., Ch. 4. Le Pen's movement has a more urban focus, although surveys show that it, like the Poujadists, has drawn its support mainly from groups which would normally support the right, especially the RPR, rather than from working-class, ex-PCF voters. Although some Communist voters undoubtedly did switch to the National Front in June 1984, it is unlikely that Le Pen has the kind of appeal that George Wallace had to certain sections of the unionized working class in the North in the primaries and the presidential election of 1968 in the United States; cf. Seymour Martin Lipset and Earl Raab, *The Politics of Unreason: Right-Wing Extremism in America, 1790–1970* (New York: Harper & Row, 1970), Chs. 9 and 10, esp. pp. 362 ff., and *Le Nouvel Observateur*, 22 June 1984.
49. Jean-Luc Parodi, 'Les logiques d'une élection intermédiaire,' *Le Monde*, 3/4 April 1983.
50. *New York Times*, 19 June 1984.
51. Cerny, 'The New Rules of the Game,' op. cit.
52. See John Frears and Jean-Luc Parodi, *War Will Not Take Place: The French Parliamentary Elections, March 1978* (London: C. Hurst, 1979).
53. Sofres survey published in *Le Figaro*, 18 April 1984.
54. A Sofres exit poll, breaking down the voting in the European elections by social category (among other things), can be found in *Le Nouvel Observateur*, 22 June 1984; this survey also examines attitudes on several relevant dimensions.
55. Results reported in *Le Monde*, 29/30 April 1984.
56. *New York Times*, 24 April 1984.
57. See note 53.
58. Cerny, 'Gaullism, Advanced Capitalism and the Fifth Republic,' in Bell, *Contemporary French Political Parties*, op. cit.
59. Edward R. Tufte, *Political Control of the Economy* (Princeton, N.J.: Princeton University Press, 1978), preface to the paperback edition (1980).
60. Cf. Kristen R. Monroe, 'A French Political Business Cycle?' in Cerny and Schain, *French Politics and Public Policy*, op cit., Ch. 7, and Joel R. Reidenberg, 'Political Business Cycles: An Analysis of France,' Honors Thesis, Dartmouth College, 1983.
61. Although any detailed comparison would be complex.
62. Tufte, *Political Control of the Economy*, op. cit., pp. 56–9, 89–94, 130–1, and *passim*.

# 2 The French Communist Party: Historic Retard, Historic Compromise, Historic Decline — or New Departure?*

*Mark Kesselman*

[What] is the historical necessity, at the end of the twentieth century, for a large communist party in a developed industrial society? By brutally reducing the PCF's electoral influence... voters made this a major question in French political life for the next decade.[1]

Although the position of the French Communist Party (PCF) was eroding for years, no one predicted the full extent of its decline in 1981. In an excellent analysis of the PCF's impasse published in early 1981, Georges Lavau speculated that PCF support might sink as low as 18 percent.[2] Several months later, Georges Marchais received less than 16 percent of the vote in the presidential elections and PCF candidates fared only slightly better in the parliamentary elections that followed. This was by far the PCF's worst electoral performance in the entire post-war period.

The PCF may reverse its downward course — recall the rebirth of the Socialist Party (PS) in 1969–71. However, several years after 1981 there was little evidence of PCF revitalization. The same leaders who presided over the PCF's crushing defeat in 1981 continued years later to shape the party's course. In cantonal, municipal and legislative by-elections in the years following 1981, the PCF share of the vote remained low and its defeats in local elections further reduced the PCF's power, patronage and legitimacy (see Chapter 3). In June 1984, the PCF received 11.3 percent of the vote in elections for the European Parliament, slightly more than the vote for the neo-fascist National Front. What are the causes of the PCF's decline? How has the party sought to counteract its setback? What might be the consequences of a weakened PCF for the future course of French politics?

## THE PCF'S HISTORICAL POSITION

Throughout the post-war period, the PCF ranked among the largest French political parties, in terms of membership size, electoral support and organizational strength. The PCF dominated the French left (an illustration: other left forces were typically designated as the 'non-communist left'). The PCF had uniquely close ties to the working class and was a major force within French intellectual life. As it demonstrated in 1977, the PCF had the capacity to prevent the left from reaching power if it deemed conditions to be unsatisfactory. Moreover, the PCF exerted a leftward tug on the Socialist Party (PS). Unlike socialist parties of Northern Europe, the PS was constantly forced to compete with a powerful opponent on its left. Given PCF strength and the Fifth Republic's majoritarian electoral laws, the Socialist Party could

* I am grateful for suggestions from Martin Schain and Richard Shryock.

**Table 2.1**   PCF electoral performance, 1936–81 (% of PCF vote at first ballot)

| Type of election | Year | Vote % |
| --- | --- | --- |
| Legislative | 1936 | 15.4 |
| Constituent | 1945 | 26.1 |
| Constituent | 1946 | 25.7 |
| Legislative | 1946 | 28.6 |
| Legislative | 1951 | 26.9 |
| Legislative | 1956 | 25.9 |
| Legislative | 1958 | 19.2 |
| Legislative | 1962 | 21.8 |
| Legislative | 1967 | 22.5 |
| Legislative | 1968 | 20.0 |
| Presidential | 1969 | 21.5 |
| Legislative | 1973 | 21.4 |
| Legislative | 1978 | 20.7 |
| European | 1979 | 20.6 |
| Presidential | 1981 | 15.6 |
| Legislative | 1981 | 16.2 |
| European | 1984 | 11.3 |

*Sources:*   Vincent Wright, *The Government and Politics of France*, 2nd edn. (New York: Holmes & Meier, 1983), p. 181; *Le Monde*, 19 June 1984.

gain power (as François Mitterrand brilliantly grasped) only by eschewing a center-left alliance in favor of a more radical stance.

This situation abruptly changed in 1981, when the PCF's popular vote plummeted by one quarter. George Marchais was fourth in the 1981 presidential elections and the PCF's parliamentary delegation was halved from eighty-six to forty-four. From the largest French political party in the post-war period, the PCF slipped to fourth by 1981.

The PCF continues to have far more members than any other French political party and possibly more than all others combined (it claims over 700,000 members). The party has an unmatched network of workplace cell organizations (12,000 compared to the PS's 1,700) and intimate links to the CGT, the largest trade union. After negotiating an agreement with the PS after the 1981 parliamentary elections, the PCF gained representation in the Socialist-dominated Government.

However, not even the usually triumphalist PCF denies how major a setback it received in 1981. Are the party's diminished fortunes the product of a historical retard, as the PCF asserts, a historic compromise, or a fundamental historical decline? Does the PCF display evidence of regaining its influence in French political life?

HISTORIC RETARD

The PCF leaders explain the party's defeat as the product of a historic retard or lag. At the 24th Congress in February 1982, the first held after the 1981 elections, delegates voted a resolution which offered a lengthy analysis of the 1981 defeat.[3] The party attributed its difficulties to tardiness in developing an appropriate strategy in the 1950s, 1960s and early 1970s. According to the 24th Congress resolution, the PCF was well attuned to France's political and economic exigencies until the 1950s. However, it failed to grasp the magnitude and character of the profound changes occurring in France (and the entire capitalist world) in the 1950s.

The development of state monopoly capitalism changed the French class structure by decimating traditional social forces and enlarging the ranks of white-collar workers (office workers, state employees, and intellectual workers like teachers, engineers and technicians). While state-stimulated economic growth initially raised living standards (prior to the crisis beginning in the 1970s) it created a host of new contradictions, including the Taylorist organization of production, urban devastation and uneven regional development. The potential was created for a vast anti-monopoly majority coalition under the aegis of a political party espousing a radically democratic, socialist vision. However, for many years the PCF underestimated the magnitude of the changes occurring in French capitalism and failed to derive the appropriate strategic consequences. Prisoner of the Soviet model of socialism, it did not seek until the 1960s to forge a socialism 'in French colors' based on a coalition of social forces reaching beyond the industrial proletariat to embrace white-collar and intellectual workers. By the 1970s, the PCF was groping toward a correct path, as evidenced by its Union of the Left alliance with the PS. (However, although the Common Program negotiated by the two parties (and the left Radicals) proposed structural reforms which could unleash a democratic socialist transition, the alliance had a number of serious deficiencies which the PCF was, once again, slow to recognize.

The Union of the Left fostered the illusion that fundamental change could be achieved by programmatic statements, summit meetings of party leaders, electoral victories and parliamentary reforms — but without the direct intervention of the masses. Moreover, the alliance obscured the PCF's distinctive identity under the umbrella of left unity — a tendency strengthened when the party chose not to contest the 1974 presidential elections. By supporting Mitterrand, the PCF fostered the illusion that the Socialist Party could adequately represent the entire left despite its social democratic orientation. Thus, PCF practice failed to reflect the party's radical democratic message.

According to the PCF, it began to rectify these errors in the middle 1970s. The 22nd and 23rd Congresses in 1976 and 1979 deepened the party's democratic commitment by describing socialism, in the words of the 22nd Congress slogan as '*démocratie jusqu'au bout*' (democracy to the fullest). At the 22nd Congress, the PCF abandoned the concept of the dictatorship of the proletariat as misleading and undesirable. By rejecting Socialist Party efforts to dilute the Common Program in 1977, the PCF forced the PS to shoulder responsibility for breaking the alliance. Henceforth, the PCF began to implement its radical democratic theory by promoting mass struggles to achieve step-by-step prefigurative reforms rather than paying lip-service to the theory while in fact practicing a top-down approach to socialist transformation.

The cruel irony, according to the PCF's post-1981 analysis, is that, although it finally overcame its historical retard in the late 1970s, it lacked sufficient time before the 1981 election to proclaim and implement its new strategy and consequently was deprived of the electoral benefits that it deserved. Whereas the left's victory demonstrated that a majority of French citizens shared the PCF's goal of radical change, many voters (including a sizeable segment of the PCF's own electorate) failed to recognize that the PCF was the sole party which proposed appropriate means to achieve this goal. By voting Socialist, French citizens chose a slower rhythm of change than that proposed by the PCF as well as a policy orientation that would inevitably fall short of overcoming the crisis. Once voters realize that more vigorous measures are needed, they will gravitate to the PCF.

The PCF asserts that the party was further damaged by two additional factors. First, because the PCF was the only genuinely anticapitalist party, it was inevitably, during a period of crisis and enormous progressive possibilities, the principal target of conservative forces (what the PCF terms ideological warfare). Second, the PCF was penalized by France's inequitable electoral laws, which unduly reward frontrunning parties. In 1981, Gaullist candidate Jacques Chirac frightened Communist voters into believing that he might outstrip Mitterrand at the first ballot, which would have eliminated the left from the second ballot (given the virtual certainty that incumbent President Valéry Giscard d'Estaing would reach the runoff). In order to prevent this situation, many PCF supporters voted 'usefully' by shifting to the PS at the first ballot.[4]

### The Retard Theory: An Assessment

The PCF is correct that, for many years, it denied the existence of profound socioeconomic changes occurring in France. (The extreme instance was when Maurice Thorez insisted on the validity of the pauperization thesis during a period when French workers were achieving unprecedented increases in living standards). Granted, too, that in the 1970s the PCF placed inordinate faith in political alliances and programs rather than locally based struggles. And granted that the Union of the Left served PS interests by legitimating the party as an adequate representative of the entire left coalition. But the PCF's retard theory obscures more than it clarifies. First, it conveniently shifts responsibility for the party's failure from Marchais and his associates to past leaders. The real villain of the PCF's rewritten drama is Waldeck Rochet — who in fact sponsored bold reforms to democratize party doctrine. Conversely, the theory also rewrites history by implying that the party's retard originated only in the 1950s. Yet, following Gramsci, one might locate the retard of the PCF and other Western communist parties in the 1920s, when they were forced to adopt an inappropriate Bolshevik model.

Third, the theory falsely implies unbroken continuity since the 22nd Congress in 1976, thereby ignoring the party's abrupt changes of direction in 1977 and 1981 — decided by party leaders without prior debate by party militants. Although the PCF continued to proclaim its commitment to Eurocommunist-style democratic socialism in the late 1970s — indeed, it asserted that it was deepening that commitment by relying on popular struggles as opposed to political machinations — the party embarked on a thoroughly sectarian course.[5] The PCF's workerist turn and bitter denunciation of the PS beginning in 1977 damaged the entire left (although, ironically, it eventually contributed to the PS triumph and PCF defeat). PCF leaders thus drew the diametrically wrong conclusion from the 1978 elections. PCF attacks on the PS were successful in the short run in partially re-equilibrating left forces (the PCF substantially narrowed the gap between the two parties). Yet, instead of seizing the opportunity to renegotiate more favorable terms in a new coalition for the 1981 presidential elections, PCF leaders redoubled their attacks on the PS. Whereas in 1978 the PCF described the PS as veering to the right, in 1981 it described the PS as part of the 'band of three,' along with Giscard and Chirac, bent on betraying the interests of French workers and the entire nation.

Thus, the PCF's retard theory needs to be turned on its head. It was not that, as the PCF asserted, voters had inadequate time by 1981 to assimilate the lessons of the 1977–8 period — but rather that they had had inadequate time by the 1978 legislative elections to comprehend the PCF's post-1977 approach — and quite enough time by 1981.

The PCF's major goal after 1977 was to discredit the Socialist Party by demonstrating that it was not a trustworthy leftist force. The PCF had flourished as a 'tribune party' (in Lavau's words) in the absence of a viable alternative to the conservative governing coalition. However, by 1981 the PS did offer such an alternative, which rendered it more attractive than the merely symbolic protest that the PCF offered (especially given the Barre Government's austerity policies). For the PCF tactic to succeed, however, the PS needed to conform to the PCF's ominous description. Mitterrand perfectly understood the necessity for the PS to stay the left course and belie PCF charges of Socialist betrayal. By contrast, Michel Rocard, Mitterrand's principal rival within the PS, urged that the PS reject its previous stance and form an alliance with centrist forces. This step would doubtless have repelled the many PCF voters whose defection contributed to the PS 1981 electoral victory.[6]

### AFTER THE DELUGE: FROM PYRRHIC VICTORY (1978) TO STRATEGIC ROUT (1981)

In the 1981 elections, the PCF designated Mitterrand as its major opponent. It insisted that the principal cleavage within French politics pitted the PCF against all other political parties. As in the PCF's other 'isolationist' periods, it adopted a workerist rhetoric and moved toward closer alignment with the Soviet Union. But, as opposed to previous periods, rather than consolidating the PCF's core support, this sectarian turn provoked the deepest split in party history — no wonder, since new PCF recruits in the 1970s were attracted by many of the elements that the party repudiated, beginning in 1977.

By 1981 the PCF reached a strategic impasse. It had abandoned hope of reaching power in a broad-based coalition and it merely sought to repeat its 1978 feat of vetoing a Socialist victory. Its rationale for shattering the left alliance was quite unconvincing, since the PS was no more reformist in the late 1970s and early 1980s than in 1972, when the PCF negotiated the Union of the Left alliance. Nor did the PCF appear to have a strategy for reaching power or rebuilding its position outside the alliance. Despite its claim in 1982 that the party had finally achieved a union of radical democratic theory and practice, the gulf was never greater between the party's words and deeds. At the doctrinal level, the PCF proclaimed its determination to support grass-roots struggles and overturn the conservative regime. Yet, in practice, it rejected grass-roots unity and local struggles while signalling a preference for Giscard's victory to 're-equilibrate' the balance of forces within the left.

However, sectarianism in the post-1978 period helped produce the very result that the PCF most feared. In 1978 PCF attacks on the PS deterred potential Socialist support. In 1981 the opposite outcome occurred, as many disgruntled Communist voters switched to the PS while PCF criticism of the

Socialist Party reassured centrist voters that the PS could be trusted to act independently.

Mitterrand's strong showing and Marchais's mediocre result at the first ballot necessitated the PCF's about-face by support for Mitterrand at the second ballot. A possible precedent, if the PCF had adopted an intransigent position, occurred in a legislative by-election in 1980, when a Radical Party candidate faced a conservative in a runoff election. Despite the PCF's call for Communist voters to abstain, they helped elect the Radical. A similar result in the presidential elections would be disastrous for the PCF. Party leaders thus weakly advocated Mitterrand's election (while some privately urged a vote for Giscard). In order to salvage the maximum benefits following Mitterrand's election, the PCF negotiated quite humiliating agreements with a the PS for the legislative elections and with a view to participating in a Socialist-dominated government. The PCF's tortured history of the past decade raises the question of how long a self-proclaimed vanguard party can lag behind history and remain a major political force.

HISTORIC COMPROMISE

The term 'historic compromise' derives from Italian political parlance, where it referred to the Italian Communist Party's attempt to participate in government by allying with the Christian Democratic Party. The PCF's entry into government in 1981 represents a historic compromise, the first in the West in generations. The key issue is on whose terms it occurred. Annie Kriegel has suggested that, by gaining representation in the government, the PCF was able to colonize the state apparatus. The PCF was also able to pursue control over the economy, with the help of the enlarged nationalized sector, industrial relations reforms legislated in 1982–3, and the PCF's new emphasis on worker intervention in industry. According to Kriegel, its approach represents a 'theoretical, strategic, political and practical offensive . . . to obtain mastery over the French economic apparatus. . . .'[7]

Kriegel believes that the PCF is acting as a Trojan Horse for the Soviet Union. Defeated in the electoral arena, the PCF seeks economic power to pursue its traditional objective of extending Communist influence on a global scale. The PCF aims to create parallel hierarchies within industry, using its workplace cell organizations and control of the CGT to challenge managerial control and weaken the French (and Western) economic base.

Although there are doubtless PCF members in the civil service, there has been no evidence of a Communist conspiracy. When trade-union leader André Bergeron, a bitter critic of the PCF, issued a report which ostensibly provided such information, the documentation was worthy of Senator Joseph McCarthy.[8] There have been a handful of Communists appointed to high administrative positions, notably the head of the nationalized coal board (who resigned in 1983 to protest government-ordered lay-offs of coalminers), the Paris subway system, one prefect, one regional educational director, and members of ministers' personal staffs. The number is disproportionately less than members of other political parties. Further, given the tight web of regulations surrounding civil service appointments, as well as the unions and other groups hostile to the PCF and vigilant to expose its influence, it is difficult to conceive that the PCF could infiltrate the state. In any case, with the resignation of PCF ministers in July 1984, new Communist appointments will be less likely.

As for the PCF's and CGT's increased economic influence since 1981, that, too, is doubtful. The CGT has failed to overcome its own deep crisis, evidenced by a substantial loss of members and support in elections to labor conciliation and public health boards (see Chapter 11). Nor did the left victory erode managerial prerogatives or unleash a wave of strikes.

In contrast to Kriegel's conservative understanding of the historic compromise, François Mitterrand could be viewed as espousing a centrist interpretation of this situation. For Mitterrand, the compromise was on the Socialist Party's terms since it progressively marginalized the PCF and, eventually, made it dependent on the PS. Despite PCF attempts (reviewed below) to establish limited autonomy from the Government, it does not appear to have used the historic compromise of 1981 to rebuild the party.

There are two leftist views of the PCF's historic compromise. First, the ultra-left regarded the compromise as rank capitulation to the right. In this version, the left government represents a new form of social democracy and a betrayal of working class interests. The PCF, along with the PS, provided a leftist cachet for austerity policies which aim to shore up capitalism at workers' expense.

The PCF offered its own leftist interpretation of the historic compromise by suggesting that, despite its own preference for a more radical orientation, voters chose to advance at a slower pace. As a party wholly committed to democracy, the PCF had no choice but to support France's first leftist government since the Liberation. At the PCF's 24th Congress, Charles Fiterman, Minister of State for Transport and member of the PCF secretariat, declared that the PCF joined the Government 'because progressive change is possible only when supported by the vast majority of citizens, as they recently expressed themselves, and according to their own rhythm and experience — and in no other way.'

According to this reasoning, why would the PCF's radical approach *ever* triumph? Basing the validity of its position on electoral returns could clearly jeopardize the PCF's vanguard role. The party's response was that historical realities demonstrated the wisdom of its position and, sooner or later, voters would draw the necessary conclusions. Given the fact that, despite the PCF's best efforts, the PS-dominated Government proposed inadequate measures to overcome the crisis, voters would eventually recognize that the PCF was the only party correctly to diagnose the causes of the economic crisis and propose an effective solution.

However, thus far, voter disenchantment with the Government has not produced a shift toward the PCF but toward the right. This raises the disturbing possibility that the PCF not only has failed to devise an attractive radical alternative, but that, as Platone and Ranger suggest, there may be structural reasons for this impasse. Before considering that possibility, PCF efforts since 1981 to revive its fortunes will be considered.

POST-1981: THE DELUGE CONTINUES

Since the 1970s, the PCF has adopted a rapid succession of divergent strategies — none of which reversed the party's decline: enthusiastic subordination of the party to the *Union de la Gauche* alliance, aggressive affirmation of the party's distinctive identity within the framework of the left alliance ('l'union est un combat'), Eurocommunism and its abandonment, rupture of the left alliance, the attempt — initially successful but ultimately disastrous — to veto a Socialist Party victory, and the PCF's humiliating retreat to support for the PS in 1981.[9] Yet, unless the party develops its own approach, distinct from the PS, there would be no reason for its decline to cease.

In an earlier analysis of the PCF, I suggested that the party 'has not yet found a new theory and strategy appropriate to the new situation.'[10] This observation continues to be accurate. Indeed, the party's orientation during the years after 1981 simultaneously displayed all the divergent tendencies of the past decade. The PCF praised the value of participting in the Socialist Government at the same time that it never retracted its violent criticism of the PS prior to 1981; it advocated broad union along the lines of the 22nd Congress, yet continued to emphasize workerist themes; it praised liberalization yet practiced sectarianism; it advocated *autogestion* yet participated in a government which exercised all the powers of the Fifth Republic's centralized political institutions.

The PCF's immediate goal from 1981 to 1984 was to use its position in the Socialist Government to restore the party's electoral, ideological and organizational influence. Yet the PCF confronted an agonizing dilemma: if the Government succeeded, this would undermine the need for more radical change spearheaded by the PCF. If it failed, the PCF would be poorly placed, as a result of its presence in government, to benefit. In 1981, remaining outside the first left government in generations was unthinkable. By 1984, however, the appointment of Laurent Fabius as Prime Minister — the chief architect of Socialist austerity — made it impossible for the Communists to continue to assume ministerial responsibility.

The PCF responded by acting as a loyal coalition partner, as long as it remained in government, claiming credit for the Government's popular measures, while seeking to distance itself from unpopular government actions. By its self-designation at the 24th Congress as a 'parti de lutte, parti de gouvernement' (party of struggle, party of government), the PCF sought to demonstrate the coherence of its orientation since 1981. According to the party, participation in government was the culmination of its strategy, elaborated since the 1970s, of promoting step-by-step change. At the same time, the PCF claimed that it had assimilated the mistakes of the Common Program period since it no longer relied merely on party alliances, codified agreements, and legislative reforms. Instead, the PCF proclaimed itself a vanguard assisting the masses to intervene directly to prefigure socialist transformation. There were two major innovations in the PCF's stance since 1981: the attempt to orchestrate participation and opposition *vis-à-vis* the Government, and a new theory that the PCF proposed to manage the economy by non-capitalist criteria.

*Coalition Politics*

The PCF sought to overcome the tensions of its divergent roles by an informal division of labor within the Communist movement. With rare exceptions, PCF cabinet ministers were models of commitment to governmental solidarity. Unlike their often fractious Socialist colleagues, they avoided public disputes with other ministers. The party sought to gain maximum credit for its presence in government by inflating the achievements of Communist ministers. (*L'Humanité* reported daily on their activity.)

Anicet Le Pors, Minister for the Civil Service, provided a reasoned defense of the party's participation in government when describing his sponsorship of a major civil service reform. The measure demonstrated 'the possibility of promoting substantial reforms . . . which are in conformity with our democratic tradition and which open up perspectives toward further progress.' Moreover, the practical experience of participation in government has been 'the source of increased consciousness, competence, and efficacy, which opposition activity could not provide.'[11]

However, other Communist forces were less circumspect about identifying governmental shortcomings. The CGT frequently criticized government measures and occasionally participated in strikes designed to reverse official policy. For example, it massively challenged the Mauroy Government's refusal in early 1982 to order that workers be compensated when the work week was reduced one hour. In face of the widespread popularity of the CGT's opposition, Mitterrand personally overruled the Government's decision. However, the CGT's bark was usually worse than its bite. For example, although it repeatedly denounced the Government's deflationary policies beginning in 1982 and warned that it would never tolerate a reduction in workers' living standards, it mounted little outright opposition — to the dismay of many workers. The CGT and PCF restrained opposition within the limits of preserving governmental stability, at considerable cost. (For example, the CGT declined sharply in works committee and other elections.)

In similar fashion, the PCF as a political party (distinct from PCF ministers) sought to orchestrate support and opposition. The party repeatedly expressed enthusiasm for participating in government and, contrary to widespread expectations, remained there long after the initial redistributive phase gave way to deflationary policies beginning in 1982. A *Le Monde* journalist speculated: 'Despite the fact that party leaders regard participation in government as a constraint with few positive benefits, the cost of withdrawing would be even greater.'[12] The PCF responded to this constraint by disclaiming responsibility for policies it opposed while emphasizing its role in the Government's popular achievements.[13] The PCF focused its criticism on foreign, economic and social policy.

Regarding foreign policy, the PCF had a fundamentally different position from the government. After 1981, the PCF persisted in arguing that the United States was a dangerous imperialist power. The official resolution of the 24th Congress asserted that world war was prevented only because of Soviet military force. PCF disagreement with the Mitterrand Government's foreign policy came to a head over nuclear armaments in 1983. In contrast to official French policy, the PCF considered that the imbalance in nuclear armaments between the United States and the Soviet Union was in favor of the United States and that the latter was solely responsible for nuclear arms escalation. The PCF organized anti-American peace demonstrations in 1982–3. It took an even more dramatic step when it flatly opposed official French policy on the issue of whether French and British nuclear missiles should be considered in negotiations between the United States and the Soviet Union on limiting intermediate range missiles in Europe. In July 1983, Marchais visited Moscow to announce PCF support for the Soviet position and, despite a stern rebuke from Mitterrand, reiterated the PCF stand.

Possibly even more consequential for the balance of forces within French politics was that the PCF engaged in increasingly frequent and outspoken criticism of government economic and social policy, on occasion nearly breaching governmental solidarity. In the Government's first year, during the 'grace period' in which the Socialists enjoyed unprecedented popularity, PCF opposition was confined to advocating more extensive redistributive measures than the Government sponsored, for example, larger increases in the minimum wage. When the Government shifted toward a deflationary course beginning in early 1982, PCF criticism increased. In April 1983, Prime Minister Mauroy sought to promote job creation by freezing certain business taxes and slowing down social reforms. The PCF faulted Mauroy for failing to extract specific concessions from business in return for these 'gifts.' The PCF was even more critical of a wage freeze in June 1982 (part of a more general series of deflationary measures). Marchais termed the freeze 'wholly unwarranted' and 'unjust.' He warned: 'Surely we cannot support this measure.'[14] PCF parliamentary caucus president André Lajoinie announced that PCF deputies would abstain on a vote authorizing the Government to issue decrees implementing the freeze (Mauroy avoided a showdown by calling for a confidence vote, with abstentions thus counting in the Government's favor).[15]

There was a running skirmish between the PCF and the Government over economic policy. In October 1982 the PCF criticized government proposals to reduce the snowballing deficit in the public health system. Lajoinie stated that the measures 'violate the government's commitments.'[16] Addressing a meeting of PCF local officials, Marchais declared: 'The current policies are not the ones we have proposed to achieve economic growth, full employment, and social justice.'[17] Each fall, the PCF sought to amend the proposed budget in a progressive direction. For example, in the parliamentary debate on the 1984 budget, the PCF proposed raising the threshhold for a proposed income surtax.

The PCF sharply distinguished between progressive and reactionary forces — and the latter were not confined to the opposition political parties and their allies. *L'Humanité* editorialized on 30 April 1983:

An important contradiction dividing France for the past two years has created new obstacles: although France is ostensibly governed from the left, its business firms, its currency, its economy are administered — how to describe it, by the right? — on the destructive basis of short-term profit considerations.

The PCF interpreted the Government's deflationary policies beginning in 1982 as quite similar to the neo-liberal policies sponsored by Prime Minister Raymond Barre prior to 1981. In both cases, government policies sought to reduce workers' purchasing power in order to increase profits which, presumably, would generate new investments, jobs and growth. The PCF rejected the logic underlying this approach, on the grounds that it was not only unjust but generated economic stagnation not expansion. The PCF's proposals for overcoming the crisis, reviewed below, went beyond Keynesian counter-cyclical policies to propose new criteria for economic decision-making.

The PCF proclaimed that it was the only political party to propose a truly progressive approach. While party leaders emphasized that the left

Government had compiled an impressive reform record, this was largely a product of the PCF's presence in government. The PCF thus continued to question (albeit in a more subdued manner than prior to 1981) the Socialist Party's progressive character.

The PCF claimed that the Socialists could not be trusted to sponsor progressive reforms without PCF pressure. The 24th Party Congress resolution criticized the Common Program of Government in the 1970s for 'fostering illusions about the PS,' presumably, that the PS was authentically progressive. Yet the PCF neither admitted that its harsh criticisms of the PS prior to 1981 were erroneous nor, if they were not, how PCF participation in a Socialist-dominated government, on the bases of Mitterrand's campaign pledges, would not foster the same illusion. The PCF's attempt to square the circle was quite unconvincing: it asserted that the PCF's presence in government provided a bulwark. For example, according to Marchais, 'If it were not for the Communist Party, on whom could workers rely against the onslaught of the right and business? Who would represent workers' interests, promote progressive change, and insist on honoring the commitments made in 1981 . . . ?'[18]

PCF leaders frequently warned that verbal endorsement of the policies proposed in 1981 was insufficient: 'It is time that the government's actions conform to its promises to voters.'[19]

The Socialist Party and Government countered these criticisms by charging that the PCF was failing to act as a loyal partner in the governmental majority. Yet, until the drastic shift in the balance between the two parties indicated in the 1984 European elections, they were forced to maintain a façade of unity or suffer greater harm pulling apart than by remaining allied. In a joint communiqué following a meeting in December 1983 to assess their relations, they praised the Government's achievements and affirmed the 'necessity to strengthen the solidarity of the governmental majority at all levels.'[20]

However, the PCF was unable to recoup its losses by the combination of support and opposition that it displayed after 1981. Given stalemate in the short run, the party sought to improve its long-run position by ambitious new proposals for overcoming the economic crisis and paving the way toward democratic socialism, a situation in which their party would play a leading role. When the PCF finally left — or was forced to leave — the Government in July 1984, it was more out of resignation than protest. Lajoinie noted: 'It is impossible for us to return to any sort of ghetto. . . . We want to build by democratic means a socialism that is itself democratic.'[21]

### THE *NOUVEAUX CRITÈRES*: A NEW DEPARTURE FOR THE PCF?

In the years after 1981, despite a turn from its Eurocommunist stance in many respects, the PCF substantially extended its emphasis on melding socialism and democracy. At the same time, this was now rooted in the PCF's analysis of France's economic crisis and the new possibilities offered by the election of a left government. In the PCF's view, the crisis derives from the manner in which capitalist social relations and the search for profit maximization have perverted the potentially emancipatory possibilities of recent changes in productive forces.

Although capitalism always accords priority to the quest for profits rather than what is socially useful, in an earlier phase of capitalist expansion benefits trickled down to the masses. In the present period, crisis derives from fundamental changes in the forces of production stemming from the third technological revolution — microelectronics, high-speed information processing, robotics, and the like. The new technology could potentially produce a substantial increase in outputs, jobs, and skills; however, capital derives greater profits from using the new technology in a diametrically opposite fashion. The result has been speculation rather than productive investments which create jobs, assaulting workers' living standards, deskilling work, and investment abroad (which thereby exports jobs). As a result, France has experienced de-industrialization, unemployment, declining demand, and rapid penetration of the French economy by foreign multinationals. (France is fast becoming an economic vassal of West German, Japanese, and American firms.)

Since the principal cause of the crisis lies in capitalist mismanagement, at the level of the individual firm, whole industries, and the entire economy, the crisis can only be overcome by reducing private capitalist control of production. More than ever before, the present crisis permits and, if it is to be overcome, dictates merging the immediate goal of maintaining living standards with the long-run goal of socializing production. Democratic socialism has thus become both a concrete possibility and the only genuine solution to the crisis.

Why? The PCF argues that new criteria for economic management must be substituted for the logic of capital accumulation. The new approach would stimulate economic growth and strengthen socialist tendencies. Whereas the criterion which guides capitalist decision-making is to maximize the ratio of profit to invested physical capital, the PCF proposes substituting the ratio of total value added to invested physical capital. According to the PCF, this shift (which, in effect, substitutes the goal of capital productivity for labor productivity) would produce a host of benefits. Rather than wage payments and job creation counting as a cost of production, they would be calculated as part of the social product. Rather than the goal of economizing on labor, which in practice has meant deskilling work, reducing wages, and eliminating jobs, the new criteria would seek to economize on raw materials and capital while creating jobs and increasing skill levels.[22]

The new criteria require that rank-and-file workers participate actively in production decisions, from shop-floor issues of health and safety to the broadest questions of investment flows and technological innovation. The present system, by contrast, seeks to expropriate workers' knowledge and convert workers into passive agents. In the new situation, rather than permitting the search for profits to devastate entire industries and regions, French workers would rebuild industry and help reconquer domestic markets lost to foreign firms. The beauty of this approach is that workers can intervene on the shop floor to help control prices, maintain product quality, and seek to increase the domestic content of manufactured goods. (*L'Humanité* is studded with accounts of successful worker initiatives of this kind.) The new criteria thus contribute to economic modernization and growth, French national autonomy, improved living standards, and workers' self-management.

Given the fact that private capitalists are determined to put profits first and refuse to share control with workers, the nationalized industries provide a more favorable terrain to introduce the new approach. The nationalized industries can be a vast social laboratory for democratizing production. Furthermore, the new approach may unleash a 'virtuous circle' of economic growth, as workers put their ingenuity and energy to the task of expanding production. Within private firms, capitalists would reap the benefits in the form of increased profits.

The PCF asserted that its new approach represents a deepening of its past commitments to defending French economic autonomy, *autogestion*, and social justice (both within France and internationally — since, in the new plan, France would enter into closer and more equitable economic relations with the Socialist world and the Third World). The approach represents a concrete way to seek socialist change by concrete step-by-step reforms, since workers in a given industry, firm or shop floor or office can intervene actively to promote the new criteria. On the other hand, the approach represents a drastic shift both from the PCF's traditional stance of outright opposition or its mid-1970s phase of supporting parliamentary socialism. Paul Laurent, member of the party secretariat, observes: 'We have abandoned an outmoded strategy of total opposition for a strategy of seeking to participate in directing the nation's affairs. This is linked to our new conception of democratic movement toward a distinctively French form of socialism.'[23]

The new mode of worker intervention promotes radical democracy by making the masses the active agent of socialist change. Rather than permitting private capital and conservative politicians to monopolize initiatives to deal with the economic crisis, with the PCF and CGT confining themselves to immediate demands and distant radical goals, the new approach integrates the two by seeking structural transformation through step-by-step prefigurative reforms.

How does this new stance differ from cogestion or social democracy — which the PCF continues to reject in favor of a more radical vision? Philippe Herzog, economist, Politbureau member, and one of the party's most gifted young leaders, asserts that the PCF does not seek a 'new social contract. We propose a distinctively French form of defending workers' rights: a combination of struggle and negotiations to affirm workers' citizenship rights in the economic realm ..., with an important place accorded to revolutionary ideas.'[24] Thus, workers must impose the new criteria approach on management by mass struggle.

### The New Criteria: An Assessment

By shifting priority from the electoral arena, where the PCF has weakened, to the economy, especially the factory level, where it is relatively strong, the PCF is seeking to serve its organizational interests. Since the new approach also accords a large role to trade union activity, the PCF would further benefit through its intimate links to the CGT. (The PCF 24th Congress urged strengthening ties to the CGT and the party sought to quell autonomous tendencies in the CGT.) Other political parties are poorly equipped to compete with the PCF on this terrain.

The point does not in itself disqualify the PCF's proposal: what political party has proposed reforms which would not serve its organizational interests? But there are more weighty objections to the new criteria. Granted that an economy shaped by the dictates of capital accumulation does not accord priority to what is socially useful, an economy shaped by the new criteria of capital productivity may also be questioned on grounds of social utility. As the Soviet economies illustrate, this approach not only maximizes employment but featherbedding and inefficiency.[25] A preferable alternative might be a procedure that sought to achieve some balance of capital and labor productivity. But it is unclear how the conflicting demands would be reconciled and, in any event, the PCF ignored this issue.

There is an even more fundamental problem: how to define the social values that production should maximize. The PCF's new criteria approach resolves this question in a wholly economistic, productivist manner by choosing the quantity of material value added as its sole standard. This is an approach which regards socialism as involving the expansion of indust-rialism, universalizing wage labor, and perpetual economic expansion. Although the 'post-industrial socialism' proposed by André Gorz has glaring deficiencies, Gorz's critique of traditional socialist conceptions such as this one seems quite cogent.[26]

In any event, however attractive the PCF proposal might be, it failed to attract much support. Two reasons seem plausible. First, given the deepening economic crisis, most concern focused on defending jobs and living standards, as is typical in a slack labor market. Second, for many citizens, the PCF had discredited itself by what was widely perceived as its erratic, destructive course of the past decade. Especially when the PCF failed to democratize its own internal structure, the gulf persisted between its radical democratic message and its authoritarian practice.

In the middle of the 1980s, the PCF remained trapped in the impasse of the previous decade. Might there be structural reasons for the PCF's dilemma that are more influential than its strategic errors in explaining the PCF's decline?

HISTORIC DECLINE

The interpretations reviewed above illuminate specific causes of the PCF's setback but fail to examine its deeper structural roots. Two such factors can be identified: changes in France's socioeconomic situation and in international politics; and the logic of liberal democracy. The PCF flourished in the post-war period, when there were sharp political and social cleavages in France. As the PCF now recognizes, this situation changed rapidly beginning in the 1950s. Economic expansion eroded the barriers separating workers from other French citizens (and immigrant workers, who replenished the ranks of the unskilled, did not possess citizenship rights and thus could not vote). Class consciousness has declined further in the most recent period. Whereas in 1976 three-quarters of French workers who designated their class membership in a public opinion poll identified themselves as belonging to the working class, in 1983 this proportion had dropped to two-thirds.[27] Ironically, the PCF's gradual acceptance since the 1960s of liberal democracy in general and the Fifth Republic in particular may have hastened the erosion of the counter-community which sustained the party.

The PCF's ability to maintain a large electoral following in the post-war period was also facilitated by cold war tensions and the fact that the USSR was an attractive model for the PCF counter-community. In French public opinion studies, pro-Soviet attitudes were influential in discriminating between PCF supporters and other citizens.

In the 1960s and 1970s, *détente* encouraged the PCF to embark on a Eurocommunist course, a hallmark of which was criticism of the repressive policies of the Soviet Union and its relevance as a model for French socialism. Despite the rise of international tensions and renewed PCF support for the USSR in the late 1970s, the PCF has been unable to rebuild popular support for the Soviet Union (especially following Soviet repression in Afghanistan and, indirectly, Poland). Moreover, the PCF partially recognizes the basis for popular disenchantment with the USSR. The PCF now praises the Soviet regime as progressive within the USSR and in global politics while continuing to deny that it should serve as a model for French socialism.

These socioeconomic and political factors have fractured the counter-community which sustained the PCF in the past.[28] Jean Badouin suggests: 'From the powerful and stable "counter-society" that formerly existed, the communist network has become a peripheral and marginalized society.'[29] This is corroborated by the crisis of the PCF press, including the disappearance of most PCF daily newspapers and the decline in readership of those that remain. With the extension of mass education and television, the PCF no longer performs the function of giving political voice to the masses.[30] The most substantial effect of the decline in the PCF counter-community was the heavy losses the party sustained in its working-class bastions in the Paris 'red-belt.' As Schain demonstrates in this volume, although the decline was obscured by the PCF's commanding position in these localities, the tendency raises questions about the PCF's continued hegemony within the working class.

At the deepest level, the PCF may have been undermined by deradicalizing tendencies associated with liberal democracy, illustrated by the success of the Socialist Party in developing a moderate alternative to the PCF.[31] (These tendencies were countered by the unusual conditions prevailing in the immediate post-war period but gained strength in the 1970s.) First, democratically elected governments are (imperfectly) responsive to broad-based demands, which undercuts the potential for a large radical opposition. Second, in order to achieve a broad base of support, any political party (including a radical one) must present a credible alternative. In a capitalist democracy, this requires reaching at least minimal accommodation with business interests, since state economic steering requires close cooperation with business. A party that earns capital's implacable hostility will probably fail to persuade voters that it can effectively manage the economy. Third, since a majority of citizens within a capitalist democracy has never expressed and embraced socialist goals, a radical party seeking power by electoral means must either dilute its program or accept marginal status.

These 'iron laws' of liberal democracy help account for the fact that radical parties have never gained an electoral majority at the national level in any advanced capitalist nation. Yet these laws do not preclude left victories — if the left forges a coalition that embraces diverse socioeconomic groups, develops a political formula that makes a credible radical appeal, and creates an organization which presents an attractive prefigurative image of the future society that the party is seeking to achieve.

In the 1970s, both the PCF and PS made considerable progress along all three of these dimensions. However, the PS proved the more successful of the two and the PCF's response was, in effect, to withdraw from the competition in 1977. Despite its subsequent doctrinal adaptations, the PCF remains an inadequate organizational vehicle to develop a broad coalition and present an attractive model.

## THE IMPACT OF THE PCF'S DECLINE FOR FRANCE'S FUTURE

If the PCF's decline is not reversed in the near and medium run (as appears likely), the shift would represent a bedrock change in French politics. The PCF's marginalization may be as significant as the PS's ascendancy — especially if it is more durable. What will be the possible impact?

An answer hinges on how one assesses the PCF's past impact. The PCF has historically contributed both to sustaining an oppositionist, contestatory, anti-capitalist current in France as well as to dividing and immobilizing the left. At its 24th Congress, the PCF rightly argued that by supporting Mitterrand in the 1974 presidential elections, it legitimated the idea that he could represent the entire left. What message, then, was conveyed by minority PCF representation in a Socialist-dominated government and by the resignation of the PCF in July 1984? The PCF's actions may help seal the decline of a radical left opposition in France in the forseeable future. Thus, the Socialist Government's failure to develop a successful new approach since 1981 produced neither a Communist resurgence (quite the opposite) nor fresh support for the ultra-left — but rather seemed to fuel the rise of the far-right. Furthermore, since the PCF first proposed much of the left's reform agenda and it was influential in propelling the PS leftward in the 1970s, the PCF's decline may produce an overall diminution of leftist energy and policy initiatives. The PCF resigned in 1984 as a result of weakness, not strength.

While the accelerating economic crisis at the end of the twentieth century provides ample historical warrant for a large radical party in a developed industrial society, this is far from suggesting that the PCF is an appropriate example of such a party. The PCF's decline may signify the exhaustion of a certain kind of radical option — but not the end of radical left possibilities. Although a more viable radical alternative appropriate to the new situation remains to be devised, it will likely embody the broad coalition of forces that the PCF unsuccessfully sought to build in the 1970s. But the program of such a coalition will probably be very different from the PCF's productivist approach: it would make a virtue of what is probably an inevitable decline in total employment (an approach anathema to the PCF) for, as a number of recent analyses suggest, the third technological revolution does not involve an increase but a reduction in employment, given the formidable increases in productivity that it unleashes. Further, the organizational vehicle that is appropriate to represent the new radical coalition is at the antipodes from democratic centralism. Thus, the decline of the PCF may well signify the demise of a certain radical option. But this does not mean the demise of the historical necessity for a radical alternative at the end of the twentieth century: it merely signifies that the PCF will probably not embody that alternative.

### NOTES

1.   François Platone and Jean Ranger, 'L'échec du Parti communiste français aux élections du printemps 1981,' *Revue Française de Science Politique*, 31, Nos. 5–6 (October–December 1981), pp. 1036–7. Also see Georges Lavau, 'Le Recul du PCF: péripétie ou déclin historique?', *Le Débat*, No. 16 (November 1981), pp. 77–83.
2.   Georges Lavau, *A Quoi sert le Parti Communiste Français?* (Paris: Fayard, 1981).
3.   PCF, *Construire le Socialisme aux Couleurs de la France: 24ème Congrès du Parti Communiste Français* (Paris: Messidor/Éditions Sociales, 1982). For an excellent analysis of the congress, see George Ross, 'French Communism with Its Back to the Wall: The Twenty-Fourth

Congress of the French Communist Party,' *Socialist Review*, No. 65 (September–October 1982), pp. 85–120. Also see Ross, 'The Dilemmas of Communism in Mitterrand's France,' *New Political Science*, No. 12 (Winter 1983).

4.  Jérôme Jaffré's analysis of the reasons for the falloff in the Communist Party vote supports this contention: Jaffré found that voters sought to improve the chances of the best-placed left candidate (Mitterrand). Jaffré, 'De Valéry Giscard d'Estaing à François Mitterrand: France de gauche, vote à gauche,' *Pouvoirs*, No. 20 (1982), pp. 5–28. However, voters continued to vote 'usefully' in successive elections: the PCF slide-off was not limited to the presidential elections.

5.  For an account of the PCF's actions in this period, see George Ross, *Workers and Communists in France: From Popular Front to Euro-communism* (Berkeley: University of California Press, 1982).

6.  Nor did the PS platform corroborate PCF charges of Socialist betrayal. Mitterrand entrusted the writing of the party's new program (the *Projet Socialiste*, ratified in 1980) to Jean-Pierre Chevènement, leader of the CERES faction, precisely in order to highlight its leftward-looking features. Although Mitterrand moderated the program for his 110-point presidential campaign platform, the PS remained further to the left than virtually any other European socialist party. But although the PS appeared to champion progressive change in a responsible fashion, the PCF seemed strident and lacking in *sérieux*.

7.  Annie Kriegel, 'Les Forces et Faiblesses du Parti Communiste dans la France de Mitterrand,' *The Tocqueville Review*, 5, No. 1 (Spring 1983), p. 204.

8.  Force Ouvrière, *L'Implantation des militants du PCF dans l'appareil d'état et dans les entreprises nationales* (Paris: Force Ouvrière, 1983).

9.  Lavau, 'Le Recul,' op. cit. Also see Vincent Wright, 'The French Communist Party during the Fifth Republic: The Troubled Path', in Howard Machin, ed., *National Communism in Western Europe: A Third Way for Socialism?* (London: Methuen, 1983), pp. 90–123.

10. Mark Kesselman, 'The Economic Analysis and Programme of the French Communist Party: Consistency Underlying Change,' in P.G. Cerny and M.A. Schain, eds, *French Politics and Public Policy* (London and New York: Frances Pinter, St. Martin's Press and Methuen University Paperbacks, 1980, p. 189).

11. Anicet le Pors, 'Le Sens d'une étape,' *Cahiers du Communisme*, 59, No. 6 (June 1983), p. 168. The title of the article is suggestive: le Pors situates the reforms sponsored by the left, those by PCF ministers in particular, within a general process of step-by-step changes leading toward socialism. The difference between this strategy and classic social democracy, which the PCF has always violently rejected, is difficult to discern.

12. Patrick Jarreau, 'L'alliance P.C.–P.S. à l'épreuve: le point limite,' *Le Monde*, 26–27 June 1983. Also see Jarreau, 'A P.C.F., champ libre pour un débat sur la politique économique et sociale', *Le Monde*, 1 December 1983.

13. For a catalog of PC–PS divergences, see *Le Monde*, 30 November 1983.

14. *Le Monde*, 24 June 1982. However, PCF leaders were no more critical than some Socialists. CERES leader Georges Sarre declared: 'The Delors Plan is at the antipodes from the Socialist program.' *Le Monde*, 1 April 1983.

15. PCF deputies had already abstained on a major government proposal to reform the radio and television system. At the time, however, Charles Fiterman, ranking PCF minister in the Government, criticized the deputies' action: 'I prefer that the various constituents of the parliamentary majority vote alike. It is preferable that they adopt precisely the same position.' *Le Monde*, 18 May 1982. Fiterman later modified his call for unanimity by asserting that PCF deputies were obliged to support the Government on important policies like the budget but not on issues 'of a less global character.' *Le Monde*, 12 October 1982.

16. *Le Monde*, 6 October 1982.

17. *Le Monde*, 17 May 1982.

18. Ibid. This represents a barely veiled assertion that the PS will not keep its promises without PCF pressure. However, French public opinion did not agree. A public opinion poll revealed that, save for PCF sympathizers, large majorities of all other partisan groupings believed that the PCF's departure from the Government would have little or no impact on government policies. *Magazine Hebdo*, 16 September 1983, p. 31.

19. *Le Monde*, 11–12 December 1983. The Government's response to this criticism (which Marchais directed against (then) Industry Minister Laurent Fabius) was also typical. Max Gallo, spokesperson for the Government, declared: 'The industrial policy developed by M. Fabius, in consultation with M. Jack Ralite, [PCF] Minister of Employment, conforms to the objectives decided by the President of the Republic.' Ibid.

20. *Le Monde*, 3 December 1983.

21. *Le Monde*, 24 July 1984.

22. The PCF described the *nouveaux critères* in its theoretical journals, notably *Économie et Politique* and *Cahiers du Communisme*, during 1982–3. For the fullest account, see Philippe Herzog, *L'Économie à bras-le-corps, Initiation aux politiques économiques actuelles* (Paris: Éditions Sociales, 1982).

23. Paul Laurent, 'Le Parti communiste qu'il nous faut aujourd'hui,' *Cahiers du Communisme*, 59, Nos. 7–8 (July–August 1983), p. 41.

24. Philippe Herzog, 'Nous lançons aujourd'hui un appel au débat, à tous les niveaux, pour une intervention constructive des travailleurs dans la gestion,' *Économie et Politique*, No. 62 (June 1982), p. 38.

25. For a critique of the new criteria along these lines, see Michel Holland and Jean Laganier, 'Contribution au débat sur les "nouveaux critères de gestion",' *Les Temps Modernes*, No. 441 bis (April 1983), pp. 221–36.

26. André Gorz, *Les Chemins du paradis, l'agonie du capital* (Paris: Les Éditions Galilée, 1983).

27. Pierre Birnbaum, *Le Peuple et les gros* (Paris: Pluriel, 1984), p. 214.

28. The leading works which describe the PCF counter-community are Annie Kriegel, *Les Communistes français* (Paris: Seuil, 1970); Ronald Tiersky, *French Communism, 1920–1972* (New York: Columbia University Press, 1972); and Lavau, *A Quoi sert . . . ?*, op. cit.

29. Jean Badouin, 'L'Échec communiste du juin 1981: Recul électoral ou crise hégémonique?' *Pouvoirs*, No. 20 (1982), p. 47.

30. Etienne Balibar, 'Après l'autre mai,' in Christine Buci-Glucksmann, ed., *La Gauche, le pouvoir, le socialisme, hommage à Nicos Poulantzas* (Paris: PUF, 1983), pp. 99–119.

31. For analyses of this issue, see Claus Offe and Helmut Wiesenthal, 'Two Logics of Collective Action: Theoretical Notes on Social Class and Organizational Form,' in Maurice Zeitlin, ed., *Political Power and Social Theory*, vol. 1 (Greenwich, Conn.: JAI Press, 1980), pp. 67–115; Adam Przeworski, 'Material Interests, Class Compromise, and the Transition to Socialism,' *Politics and Society*, 10, No. 2 (1980), pp. 125–53; and Przeworski, 'Social Democracy as a Historical Phenomenon,' *New Left Review*, No. 122 (August–September 1980), pp. 27–58.

# 3 Conditional Support for Communist Local Governments in France: Alienation and Coalition-Building*

*Martin A. Schain*

The essential difference is that the Communists are more dissatisfied, more outraged by the State of Things, and consequently their protest vote is even more violent. They vote as far to the left as they can. If there were a party to the left of the Communist Party, they would vote for it. Furthermore, by voting Communist they are voting against their neighbors who vote Socialist and Socialist Radical. A Communist vote permits them to express their contempt of the inside *ils* and the outside *ils* at the same time.... However, it is only on this negative aspect of the Communist program that the members of the party find themselves in agreement.[1]

Communism in France has been generally understood from the perspective of protest and opposition. Supported by dissatisfied, deprived and alienated voters, the attractiveness of the party has been related more to its implacable anti-regime opposition than to its revolutionary vocation. In fact, so widespread has been the assumption of a link between Communist support and protest and alienation, that social scientists have frequently turned the relationship around and considered party membership and support as a measure in itself of the scope of alienated opposition in France.

However, the very nature of the support is the Achilles' heel of the movement, since it is argued that support for the French Communist Party (PCF) should inevitably diminish as the conditions responsible for alienation recede. A party with little positive support, moreover, gains only as opposition, and is unlikely to gather support as a party with a serious chance of actually governing.

In recent years, this view of the PCF, and of support for the party, has been effectively challenged.[2] However, support for the PCF at the one level of government where the party has held governing power for almost fifty years — the commune — has remained a neglected area of enquiry.

But paradoxically, while 9 million Frenchmen [in 1983] live today in these [Communist-governed] communes, while numerous specialists are in agreement in their recognition that the strength of the PCF is largely found in its local implantation, the world of research and of the university is not interested in this phenomenon ... Another paradox, if dozens, even hundreds of books have appeared to clarify the PCF from within, not one has yet focused essentially on the municipalities of the party. A veritable law of silence sems to be imposed, stronger than the one that reigns within the national directorate [of the party].[3]

This neglect is particularly puzzling because, far from being exceptional,

* This chapter is part of a larger study of Communist-governed cities, *French Communism and Local Power: Urban Politics and Political Change* (London: Frances Pinter, 1985). An earlier version was presented at the Annual Meeting of the American Political Science Association, The Palmer House, Chicago, Ill., September 1983, and a shorter version was published in *Contemporary French Civilization*, **VIII**, Nos. 1 and 2 (Fall/Winter, 1983–4).

Communist government at the municipal level has been widespread and well established since the Second World War. In the provisional elections in 1945 almost 1,500 towns elected Communist mayors, including 46 of the 110 cities with more than 30,000 population. While many of these towns were lost in the Gaullist sweep of 1947, support for Communist local candidates and lists remained steady and strong during the Fourth and Fifth Republics, and the number of towns with Communist mayors grew steadily after 1947. Between 1959 and 1983, no Communist-led local government in a town with more than 30,000 population lost an election, and in each election the number of towns with Communist mayors increased. By 1965, Communist mayors governed more large towns than any other single party. Although this was no longer true after 1977, the Communist group has remained second only to the Socialists. (See Table 3.1.)

Table 3.1  The number of towns with mayors of different parties during the Fifth Republic (cities with over 30,000 population)

|  | 1959 | 1965 | 1971 | 1977 | 1983* |
|---|---|---|---|---|---|
| PC | 25 | 34 | 45 | 72 | 57 |
| PS (MRG) | 41 | 33 | 40 | 83 | 63 |
| Misc. Left | 17 | 14 | 9 | 8 | 0 |
| Radical | 6 | 6 | 4 | 2 | |
| Centrist | 12 | 13 | 26 | 9 | |
| Independent | 15 | 13 | 11 | 13 | 40 |
| R.I. | 8 | 8 | 12 | 15 | |
| UNR–RPR | 24 | 25 | 30 | 15 | 39 |
| Diverse | 10 | 12 | 15 | 3 | 21 |
| Total | 158 | 158 | 192 | 221 | 220 |

* These balances do not reflect simply the gains and losses of larger towns. They also reflect the results of population gains and losses. Thus ten towns that had 30,000 population in 1977, fell below that number in 1983, while nine towns grew beyond that level. These demographic changes decreased the number of larger Socialist governed towns.

*Sources:*  *Le Monde*, March 23, 1965, March 23, 1971, March 22, 1977; Gérard LeGall, 'Un recul du "bloc au pouvoir" moindre en 1983 qu'en 1977'. *Revue Politique et Parlementaire*, April 1983, p. 31.

In the local elections of 1983, cities governed by Communists lost support for the first time since the establishment of the Fifth Republic, and the number of large towns governed by Communist mayors declined. This loss of support was not unexpected, since it confirmed the serious Communist losses in the presidential and legislative elections of 1981, as well as a reaction to the economic problems of the country, but it did indicate the limits of a long period of expansion of Communist local government. Nevertheless, it is clear that for many years a large number of voters have been willing to support Communists not simply as opposition, but as decision-makers and leaders of government.

We will argue here that the protest and opposition perspective, at least as it is generally presented, is an explanation that does not conform to the development or structure of support for Communist local government. The expansion and growth of electoral support was accomplished through a careful process of social and political coalition-building, while the decline in 1983 indicates some of the limits of that process. We shall argue that the expansion and decline reflect the strengths and weaknesses of established Communism in France, rather than the level of alienation in the country.

## EXPLAINING SUPPORT FOR ESTABLISHED COMMUNISM

Studies going back to the 1950s have emphasized the uniqueness of those who vote for the PCF, and have generally explained its electoral success in economic, sociological and psychological, rather than political, terms. Thus, the basis of Communist support is purported to be enduring poverty accentuated by large gaps between rich and poor.[4] Support is also nurtured by the isolation of some groups of workers from the rest of society. Therefore, support may be fixed in time to a transitional period of rapid industrial development, or fixed in social space (for railway workers, for example) or geographic space (for miners).[5]

The cumulative effect of these conditions, it has been argued, tends to foster working-class rootlessness and alienation, which forms the seedbed within which Communist support is established and grows. In this sense, Communism is 'the religion of the rootless' and support is the protest of the alienated.[6]

While work of Lipset and Kornhauser focuses on the conditions that form the context within which working-class alienation develops and is expressed, other studies deal directly with the nature of the alienation itself. What emerges is a pattern of strong, negative opposition. The Communist voter above all is opposed to 'the abstractions he feels are holding him back.' Support for the Communist Party has little to do with any positive agreement with the positions of the party, its programs and personnel; rather, it is simply the strongest expression of opposition to the existing system. Between the party and its supporters there is no shared perspective that goes beyond opposition and hostility towards the established political, social and economic order.

It will have been noted by now that the one thing lacking in the reality world of the protest voter is some encompassing intellectual abstraction he is really and enthusiastically for: one consistent with the feelings he shares with so many others and with his most satisfying personal experiences; one that he and others can communicate and can rally around; one that rings as true for him today as the great political slogans of the eighteenth century did in their time.[7]

Given the sources of Communist strength, and the almost pure opposition that unites Communist support, the primary role of the party must be to maximize the political expression of discontent. In the short run this increases support: 'The social, economic and political issues remain, and with them, the impressive scope of Communist power to act as a disintegrating and corrupting element within our society.'[8] In the long run, however, modernization will eliminate the seedbed of protest support, and electoral support for the Communist Party will inevitably decline.

. . . If one admits that the true social revolution is taking place now through modernization, Communism seems fated in the West either to disappear or to remain only as an instrument of Soviet imperialism.[9]

Thus, the short-run stability of Communist support can be understood in terms of continuing sources of discontent and alienation. The logical consequence of this argument about the sources of Communist strength is to accept Communist electoral support as a measure, in itself, of the depth and breadth of systemic opposition, of widespread alienation and of weakness of the social fabric.

Voting for a radical party is an aggressive form of alienation oriented against the existing socio-economic system, which aims at replacing the system with another. The percent of the radical vote is a good indicator of the extent of this kind of alienation.[10]

Other studies, however, offer a political explanation for the durability of Communist support that goes beyond alienation and that is related to the ability of the party to develop an effective organization. If Communist electoral support emerges from alienation, it is perpetuated through an isolating political subculture. Within the working-class core, the PCF has built political and electoral support on a counter-community structure.

Stable Communist strength, that is, little fluctuation up or down, is associated with the older industrial areas in which the party has been strong since the Russian revolution ... In such regions, the Communists have created an elaborate network of party-linked voluntary associations and leisure activities, so that, as in parts of France and Italy, one almost has a functioning subculture unaffected by political events ... When the party is strong, it endeavors ... to isolate its base from serious influence by non-Communist sources.[11]

Where they actually govern, they are in a stronger position, of course, to build a solid, oppositional counter-community.

As the actual governors of a community, capable of producing political outputs more visibly than elsewhere, the Communists are able to serve this role in three ways: by answering the bread-and-butter interests of their clientele ...., by making full use of a privileged channel of political communication, and by creating a network of solid Party bastions for use in both offensive and defensive strategy, depending on the exigencies of the moment. In other words, Communist local governments are important supports of the generalized roles of the tribune and countercommunity ...[12]

Atomized, alienated, aggressive and even organized support, however, is quite different from support for the party as such, it is argued. Support for the party as opposition may be considerable, and even organizable, but this in no way presumes support for Communist Party power. The party voter, 'measures his own satisfactions of life, not on Communist Party standards, but on middle class, bourgeois standards.'[13]

Thus the opposition–protest orientation of Communist support would appear to lock the party into a role of permanent opposition, since there always exists the danger of voters moving further to the left (or to the protest right for that matter). This analysis also implies that the Communist base is either highly politically unstable, or, alternately, subject to the influence of totalitarian controls.

Clearly, there are problems with this view of Communist electoral support as protest. Even if we accept the Communist Party as the party of the alienated and the politically disinherited, Georges Lavau has presented an impressive case that by effectively disengaging itself from revolutionary activity, and by committing itself to the electoral game, the PCF has provided an integrating bridge between the alienated and the Republic.[14] While this view certainly has not gone unchallenged, Lavau presents extensive survey data to demonstrate that large numbers of voters — those who have voted Communist and those who have not — have *perceived* the Communists as 'tribunes' for the well-being of the dispossessed, rather than simply regime opponents.[15]

There is also evidence that the protest voter image of the PCF supporter has, at the very least, been exaggerated. For example, it is not at all clear that the Communists draw their support from the most impoverished groups. In various surveys taken during the Fifth Republic, the poorest categories gave more support to almost every major party over the PCF.[16] Nor was the income structure of PCF voters much different from that of any major party during the Fifth Republic; in fact, every major party drew a larger percentage than the Communists of its electorate from the lowest income groups.[17] With about half its votes coming from blue-collar workers, the PCF is certainly more dependent upon the working class than any other party. However, only about a third of blue-collar workers voted Communist in 1967, 1968, 1973 and 1978 (up from about a fifth in 1962) and fewer than a quarter voted Communist in the first round of the 1981 legislative elections. Moreover, it is important to remember that almost as many workers appear to have voted Gaullist in 1967 and 1968; the parties of the right lost working-class votes after 1973, but apparently to the Socialists. Finally, the unskilled, assembly-line workers were less likely than the skilled workers to vote for the PCF.[18] Thus, while alienation may be nurtured in an environment of relative deprivation, the Communist Party does not appear to have either an exclusive or a dominant claim on either the deprived or the working class.

Moreover, the claim that Communist Party supporters are alienated protest voters has to be analyzed in the context of French political culture. Statements describing a conflict society, or proposing that there is great injustice in France regularly receive a high level of agreement across party lines and class lines. Fifty-six percent of PCF respondents in 1968 agreed that 'class conflict is a reality;' but so did 50 percent of the Socialists and 40 percent of the Gaullists.[19] Also in 1968, fully two-thirds of the respondents agreed that increased wealth was being inequitably distributed, with little difference in the breakdown by party or class.[20] One analysis of mass orientations towards politics concluded that by the last months of the Fourth Republic, there was 'a tendency towards a national consensus against the parties and parliament.'[21]

Attitudes of alienation and opposition to various aspects of the political system have been quite common in France, and it is not clear that Communist supporters are different in this respect. PCF supporters do think of themselves, and are thought of by others as 'a useful force of opposition' and articulators of discontent.[22] However, Sidney Tarrow found that, in the early 1970s, political involvement among working-class respondents tended both to increase commitment to the left and decrease hostility to political leaders; among the working-class respondents, those most hostile to political leaders were least likely to be involved in politics and likely to support parties of the right.[23]

What has distinguished PCF supporters from those of other parties is not so much the negative bond of mere protest, but a much stronger bond of commitment. The response of Communist voters to questions concerning international events and the working-class condition has been strikingly different from that of other voters, and generally consistent with the party world view. PCF voters have also shown the strongest consistent loyalty to their party from election to election, and before 1982 were consistently favorable to participation of the party in responsible governmental positions.[24] In fact, if we take the attitudes and electoral behavior of Communist supporters as our guide, there seems to be more evidence of strong, widespread commitment to the PCF than to any other party. Whatever anger, protest or commitment attracts supporters to the party, the negative bond of protest seems to be an insufficient explanation for the stability and the growth of the Communist constituency until 1981.

Moreover, at least two studies of departments undergoing rapid industrial development show no consistent relationship between transitional economic development and changes in Communist support. The dislocations of development have increased PCF support under some circumstances, but have also increased support for the right under other conditions.[25]

Thus, analyses of voter attitudes and voting patterns bring into question the link between alienated protest and electoral support for the PCF. Nevertheless, it would be useful to pursue this analysis at the level where Communists have actually governed and held power, where the ability of the Communists to organize, isolate and perpetuate a counter-community has acquired mythical dimensions.[26]

### THE EXPANSION AND GROWTH OF ELECTORAL SUPPORT AT THE LOCAL LEVEL

An analysis of voting patterns at the local level presents a complex picture that challenges both the link between protest voting and Communist support, as well as many of the prevailing assumptions about the ability of the PCF to organize politically and to perpetuate a counter-community. The establishment and expansion of Communist governments at the local level has always been conditional, and has been related more to their will and ability to operate within the political system, than to their desire to challenge the system directly. Until 1983, the electoral support for Communist local governments increased most during those periods when the party has either aspired to gain national governing power (1935 and 1977), or has actually held positions in the national government (1945-6). The greatest declines in support for Communists at the local level have occurred when the party has been most militantly revolutionary and has most openly challenged the regime.

The first breakthrough for the PCF in local elections was in 1935, when it doubled the number of cities under its control, from 150 to 297.[27] Ten years later, the second breakthrough occurred at a time when Communists held ministerial positions for the first time, and when the party was part of the governing coalition. The vote for Communist lists in local elections reached an all-time high in 1945 (5.5 million votes) and the number of towns with Communist mayors increased to almost 1,500.[28]

Local electoral support generally declined after the breakdown of the tripartite coalition in the spring of 1947 and local electoral success (i.e. actually winning elections) diminished rapidly. By 1965, the number of Communist local councilors and the number of towns with Communist mayors declined to about half the 1945 level.[29] As momentum increased in negotiations within the left on a common program, however, both electoral support and success increased. By 1977, the total number of towns with

Communist mayors rose to about the same level as it had been in 1945.[30] Almost ten million people lived in towns with Communist mayors.

The general pattern of electoral success and failure until 1983 provides evidence that when the commitment of the PCF to govern was strong and clear, support and success increased, and declined when this commitment was ambiguous. In 1983, for the first time since the period of the liberation, local elections took place with the left actually in power at the national level, and with Communists holding ministerial positions. Once again voters were offered the possibility of voting their judgment of the Communists (and the Socialists) as national as well as local decision-makers and the judgment was 'globally negative.' For the first time during the Fifth Republic, the Communists suffered important losses in the larger towns (over 30,000 population). Electoral support declined by about 7 percent, and sixteen of the seventy-two towns with Communist mayors were lost to the right.[31] Communist-led lists lost votes in all but one of the towns controlled by the party. During the following year the Communists lost six more by-elections, held because of voting irregularities in March.

Although the scope and pattern of their losses were comparable to those of the Socialists, and less serious than those sustained by the right in 1977, they were quite serious from the point of view of the party organization. In areas in which the number of Communist-led governments had recently expanded, and where their defeats were concentrated, decline in electoral support was marginal. However, in areas where they had been in control the longest — the 'bastions' — decline was most pronounced, although there were few actual defeats of incumbent governments. (See below, pp. 73–4.)

If past patterns indicated a willingness by increasing numbers of voters to support Communists aspiring to attain national governing power, the 1983 local election results demonstrated a clear reaction to the way that power had been used. While support for Communist local government has always been conditional, the results also reflected the growing number of complex conditions that have underpinned the expansion and growth of support for Communist local government during the Fifth Republic.

EXPANSION OF SUPPORT AND COALITION-BUILDING

Changes in the electoral fortunes of Communist local governments cannot be attributed to changes in electoral support alone. Electoral success since 1925 has also been related to such factors as electoral laws and, most of all, to cooperation within the left. (Of course, cooperation has also been related to periods when the PCF has pursued an electoral strategy.) Cooperation has usually benefited all parties, either through withdrawal in favor of the best-placed list in the second round of local elections, or through formation of combined 'popular-front' lists. Such agreements have increased success by eliminating destructive competition, even where actual voter support has changed very little.

Although widespread local agreements have been generally limited to periods when there has been agreement among the national parties, there have been local agreements even during the worst periods of internecine warfare on the left. In 1925, for example, in two of the five towns that elected Communist mayors in the Paris region (Malakoff and Vitry), there were local united lists with the S.F.I.O.[32] In 1947 and 1953, on the other hand, cooperation at the local level was rare, and the Communists suffered massive defeats.

In 1947, Communist-led lists were defeated in thirty-five of the forty-six larger towns that they had governed since 1946. Twelve of these were clearly lost in 'duels' with the RPF, but the remainder of the defeats were due to the breakup of popular-front alliances with the Socialists. In numerous cities, Socialist town councilors voted with the Gaullists for either a Gaullist or Socialist mayor.[33] In the Paris region, the PCF lost forty of the sixty towns it controlled in 1946. In twenty-five of these towns, the Socialists were in a position to 'arbitrate,' and in twenty-one they used their position to gain the mayor's office, although in no case were they the strongest party.[34]

By contrast, in 1959, in the first local elections under the Fifth Republic, there were united lists in almost 20 percent of the 411 cities with more than 9,000 population. There were also numerous mutual withdrawals in the second round of the elections, despite efforts by the national Socialist Party to keep the Communists isolated. As a result, there were important gains for both parties.[35]

The importance of the combined effects of the electoral law and electoral cooperation can be seen through an analysis of Communist victories in towns with over 30,000 population during the Fifth Republic. Of the seventy-two large towns governed by the Communists prior to the 1983 elections, only sixteen had been in their control after the 1947 Gaullist sweep. In each succeeding election the PCF was able to increase the number of larger towns under its control.

Increased electoral support was only marginally important for most of the initial victories in each election. The first large increase in the number of municipalities with Communist mayors occurred in 1959, and can be attributed more to the operation of the new election law, than to any massive shift of voters in favor of the Communists. The new law substituted a winner-take-all system (in municipalities with between 30,000 and 120,000 people) for the previous system of proportional representation. Three of the ten victories in 1959 were achieved by a plurality in the second round; these municipalities probably would have gone to a non-Communist coalition under the old system. In three others, the Communists owed their victory to the organization of popular front lists (Noisy-le-Sec, Patin and Choissy-le-Roi.)[36] In only three of the remaining five was there a decisive Communist electoral victory with a majority on the first round. The mean vote in the first round for the Communist-led lists was only 44.8 percent, three points higher than in the previous election.

Similarly, of the eight large municipalities that elected Communist mayors in 1965, four were won with joint lists, and one other with withdrawal of the Socialist list in the second round. In two of the remaining three, the Communist list won a plurality in both rounds. In the last, le Havre, the Communist list, led by a former mayor, gained a majority in the second round. However, because the Communists did not have a majority in the first round, they gained control of the city council only because the election rules for cities with more than 120,000 population were changed in 1965 from proportional representation to winner-take-all in the second round.[37]

By 1971, the movement towards unity on the left had begun in earnest, and five of the six new municipalities that elected Communist mayors, did so with Communist–Socialist lists. The 1977 municipal elections marked an unprecedented victory for the united left in general, and the Communists in particular. The number of Communist-governed municipalities increased by twenty-two. Twenty of these lists were union of the left coalitions with the Socialists. In the remaining two, La Ciotat and Noisy-le-Grand, the Socialist Party split, enabling the United Left list to win a first-round victory, and in the second, the Socialists withdrew their list for the second round. However, in no case can the PCF victory be attributed to an upsurge in support for the Communist Party.[38]

Therefore, the electoral laws since 1959, which have generally favored party coalitions and cooperation, combined with increasing cooperation among the parties of the left, have provided a framework within which the Communists have been able to maneuver either to win all of the municipal council seats with a plurality of votes, or (increasingly) to expand their local influence through the development and the enforcement of left-unity. The point is that increased voter support has been of only marginal importance for most of the initial victories, and that the alteration of the political environment has been of far greater importance — at least for the initial victory.

Aside from the election laws, the second important change in political environment has been the restructuring of the Socialist Party at the local level. Despite the national strategy to which the PS was committed after 1972, thirty of the forty-six municipalities with Socialist mayors before the 1977 elections were governed either by non-Communist-left or 'Third Force' coalitions.[39] This reflected the reality of the Socialist Party at the grass roots when the feeling was still strong that the strength of the party lay in its ability to form either coalitions of the center or the left, depending on the local situation, and that it could maximize its strength nationally through local flexibility. In addition, many of the party's important local notables had built their careers on fighting and defeating the Communists at the local level.[40]

The PS was changing, however, particularly in the larger cities. With considerable caution, the new party leadership had begun to break up some of the old Third Force alliances at the local level even before the 1971 local elections.

In 1965, and even more in 1971, a 'new' Third Force tactic was not likely to be successful, particularly not in a large city for the simple reason that its acceptance almost always implied the disruption of the local Socialist section and favored the establishment of rival Socialist factions thus splitting the Socialist electorate.[41]

Frequently, Socialist leaders at the department level intervened directly to prevent the formation of Third Force coalitions, and at times PS and PCF section leaders at the local level intervened as well. Where higher party intervention at the local level was resisted, advocates of Third Force strategy were sometimes either dismissed from the party, or resigned in anticipation of dismissal. Thus, after 1965, there was a gradual 'nationalization' of Socialist politics that permitted an expansion of Communist influence at the local level.[42]

In anticipation of the 1977 municipal elections, the Communists now demanded that the PS intensify its efforts to restructure the party at the local level. In the short run this would be a test of viability of the united-left strategy; in the long run it would serve to neutralize the most anti-Communist elements within the PS. As a result, an agreement was reached at the national level on 28 June 1976 that required the departmental and local organizations of both parties to negotiate united lists for the first round of the elections.[43]

For the Communists, there were several important results of the general success of this operation. The united-left coalitions enabled both parties to expand their presence at the local level, and for both the gamble was fully justified by the results. Despite the turmoil that accompanied the restructuring in numerous cases, party loyalty remained generally strong, and united-left lists were victorious in fifty-seven new municipalities: twenty-two where the PCF headed the list and thirty-five where the PS headed the list. Perhaps more important, the Communists lost none of the municipalities they held before the elections, while the Socialists lost only six (one to the Communists). Thus, the viability of the coalition was demonstrated. Also, the PCF entered the governing councils of twenty-five cities that were formerly governed by non-Communist-left or Third Force coalitions (the PS entered the councils of nine PCF-governed cities from which they had been previously excluded). This breakthrough, and the forced resignation or dismissal of five Socialist mayors, was of long-term importance for the Communists, since the strategy of cooperation set into motion a process that greatly expanded the presence of the party.[44]

This process contradicts the widely-held belief that the expansion of Communist government at the local level was '. . . above all due to an anti-Gaullist reflex among a large number of voters.'[45] During the Fifth Republic, many of the Communist victories were at the expense of Socialist or centrist Third Force coalitions. Although a number of more recent victories were 'duels' between left and right coalitions, the record does not support the contention that Communist expansion was basically a reactive and negative reflex. The expansion of Communist local government (and therefore the limit to that expansion) can be attributed, in large measure, to the slow disintegration of Third Force coalitions at the local level under the pressure of left unity. Of course, this too can be seen as a reflex against the right, but by the parties, not the voters. This process also greatly altered the social environment within which the Communists held local power.[46]

THE CHANGING SOCIAL ENVIRONMENT

Cities in which PCF mayors have held power since 1947 are mostly the working-class suburbs of Paris; only two are outside the Paris region. Municipalities that have elected Communist-led lists since 1953, however, have been increasingly less working class and are in other parts of the country. In 1968, a third of the larger towns governed by Communists had working-class majorities, but by 1978, only 13 percent were predominantly working class. In 1968, fewer than a quarter of the Communist-governed towns were outside the Paris region, but by 1978, 40 percent were in the provinces. (See Table 3.2.)

Three kinds of changes have contributed to this altered environment. The most important is the development of coalition politics within the left, which made possible a large number of victories of Communist-led lists during the Fifth Republic. Only three of the forty-two larger towns won by the Communists after local coalition-building began (in 1965) had majority working-class populations. Second, the social structure of the population has

**Table 3.2**   The distribution of Communist-governed towns in 1968 and 1978 by location and by working-class population (percentage of towns over 30,000 population)

| | *1968 (N = 34)* | | | *1978 (N = 72)* | | |
|---|---|---|---|---|---|---|
| | *High working class** % | *Low working class** % | *Total 1968* % | *High working class** % | *Low working class** % | *Total 1978* % |
| Paris region | 24 | 52 | 76 | 5 | 54 | 59 |
| Provinces | 9 | 14 | 23 | 8 | 32 | 40 |
| Total | 33 | 66 | 100 | 13 | 86 | 100 |

* Cities with over 30,000 population and more than 50 percent blue-collar workers.
*Sources:*   Population figures are taken from *Le Recensement de la population, 1968 et 1975* (Paris INSEE, 1970 and 1978).

**Table 3.3**   Distribution of towns governed by different parties — 1983 (before the elections) by working-class concentration (cities with over 30,000 population)

| *% Working class* | | *PC* | *PS/ MRG* | *MOD* | *Gaullist* | *Local* | *Total* |
|---|---|---|---|---|---|---|---|
| 0–30 | Number | 4 | 12 | 9 | 6 | 3 | 34 |
| | Percent | 5.4% | 14% | 23.7% | 60% | 30% | 15.6% |
| 31–50 | Number | 60 | 62 | 29 | 4 | 7 | 162 |
| | Percent | 81% | 72.9% | 76.3% | 40% | 70% | 74.7% |
| 50%+ | Number | 10 | 11 | 0 | 0 | 0 | 21 |
| | Percent | 13.5% | 12.9% | 0 | 0 | 0 | 9.7% |
| Total | Number | 74* | 85 | 38 | 10 | 10 | 217 |
| | Percent | 100% | 100% | 100% | 100% | 100% | 100% |

* includes two towns where the population exceeded 30,000 by 1983.
*Sources:*   population figures are taken from *Le Recensement de la population, 1975* (Paris: INSEE, 1978).

been changing since the Second World War, even in the older bastions. Among the sixteen larger towns governed by Communists since 1947 (or before), almost 60 percent had working-class majorities in 1968, but this diminished to 25 percent by 1975. Finally, an increasing percentage of this working-class population in the older bastions was composed of immigrant workers who could not vote, thus diluting working-class electoral strength even more.[47]

By 1983, as a result of these changes, the network of Communist-governed municipalities was somewhat more working class than towns governed by other parties, but not strikingly different from those governed by the Socialists. (See Table 3.3.) Indeed, the class profile of Communist-governed towns (and those governed by the left in general) was far more typical of larger cities in France than the class profile of cities governed by the right. If the 'typical' Communist town has been understood as a working-class suburb of Paris, the 'typical' town that elected a new Communist mayor during the Fifth Republic was a provincial town with a working-class minority.

THE GROWTH AND DECLINE OF COMMUNIST ELECTORAL SUPPORT

Although increased support for the PCF has been less important than coalitions and changing support in accounting for initial Communist victories in most cases, once the Communists were in power support grew impressively until 1983. Eleven municipalities elected PCF-led councils in 1959. In the first round of the elections, the mean vote for these lists was 41.1 percent. In 1965, it increased to 58.4 percent, in 1971 it stayed about the same, and rose to 63.5 percent in 1977. Similarly, in 1965 nine large municipalities elected a Communist list for the first time with an average of 43.4 percent of the votes in the first round. This rose to 56.1 percent in 1971 and 60.2 percent in 1977.

In general, those towns that have been governed by Communists for the longest period of time voted for them in the highest proportions. (See Table 3.4.) The vast majority of the towns that were governed by Communists for

**Table 3.4** Electoral support for Communist-governed towns in 1977 and 1983, by years in power (towns with over 30,000 population — percentage in first round of local election)

|  | *Years in power in 1983* | | | | | | |
|---|---|---|---|---|---|---|---|
|  | 36 | 30 | 24 | 18 | 12 | 6 | Total |
| 1977 | 76% | 70% | 63% | 60% | 58% | 48% | 61% |
| 1983 | 61 | 60 | 53 | 51 | 47 | 47 | 53 |
| Mean loss | 15 | 10 | 10 | 9 | 11 | 1 | 8 |
| No. of towns | 16 | 7 | 11 | 9 | 7 | 22 | 72 |

*Sources: Le Monde*, March 15, 1977; March 8, 1983.

twelve years or longer in 1977 gave them more than 60 percent of the vote. While this comfortable margin was sharply reduced in 1983, the relationship between level of electoral support and length of time in office was confirmed. Thus, if the changing political environment facilitated the *emergence* of Communist-led governments in a growing number of cities with more complex class structures, the experience of voters with these governments resulted in an *increase* of support in subsequent elections, at least until 1983.

The 1983 municipal elections somewhat altered these trends of the past twenty-four years. For the first time during the Fifth Republic, recently-elected Communist municipalities failed to increase their proportion of the vote, and in the oldest bastions of Communist strength there was a heavy erosion of electoral support for the first time since the Second World War.

In the most competitive marginal towns (from an electoral point of view), those won in 1977, Communist-led lists lost less than 1 percent of their 1977 vote. Even in towns that were lost to the opposition, the loss was 3 percent. A large number of the defeats that were sustained can be attributed to a weakening of the political coalition between the Communists and the Socialists at the local level, and a comparative strengthening of the coalition of the right. In seven of the sixteen towns that were lost by the Communists, the parties of the left ran separate lists in the first round; three of these towns were lost in the first round to a more unified opposition. In the second round, at least three more were lost because of a weak transfer of votes from the Socialists (who had withdrawn) to the remaining Communist list.[48] Thus the election demonstrated the strength of the social coalition upon which the expansion of Communist local governments was based, while it also showed the fragility of that political coalition, and the degree to which the maintenance of Communist local government is based upon political agreement.

The 15 percent decline of electoral support in the oldest bastions was far more serious, and accentuated some differences between areas of established Communist strength and the more marginal areas, particularly at times when electoral trends were changing nationally. The last important decline of electoral support for the Communists at the local level was in 1947, a decline that we have attributed to a protest against the movement towards an oppositional position by the party nationally. Although the loss of votes nationally was substantial in 1947, it was only marginal in the bastions of the Paris region.[49] In 1983, the most substantial losses, and the highest rates of abstention were in the 'bastions.'[50]

Voting patterns during the Fifth Republic do not support the thesis that support for Communist local governments is simply a manifestation of negative protest against the central authority of governments of the right. Local support has been stable and has grown as these governments have become better established, and stable voting patterns are not usually characteristic of the protest voters.[51] Moreover, many of the same voters who have voted for Communist governments at the local level have voted for center–right candidates at the national level, behavior that would certainly contradict an interpretation of their local voting as a protest against the right. (See below.)

On the other hand, voting patterns reveal a pattern of protest directed against the Communists at particular moments: in 1947, in the marginal towns, against the shift of PCF policy in the Cold War; in 1983, in the bastions, against the policies of a government of the left in which the PCF shared responsibility. While willing to support Communist local governments when the party was in opposition, large numbers of voters in the bastions now cast their votes in reaction to their strong feelings about key national issues, experienced more acutely in the older industrial towns than in the newly-won towns. (See below, pp. 76–7.)

In the bastions, as in other towns, the electoral support for Communist lists has been far in excess of the number of working-class voters during the Fifth Republic, and the high levels of support have been due to the votes of white-collar workers. It appears from national surveys that while working-class voters remained most loyal to the left in 1983, particularly in towns governed by Communist or Socialist mayors, white-collar workers deserted the left in the highest proportions.[52] Therefore, by 1983, even the bastions were dependent on white-collar support, and vulnerable to white-collar concerns and disappointments. This protest vote, directed against the Communists, is clearly different, however, from a protest vote in favor of the Communists and against the right.

### THE MAINTENANCE OF SUPPORT: THE 'BREAKING EFFECT' AND THE ISOLATED WORKING-CLASS COMMUNITY

Nevertheless, throughout the Fifth Republic electoral support for the Communist-governed municipalities has been strong and stable. However, it is certainly possible that this support can be explained more by working-class loyalties and by the effectiveness of local party organizations, than by the attractions of Communist local government.

Because of a combination of class solidarity and the pressure exerted by a large working-class community, we would expect to find disproportionately high levels of support for Communist candidates in cities with larger working-class populations — a phenomenon referred to by Robert Lane as 'the breaking effect.'[53] Also, because the party organization is more solidly entrenched in the older bastions, particularly those with large working-class populations, we would expect to find consistency of electoral support in these towns.[54]

Support for Communist-led lists, however, has not been affected in any predictable way by working-class concentration. Support levels in 1977 and 1983 varied with length of time in office, regardless of working-class population. If, for example, we compare the cities where Communist governments were elected in 1947 or before with those where Communist mayors were first elected in 1977, we find that in the 1977 and 1983 elections the level of electoral support was highest where the concentration of working-class population was smallest for the 1947 group, indicating no breaking effect. (See Table 3.5.) However, the towns with the largest working class

Table 3.5   Percentage of the vote won with Communist-led lists in 1977 and 1983 by working-class concentration (cities of over 30,000 population)

| *Percent working class (1975)* | *Elected 1947 or before* | | | | *Elected 1977* | | | |
|---|---|---|---|---|---|---|---|---|
| | *(N)* | *% 1977* | *% 1983* | *Difference* | *(N)* | *% 1977* | *%1983* | *Difference* |
| 50–9% | (4) | 73.8% | 61.8% | −12% | (1) | 50.3% | 49.2% | −1.1% |
| 40–9% | (9) | 75.3% | 58.6% | −16.5% | (9) | 48.3% | 51% | +2.7% |
| 30–9% | (3) | 83.2% | 67.2% | −16% | (12) | 47.3% | 48.9% | +1.6% |

populations suffered smaller losses of votes in 1983, indicating greater working-class loyalty, or the effectiveness of the local party machine.

In the marginal towns captured in 1977, the breaking effect should be more important, since the party machine did not have time to take root in 1977. However, there was very little variation in support levels in 1977 and 1983. In fact, those with the largest working-class populations lost votes relative to 1977, while the others actually gained votes. (See Table 3.5.)

It is also possible that Communist electoral stability can be explained by the successful work of local parties in creating an isolating political culture from a more dynamic and complex social base. One way to explore this hypothesis is to compare the consistency of local and national election results in those towns where the party organization can be presumed to be strongest. If the link between effective party domination and electoral success is strong, party influence should be as strong in national as in local elections.

However, there is considerable evidence that the party machine is less effective than its reputation. In the 1973 National Assembly elections, when the Communists generally regained their 1967 level of electoral support, the PCF reported that 58 percent of the towns governed by Communists (with greater than 10,000 population) lost votes compared with 1967. Among the 42 percent that gained votes over 1967, the gains were greatest in the *newer*, less-established municipalities. Thus, the party argued that its organizational strength in more established towns did not seem to aid their national electoral success. Indeed, the party committee argued that the less-established municipalities were more successful because of '. . . the impact of renovation and reinforcement of the party and the working class.'[55]

Similarly, in 1978 the PCF vote remained stable nationally, and there were gains in forty-four departments, compared with 1973. However, in the Paris region there was a general decline in the vote for the Communists '. . . including the two strong bastions of the Seine-Saint-Denis, where the PCF progressed only in the ninth circumscription, and in the Val-de-Marne, where it generally declined, often seriously.'[56]

If we compare the vote for the Communist-led lists in the bastions of the Paris region in the first round of the 1977 local elections with both the first rounds of the legislative elections a year later and the presidential election four years later, once again we find that political implantation is not easily transformed into political effectiveness. (See Table 3.6.) With a mean vote of 75 percent, Communist-led lists mobilized more than 60 percent of the vote in 1977 in all but one of the twenty-one bastions. In the legislative elections a year later, electoral support for Communist candidates was much less impressive. In many of the bastions, Communist candidates confronted opponents from the left, as well as the right. The mean PCF vote was 51.3 percent, and in none of these towns did the Communist candidate receive more than 60 percent of the vote. In a third of the bastions the candidate attracted less than half the vote. In the second round, when there was no longer any opposition from the left, the mean vote rose to 68 percent, seven points below the 1977 showing. This gap between local and national support confirms the findings of Dupoirier and Grunberg for the 1965–71 period.[57]

In the presidential election of 1981, the First Secretary of the PCF was unable to command a majority in any of the bastions in the first round. Indeed, he received a mean of only 36 percent of the vote in these towns (with little deviation from this mean). Despite the setbacks in the 1983 elections in

**Table 3.6** Distribution of votes for the PCF in the 21 bastions* in the Paris Region in 1977, 1978, 1981 and 1983 (Number of towns in each category – 1st round of each election, percentage of votes cast)

|  | 1977 (munic.) | 1978 (legis.) | 1981 (pres.) | 1983 (munic.) |
|---|---|---|---|---|
| 70% + | 16 |  |  | 4 |
| 60–9% | 4 | 1 |  | 10 |
| 50–9% | 1 | 13 |  | 7 |
| 40–9% |  | 5 | 4 |  |
| 30–9% |  | 2 | 16 |  |
| 20–9% |  |  | 1 |  |
| Total | 21 | 21 | 21 | 21 |
| Mean vote | 75.3% | 51.3% | 35.6% | 67.7% |

* Cities governed by Communist mayors before the Fifth Republic — cities over 30,000 population.
*Sources: Le Monde*, March 15, 1977; March 15, 1978; March 8, 1983.
  *Le Monde, L'Élection présidentielle 26 avril–10 mai, 1981 (Supplément aux dossiers et documents du monde*, mai, 1981), pp. 153–190.

the bastions, the results confirm that local support cannot be transferred easily. The mean of 67.7 percent is far below the 1977 level, but far above the support levels of 1981 and 1978.

Therefore, if we use electoral support for Communist candidates as a rough index of party effectiveness, we must conclude that the influence and the ability of the party to mobilize electoral support is qualified and limited. Able to mobilize impressive support in local elections, where candidates may be known, are close to home and have developed a record in governing, the party is far less effective in mobilizing support for Communist candidates in the broader electoral arenas. The emphasis on both the breaking effect and organizational control as explanations for the maintenance of local support appears to be exaggerated, since electoral support mobilized in this way should be transferable to different kinds of elections. Voters who give overwhelming support to Communist local candidates are quite capable of withdrawing that support from other candidates. In fact, local Communist governments appear to attract support in their own right.

CONDITIONAL AND IDEOLOGICAL SUPPORT

There is some limited evidence that what has attracted voters to support local Communist governments is both positive and somewhat different from what has attracted voters to other alternatives. Communist voters are more politicized in the sense that they tend to link local and national party politics, and that they think that this linkage is a good thing. On the other hand, they profess relatively strong faith in the liberty of action of local government as more positive and more innovative than do voters for other parties. (See Table 3.7.) Thus, one survey indicated that the highest priority among those voting

Communist on the local level is the development of public services. While this was a priority for those voting for other left parties (mostly Socialist), in contrast to those voting for the right, far more Communist voters also ranked greater citizen participation as a priority in contrast to those voting for other

**Table 3.7**   Voters' orientations toward local governments

| | PCF | Party preference Non-Comm. left | Centrist | RI | UDR |
|---|---|---|---|---|---|
| 1. Do you feel it is a good thing or a bad thing that a mayor has a political tendency? %age who feel it is good: | 52% | 39% | 26% | 29% | 31% |
| 2. Mayors do not have enough freedom to direct their communes. %age who disagree: | 32% | 20% | 24% | 27% | 25% |
| 3. It is better that communes do not have budgets that are too large because they do not know how to use them. %age who agreed: | 17% | 19% | 17% | 23% | 24% |

*Sources: Sondages* 1971, Nos. 1 and 2, pp. 79 and 82.

**Table 3.8:**   Of the following municipal functions, which do you regard as the most important?

| | Traditionalist | | Modernist | | Participationist | |
|---|---|---|---|---|---|---|
| | Satisfactory administration of local services | Champions local interests vis-à-vis the central government | Develops public services | Prepares for further development | Secures greater participation by inhabitants | Represents political attitudes |
| Total | 49% | 40% | 45% | 38% | 21% | 1% |
| Party Pref: | | | | | | |
| PCF | 43 | 36 | 49 | 33 | 30 | 3 |
| Non-Comm. left | 45 | 39 | 49 | 41 | 22 | 3 |
| Center | 56 | 51 | 39 | 27 | 25 | |
| Gaullist | 53 | 38 | 40 | 40 | 23 | |

*Sources:*   Derived from Jack Hayward and Vincent Wright, 'The 37708 Microcosms of an Indivisible Republic: The French Local Elections of March, 1971,' *Parliamentary Affairs,* Autumn, 1971, p. 234.

parties. In addition, fewer Communist supporters regarded the defense of local interests as a priority compared with other voters. (See Table 3.8.) Sidney Tarrow found that Communist mayors tend to justify their actions in terms of 'the public interest' far more than mayors from other political parties, and are deeply involved in the administrative complexities of developing local projects and services. Thus, their actions seem to reflect the orientation of their voters.[58]

Until 1981, these orientations probably helped to maintain and increase the levels of support for Communist local government. However, after 1981, the opposite was probably true. The orientation towards local–national party linkage facilitated a left protest vote that was most evident where support had been most stable and durable. About 4 of the 14 percent of the electorate that voted for Mitterrand in the second round of the 1981 presidential election, but voted for the right in 1983, changed their vote for 'local reasons,' and most of these voted in towns dominated by the right. Most of the remaining 10 percent, those concerned with national issues, voted in towns governed by the left.[59]

Almost 40 percent of those who changed their vote to the right were concerned about unemployment (which was also the dominant concern for 64 percent of those who continued to vote for the left and 45 percent of the general electorate). Two national issues, however, concerned many more of those who switched to the right than other voters: security and immigrants, issues that most easily link local politics to national responsibility.[60]

If support for Communist local government has been more than merely the rejection of the right, rejection of Communist local government is linked to rejection of the policies of a national government with which the Communists have been associated. Although 52 percent of those who responded (to a SOFRES survey) in February 1983 were more confident of the left to run local government than of the right, 61 percent declared their desire 'to manifest their discontent with the left.'[61]

\* \* \*

We have found that the more conventional, oppositional interpretation of support for Communist local government is helpful neither for understanding the development and maintenance of that support, nor for understanding the changes indicated by the results of the 1983 local elections. The view of electoral support as a manifestation of working-class alienation and party manipulation both overestimates the effectiveness of the party and ignores important elements with which support has been built.

Closer investigation reveals that even in areas of working-class strength, the party has not been able to mobilize a consistent, dependable constituency, and that electoral support for Communist-led local governments almost always exceeds support for Communists running for national office in the same towns. Increasingly, stable support has expanded to areas outside of the older core areas, but this support has also been conditional. The results of the 1983 elections confirm the stability of this support, but also confirm the conditions that make it possible, the most important of which is the ability of the Communists to attract multiclass support, which is related to continuing political cooperation within the left.

The oppositional interpretation of electoral support implies a level of unconditional ideological commitment by voters to the PCF that may never have existed. As Communist government expanded at the local level during the Fifth Republic, it was built on a complex set of conditions. Voters were asked to vote for Communist-led lists in order to achieve local change and reform and to manifest their support for the unity of the left, and voters from diverse backgrounds responded in growing numbers. The results of the 1983 elections serve to remind us that social and political bases for Communist local government have changed during the Fifth Republic. Political coalitions, built around programs, objectives and diverse party loyalties have modified, and perhaps replaced, the old ideological community. The party seems to have succeeded in building a different kind of electoral support, at once broader and more conditional. However, it is not clear that the PCF is aware of this success.

NOTES

1.  Laurence Wylie, *Village in the Vaucluse* (New York: Harper, 1964), p. 219.
2.  In, for example, Georges Lavau, *A quoi sert le parti communiste français?* (Paris: Fayard, 1983). Lavau, however, presents a functional argument that 'the PCF legitimates the system, while constantly crying about its legitimacy . . .' by acting as a 'tribune' for the alienated while acting within the confines of the rules of the game. Thus, alienated opposition is channeled into the system in legitimate ways. See pp. 34–8. Also see Richard Hamilton, *Affluence and the French Worker in the Fourth Republic* (Princeton: Princeton University Press, 1967), Introduction and pp. 290–8.
3.  Raymond Pronier, *Les Municipalités communistes* (Paris: Balland, 1983), p. 12. Pronier somewhat exaggerates. There are a few studies of Communist municipalities that will be referred to below. However, interest has certainly been peripheral. Although Elisabeth Dupoirier and Gerard Grunberg of CIVIPOF in Paris have collected extensive data on voting at the municipal level, there has been no important study of voting patterns in Communist municipalities. Pronier's study (475 pages) devotes little space to electoral support.
4.  Seymour Martin Lipset, *Political Man* (New York: Anchor, 1963), pp. 45 and 125.
5.  William Kornhauser, *The Politics of Mass Society* (New York: Free Press, 1959), p. 213 and Ch. 5, *passim*.
6.  Ibid., p. 157.
7.  Hadley Cantril and David Rodnick, *On Understanding the French Left* (Princeton: Institute for International Research, 1956), p. 151.
8.  Mario Einaudi, 'Communism in Western Europe,' in Einaudi, Domenach and Garoschi, *Communism in Western Europe* (Hamden: Anchor Books, 1971), p. 51.
9.  Pierre Fougeyrollas, 'France,' *Survey* (June 1962), p. 124.
10. Glaucio Soares and Robert L. Hablin, 'Socio-economic Variables and Voting for the Radical Left in Chile, 1952,' *American Political Science Review* (December 1967), p. 1053.
11. Seymour Martin Lipset, 'The Changing Class Structure and Contemporary European Politics,' *Daedelus* (Winter 1964), p. 290. Also, see Hamilton, op. cit.
12. Ronald Tiersky, *French Communism 1920–1972* (New York: Columbia University Press, 1974), p. 352.
13. Cantril and Rodnick, op. cit., p. 151.
14. Lavau, op. cit. Also see his article, 'The PCF, the State and Revolution,' in Donald Blackmer and Sidney Tarrow, *Communism in Italy and France* (Princeton: Princeton University Press, 1975). Lavau's views have not gone uncontested. See the article by Annie Kriegel, 'The French Communist Party and the Fifth Republic,' in the same volume, as well as *Les Communistes* (Paris: Éditions du Seuil, 1970) pp. 238–47.
15. We should add that perceptions aside, the PCF has not been in the lead of protest mobilization for some time. The most determined protests during the Fifth Republic have been organized by former Catholic trade unionists and peasant militants, as well as violently anti-Communist students. Lavau notes that in Stanley Hoffmann's article, 'Protest in Modern France' (in Morton Kaplan, *The Revolution in World Politics*) the PCF is not mentioned a single time. Lavau, 'Le Parti communiste dans le système politique français,' in Frédéric Bon *et al., Le Communisme en France* (Paris: Armand Colin, 1969), pp. 28–31, 39.
16. See *Sondages*, 1963, No. 2, p. 64. In the first round of the presidential elections in

1981, Georges Marchais, the candidate for the Communist Party, received a lower percentage of the vote than any other major candidate in two income categories — the lowest and the highest. See *Le Nouvel Observateur*, 1 June 1981, p. 40.

17. *Sondages*, No. 2, 1966. For additional comments, see Thomas Greene, 'The Electorate of Non-Ruling Communist Parties,' *Studies in Comparative Communism* (July–October 1971), p. 82.

18. *Sondages*, 1967, No. 3, p. 55; 1968, No. 2, p. 102; 1973, No. 1, p. 21; 1978, No. 1, p. 22. *Le Nouvel Observateur*, 4 July 1981. In fact the proportion of working-class votes among the PCF electorate has declined slightly from 53 percent in 1973 to about 49 percent in 1981.

19. *Sondages*, 1968, No. 1, p. 45.

20. Ibid., p. 43.

21. Pierre Fougeyrollas, *La Conscience politique dans la France contemporaine* (Paris: Denoël, 1963), p. 185.

22. Lavau, 'Le Parti communiste . . .,' op. cit., pp. 30–1.

23. Sidney Tarrow, 'Urban–Rural Cleavages and Political Involvement: The Case of France,' *American Political Science Review* (June 1971), p. 350.

24. Fougeyrollas, *La Conscience* . . ., op. cit., Ch. 2, and Greene, 'The Electorate of Non-Ruling Communist Parties,' op. cit., pp. 73–89.

25. Greene, op. cit., p. 101. Also see François Goguel, *Modernisation économique et comportement politique* (Paris: Armand Colin, 1969), pp. 81–7.

26. For example, see the volume by the journalist Jean Montaldo, *L'État Communiste* (Paris: Albin Michel, 1978), especially Chapters 4 and 5.

27. Daniel Brower, *The New Jacobins* (Ithaca: Cornell University Press, 1968), p. 86.

28. *L'Année Politique*, 1944–45 (Paris: Presses Universitaires de France, 1946), p. 491; *L'Année Politique*, 1947, p. 364.

29. *Le Monde*, 23 April 1971, p. 10.

30. For a listing of towns and their Communist mayors, see *Communes d'Aujourd'hui*, No. 10 (1977), p. 43.

31. See Gérard Le Gall, 'Un recul du "bloc au pouvoir" moindre en 1983 qu'en 1977,' *Revue Politique et Parlementaire* (April 1983).

32. François Platone, 'L'Implantation municipale du Parti communiste dans la Seine et sa conception de l'administration communale,' (unpublished mémoire, DES, FNSP, Paris, 1967), p. 12.

33. Frédéric Bon and Jérôme Jaffré, 'Les Résultats des élections municipales de 1947,' FNSP, colloque des 4 et 5 décembre, 1981, pp. 14–20.

34. Platone, op. cit., p. 32.

35. *Le Monde*, March 19, 1959. Also see Roy Macridis and Bernard Brown, *The De Gaulle Republic* (Homewood: Dorsey Press, 1960), pp. 279–82.

36. *Le Monde*, 19 March 1959, p. 5.

37. *Le Monde*, 16 and 23 March, 1965.

38. Indeed, Jean Charlot found that the victories for the left were probably due more to support for the Socialists. See Charlot, 'Avant l'empoignade du 2e tour,' *Le Point*, 4 March 1977.

39. See Jean Charlot, 'La Politisation des municipales,' *Projet* (February 1977), p. 139.

40. See Denis Lacorne in Blackmer and Tarrow, op. cit., pp. 335–9.

41. Ibid., p. 321.

42. The definitive book on the development of unity of the left at the local level is Denis Lacorne, *Les Notables rouges* (Paris: Presses de la FNSP, 1980). On the intervention of the national Socialist Party, see pp. 153–61.

43. Ibid., p. 162. Also see Jack Hayward and Vincent Wright, 'Governing from the Center, the 1977 French Local Elections,' *Government and Opposition*, Autumn 1977, pp. 40–1.

44. For the results of the elections, see *Le Monde*, 15 and 22 March 1977, and *Regards sur l'Actualité*, Ministry of the Interior, April 1977, pp. 58–64; report of Roger Fajardie of the PS, *Le Monde*, 27–8 March 1977.

45. *L'Année Politique*, 1965, p. 26.

46. See Lacorne, *Les Notables rouges*, op. cit., p. 125.

47. Immigrants comprised 13.2 percent of the population of the bastions in 1968, and 16.4 percent in 1975. This percentage has certainly increased since 1975. In 1975 all Communist-governed cities had a mean immigrant population of 12 percent, higher than that of groups of cities governed by any other party. On the question of immigrant workers and local politics, see my article, 'Immigrants and Politics in France: Local Politics, Socialism and Race,' in John S. Ambler, ed., *France Under Socialist Leadership* (Philadelphia: Institute for the Study of Human Issues, forthcoming).

48. Jean-Luc Parodi, 'Dans la logique des élections intermédiaires', *Revue Politique et Parlementaire*, April 1983, p. 64

49. *L'Année Politique*, 1947, pp. 193–4.

50. Le Gall, op. cit., pp. 16–17.

51.   On this question, see Angus Campbell, Philip Converse, Warren Miller and Donald Stokes, *The American Voter* (New York: Wiley, 1967), pp. 223–30; and Duncan Macrae Jr., *Parliament, Parties and Society in France, 1946–1958* (New York: St. Martin's Press, 1967), Ch. 9.
52.   Parodi, op. cit., pp. 60–1.
53.   See Robert Lane, *Political Life* (New York: Free Press, 1959), pp. 261–4; Robert Putnam, 'Political Attitudes and the Local Community,' *American Political Science Review*, 60, No. 3 (1966).
54.   Pronier, op. cit., is particularly good in analyzing the entrenchment of the party at the local level. See Part I, *passim*, as well as Chs 6 and 7 of the second part.
55.   *Bulletin de l'Élu Communiste*, No. 45–6 (1973), pp. 2–3.
56.   *Le Monde, Les Élections législatives de mars, 1978 (Supplément aux dossiers et documents du Monde*, mars 1978), p. 76.
57.   See Elisabeth Dupoirier and Gérard Grunberg, 'Vote municipal et vote législatif,' *Revue Française de Science Politique*, 22, No. 2 (April 1972), p. 267. The findings can be compared if we consider the somewhat different sample, and recalculate their table as percentages of expressed, rather than registered, voters. Also see *Le Monde*, 21 March 1978.
58.   See articles by Tarrow and Milch in Blackmer and Tarrow, op. cit., pp. 164–5 and 353.
59.   Parodi, op. cit., p. 60.
60.   Ibid., p. 63. The linkage between national political considerations and local elections has been stronger on the left than on the right for some time. However, linkage has gradually become more generalized on the right as well. See *Sondages*, 1978, Nos 2 and 3, pp. 86–7.
61.   *Le Figaro*, 15 February 1983.

# 4 Socialism in One Country: Mitterrand and the Struggle to Define a New Economic Policy for France*

*Peter A. Hall*

In May 1981 the French people elected a Socialist President for the first time under the Fifth Republic. A month later they ended twenty-three years of conservative rule by returning a Socialist majority to the National Assembly. President François Mitterrand formed a coalition government from the Socialist and Communist Parties. These elections were a decisive act of political will; yet the underlying motivation was largely economic. Formerly cautious French voters gambled on Mitterrand's ability to pull the nation out of six years of recession.[1] He promised to change the economic policies and performance of France.

Has the Mitterrand Government been able to implement an alternative economic strategy? What effect has it had on the performance of the French economy? Can a change of party within the state itself alter the functioning of a capitalist economy? These are the questions this chapter addresses.[2] There is more at stake than the health of the French economy. The world is watching the Mitterrand experiment to judge the ability of socialism to develop a viable response to recession.

## THE ECONOMIC BACKGROUND

To understand the Socialists' performance it is essential to understand the economic situation they inherited. Structural trends had already transformed the French economy. The opportunities and constraints that faced François Mitterrand were different from those presented to Léon Blum or even Charles de Gaulle.

On the one hand, Mitterrand could count on long-term industrial strength. Under the impetus of demographic change, entry into the European Economic Community and *dirigiste* economic policies, France finally experienced rapid industrialization in the post-war period. The volume of French production increased from only $US1,200 to $US1,400 between 1912 and 1947 but tripled to $US4,700 per capita between 1947 and 1982. In the process, the very shape of French industry changed. The small family firms and neo-Malthusianism of the pre-war economy gave way to massive conglomerates with a powerful presence on world markets. Capital was already organized and the state enjoyed control over the flows of funds in the economy.[3]

On the other hand, long-term changes in France's international economic

* The author is grateful to Philip Cerny, Gilles Oudiz, Christian Stoffaës, and George Ross for many helpful conversations and for the assistance of Harry Brown.

position placed new constraints on French policy-makers. French production was now closely integrated into the world economy; and there were trade, energy and monetary dimensions to this interdependence. On the trade side, imports and exports, worth 13 percent of gross domestic product (GDP) in 1953, accounted for 23 percent of GDP by 1983. Therefore, international recession was more likely to depress French industry and domestic expansion was more likely to result in rising import levels and balance of payments problems. With regard to energy, France depended on imports for 80 percent of her requirements. Any increase in international energy prices could throw the balance of payments into immediate deficit, as the oil price rises of 1974 and 1979 demonstrated. Since 37 percent of French imports were now denominated in American dollars, the nation was also vulnerable to changing exchange rates. For every 10 centimes that the franc fell against the dollar, the French import bill rose by 2.5 billion francs.[4] While the French economy was more vulnerable to balance of payments crises, the state's ability to counter such crises by devaluing the franc was more limited: if devaluation spread to the dollar-franc exchange rate, the balance of payments simply worsened. A pattern of policy on which French government relied for thirty years — devaluation to counter domestic inflation — lost its viability. A substitute would have to be found; and the principal alternatives seemed to be trade barriers, an incomes policy or more frequent recourse to deflation.

On the domestic front as well, structural changes were posing new problems for French policy-makers. Some developed in the labor market. The industrial shake-out that followed the 1974 oil crisis resulted in the loss of 684,000 jobs. However, demographic trends promised to expand the labor force by 230,000 people a year through 1990.[5] To avoid rising unemployment, a quarter of a million new jobs had to be found each year in France.

The corporate sector also faced disturbing trends. Since 1974, neither wages nor government spending had fallen to absorb the cost of increased energy prices to the French economy. Instead that cost was borne by profits. Between 1975 and 1981 the share of value-added going to profits fell from 17 percent to 9.6 percent while the share going to wages rose from 6.8 percent to 7.5 percent and that of taxes increased from 2.7 percent to 4.3 percent.[6] Profits were squeezed and an investment crisis ensued. The volume of private investment in France fell by 14 percent between 1971 and 1981.[7] At the same time, corporate debt rose precipitously and the rate of *autofinancement* fell. This, in turn, weakened the ability of the French state to stimulate investment by expanding demand. Low profit margins and high debt levels meant that French firms were slow to respond to a demand stimulus and a lengthy stimulus brought immediate balance of payments problems in the more open economy of the 1980s.

Therefore, the Socialists faced depressed levels of investment and a policy dilemma. They could use traditional Keynesian techniques to stimulate demand; yet this would bring balance of payments problems before it began to affect investment. Another option was to raise profit levels directly by depressing wages or taxes; yet this meant the Socialists would have to discipline the workforce or cut social spending. The first tactic was economically dangerous; the second was politically unpalatable. In large measure, the history of the early Mitterrand years is the story of how the Government moved from one option to the other before seeking a third way out of the dilemma.

The conjunctural policies pursued by the preceding administration under Valéry Giscard d'Estaing intensified the structural problems that Mitterrand faced. Giscard's industrial policy, which channelled resources into diplomatic exports (such as arms, airplanes, and turn-key plants) and massive capital projects (such as the telephone system, nuclear plants and rapid transit), improved French exports and the infrastructure but left the consumer goods sector of the economy vulnerable to import competition. While France sold arms to the OPEC nations, the Germans and Japanese were penetrating French markets for automobiles, electronics, and consumer durables. Only too late did the attention of the regime shift from the 'challenge of the Third World' to the 'reconquest of the domestic market.'[8] By this time, small and medium-sized firms producing for domestic consumption were in a weakened position.

Prime Minister Raymond Barre's macroeconomic policies also intensified the underlying problems of the economy. In distributional terms, the burden of adjustment following the oil price shocks of the 1970s was imposed on profits and the unemployed. The rate of unemployment increased from 2.6 percent in 1973 to 7.6 percent in May 1981 while real unemployment benefits declined. By contrast, the French middle classes remained unscathed. Wages were allowed to climb, and household spending grew by 3.5 percent a year between 1975 and 1980 despite stagnant economic growth. Most forms of government spending continued to rise without substantial changes in the structure of taxation. On the one hand, these policies reinforced the longstanding inegalitarianism that had characterized the French pattern of growth.[9] On the other hand, they left the economy in a precarious position. Inflation was allowed to hit 13 percent and the balance of payments ran 60 billion francs into deficit before the Socialists even took office. That rendered devaluation of the franc and domestic deflation almost inevitable. Although Barre talked of 'austerity', he hesitated to impose it on the French middle classes before the 1981 elections. Mitterrand was left with an economic and political bill to pay.

This was the economic inheritance of the Mitterrand Government. Its actions must be understood and judged in this context.

### THE REDISTRIBUTIVE KEYNESIANISM OF 1981-2

The Government also entered office with a political legacy of ideas and aspirations formed during twenty-five years in opposition. Although their leader was a highly pragmatic politician, the Socialist Party (PS) took ideas seriously. 'Our responsibility is to invent the future,' declared one of the electoral brochures.[10] The party itself was less a unified force than a collection of competing *tendances*, and it came to power in coalition with a Communist Party (PCF) that had only four ministers in the Cabinet (*conseil des ministres*) and forty-four seats in the Assembly but considerable influence over France's largest trade union (the CGT) and a solid 15 percent of the vote. The tenuous alliances which held these competing political currents together were forged around agreement on a commmon electoral program that called for a radical shift in policy toward fiscal expansion, income redistribution, nationalization, industrial relations reform and decentralization.[11] It had taken years to forge such an agreement and to persuade the French electorate to vote for a change.

84 Peter A. Hall

*Over enthused* Therefore, the new administration was more committed than most to the implementation of its electoral platform. The unity of Government, its good faith in the eyes of the electorate, and the multiple aspirations of its followers seemed to be at stake. Economically, all the politicians needed was some indication that their policies might succeed. In 1981 most economic forecasters supplied such an indication when they predicted that world economic recovery would generate new markets for French exports by 1982. If this had been true, France might have been able to expand her economy and finance the resulting balance of payments deficit until world recovery improved the trade balance. The policy was an economic gamble, but political considerations suggested that it should be taken. Mitterrand later explained why he accepted such optimistic predictions: 'I was carried away by our victory; we were intoxicated. Everyone . . . predicted the return of growth by 1983. Honestly, I lack the necessary knowledge to say they were wrong.'[12]

Accordingly, the Government began to implement the economic strategy of its electoral platform which called for an economic expansion to be generated by government spending designed to increase the incomes of the low-paid and to provide jobs for the unemployed. One policy served two purposes. The redistribution of income and employment was supposed to spark off a consumer boom that would revive French industry. We can think of it as 'redistributive Keynesianism.' Immediately after the Socialist victory a series of dramatic measures were taken in this direction.

Family allowances were raised by 81 percent for families with two children and by 44 percent for those with three children in the two years from May 1981. Housing allocations for the low-paid were increased by 25 percent in 1981. Health insurance benefits were made more widely available to part-time employees and the unemployed. Old-age pensions were increased by 300 francs a month to 1,700 francs for a single person and 3,700 francs for a couple. The purchasing power of social transfers rose by 4.5 percent in 1981 and by 7.6 percent in 1982. Most significantly, the minimum wage (SMIC), to which the salaries of 1.7 million workers were tied, was raised by 15 percent in real terms between May 1981 and December 1982.

A striking series of measures were also taken to reduce unemployment. First came statutory reduction in the regular hours of work. In July 1981 the work week was reduced from 40 to 39 hours and the workforce was given a *party unity* fifth week of vacation. The left wing of the PS and the PCF argued against corresponding reductions in pay, while centrist Socialists argued for them. Mitterrand resolved the debate by leaving the decision to local negotiators who generally decided against salary reduction. As a result, the policy improved the quality of life for many employees but had little effect on unemployment. Only a fifth of all firms took on new employees and no more than 28,000 jobs were created by the reduction of the work week.[13]

A second program of January 1982 encouraged firms to negotiate 'contracts of solidarity' with the Government. One formula allowed employees aged 55–60 to retire on 70 percent of their salary which was provided by the state if the firm replaced them with younger workers. That scheme created 100,000 jobs in 1982. Under a second formula, employers who reduced the work week below 39 hours and hired additional employees as a result could be forgiven their social security payments for the latter. In all, 13,300 positions were created in this way during 1982. Under a third program, older employees could go on half-time work at 80 percent of their former salary (with the additional 20 percent paid by the state), if younger employees were hired to replace them. Under this formula, 1,500 people were employed in 1982.[14]

In March 1982 the Mitterrand Government also introduced an early retirement program with effect from April 1983. Anyone who had paid social security contributions for 37.5 years could retire at 60 on an amount ranging from 80 percent of the former salary of a *smicard* (employee earning the minimum wage) to 50 percent of the salary of a *cadre* (middle management). While some *cadres* lost the right to retire at 60 with 70 percent of their salary under this scheme, there were 360,000 potential beneficiaries, of whom a quarter were expected to retire and open up positions for younger employees.[15] Finally, the Government hired an additional 200,000 employees in 1981–2.

In distributive terms these measures were a great success. The position of the poor, aged, and lower-paid was substantially improved. Many of the least advantaged French workers were able to take early retirement and longer vacations without loss of income. When most other nations were trimming transfer programs and work-force privileges, France took a dramatic step forward. At the same time, these policies slowed the rising tide of unemployment. Although 140,000 formerly illegal immigrants joined the labor force under a government amnesty, unemployment rose only 4 percent in France during 1982, against a rise of 29 percent in Germany and 22 percent in the US. No other Western nation had been able to reduce the growth of unemployment so significantly.

However, the cost of these policies was high. French industry struggled to remain competitive under the 34-billion-franc increase in wages and social security contributions that these programs entailed.[16] Public expenditure rose by 11.4 percent in volume during 1981 and 1982, and the budget deficit increased from 0.4 percent to 3 percent of GDP in 1982. Under this stimulus, the economy grew by 2 percent over two years, when growth in most other European nations was stagnant. But real disposable income grew twice as fast as production, and the difference was spent on imports. Imports of autos rose by 40 percent, of electrical appliances by 27 percent and of consumer goods by 20 percent in 1982. As a consequence, the trade deficit ballooned from 56 billion francs in 1981 to 93 billion francs in 1982, and price inflation remained at 12.5 percent for 1981, 11 percent for 1982 and 9.3 percent for 1983 (well above falling rates abroad). The result was a balance of payments crisis that brought the value of the franc under severe pressure on the foreign exchanges as the expected world recovery failed to appear.

## THE POLITICS OF AUSTERITY, 1982–4

By the autumn of 1981, it became clear to French forecasters that the international economy would not expand sufficiently to rectify the balance of payments. Devaluation of the franc and domestic deflation became inevitable. One would restore the competitiveness of French exports; the other would restrain spending on imports by reducing domestic incomes. Both were politically unpalatable. After the triumphant expansion of the first year, the second and third years of the Mitterrand presidency would be marked by a reversal toward austerity. The Government tried to implement this about-turn by proceeding in stages.

The most important item on the agenda was realignment against the German mark because Germany provided the principal market for French exports and French prices were rising at twice the rate of competing German products. Accordingly, the franc was devalued against the Deutschmark on three occasions — 4 October 1981, 12 June 1982 and 21 March 1983 — for a total decline of 27 percent in two years. French figures suggested that such a devaluation would improve exports by 3 percent, GDP by 1 percent, employment by 120,000 people and the trade balance by 24 billion francs over three years.[17]

Although most French exports go to Germany, many of their imports are denominated in American dollars. Therefore, they would prefer the franc to remain low against the Deutschmark but high against the dollar to reduce their import bill. Instead, rising interest rates in America and speculation against the franc carried the currency from 4.20 against the dollar in 1980 to 5.35 in April 1981 and 8.60 by 1984. In vain, Mitterrand tried to persuade the Reagan administration to lower its interest rates. The effects on the French economy were catastrophic. The rise in the dollar reduced the French growth rate by 1 percent in 1982, raised unemployment by 24,000, inflation by 3–5 percent, and the public sector deficit by 36 billion francs. Its effect on import prices alone lifted the trade deficit by 57 billion francs in 1982.[18] This, in turn, renewed speculation against the franc. Many of the problems Mitterrand faced in 1982-3 were not of his own making.

The Government was forced into domestic deflation to rectify the balance of payments. As part of the realignment of parities within the European Monetary System (EMS) in October 1981, Germany insisted that France eliminate 15 billion francs of spending from the 1982 budget. As early as 29 November 1981, the French Finance Minister indicated that 'it will be necessary to pause before announcing further reforms.'[19]

However, the real break came on 13 June 1982, after the franc was again devalued against the German currency. The Government implemented a serious austerity plan, whose object was to limit the public sector deficit to 3 percent of GDP and improve the deteriorating financial situation of private enterprise. Public spending for 1982 was cut by 20 billion francs. All wages, except the SMIC, and most prices were frozen until the end of October 1982. The level of employers' social security contributions was frozen for a year; company tax was reduced by 10 percent; a portion of the cost of family allowances was transferred from employers to employees; value-added tax was removed from tools for three years, and accelerated depreciation provisions introduced. In total, these measures meant that the wage and benefits bill facing French industry in 1982–3 would grow at only half the rate of the preceding year.[20]

Within the Government, these measures reflected a shift in power toward the economic hardliners. The Ministry for National Solidarity was renamed the Ministry for Social Affairs, and Nicole Questiaux was replaced as Minister by Pierre Bérégovoy, Mitterrand's right-hand man at the Elysée. Questiaux had embarked on the system of retirement at 60 with little concern for its cost. In the following year, Bérégovoy was to engineer a radical reduction in the social security and unemployment insurance deficits through increased charges and reduced benefits for the schemes.[21]

The measures of June 1982 were significant for two reasons. First, they marked the end of the fiscal expansion on which the Government initially pinned its hopes for economic recovery. Secondly, they reflected a reversal in the distributive priorities of the Government. In its first year, the Government's primary concern was to redistribute income toward the unemployed and those on lower incomes who were suffering from the effects of the two oil shocks. In so doing they ignored the higher costs being paid by business. By June 1982, policy-makers had concluded that French employers also needed relief, and imposed higher costs on workers and social beneficiaries to lift the financial burden on French enterprise.

In March 1983, a second wave of austerity became necessary. In part because the deflationary impact of the 1982 measures was low, the trade deficit continued to rise until further devaluation against the German mark was secured. Along with this, the Government announced a new austerity plan on 23 March 1983 which marked a new stage in policy beyond that of June 1982. For the first time, real costs were imposed on the French middle classes. Taxes were raised by 40 billion francs and public spending was slashed by 24 billion francs in 1983. Out of 22 million taxpayers, 15 million would pay a new 1 percent surcharge on taxable income, and 8 million were to make a compulsory loan to the Government of 10 percent of their taxes repayable in three years. Public enterprise prices were raised an average of 8 percent, along with taxes on tobacco, alcohol and petrol. An 8 percent limit was imposed on wage and price increases over the following years. In addition, French tourists were prohibited from taking more than 2,000 francs out of the country. Élysée officials argued that to secure an equivalent balance of payments improvement by other means would have required a 1 percent reduction in real disposable income, but this was an enormous psychological blow to a nation which spent 30 billion francs on foreign travel in 1982.[22]

The political consequences of such moves were bound to be serious. In the first instance, travel agents and other middle-class groups adversely affected by the Government's policies demonstrated in the streets of Paris in the spring of 1983. Fifteen years after the famous events of May 1968, it was the farmers, shopkeepers, and middle classes who took to the streets. By the summer of 1983, the President's popularity had fallen dramatically; only 32 percent of the electorate approved of his policies.

Within the Socialist Party itself, the illusions of Keynesianism in one country had been dashed. The Government's hopes for domestic economic expansion foundered in the face of a rising American dollar and continuing world recession. That inspired a profound re-evaluation of France's ability to undertake expansion, perhaps even redistributive socialism, alone. The Prime Minister declared:

> Quite simply, a real left-wing policy can be applied in France only if the other European countries also follow policies of the left . . . I want to change the habits of this nation. If the French resign themselves to living with an inflation of 12%, then they should know that, because of our economic interdependence with Germany, we will be led into a situation of imbalance. France must rid herself of this inflationary disease.[23]

The Government decided to remove inflationary habits from a nation that had always depended on them in order to generate growth.

There were those in the party who argued that an alternative strategy, based on neo-protectionism, was possible. On this view, France would unilaterally withdraw from the EMS in order to devalue, free of German demands for spending cuts, and use a system that imposed mandatory deposits on importers to improve the trade deficit without recourse to deflation. Italy had once employed such a scheme without leaving the EEC. Several ministers, such as Jean-Pierre Chevènement, Laurent Fabius, and Pierre Bérégovoy, as well as Jean Riboud, the industrialist closest to Mitterrand, were interested in such a scheme.[24] They suggested that France could develop a new economic strategy based on monetary independence and economic expansion behind rising trade barriers.

The critical juncture when policy might have turned in this direction came during the third week of March 1983 between the two rounds of the municipal elections. The Socialists sustained losses in the first round, and Mitterrand considered replacing Prime Miniter Pierre Mauroy and Finance Minister Jacques Delors, who were the principal advocates for a new round of austerity. By this time it was clear that the franc would have to be devalued against the mark once more; and as the Government spent 40 billion francs on the foreign exchanges to defend the franc, the President pondered his options. Two factors seemed to swing the decision against neo-protectionism. Mauroy and Delors successfully persuaded the Germans to revalue their currency by 5.5 percent in exchange for a mere 2.5 percent devaluation in the franc. No doubt the imminent threat that France might leave the EMS helped persuade the Germans to bear the disproportionate share of realignment. This was a coup for the French negotiators and a fillip for the EMS. Secondly, Élysée studies told the President that even the neo-protectionist option would have to be accompanied by deflation if frustrated demand for imports were not to bring domestic inflation.[25] With this in mind, Mitterrand confirmed Mauroy and Delors in their positions and agreed to the deflationary program of March 1983.

The austerity of 1982–3 forced the Government to develop another strategy for regenerating growth and employment. It was no longer possible to generate investment by expanding demand. Therefore, the Socialists resorted to two tactics, one conservative and the other more radical. On the one hand, they tried to raise profits directly by depressing wages and corporate taxes so as to encourage private investment and the maintenance of employment. The corporate tax concessions and extension of wage control in 1982 were designed for this purpose. 'We want to have wages rise more slowly than prices in order to curb consumer purchasing power and increase profitability,' explained the Prime Minister.[26] The Socialists acquired an unusual concern for profitability and used their credibility with the trade unions to restrain wages.

On the other hand, the Government used the nationalized sector to channel vast sums of money directly into industrial investment. The object was to increase the rate of capital formation despite the limits which austerity imposed on the stimulation of demand. In order to make funds available for investment, while maintaining tight budgetary constraints, the Government reduced public spending on *both* social programs and defense. The Minister of the Budget said that the Government had reconsidered its priorities:

We will hold spending down in 1983 by cutting many social programs. And in coming years, we plan to cut government spending from 46% of gross domestic product to 42% by further cutting on social programs and aid to municipalities. There are maybe 15,000 public swimming pools in French municipalities; we have to ask ourselves if we need 20,000.[27]

Simultaneously, 30 percent of the military equipment purchases authorized for 1982, worth 15 billion francs, were cancelled; and manpower in France's conventional forces was severely cut back to save expenditure in succeeding years. Only the nuclear *force de frappe* remained untouched.[28] In short, when most nations were cutting either defense or social spending, the French had found a third way. They were trimming both defense and social programs to pass public resources into industrial investment.

NATIONALIZATIONS: BUT TO WHAT END?

The keystone of the Government's new economic strategy was the nationalization program completed in February 1982. Although the largest French banks were already under state control, the Government nationalized thirty-six smaller banks, two investment banks, Suez and Paribas, and the remaining minority of private shares in the Crédit Lyonnais, Banque Nationale de Paris, and Sociéte Générale. It acquired 100 percent of the shares in six industrial conglomerates: the Compagnie Générale d'Electricité (CGE), the Compagnie Générale de Constructions Téléphoniques (CGCT) and Thomson-Brandt in electronics and in telecommunications, Rhône-Poulenc in textiles and chemicals, Péchiney-Ugine-Kuhlman (PUK) in aluminum and chemicals, and Saint-Gobain-Pont à Mousson in glass, paper and metals. State debt in the two major steel firms, Sacilor and Usinor, was converted into a majority shareholding; and the Government acquired 51 percent of the shares of the two arms and aeronautical manufacturers Dassault-Breguet and Matra as well as control over CII-Honeywell Bull in computers and Roussel-Uclaf in pharmaceuticals.[29] The state now owned thirteen of the twenty largest firms in France and a controlling share in many other French companies. State holdings accounted for 2 percent of the employees, 3 percent of the sales, 30 percent of the exports, and 60 percent of the annual investment in the industrial and energy sectors of the French economy.

The cost of the nationalizations was not negligible. The state would pay about 39 billion francs in capital and 47 billion francs in interest over fifteen years for its purchases. In 1983 its payments totaled 9 billion francs. Most dispossessed shareholders were amply compensated; for instance, each share of Rhône-Poulenc, which had recently traded as low as 45fr., was exchanged for a bond worth 126fr. paying 16 percent interest.[30] Ministers such as Rocard and Fabius had argued that the state could save 30 billion francs by nationalizing only 51 percent of each company, but they were overruled by Mitterrand, who was anxious to satisfy his Communist coalition partners.[31]

What purpose did the nationalizations serve? Prior to the election, the very ambiguity of the project helped unite diverse factions on the left. Each group saw the nationalizations as a means toward its end, whether that was the implementation of workers' control, the elimination of private profit, the strengthening of the unions or the rescue of France's industrial base. As a project, nationalization could be all things to all people. Therefore it was a powerful unifying device. After the election, however, the project had to be defined more concretely and it became a source of division within the Government.

Those who expected the nationalized firms to spearhead the drive toward workers' control were largely disappointed. The new administrative councils of each enterprise contained six state appointees, six outside experts, and six representatives from the workforce. Workers were given a voice, but not control over the enterprise.

Similarly, contention continued with the Government over the degree of influence it was to exercise over the nationalized industries. The rapid turnover in Ministers of Industry reflected this struggle. In the space of two years, Pierre Joxe, Pierre Dreyfus, Jean-Pierre Chevènement and Laurent Fabius all held the position. When Dreyfus replaced Joxe, a tight rein was supposed to give way to the arm's length relationship that Dreyfus had established at Renault. Chevènement, however, reintroduced intervention on a daily basis in the decisions taken by the heads of the public enterprises, and their complaints to the President were instrumental in   securing his dismissal.[32] The appointment of Fabius in May 1983 reflected Mitterrand's new determination that 'the nationalized industries should have total autonomy of decision and action.'[33]

Of course, the newly nationalized enterprises would never receive total autonomy; but it was equally hard for the state to acquire effective control over them. Formal ownership was only the beginning. Real power consists in the ability to direct an enterprise so as to achieve one's ultimate goals. The French state still had to clarify its goals and learn how to point such enterprises toward them. In 1982–3, these companies faced the worst of both worlds: they lacked global directions from the state to guide their long-term strategy, yet were subject to sporadic intervention into their daily operations. Because the state also faced more intense political pressure to avoid lay-offs than private firms, its capacity to restructure French industry might even have been reduced by the nationalizations.

After all, the measures of 1981–2 simply consolidated the longstanding influence of the French state over industry. The large state banks, which had been important since the Caisse des Dépôts was formed in 1816, and the practice of rediscounting loans at the Bank of France already enabled the state to control the flows of funds in France; and by 1980 the Government was already the major shareholder in 500 firms and a minority shareholder in 600 others.[34] French officials had always been able to put a good deal of pressure on selected industries. As one officer of Saint-Gobain explained, nationalization made little difference: 'It is the state who told us to replace CGE in CII-Honeywell Bull in 1978, and it is the state who told us to get out of it in 1982.'[35]

Nevertheless, by 1983 it was clear that the nationalizations were serving two purposes. They allowed the state to accelerate the pace of rationalization in several sectors, notably chemicals; and they were used to ensure that several sectors of French business continued to invest heavily despite the world recession. In 1982, the newly nationalized industries lost 16 billion francs, and the older public enterprises of EDF (electricity), GDF (gas), SNCF (railways), RATP (Paris transport), Air France and Charbonnages (coal) lost 27 billion francs, compared with total losses of 19 billion francs in 1981 and 2.2 billion francs in 1980 for all these firms.[36] Similar deficits were expected for 1983. Therefore, the state was keeping a significant portion of French industry afloat. It hoped to overcome one of the classic structural constraints of capitalism — the dependence of investment on 'business confidence.' No matter how low that confidence was to ebb, half of the investment in the French economy would be assured.

Funds for investment were made available to each enterprise in return for its agreement to a three/five-year 'planning contract' signed with the Ministry of Industry. On this basis the newly nationalized industries received 20 billion francs in 1983, of which 12.6 billion francs came from the budget and the rest from the nationalized banking sector.[37] Additional funds were to be raised through the capital markets and various forms of research and regional aid. In return, the newly nationalized industries were to invest 31 billion francs in 1983 (22 billion francs of it within France), equivalent to 50 percent of total industrial investment in France and roughly 20 percent more than they had otherwise planned. As Table 4.1 indicates, half of these funds went to the steel and chemical sectors alone. In addition, the older public enterprises received 43.5 billion francs in 1982 and 56.8 billion francs in 1983, almost half of which went to the railways.[38]

**Table 4.1**   Direct aid to nationalized industries, 1983 (billion francs)

| | |
|---|---|
| Charbonnages-Chemicals | 1,000 |
| CGE | 870 |
| CIT-Honeywell-Bull | 1,500 |
| EMC | 250 |
| PUK | 2,400 |
| Renault | 1,650 |
| Rhône-Poulenc | 1,800 |
| Saint-Gobain | 750 |
| Snecma | 300 |
| Thomson | 1,600 |
| Steel | 6,450 |
| Chemicals | 1,650 |
| TOTAL | 20,220 |

*Source:*   *Le Monde*, 11 February 1983, p. 26.

The nationalization of the banking sector reinforced this strategy. Three months after the banks were supposedly guaranteed operating autonomy, they were instructed to lend 6 billion francs to the nationalized industries, purchase 7 billion francs in state debt during 1983, and maintain their industrial rates at 14 percent. In effect, the banks were subsidizing loans to the state and industry. Small and medium-sized enterprises were also supposed to benefit from such loans. In order to use the banks as an instrument of policy, their *tutelle*, or traditional supervisory responsibility, was transferred to a new monitoring unit at the Ministry of Economics and Finance, and the National Credit Council was reorganized. The French banks had been subject to the *encadrement du crédit* (government controls on lending above authorized ceilings), but since 1972 loan recipients were more fully specified and some banks were expected to orchestrate the rationalization of entire industrial sectors.[39]

### INDUSTRIAL POLICY: A WINNING STRATEGY?

Under Mitterrand, the French tradition of *dirigiste* industrial policy remains unbroken. Behind its free market rhetoric, the Barre Administration pursued an active program of industrial aid. The Socialist Government has simply changed some of the agencies and a few of the goals. One set of agencies assisted the declining sectors; another fostered *industries de pointe*.

During the presidency of Valéry Giscard d'Estaing, large firms in financial trouble received aid from CIASI and small firms were supported by the departmental committees of CODEFI. Between 1974 and 1981, these agencies handled 660 corporate rescues where 300,000 jobs were at stake.[40] Mitterrand replaced CIASI with an interdepartmental committee, named CIRI, that is chaired by the Minister of Finance and staffed by a twenty-person secretariat handling over 200 cases a year. Six regional committees (CORRI) have been established to decentralize the operations of CODEFI.[41] While these bodies consult the unions more frequently than their predecessors, the basic administration of aid has not changed. Within three to six months, the committees usually arange a transfusion of state aid into a failing firm and often merge it into another enterprise.

In 1979, Giscard established CODIS and its analogue for small business, CIDISE, to fund innovative projects in growth areas, such as robotics, biotechnology, electronics, office automation, energy-saving devices, underwater exploration and synthetic textiles. Selected firms received government subsidies, public orders, export aids or import controls in return for signing a 'development contract' that specified performance targets to be met over the three/five-year life of the contract. In total CODIS spent 3 billion francs to initiate investment projects worth 20 billion francs, and CIDISE spent 18 billion francs to provide equity participation or interest-rate subsidies to over 450 projects.[42]

The Mitterrand Government has replaced CODIS with Le Fonds de Modernisation Industrielle (FMI), that will spend 3 billion francs appropriated from the Caisse des Dépôts in 1983 and another 5 billion francs in 1984 to be raised from a new savings bond, the CODEVI, whose interest will be tax-free for three years. The FMI will provide loan guarantees, long-term debentures, and interest subsidies to growth-sector firms investing in new plant or technologies.[43] The list of preferred sectors is very similar to that of CODIS, and the Fund is supposed to dispose of all requests for aid within eight weeks of their receipt. The design of the Fund reflects several important political decisions. Whereas CODIS was run from the Treasury, FMI has been placed under the Ministry of Industry which, after gaining control of research, has become the locus of power over industrial policy-making. The use of a state agency to dispense this money also reflects a retreat from the Government's promise to utilize employee-administered funds for that purpose. Mitterrand seems unwilling to entrust these sums to potentially oppositional unions. At the same time, he has moved away from the Government's original reluctance to favor some sectors over others by picking 'industrial winners.'

The one agency which the Mitterrand Government has retained in its original form is ANVAR, established in 1979 to sponsor research and development. Over three years, ANVAR and its twenty-two regional committees handled over 4,000 cases, and in 1983 it distributed 900 million francs mainly in equity loans.[44] That reflects the Government's commitment to raise French expenditure on research to 2.5 percent of GDP by 1988.

In addition, Mitterrand has taken steps to improve the flow of savings into private investment. Besides the new CODEVI bond, another savings bond indexed to inflation (the *livrêt d'épargne populaire*) has been issued to encourage saving among the 11 million households who pay less than 1,000 francs tax. To increase investment in the stock market, the complicated and heavy system of capital gains tax has been replaced by a flat rate of 15 percent; and a second market, where issuers need place only 10 percent of their stock, has been created to give small business access to equity capitalization.[45] Finally, businesses started in 1983 have been forgiven half their taxes for the next three years.

The Socialists also continue to emphasize the export of arms and turn-key plants. Foreign orders for French arms rose from 22 billion francs in 1980 to 42 billion francs in 1982; and exports of major infrastructure projects are to increase from 20 billion francs in 1981 to 40 billion francs in 1986.[46] These sales are heavily dependent on subsidized loans from the French Government, such as the $2 billion it lent to Iraq in 1983. As justification, the Government notes that 1 million jobs depend on arms sales alone, and that the trade surplus on arms was greater than that for all of the rest of industry in 1982.[47]

At the sectoral level, the Mitterrand Government devised rescue plans for no less than eight major industries in 1981–3 including steel, chemicals, textiles, machine tools, furniture, leather goods, toys, and electronics.[48]

In steel, where the unions are particularly strong, the watchword until 1984 was expansion whatever the cost or projected market. The Government accepted the recommendation of the Judet report to expand production from 19 million tons in 1981 to 24 million tons in 1986, despite EEC estimates that the market will bear no more than 21 million tons.[49] A total of 17 billion francs will be spent over four years to modernize the productive facilities of Usinor and Sacilor. The tightening of the austerity program in 1984 will lead to at least 20,000 more lay-offs in the industry, whose workforce will have been cut by over half since 1978. The French steel industry will have received 60 billion francs in public aid over the eight years since 1978, but the Government has targeted 1987 as the year when steel is expected to break even.

By contrast, the Government's principal object in chemicals from the start has been to restructure the industry into a few massive and specialized firms. The heavy chemicals section of PUK has been hived off to Elf-Acquitaine, and a series of mergers were enforced to regroup the industry around three large public firms, CDF-Chimie and Elf-Aquitaine in heavy chemicals, and Rhône-Poulenc in speciality chemicals. Pharmaceutical production has been concentrated in three firms, Sanofi tied to Elf, Roussel-Uclaf and Rhône-Poulenc. If size and specialization were all that mattered, this would be a winning strategy; but the French industry remains beset by many problems, related to the high cost of raw materials, that this plan does not resolve.[50]

In textiles, the Government's actions have been designed to save jobs at the cost of increasing state support for a largely uncompetitive industry. The two foundering giants, Boussac-Saint-Frères and Bidermann have been rescued. In total, an industry which suffered 8 billion francs worth of losses in 1982 has been given 820 million francs a year in subsidies or loans and a 12 percent reduction in social security taxes worth 3 billion francs a year, in return for increased investment and the restriction of lay-offs from 8 percent of employees in 1981 to 1 percent in 1982.[51]

The plan for machine tools regroups 130 firms into larger entities while providing 3 billion francs in grants and 4 billion francs in loans over three years to the industry. Public orders will be used to stimulate the production of numerically controlled machine tools and to reduce the rate of imports of machine tools from 60 percent to 30 percent. Similarly, funds raised from a special tax on home furnishings will be invested in the French furniture industry in return for their distributors' agreement to cut imports from 20 percent to 15 percent of French sales.[52] In these sectors, the state is determined to maintain a French industry despite serious European competition.

The Government's most ambitious plans, however, have been reserved for the electronics sector, which President Mitterrand described as 'our weapon of the future.'[53] Over five years, 140 billion francs will be spent to redress the commercial balance in the sector, create 80,000 jobs, and increase production by 9 percent a year. Public orders will be used to stimulate technological progress in microelectronics, computers, robots and office communications. Several firms have already been forced out of the industry, which is being regrouped around four giant public enterprises supervised by a national advisory committee of fifty officials.[54] The jurisdiction of the Ministry of Industry has been extended again to cover the profitable post and telecommunications ministry so that its resources may be used on this project.

Together these programs will pump vast sums of money into French industry, in keeping with President Mitterrand's assertion that 'industry is a priority that overrides all others.'[55] In 1981, public aid to industry totaled 100 billion francs or 3.5 percent of GDP. That included 40 billion francs spent on research and development, 16.5 billion francs in export subsidies and insurance administered through COFACE, 13.2 billion francs in direct industrial subsidies, 11.3 billion francs to cover losses in sectors such as shipbuilding and steel, 12 billion francs in tax incentives for investment, 6.5 billion francs under various programs designed to increase employment, and 1.8 billion francs in regional aid. The figures for 1982 and 1983 were even higher.[56] Clearly-visible loans and grants to the private sector rose from 20 billion francs in 1980 to 35 billion francs in 1982 and 45 billion francs in 1983.[57]

However, we can also ask if this constitutes a coherent industrial policy. The success of an industrial policy depends on the criteria used to select the projects to support and which to abandon. Inadequate criteria mean that crucial resources are wasted on products that cannot be sold and on firms that cannot compete on world markets. This was a hard lesson learned by the preceding regime. By 1978, wasted resources on the Concorde supersonic transport, the Plan Calcul for computers and other 'lame ducks' led the *Giscardiens* to experiment with new kinds of criteria for industrial aid. Some tried to solve the problem by generalizing the criteria of the Boston Consulting Group to the level of national sectors in order to direct resources to those niches in fast-growing markets for products with high value-added where France was likely to be competitive.[58] This became known as a *politique de créneaux*. Others provided 'seed money' to several firms in the same sector and made future aid contingent on market performance.[59]

The Mitterrand Government initially ignored these lessons. It rejected the very distinction between rising and declining sectors. Pierre Dreyfus's phrase was constantly repeated: 'There are no condemned sectors; there are only outmoded technologies.'[60] And even Laurent Fabius declared: 'The distinction between leading sectors and those described as traditional is irrelevant. The new technologies should permeate all industrial sectors.'[61] In this way, the new regime avoided industrial *triage* in favour of a *politique de filières* whose object was to strengthen the entire range of products in each sector so that no part was lost to imports. On this view, France could produce everything.

The political advantages of such a policy are obvious. In the struggle against unemployment no battlefields need be conceded to the enemy. The policy meshed well with the line of the PCF and CGT who tended to defend all sectors to the point of autarchy. It postponed the need to make hard choices; and the *politique de filières* was another of those concepts sufficiently ambiguous to appeal to all currents within the Government.[62]

However, the economic virtues of such a policy are unclear. It relies on three principal techniques to generate growth: the creation of very large firms specialized in a particular product line with a virtual monopoly over the French market; massive infusions of capital for investment; and the intensive promotion of new technologies. In these respects, Mitterrand's policy seems to skip over the Giscardian experiments and return to the approach of the Gaullists in the early 1970s. Once again, high technology is a magic word; consumption is being squeezed to supply investment; and enormous national champions are being groomed in each market. The policy resembles nothing so much as the Sixth Plan.

One can ask if this is an appropriate industrial policy for the 1980s? It assumes that future growth will come from high volumes of mass-produced commodities that compete on price terms in world markets, when several analysts suggest that growth will be generated in the 1980s primarily by smaller firms employing craft-based production techniques and short production runs to generate specialized goods that compete on quality terms.[63] Similarly, increases in capital and the scale of production do not always improve the efficiency of a firm; for many years, increasing state aid to the French steel industry simply led to growing overcapacity in world markets and the postponement of effective rationalization.[64] It is possible that the Government's desire to support all segments of all sectors will intensify the rigidities in French industry and delay the reallocation of resources to growth areas. The policy seems to assume that France can compete in most sectors when growing international interdependence and specialization suggest that the nation must concentrate on developing a comparative advantage in a few areas if it is to compete on domestic and world markets. France runs the risk of developing huge stockpiles of steel, chemicals, and electronics that it cannot sell at competitive prices without either increasing its tariff barriers or permanently subsidizing sales. In that case, the policy could bring complaints from the EEC under articles 90, 92 and 93 of the Treaty of Rome and ultimately drive France into neo-protectionism.[65] One policy stage would lead to another.

On the other hand, the Mitterrand Government found a way to preserve France's industrial base and generate investment despite continuing world recession and low business confidence. Its shotgun approach to the allocation of funds seems likely to produce some successes and some disasters. The sheer magnitude of the effort, when investment elsewhere is more limited, may give France an initial advantage over her competitors. In the long run, however, industrial success will depend on reallocating resources from declining sectors and firms to those which can grow and compete internationally. If French policy-makers are unable to do this because of inadequate investment criteria, unwillingness to make hard choices, or an aversion to lay-offs, they will have weakened, rather than reinforced, the industrial power of the nation.

In many respects, the industrial policies of 1981–4 were only the first stage of an unfolding process. By 1984, macroeconomic pressure to reduce public spending was already forcing the government to allocate industrial aid more selectively and to accept lay-offs in depressed sectors such as automobiles, coal, and steel. These measures brought the government into direct conflict with the unions and many parts of its own coalition. They marked the end of a broad *politique de filières* and the acceptance of short-term unemployment, expected to reach 2.5 million people by 1985. Nevertheless, direct aid to industry remained the Government's principal spending priority and the key to its economic strategy.

## THE POLICY-MAKING PROCESS UNDER MITTERRAND

There have been surprisingly few changes in the process of policy-making under Mitterrand. Within the civil service, about half the posts at director level changed hands, and a quarter of the new appointees had ties to the political left. The Ministerial *cabinets*, of course, changed with their ministers and 60 percent of their new officials were affiliated to the PS.[66] Many also had ties to the union movement, although most were still civil servants. In short, the change of administration brought a turnover of personnel that reflects a long-term trend toward politicization of the French bureaucracy; but there were few purges, and those who left generally moved to other influential positions within the state.[67]

Ministerial *cabinets* looked more heterogeneous under the new Government. About half their members came from the prestigious École Nationale d'Administration or Polytechnique and half were of upper-middle-class origin.[68] This is not surprising since many Socialist militants are professionals, and fully 34 percent of the deputies elected to the National Assembly in 1981 were teachers. However, the famous *grands corps* that supplied 60 percent of the advisors to previous presidents filled only 19 percent of the posts in the Elysée under Mitterrand. Instead, the lesser known corps of *administrateurs civils*, which had often attracted Socialists, rose to new prominence.[69] In short, the left brought, not a dismantling of the old elite, but a circulation within it.

Similarly, instead of decentralizing authority to the ministries, the new regime still concentrated power in the Élysée. Ministers remained advocates before the President rather than autonomous centers of decision-making. Power revolved around a few of the President's closest economic advisors, such as Alain Boubil, Jacques Attali and Christian Sautter. As one civil servant explained: 'Under the institutions of the Fifth Republic, access to the chief of state is vital for a Minister — but even more in the Mitterrand system where everything depends on the personal relations the President has with a few men.'[70]

The most pronounced change in policy-making under Mitterrand has been the extensive use made of interdepartmental committees to handle major problems. A total of 459 interdepartmental meetings were held in the first three months alone of 1982 versus 328 in 1980; and the number of such committees rose from eight in 1980 to thirty-six in 1982.[71] Once again, however, this reflects a long-term trend away from the traditional French reliance on rule-based administration and carefully isolated spheres of responsibility to a more flexible form of bargaining among interdependent administrators.[72]

At the political level, the Mitterrand administration has been characterized by frequent conflict between ministers who speak for the diverse currents of the Socialist Party. Jean-Pierre Chevènement, from the CERES group on the left of the party, waged a bitter campaign to build up his Ministry of Research and Industry, extend state intervention, and safeguard industrial funds from budgetary cuts that brought him into conflict with the pragmatic Minister of Finance and Economics, Jacques Delors.[73] In the end, he lost that ministry and retired to build support for neo-protectionism and further expansion among the back benches. Michel Rocard argued with no more success for 51 percent nationalizations, earlier austerity, and salary cuts to accompany work-week reductions.

The principal casualty of these maneuvers was economic planning. It had been a distinctive feature of the French policy-making since Jean Monnet established the First Plan in 1948. The Socialists were committed to planning and even set up a Ministry for this purpose under Michel Rocard. It quickly prepared an Interim Plan for 1981–3, and appointed a new Commission Nationale de Planification, with seven sub-committees and multiple working groups, to draw up a Ninth Plan for 1984–8. Its deliberations were to culminate in the passage of a global outline plan and then detailed financial provisions through the National Assembly in the spring and autumn of 1983.[74] For the first time, regional plans to implement the national scheme were then to be negotiated with the new regional governments; this was a striking institutional innovation.

Within a short time, however, it became apparent that the planners were having almost no effect on government policy. As one senior economic official said: 'In this ministry, the Plan has no influence at all. We occasionally use it as a debating point but it does not affect our decisions.'[75] The Planning Minister was never influential with his colleagues. He lost successive battles to place a planning official in each ministry, to gain representatives on the administrative councils of the nationalized industries, and to persuade regional leaders to join the National Planning Commission.[76] His pessimistic outline for the Ninth Plan was sent back by the Elysée for redrafting.

In part, the limited influence of the planners can be attributed to the circumstances of the new Government. As a former rival for the presidency, Rocard was not overly influential with Mitterrand; the PCF and CERES group in the party also tended to oppose many of his moves. Most seriously, however, real power over the daily decisions that would actuate the plan belonged to a Minister of Finance, who was preoccupied with the exchange rate, and a Minister of Industry, who was interested in arrogating most planning functions to himself. In part, because everyone wanted to be a planner in the new Socialist Government, they were unwilling to delegate that function to the planning commission.

Long-term developments also attenuated the importance of the plan. Slow and unpredictable rates of growth meant that the planners had fewer resources to allocate, gloomier forecasts to promulgate, and greater difficulty devising any economic predictions at all. This was politically embarrassing. For some time, therefore, the Plans had given up making extensive quantitative forecasts and done little more than recite the pre-existing financial priorities of the Government. *Déplanification* began long before the Socialists took office.[77]

However, the Mitterrand Government followed suit. The optimistic projections of the Interim Plan were soon rendered obsolete by austerity. The Ninth Plan reiterated and rationalized the Government's decision to give priority to industry and noted that austerity would continue until 1985, but it contained few quantitative forecasts or new observations. The 35-hour week appeared as a distant ideal rather than a commitment. Rocard himself called the Plan 'a theatrical exercise in collective psychodrama.'[78] It received a cool reception in the Assembly, and in March 1983 the Ministry of Planning was abolished. The work of the National Planning Commission continued under Jean Le Garrec at the Prime Minister's office; but the once central concept of planning became a peripheral element in the Socialists' economic policy. Even Le Garrec expressed the puzzled disillusionment with which the Government treated its former hopes for planning, saying: 'Today, given that nothing is predictable any more, one wonders how to plan.'[79]

The other casualty of the Government's initial years in office was the program of workers' control that had played such a large role in the Socialist party's thinking over the past decade.[80] *Autogestion* was another one of those ambiguous concepts whose multifaceted appeal had served to unify the party. Like the other concepts, however, it had to be defined more clearly to be implemented, and the process of definition itself exposed a series of latent conflicts and political obstacles to progress on this front. As a result, the new Government's steps in this direction were hesitant. Only two measures were taken. One-third of the members on the administrative councils of the nationalized industries were drawn from the workforce; and fifteen out of twenty-five members on the administrative commissions for social security were chosen via elections among those insured by the fund.[81]

The new Government did undertake an extensive reform of industrial relations, based on four laws which the Minister of Labor, Jean Auroux, pushed through in April 1982. The first obligated all firms with fifty employees to negotiate each year on wages and working conditions. The second guaranteed workers certain basic liberties and the right to file grievances when these were infringed. The third extended representative works committees to almost all firms, increasing their access to information and resources. Finally, health and safety committees were amalgamated and reinforced in each plant.[82]

In France, that was a far-reaching achievement. Like the American Wagner Act of 1934, the reforms institutionalized collective bargaining, and finally brought France into line with European practice. They also strengthened the hand of the unions at the plant level. However, these were moves designed to extend contractual relations in French industrial relations rather than to put workers in control of the management of industry. The reforms actually reinforced the separation of workers from management by identifying two separate sides, defining autonomous spheres of responsibility for them, and mandating negotiation of a traditional sort between them. The watchword of the Government's initiatives in this area was *contractualisation* rather than *autogestion*.

What happened to *autogestion*? It was largely the victim of fragmentation within the left. Many groups, including several trade unions and political parties, claim to speak for the workers in France. Therefore, any scheme of workers' control is likely to transfer power from some of these groups to others, depending on its configuration. Agreement on the principle then gives way to bitter conflict over the character of any concrete program. It is not surprising that the Government was reluctant to proceed. In particular, the balance of power within the Government, which favored the Socialists over the Communists, was the reverse of the balance in the workplace where the Communist CGT was far larger than the Socialist CFDT or FO unions. Therefore, union-based schemes of *autogestion* were likely to leave the CGT in control of many industries, especially in the nationalized sector.[83] As a result, the Government could lose control of even the nationalized industries if a split opened up in the left. Schemes for *autogestion* which did not reinforce the power of the unions would, of course, be opposed by these allies of the Government. Thus, the Auroux laws represented a compromise which slightly strengthened the unions but in a way that actually reduced their potential threat to the Government.

One of the Government's longstanding problems has been to find a means of regulating its relationship with the unions. Such a dilemma faces every social democratic government; it is intensified in times of austerity. The politicians want to retain union support without becoming hostages to union demands. At the same time, the French unions are torn between the desire to remain solidaristic with a government that shares their ideals, and their wish to remain independent instigators of social ferment and the true interpreters of working-class concerns.

To date, the French have not found a stable solution to this problem. The CGT and CFDT have cooperated to a remarkable extent with the Government's austerity policies. Strike rates in 1982 were the lowest in years. However, those unions without strong ties to the left, the CGC (which represents *cadres*), FO and CFTC, who lost their position as privileged interlocutors under Giscard, have been hostile to the new policies, and are picking up rank-and-file support that will ultimately threaten the two larger unions.[84] As increasing austerity and industrial restructuring bring lay-offs, even the left-wing unions will feel pressure to break with the Government, as their reaction in 1984 to cutbacks and lay-offs in steel, coal and shipbuilding demonstrates. Therefore, the equilibrium remains precarious.

Similarly, the influence of the unions over the Government remains ambiguous. On the one hand, their informal channels of influence have grown. Twenty-five percent of the members of ministerial *cabinets* are trade unionists, and union leaders enjoy frequent access to the Elysée.[85] On the other hand, a divided union movment makes it difficult for the state to establish formal mechanisms for peak-level bargaining with the trade unions.

The employers' association (the CNPF) is also in a transitional stage. The nationalized industries now make up one-third of its membership, and the CNPF is being pressured to play the role of co-manager of the economy in alliance with the state that it assumed under Giscard. The Government's new emphasis on industrial development makes this an attractive offer. On the other hand, many of its members are demanding that the CNPF undertake a more aggressive defense of business interests against creeping socialism and threaten to withdraw to the more militant SNPMI and AFEP unless it does so.[86] Yvon Gattaz, the new president of the organization, is walking a political tightrope.

The Mitterrand Government has been dealing with these problems on an *ad hoc* basis. Its most consistent initiative has been to extend contractual relations to ever broadening spheres of state–society relations. The Ninth Plan is to be elaborated via *contrats État–Entreprises* and *contrats État–Régions*; and development contracts have already been used to regulate relations between the state and the nationalized industries. Serious bargaining with the unions and CNPF was central to the unemployment insurance reforms of 1982–3 and further reduction of the work week.[87] In effect, the state is trying to force social actors to bargain with one another and with the Government. This extends a tradition which may ultimately break down the longstanding *étatisme* of the French state.[88] The trend is by no means complete, but corporate actors who were once 'two solitudes' are now pragmatic and frequent negotiators with each other and the state.

CONCLUSION

By the winter of 1984, the Socialist Government was half-way through its first term in office. A preliminary assessment would have to conclude that the high aspirations of its supporters had not been met but neither were the worst expectations of its detractors confirmed.

The Government made some mistakes. The expansion of 1981 intensified the nation's balance of payments problems and could be seen as an error. However, the employment effects of the policy were substantial and contractionary measures would have generated legitimate political dismay. Mitterrand gambled and lost, but the ensuing problems were equally attributable to the inherited trade deficit and rising American dollar. In fact, France's overall economic performance during 1981–3 was quite good in comparison with those of her trading partners and the preceding three years (see Tables 4.2 and 4.3). GDP grew by 2.4 percent versus 0.3 percent for the EEC as a whole, and capital formation fell by only 1.9 percent versus 2.7 percent on average in the EEC. Price controls successfully reduced inflation from 14 percent in 1981 to 9.3 percent in 1983; and France, alone among the European nations, was able to keep her increase in unemployment below 10 percent a year until 1984. Inspired by freer credit and the falling franc, the

Table 4.2   Economic performance in Europe, 1981–3

|  | France | Germany | UK | EEC |
|---|---|---|---|---|
| GDP (total volume change %) | 2.3 | 0.6 | 0.4 | 0.8 |
| Unemployment (total change in % labour force) | 2.9 | 4.9 | 5.6 | 4.2 |
| Investment (total % change in GFCF) | −4.5 | −9.2 | −4.3 | −11.0 |
| Inflation (average rate in %) | 10.8 | 4.9 | 8.9 | 10.1 |
| Earnings (total % change real earnings) | 3.5 | −0.1 | 4.4 | 2.0 |
| Imports (total % change) | 0.7 | 2.5 | 11.3 | 3.7 |
| Exports (total % change) | 4.8 | 14.8 | −1.3 | 2.8 |
| Budget deficit (PSBR as % GDP) | 2.9 | 4.0 | 1.2 | 4.9 |

*Source:   European Economy* (1983), various issues. Figures for 1983 are estimates.

**Table 4.3** French economic performance under Giscard and Mitterrand

| | Average 1978-80 | Average 1981-84 | 1978 | 1979 | 1980 | 1981 | 1982 | 1983 | 1984 | 1985 |
|---|---|---|---|---|---|---|---|---|---|---|
| GDP growth (% volume) | 2.6 | 1.1 | 3.5 | 3.0 | 1.4 | 0.4 | 2.1 | 0.9 | 1.0 | 1.5 |
| Investment (% change GFCF) | 2.4 | -1.8 | 1.5 | 3.3 | 2.0 | -1.8 | -2.4 | -2.4 | -0.4 | 1.4 |
| Industrial production (% change) | 1.9 | -0.1 | 2.3 | 4.0 | -0.5 | -0.7 | 0.1 | 0.2 | 4.0 | 5.0 |
| Imports (% change) | 7.0 | 0.1 | 5.1 | 10.4 | 4.5 | -1.3 | 2.8 | -3.1 | 2.0 | 4.0 |
| Exports (% change) | 5.4 | 2.4 | 6.4 | 6.5 | 2.5 | 4.8 | -2.2 | 2.3 | 4.5 | 4.0 |
| Consumer prices (% change) | 11.0 | 10.0 | 8.8 | 10.9 | 13.6 | 14.0 | 9.7 | 9.3 | 7.0 | 6.0 |
| Earnings (% change) | 13.3 | 11.4 | 12.6 | 12.8 | 15.4 | 16.3 | 12.6 | 9.8 | 7.0 | 6.7 |
| Unemployment (% change) | 10.7 | 8.9 | 8.8 | 15.7 | 7.5 | 7.8 | 8.9 | 10.0 | 11.3 | 11.0 |
| Trade deficit (billion francs) | -22 | -55 | 0 | -10 | -57 | -56 | -93 | -42 | -30 | -15 |
| Budget deficit (% GDP) | 1.4 | 2.9 | 1.6 | 1.6 | 1.1 | 2.6 | 2.9 | 3.1 | 3.2 | 3.3 |
| Household consumption (% change) | 3.2 | 1.6 | 4.7 | 3.3 | 1.3 | 1.7 | 3.1 | 0.9 | 0.7 | 1.5 |
| Social transfers (% change) | 5.1 | 5.5 | 8.7 | 4.7 | 2.0 | 4.5 | 7.0 | 5.0 | — | — |
| Direct tax revenue (% change) | 4.6 | 4.4 | 3.6 | 2.5 | 7.8 | 1.0 | 7.1 | 5.1 | — | — |
| Real disposable income (% change) | 2.1 | 1.3 | 4.9 | 1.3 | -0.2 | 2.9 | 2.7 | -0.3 | 0 | 1.0 |

*Sources:* *European Economy* (1983), various issues; OECD, *Economic Outlook* (December 1983), *L'Expansion* (6 July 1984).
Figures for 1984 are estimates; those for 1985 are forecasts.

French stock market hit new highs in 1983; the rise continued through January 1984, after which it leveled off.

The Government's more serious mistake was its failure to devalue the franc as soon as it took office. A 25 percent devaluation against the Deutschmark was dictated by the changing terms of trade. Immediate devaluation would have delivered a faster and greater stimulus to exports than the slow decline that ensued and might have reduced the subsequent need for austerity. Most importantly, the nation might have avoided the need to borrow heavily to prop up the currency. As pressure against the franc mounted, France borrowed over $20 billion abroad, taking the total foreign debt from 120 billion francs in 1980 to 330 billion francs by March 1983.[89] Several consequences followed from this. First, in return for foreign loans, the Government had to commit itself to domestic deflation and continued membership in the European Monetary System. France's policy options were significantly constrained. Secondly, interest payments on these debts have been rising with the dollar, since most are denominated in dollars, and massive payments will become due from 1985. The outflow of capital could leave France with a balance of payments deficit even if its export drives and domestic austerity succeed. That could condemn the nation to a weak exchange rate and continuing austerity just as the 1986 elections approach. The Government may have mortgaged its own future.

This is a pattern that is repeated elsewhere in the economy. The secular decline in rates of profit has forced many French firms to terminate their investment programs or go heavily into debt. The Government has been urging them to invest, and the debt–equity ratios of French industry are rising dramatically. The portion of investment financed from retained earnings fell from 78 percent in 1979 to 34 percent in 1982. Simultaneous increases in interest rates mean that the cost of debt service alone for French firms has doubled as a percentage of value-added since 1979. In 1982, 24 percent of the value-added of the nationalized industries went to pay interest charges. Many of these firms have also been borrowing heavily abroad, and as the exchange rate of the franc falls, the cost of these loans multiplies. The SNCF borrowed 8 billion francs and EDF 12 billion francs during 1982 alone.[90]

Table 4.4    The impact of domestic and external factors on French economic performance in 1982

|  | Growth (%) | Inflation (%) | Unem- ployment (000's) | Trade balance (bF) | Public deficit (bF) |
|---|---|---|---|---|---|
| Domestic expansion, 1981–2 | 0.9 | 0.2 | −64.7 | −27.0 | 51.5 |
| Other domestic policies, 1981–2 | −0.4 | −0.3 | −106.0 | −0.2 | −18.4 |
| EMS realignmnent, 1981–2 | 0.5 | 1.5 | −15.2 | −17.9 | 2.3 |
| Change in US dollar and interest rates | −0.9 | 3.5 | 24.0 | −57.4 | 35.8 |
| TOTAL | 0.1 | 5.5 | −161.9 | −102.1 | 71.2 |

Source:    Calculations by Raymond Courbis and André Keller on the MOGLI econometric model reported in Le Monde (24 March 1983) and in Prévision et Analyse économique, 4, 1 (1983).

On the domestic front, the state has been encouraging firms to take *prêts participatifs*, or loans that are technically designated as equity in the firm. Over 15 billion francs were allocated to industry in this way during 1982 and 1983.[91] Enterprises find such instruments attractive because they are tax-deductible and technically decrease debt–equity ratios, increasing their ability to borrow even as they borrow. Unless interest and principal on these loans are readily forgiven, however, French industry may find itself with a level of indebtedness that discourages further expansion.

On all these fronts, a Socialist economic policy has been paid for by borrowing. The Government is gambling again. If these funds do not make growth possible in the near future, the French economy may be saddled with levels of debt that will seriously inhibit growth. This could constitute the structural change that will be Mitterrand's legacy to the French economy.

In redistributive terms, the Government can claim some solid accomplishments. These include: the 39-hour week, a fifth week of vacation, retirement at 60, a 12 percent increase in the purchasing power of the minimum wage, higher family allowances, and slightly more progressive taxation of higher incomes. In an era when conservative governments are trimming the welfare state, these measures represent a distinctive step forward.

To the French populace, however, such edicts do not seem to be a radical departure from past policies. Although the real value of social transfers increased by 5.4 percent between 1981 and 1983, their value had already been rising by 6.6 percent a year since 1974.[92] If tax revenues rose from 42 percent of GDP in 1980 to 44 percent in 1983, they had already grown from 36 percent in 1974. Even the move to a 39-hour week was in line with a long-term decline from 43.5 hours in 1973 to 40 hours in 1981. The promised shift from indirect to direct taxation has barely begun. Although these policies diverge from international trends, they display profound continuities with the history of policy in France.

Similarly, the interventionist industrial policies of Mitterrand draw upon a long French tradition of using the national enterprises, a public banking system, state procurement policies, price control, and extensive subsidies to rationalize the private economy. Within an international context, this appears to be a genuine alternative to conservative responses to recession that depend on reduced public spending, market forces, and a revival of business confidence to revive the economy. In France, public funds and state pressure have replaced market incentives in many sectors of the economy. Such a policy may modernize the French industrial base, as that of Britain shrinks. However, two questions hang over the outcome. Will the electorate tolerate the levels of public spending and taxation that become necessary as most industrial investment is channeled through the state? And will the Government find criteria which enable it to fund internationally efficient projects rather than persistently uncompetitive firms? By channeling more aid through the banking system, the Government has made progress on the first problem; and as public funds become increasingly scarce, it will have to tackle the hard choices implicit in the second more directly.

At the macroeconomic level, continuing austerity has begun to reduce the trade deficit (down by more than half in 1983) and lower inflation; but at the cost of stagnant growth and rising unemployment in 1984. It is arguable that the deflation has been *too* severe. Real disposable income fell in 1983 for the first time since the war; and the Government has lost its room for further redistribution. It can only hope that external equilibrium is restored in time to expand the economy before the 1986 legislative elections. In the end the success of the policy depends heavily on developments in the international economy. If the value of the dollar and the cost of oil fall by 10 percent alone, France's current account deficit would be cut in half.[93] A German recovery would also stimulate French production. Mitterrand cannot fully determine his own fate.

The most serious problems generated by these policies have occurred at the political level. As austerity intensified, French politics became increasingly conflictual. Trade unionists began active resistance to the lay-offs implied by a more selective industrial policy. Opponents of the Government's educational reforms were able to assemble 1.5 million people for Paris street demonstrations in June 1984. In the European elections of that month, the PS received only 21 percent of the vote and the Communists 11 percent, barely more than the extreme right-wing party of Jean-Marie Le Pen. The traditional working-class base of the Communists was disappearing and the Socialists were losing the floating middle-class vote on which their ascent to power had depended. Many members of the 'new working class' white-collar technicians, cadres, and service personnel to whom the Socialist appeal had been directly pitched, were bearing the brunt of tax increases designed to reduce domestic spending and the external deficit. In the face of austerity, the Government's electoral coalition was dissolving.

President Mitterrand responded to these developments by promising to reduce taxes by 5 percent in 1985 and by shuffling his ministers. In July 1984, Laurent Fabius became France's youngest Prime Minister in 150 years and Pierre Bérégovoy the new Finance Minister. The PCF took advantage of this shift to leave the majority. With these changes, the Government moved closer to the center of the political spectrum. Although Fabius was a strong supporter of industrial modernization, Bérégovoy was a fiscal conservative. They announced a new initiative against youth unemployment. However, to cut taxes on French employers and the middle classes without raising the public sector deficit much above 3 percent of GDP, increases in the price of public utility products and reductions in state spending would have to follow. The Government seemed likely to move even farther away from redistributive policies toward those designed to raise private sector investment and middle-class purchasing power in the hope of attaining higher levels of economic growth before the 1986 legislative elections.

By the end of 1984, Mitterrand was presiding over a socialism beseiged. Paradoxically, a government that stressed decentralization of decision-making and consultation with social groups more than any preceding French administration had been peculiarly unsuccessful at mobilizing consent for its policies. Sniping from the unions, the PCF, and the Socialist Party's own political wings became a barrage. Similarly, a forceful left-wing administration in control of an *étatiste* state found that its room for maneuver was still heavily constrained. The authority of the state itself was being called into question. Many conservative politicians were beginning to advocate a Reaganite 'neo-liberalism' and many voters were turning away from politics altogether.[94]

The French left seemed to be engaged in an extended process of social learning. Many of the intellectuals who were such avid partisans of socialism retreated into skeptical reflection.[95] The Socialist Party and CFDT had always been organizations that looked as much for the transformation of society as the expropriation of capital. Yet even the Government's most radical moves, such as the reform of regional administration, the extension of social transfers, and the nationalization of industry had extended rather than revolutionized longstanding patterns of political behavior. Most social relations remained untouched. The profound *étatisme* of Mitterrand's socialism led many to see it as 'socialism trapped within the state.'[96] As a result, many Socialists themselves have had to search to new conceptions of their mission. As one said: 'When we look in the mirror, we no longer recognize ourselves.'[97] Therefore, the following years may bring more than a verdict on the viability of Mitterrand's policies. They may inspire a redefinition of socialism and the role of the state itself in France.

## NOTES

1. *Le Point*, 2 May 1981, p. 51.
2. For overviews of this period see: Stanley Hoffmann, 'Year one,' *New York Review of Books* (12 August 1982), pp. 37–43; Michel Beaud, *Le mirage de la croissance* (Paris: Syros, 1983); Bela Belassa, 'Une année de politique économique socialiste en France, *Commentaire* (1982), pp. 415–28; Philippe Simonnet, *Le grand bluff économique des socialistes* (Paris: Lattes, 1982); Volkmar Lauber, *The Political Economy of France* (New York: Praeger, 1983); Mark Kesselman, 'Socialism without the Workers: The Case of France,' *Kapitalistate*, No. 10/11 (1983).
3. *L'Express*, 22 April 1983, p. 43 in $US of 1970; see Bertrand Bellon, *Le pouvoir financier et l'industrie en France* (Paris: Éditions du Seuil, 1980); B. Bellon and J.-M. Chevalier, *L'Industrie en France* (Paris: Flammarion, 1983).
4. *9e Plan de développement économique social et culturel 1984–1988* (Paris: Documentation française, 1983), Vol. II, p. 110.
5. *Regards sur l'actualité*, March 1983, p. 6; *Le Monde*, 28 May 1983, p. 1.
6. Pierre Rosenvallon, 'Les tendances de la négotiation collective et des relations industrielles en France,' mimeo, p. 5; see also Alain Lipietz, 'L'échec de la première phase,' *Les Temps modernes* (April 1983), pp. 34–57.
7. *L'Expansion*, 19 December 1982, p. 44.
8. Yves Berthelot and G. Tardy, *Le Défi économique du tiers monde* (Paris: Documentation française, 1978).
9. Jane Marceau, *Class and Status in France* (Oxford: Oxford University Press, 1977); Philippe Lefournier, 'Septs Ans de Malheur,' *L'Expansion*, 6 (March 1981), p. 65.
10. *Le Projet Socialiste* (Paris: Club Socialiste du Livre, 1980), p. 141.
11. See Jane Jenson and George Ross, 'Crisis and France's "Third Way",' *Studies in Political Economy* (Spring 1983), pp. 71–103; *Le Monde dossiers et documents: l'élection présidentielle 26 avril–10 mai 1981* (May 1981).
12. *Le Témoignage chrétien*, 11–17 July 1983, p. 7.
13. Oliver Marchand et al., 'Des 40 heures aux 39 heures: processus et réactions des entreprises,' *Économie et Statistique*, 154 (April 1983), p. 11.
14. *Le Monde: Bilan économique et social 1982* (January 1983), p. 66.
15. *Le Monde*, 2 April 1983, p. 21.
16. *Le Monde*, 5 July 1983, p. 30. The total includes taxes 10.4, social security 6.6, unemployment insurance 7.0, SMIC 0.6, Auroux laws 0.6, worktime reduction 8.3, and urban transport 0.2 billion francs.
17. M. Debonneuil and H. Sterdyniak, 'Apprécier une dévaluation,' *Économie et Statistique*, 142 (March 1982), pp. 41–61.
18. *Le Monde*, 24 March 1983, p. 40.
19. Ibid., p. 9 and *Le Monde*, 1 December 1981, p. 1.
20 *L'Express*, 25 June 1982; *Le Monde*, 1 January 1983, p. 17.
21. *Le Monde: Bilan économique et social 1982*, p. 68.
22. See *Le Monde*, 26 and 27 March 1983.
23. Pierre Mauroy quoted in *L'Express*, 8 April 1983, pp. 38–9.
24. *Le Nouvel Observateur*, 30 May 1983.
25. Interviews with French officials, July 1983.
26. *Business Week*, 10 January 1983, p. 67.

27. Ibid.
28. Yves Laulan, 'La Défense nationale à l'heure de l'austerité,' *Chroniques d'actualité de la SEDEIS* (15 March 1983), pp. 11–146.
29. See André Delion and Michel Durupty, *Les Nationalisations 1982* (Paris: Economica, 1982) and *Revue Économique* (May 1983).
30. *L'Express*, 14 June 1983, p. 40.
31. *L'Express*, 1 October 1982 and Delion and Durupty, *Les Nationalisations*, op. cit.
32. See *Le Monde*, February 5, 1983, p. 33; *L'Expansion*, 10 September 1982; *Le Monde*, 7 August 1982.
33. *Le Monde*, 28 May 1983, p. 1; *Le Monde: Bilan économique et sociale 1982*, p. 168; *Le Monde*, 2 April 1983, p. 1.
34. J. Hough, 'Government Intervention in the Economy of France,' in Peter Maunder, ed., *Government Intervention in the Developed Economy* (London: Croom Helm, 1979), p. 191. See John Zysman, *Governments, Markets and Growth* (Ithaca: Cornell University Press, 1983), Ch. 3.
35. *Le Monde*, 5 February 1983, p. 33.
36. Électricité de France, Gaz de France, Société Nationale des Chemins de Fer Français, Régie Autonome des Transports Parisiens and Charbonnages de France. *L'Express*, 27 May 1983; *Le Monde*, 21 April 1983, p. 29.
37. *Le Monde*, 11 February 1983, p. 26.
38. Xavier Greffe, 'Les entreprises publiques dans la politique de l'Etat,' *Revue Économique*, 34, 3 (May 1983), p. 510; *Le Nouvel Économiste*, 9 May 1983, p. 38; *Le Monde*, 21 April 1983, p. 29.
39. *The Economist*, 26 March 1983; International Banking Survey, p. 59; *Euromoney*, November 1982; *Le Monde*, 17 February 1983, p. 1.
40. CIASI: Comité interministériel d'aménagement des structures industrielles; CODEFI: Comités départementaux d'examen des problèmes de financement des entreprises; see *Alternatives Économiques*, 17 (15 July 1983), p. 9; see also Diana Green, 'Administered Industrialisation: Managing Industrial Crisis in France,' in K. Dyson and S. Wilks, eds, *Managing Industrial Crisis* (London: Martin Robertson, 1984).
41. CIRI: Comité interministériel de restructuration industrielle; CORRI: Comités régionaux de restructuration industrielle; *The Economist*, 26 March 1983, p. 58.
42. CODIS: Comité de développement des industries stratégiques; CIDISE: Comité interministériel pour le développement industriel et le soutien de l'emploi; *Le Nouvel Économiste*, 9 May 1983, pp. 38–9.
43. *Le Monde*, 29 July 1983.
44. *Le Nouvel Économiste*, 9 May 1983, p. 38.
45. *Sunday Times* (London), 4 September 1983; *L'Express*, 23 April 1982.
46. *9e Plan*, II, pp. 1, 63–4; *Le Nouvel Observateur*, 3 June 1980, p. 38.
47. *Le Monde: Bilan économique et social 1982*, p. 45.
48. See André de Lattre, M. Pebereau and Christian Stoffaës, *Politique Économique de la France* (Paris: IEP les Cours de Droit, 1983), Ch. 7, for an excellent discussion.
49. *Le Monde: Bilan économique et social 1982*, pp. 168–70.
50. De Lattre, Pebereau and Stoffaës, *Politique économique de la France*, op. cit.
51. *Économie et politique*, March 1983, p. 38; *Business Week*, 28 December 1981, p. 70.
52. Ibid.
53. *Financial Times* (London).
54. *Le Monde*, 22 January 1983, p. 29; *L'Express*, 19 November 1982.
55. *Le Monde*, 3 January 1983, p. 1.
56. De Lattre et al., *Politique économique*, op. cit., pp. 165–6.
57. *L'Express*, 7 January 1983, p. 28.
58. Cf. Christian Stoffaës, *La Grande Menace industrielle* (Paris: Calmann Lévy, 1978) and Suzanne Berger, 'Lame Ducks and National Champions,' in W.G. Andrews and Stanley Hoffmann, eds, *The Fifth Republic at Twenty* (Albany: SUNY Press, 1981).
59. See Diana Green, 'Giscardisme — Industrial Policy,' in Vincent Wright, ed., *Continuity and Change in France* (London: Allen & Unwin, 1984).
60. *Le Monde*, 24 March 1983, p. 16; *L'Express*, 19 November 1982, p. 44.
61. *Le Monde*, 13 April 1983, p. 43.
62. See Jean Monfort, 'A la recherche des filières de production,' *Économie et Statistique*, 151 (January 1983), pp. 3–12.
63. Cf. Michael Piore and Charles Sabel, *The Second Industrial Divide* (New York: Basic, 1984).

64. Cf. Jean Delatte, *Crépuscules industrielles 1945–1985* (Paris: Édigéon, 1979).
65. See *OJL* 795/35, 29/7/780.
66. Monique Dagnaud and Dominique Mehl, *L'Élite rose* (Paris: Éditions Ramsay, 1983), pp. 43, 326.
67. See Ezra Suleiman, *Elites in French Society* (Princeton, N.J.: Princeton University Press, 1978); Pierre Birnbaum *et al.*, *La Classe dirigeante française* (Paris: PUF, 1978).
68. Dagnaud and Mehl, *L'Élite rose*, op. cit., p. 326.
69. Ibid., p. 243. Long-term change became possible, however, as the Socialists opened entry into the École Nationale d'Administration up to more mid-career civil servants.
70. *L'Expansion*, 22 April 1983, p. 87 also quotes Laurent Fabius: 'My role as regards the President is not to make a decision on one side or another but to weight the pros and cons in front of him until he comes down with a decision.'
71. Dagnaud and Mehl, *L'Élite rose*, op. cit., p. 217.
72. See Peter A. Hall, 'Policy Innovation and the Structure of the State,' *Annals*, **466** (March 1983), pp. 43–59.
73. *L'Express*, 8 April 1983.
74. Le Commissariat Général du Plan, *Plan intérimaire: stratégies pour deux ans 1982–83* (Paris: Documentation Française, 1982); *Le Monde*, 10 April 1983, p. 21; Commission de Réforme de la Planification, *Rapport final au Ministre d'État* (Paris:Documentation française, 1982).
75. Interview with French official, July 1983.
76. *Le Monde*, 30 July 1983, p. 18; *L'Express*, 1 October 1982.
77. See Peter A. Hall, 'Economic Planning and the State: the Evolution of Economic Challenge and Political Response in France,' in Maurice Zeitlin *et. al.*, eds, *Political Power and Social Theory*, Vol. III (Greenwich Conn.: Jai Press, 1982).
78. *Le Monde: Bilan économique et social 1982*, p. 56.
79. *Le Monde*, 30 July 1983, p. 18.
80. See H. Portelli, *Le Socialisme français tel qu'il est* (Paris: PUF, 1980).
81. *Le Monde: Bilan économique et social 1982*, p. 68.
82. J. Auroux, *Les Droits des travailleurs: rapport au Président de la Republique et au Premier Ministre* (Paris: Documentation Française, 1981); *Le Monde*, 24 March 1982, p. 10.
83. See Pierre Rosenvallon, *Misère de l'économie* (Paris: Éditions du Seuil, 1983), Ch. 12.
84. *Le Monde*, 28 April 1983, p. 31; *Le Monde: Bilan économique et social 1982*, p. 67.
85. Dagnaud and Mehl, *L'Élite rose*, op. cit., p. 160.
86. *L'Express*, 12 December 1982. SNPMI: Société nationale de petites et moyennes entreprises; AFEP: Association française des entreprises privées.
87. *9e Plan*, II, pp. 137, 294; *L'Express*, 26 November 1982, 3 December 1982.
88. See Michel Crozier, *The Bureaucratic Phenomenon* (Chicago: University of Chicago Press, 1964); Alain Peyrefitte, *Le Mal Français* (Paris: Flammarion, 1980); Hall, 'Economic Planning and the State,' op. cit.
89. *L'Express*, 13 April 1983, p. 44.
90. *Le Monde*, 21 April 1983, p. 29 and Elizabeth Versillier, 'Aspects financiers des nationalisations,' *Revue Économique*, **34**, 3 (May 1983), p. 483.
91. See Daniel Barbe, 'Prêts participatifs: Les limites du succès d'une innovation financière,' *Chroniques d'actualité de la SEDEIS* (15 April 1983), pp. 162-70.
92. *9e Plan*, II, p. 122.
93. *L'Express*, 7 June 1983.
94. See *Le Monde*, 6 September 1984.
95. See the debate in *Le Monde* from 23 July 1983 initiated by Max Gallo's contention that the intellectuals had deserted the Government.
96. P. Viveret, 'La gauche piegée dans l'État,' *Projet* (June 1983).
97. Robert Chapuis, député from the Ardèche, *L'Express*, 3 December 1982, p. 40.

# 5 Defence Policy under François Mitterrand: Atlanticism, Gaullism or 'Nuclear Neutralism'?

*Jolyon Howorth*

The French Socialist Party has, from its very origins in the late nineteenth century,[1] been a tense coalition between a congeries of fissiparous ideological factions whose unity has been based as much on shared hostility to other political formations as it has on any clear agreed project for society. These factions have usually succeeded in finding a form of words (a 'resolution') representing a compromise political line which will allow them to remain united. This is as true on defence issues as on any other aspect of public policy — with two significant differences.

First, Socialists have traditionally fought shy of coping with (or even thinking about) defence policy, which has seemed to many to be antithetical to socialist ideals. Unlike most other fields of public policy, there has, with one notable exception,[2] been no serious attempt to theorize a socialist defence policy — at least until the early 1970s. Socialists in the twentieth century have tended to oscillate between two different approaches to their responsibilities in matters military. Either (1920–39) they retreated into a struthious form of pacifism, pinning all their faith on international organizations (League of Nations) to avoid war; or (1945–72) they threw themselves headlong into an integrated military alliance in which the ultimate responsibility for national defence was shuffled off on to other shoulders. More recently, influenced by the national consensus which has formed around Gaullist notions of an independent nuclear 'deterrent', they have tended to see salvation in the bomb.

The second difference between defence issues and other issues of public policy is the international dimension which injects into the policy-making equation a new and complex set of variables. Some are subjective: assessment of enemy *intentions*, perceptions of great power status and national *grandeur*. Many are purely speculative: trade-offs between allies or adversaries involving known sacrifices and anticipated recompenses. In the nuclear era, most are purely hypothetical: the rules of the game since 1945 have involved convincing an enemy through discourse rather than constraining him through battle.[3] For socialists, this international dimension is rendered more complex on account of the 'natural' antipathy between the capitalist ideology of the Western World and the aims of socialism.

Any socialist government therefore has to tread a very wary path between these different constraints. The task is made even more difficult in times of economic crisis when the government's margin of manoeuvre is considerably reduced both by the international financial community, on whose goodwill it becomes more dependent, and by the national business community, without whose cooperation its task becomes even more problematic. These various levels of constraint are a necessary backdrop to any understanding of the defence policy of a socialist government in France. They explain and illustrate the three conflicting options which divide the French Socialist Party in this domain: Atlanticism, Gaullism and 'Nuclear Neutralism'.

Since 1945, the dominant variable in strategic thinking has been the division of the world into two blocs subjected to superpower hegemony. In France, the dominant issue has been how to relate to what is known as 'Atlanticism'. Ever since 1917, the French Socialist Party has contained a solid phalanx of members committed to American leadership of the 'free world'. This tendency, which became dominant in the SFIO after 1947, considers that, in a bipolar world, all nations have to make a choice of camp. Since social democrats have always seen communism as a greater evil than liberalism, that choice is self-evident. Since socialist principles of equality and justice cannot countenance, either economically or politically, spending vast sums on military preparations, defence must be left in the hands of a greater unit than the nation. That unit is, in any case, called for in the internationalist aspiration of socialism. These ideas, typified from 1946 to 1962 by Guy Mollet and, more recently, by Robert Pontillon,[4] remained relatively unchallenged within the old SFIO until the early 1970s. They implied very close ties with NATO and the USA; total rejection of the *French* nuclear weapon as both an unacceptable extravagance and a strategic spoilsport; and vociferous criticism of Gaullist nationalist pretensions. So strong was this current within French socialism that, even after the founding of the new Socialist Party[5] in 1971, it gathered 75 per cent of the votes at the national convention on defence in 1972.[6]

However, by the early 1970s, other voices were beginning to make themselves heard within the party. The strategic debate which had been generated in France after Robert MacNamara's adoption of 'flexible response' in 1962[7] had a profound impact not only on the Gaullist movement, but also on the left. An important fraction of the Socialist Party, under Charles Hernu,[8] began to plead openly for a pseudo-Gaullist defence policy based on an independent French nuclear capability within the Atlantic Alliance. Another group, around Jean-Pierre Chevènement and the CERES,[9] went one stage further and argued that the prospects of survival for an 'experiment in socialism' in France depended on withdrawal from the Atlantic Alliance and the development of a totally neutral nuclear arsenal capable of keeping *both* superpowers in check. Gradually, as these ideas began to germinate in the minds of the members of the PS defence commission, and as François Mitterrand began to identify himself more and more openly with them,[10] the non-nuclear Atlanticist majority became a minority. At the PS convention on defence held in January 1978, the party adopted a resolution inspired by Charles Hernu. The non-nuclear Atlanticists allowed themselves to vote for it because of the firm promises that a socialist France would regard the Atlantic Alliance as its natural ideological and strategic 'home', and because acceptance of the bomb was presented as a temporary measure pending universal disarmament; the CERES (after suffering a humiliating 71–15 per cent defeat for its anti-Atlanticist motion) decided to vote for it because it did at least give France her independent nuclear arsenal. Both of the 'non-Hernu' factions were willing to reach a compromise since the convention was taking place only weeks before the vital general elections of 1978. But the resolution nevertheless failed to disguise the fact that the Socialist Party was as divided as ever on questions of defence.[11]

Between the PS defence convention of January 1978 and the coming to power of François Mitterrand in May 1981, vast geological shifts took place in the substratum of socialist, French and international politics. Inside the Socialist Party, a challenge to François Mitterrand from the 'right-wing' leader, Michel Rocard, precipitated a hasty political alliance between Mitterrand and the CERES. The latter were charged with the drafting of the 'Socialist project' for the 1980s, which was to serve as the basis of the presidential candidate's campaign for the 1981 elections. The defence chapter of that document[12] spelled out a far more pro-nuclear and anti-Atlanticist line than the motion adopted in 1978. As for French domestic politics, the disintegration of the Gaullist–Giscardian alliance, the worsening of the economic crisis and the electoral collapse of the Communist Party finally created the conditions for the coming to power of a Socialist government. By the time the Government was elected, however, the international situation had changed radically in relation to 1978. The collapse of *détente*, heralded in the late 1970s by the decision of both superpowers to deploy new generations of nuclear missiles, had become total. Despite the hopes raised by the signing of the SALT 2 agreement in Vienna in 1979, those agreements were never ratified by the US Senate. Instead, NATO decided, in December 1979, to deploy Cruise and Pershing 2 missiles in several European countries if there was failure to reach agreement with the USSR on general disarmament of intermediate range weapons by 1983. Several weeks later, the USSR invaded Afghanistan. By the end of 1980, the Atlantic Alliance was dominated by two extreme right-wing governments committed to wholesale escalation of the nuclear arms race. Meanwhile, the Soviet Union was deploying one new SS-20 missile pointed at Europe every three days. How was the incoming President to respond to the conflicting pressures which this threefold set of constraints imposed upon him?

### DEFENCE ISSUES IN THE PRESIDENTIAL CAMPAIGN

Mitterrand's manifesto, drawn up at a special Socialist Congress on 24 January 1981, had been a far cry from either the 1978 motion of the defence chapter or the 'Socialist Project'. Vague reference was made to the objective of simultaneous dissolution of the military blocs, alongside a promise that the new President would renegotiate certain aspects of the Atlantic Alliance. There was a commitment to avoid nuclear proliferation, a call for a European disarmament conference, a suggestion that the SS-20s be withdrawn and the new NATO missiles cancelled, and a promise to construct two new nuclear strike submarines (SNLEs). In other words, the package was as broad as possible, designed to offend nobody on the left, and even to attract disillusioned Gaullists.

Defence issues, however, played virtually no part in the campaign, except for a clash over numbers of nuclear submarines.[13] Mitterrand remained curiously silent about the specific clauses of the Alliance that he wished to discuss, unforthcoming about his view of the balance of forces in Europe, and noncommittal about the way in which he saw France's role in the defence of the continent. He also said nothing about French strategic doctrine. The CERES group tried to force some discussion of these vital defence issues on to the campaign agenda through a series of articles in *Le Monde*.[14] The real debate, they insisted, was about bloc politics. Giscard, they charged, had realigned France with NATO and thereby demolished all her credibility as an arbiter or intermediary between the superpowers. Only a strong, nuclear France, totally neutral as regards both blocs, could take the sorely needed initiative on European disarmament. The implication was clear. If François Mitterrand did harbour temptations of an Atlanticist nature, the CERES was serving a warning that he should not repeat the errors of the Giscard presidency.

## DEFENCE POLICY IN FRANCE UNDER PRESIDENT MITTERRAND

During the final year of the Giscard *septennat*, owing to the deep-rooted contradiction between the Atlanticism of the UDF and the Gaullism of the RPR, defence policy had remained in a state of suspended ambiguity. There were four important issues on which defence experts looked to the Socialists for a clear lead. First, what line would the new Government take on the burning issue which was convulsing the entire continent: the euromissile controversy? Secondly, which way would the Socialists swing the balance of priorities as between nuclear and conventional defence systems? How would they react to rapid advances in defence technology and the need for 'modernization' which was being pressed on successive governments by the military planners? Third, what strategic doctrine would underpin the choice of weapons systems? If the priority were given to nuclear weapons, would this involve a return to Gaullist precepts of strategic 'deterrence', or would continued emphasis be placed, as it had under Giscard, on battle-fighting, tactical systems? On the other hand, if there was to be a major effort in the field of conventional weapons, would this signal closer links with NATO? Fourth, how would the Socialists handle the long-overdue question of the restructuring of the land army? Would the new, professional force which seemed bound to emerge have a new role to play in the forward defences of Europe?

A flurry of defence activity followed Charles Hernu's appointment as Defence Minister on 22 May 1981, but there were to be no early signs of a clear Socialist defence policy. Arguing that there had been massive delays in implementing the previous (Giscardian) defence white paper, Hernu postponed the drafting of a Socialist white paper until the provisions of the previous one had been carried out. This hardly spelled revolution. Although the decision to scrap the controversial plans for extension to the Larzac military camp and the temporary cancellation of nuclear tests in Polynesia were seen as triumphs for 'the spirit of 10 May', they turned out to be triumphs of public relations more than anything else.[15] In a refreshing public return to Jaurésian principles, Hernu insisted that defence depended above all on national unity and solidarity. In this sense, he suggested, the Minister of Labour, by putting men back to work, and the Minister of Education, by instilling a notion of justice and history in young people's minds, were also 'Ministers of Defence'. He, of course, was merely the 'Minister of Military Defence'.[16] However, it was not long before the new Government was obliged to take a firm stand on the first major issue on the defence agenda: the euromissiles.

## THE EUROMISSILES AND THE PROBLEMS OF NUCLEAR DIPLOMACY

It was only weeks after his election that President Mitterrand first came out openly, in an interview in the German magazine *Stern*, in support of the deployment by NATO of Cruise and Pershing 2 missiles.[17] Ever since 1980, he had gradually been coming round to the idea of linking withdrawal of the SS-20 to non-deployment of Pershing 2 and Cruise.[18] Curiously enough, Charles Hernu had, until comparatively recently, held very different views. In a book published in December 1980 (one year after the NATO '2-track' decision), he had summarily rejected all talk of Soviet superiority in Europe or elsewhere as NATO propaganda, referring scornfully to the 'circulation of the most fantastic figures and statistics'. In strategic weapons, he argued that the USA had a commanding lead, in warheads, guidance systems, fuel systems and undetectability: 'On the whole range of weapons systems, the USA has about a generation's advance over the USSR [. . . .] To speak of an imbalance in favour of the USSR is simply not serious.' He accepted that the SS-20 was a qualitatively different weapon from the SS-4 or the SS-5, but even so did not feel that it had altered the balance of forces in Europe as a whole. He waved aside the oft-repeated assertion of a 5:1 Soviet advantage in tanks as 'meaningless' in view of the West's anti-tank weapons. After reviewing naval and air forces, he concluded unequivocally: 'The truth is that American superiority is total'.[19] Hernu's book was unavailable in bookshops by the summer of 1981, and even the PS's own bookshop could not seem to locate a copy . . .[20]

For by that time, Mitterrand's own views on these matters were diametrically opposed to those expressed by his Defence Minister only six months previously. The matter was already very complex, but two interrelated secondary issues rendered it even more so: first, Mitterrand's stated intention of 'renegotiating' certain aspects of the Atlantic Alliance; and, second, his decision to appoint four Communists to his Government. Vice-President Bush, visiting Paris immediately after this latter decision, ominously warned that relations between France and her Alliance partners could be seriously affected by the appointment of Communist ministers. Mitterrand's margin of manoeuvre was tightly circumscribed. Retreat into a defence strategy based solely on France was as politically hazardous as was complete reintegration of NATO. He could not afford to alienate the Americans for two reasons: France still depended on US satellite and other technology for her own defence systems; and US potential for economic sabotage of the French socialist experiment was considerable. All these considerations no doubt help to explain the President's decision, in July 1981, to offer enthusiastic support for the deployment of Pershing 2 and Cruise:

I believe that peace is linked to the balance of forces in the world. The installation of the SS-20s and the Backfires has disturbed this balance in Europe. I cannot accept this and I believe that Europe must rearm in order to re-establish equilibrium. . . . I believe . . . there is a Soviet supremacy in Europe and I see a real danger there. But the USA has the means to re-establish the balance.[21]

It is clear from the outset that Mitterrand's enthusiastic support for the NATO '2-track' decision was based more on a diplomatic gamble than on strategic principle. Irrespective of the eventual outcome of the euromissile crisis, the risks for France in open support for NATO were considerable. First, there was the risk of blurring the distinction between superpower strategic systems and the French strategic system — a distinction which had kept the French arsenal out of the SALT talks. Second, there was the danger of prejudicing France's hopes of acting as an 'honest broker' between the US and the USSR with a view to bringing them to the negotiating table (the stated principal aim of socialist diplomacy).[22] Finally, such a stance was likely to be very destructive of the political bases of the Government's internal support. On the other hand, Mitterrand felt there was much to be gained from demonstrations of Franco-Atlantic solidarity. The sympathy of Ronald Reagan and Helmut Schmidt was essential for the defence of the franc, which was already under intense pressure on the money markets. It was also necessary to 'buy' a certain amount of domestic 'peace' from the French right.[23] Finally, Mitterrand clearly believed that 'nuclear diplomacy' works and that the Soviet Union would eventually concede to a united Western front what it would not have yielded to a less resolute negotiating partner.

The military or strategic aspect of the question is of far less immediate importance to Mitterrand. Having, in his July 1981 interview in *Stern*, spoken of clear Soviet superiority in Europe, he later stated, in the same interview, that he 'would like to know precisely what the state of the forces [was] between the two camps' and promised to 'study this matter very carefully'. What was it he did not yet know? Evidently a good deal, since only ten weeks later, in his major press conference of 24 September 1981, he reversed his previous judgement on Soviet superiority and accepted, as did Charles Hernu, the notion of approximate parity between the superpowers. On these occasions, the decision to support NATO policy was justified on the grounds of a *potential* Soviet lead later in the decade.[24]

In the long term, of course, Mitterrand is clearly very concerned about the military–strategic aspect of the euromissile question. He was disarmingly frank, in December 1981, in acknowledging that if the SS-20 had caused an imbalance in one direction, Pershing 2 would create another, equally intolerable imbalance in the other direction.[25]

Yet the basic tactic of the Mitterrand Administration has been to play to the full the game of nuclear diplomacy. In an important speech to the Institut des Hautes Études de Défense Nationale (IHEDN), Charles Hernu candidly admitted that what was important was not the missiles themselves, but 'the fact of announcing' the new deployments.[26] Similarly, Foreign Minister Claude Cheysson, in welcoming Reagan's 'zero option' proposals, analysed them in purely diplomatic terms. First, he said, they were intended to reassure Europeans who had been alarmed by previous statements from the White House about 'limited nuclear war-fighting in Europe'.[27] Second, Cheysson interpreted the Pershing 2 missile as essentially a *political* weapon with which to counter the 'decoupling' propensities of the SS-20.[28] And finally, according to Cheysson, once the superpowers had been led to the negotiating table, they would be sure to find a satisfactory formula.[29]

Nuclear diplomacy is not seen by Mitterrand simply as a way of entering into the debate between the superpowers. It also has a *bilateral* dimension to it. The aim is to show both superpowers that France remains mistress of her own destiny. Thus, while Claude Cheysson, in the interview referred to above, insisted on France's desire to improve relations with the Soviet Union at every level, the President continued to refuse to meet the Soviet leaders while they maintained troops in Afghanistan. Yet, at the same time, France vigorously resisted US attempts to impose commercial sanctions on the Communist bloc and, after the imposition of martial law in Poland, successfully killed off US attempts to prevent European states from signing gas pipeline contracts with the USSR. Similarly, although Mitterrand has been vociferous in his support for Reagan's nuclear diplomacy, he has been outspokenly opposed to American foreign policy on almost every other issue: Central America, North South, Africa, and international economic policy.

The main bilateral thrust of Mitterrand's nuclear diplomacy has come in the field of Franco-American relations. It was in the context of his much publicized desire to 'renegotiate' aspects of the Atlantic Alliance that he made his dramatic flying visit to Washington on 12 March 1982. The object of the exercise, it was argued by many, was for Mitterrand to consecrate his position as 'spokesperson for Europe' which he felt France's nuclear arsenal gave him the right to claim. What he actually said to Reagan is still subject to conjecture, but a certain consensus has emerged around the likelihood of his having raised four basic points. The first was that the Alliance had to be seen as a comprehensive unit in which mutual duties and responsibilities, diplomatic, political and economic as well as military, needed to be carefully weighed.[30] Second, that at the European end, the most vital task was to ensure that Germany be recemented to the Western bloc and prevented from sliding towards 'neutralism'. In order to achieve this, Mitterrand discussed with Reagan the prospect of much closer military collaboration between the two continental European powers. His third aim was to persuade the American President that, while nuclear diplomacy was a necessary game to be played, it had to be played sincerely and intelligently. It was, he argued, vital not to provoke the Russians, not to bury *détente* altogether, and not to scuttle the Europeans' chance of establishing a viable *modus vivendi* with their Eastern neighbours. Finally, he wished to reassert France's absolute refusal to consider participating in the INF talks in Geneva. In this way, while offering France's enthusiastic support for one aspect of US nuclear diplomacy, Mitterrand was able to suggest to the Americans that he was by no means a slave to the Pentagon. The same trip had the collateral effect of reminding the Russians, in case they should imagine that the gas pipeline contracts signalled a 'weakening' of Western resolve, that Washington was only three hours away on Concorde, even if it did mean eating two breakfasts.[31]

While Mitterrand was pursuing nuclear diplomacy, the PS leaders were tussling with the need to prepare a statement on disarmament for the United Nations Special Session on the issue due to be held in New York in June 1982. In view of the party's support for both French and American contributions to the arms race, this was a difficult document to draft, and the finished product reflects these difficulties. The document is a curious mix of paradox and contradiction.[32] While proudly reasserting the traditional Socialist concern for 'peace', it scornfully denounces 'pacifism' as an impasse (many people would have been forgiven for believing that 'pacifism' *was* the traditional Socialist approach to peace). While asserting that the PS has a 'realistic' understanding of the requirements for maintaining peace, there is a complete absence of any theoretical assessment of those requirements. While reiterating Socialist calls for disarmament, it repeats just as regularly the Socialist call for France to build up her nuclear arsenal. While demanding the dissolution of the military blocs, it offers unequivocal support for the NATO position at Geneva. While recognizing that all over Europe the political credibility of nuclear deterrence is being challenged and questioned, it asserts that the French 'deterrent' works and that the French people feel quite secure in the midst of their nuclear stockpile. Two concrete proposals somewhat enhance the value of this confused compromise text which is clearly trying to placate the three contending factions within the Socialist Party. The first is a renewed call for a European Disarmament Conference comprising all the nations involved in the 'Helsinki process'. The second is for a conference of all five nuclear powers with a view to producing a global approach to nuclear disarmament. In July 1983 the former of these proposals was finally accepted and the Conference on European Security and Cooperation, meeting in Madrid, finally agreed to organize an all-European disarmament conference which held an inconclusive meeting in Stockholm on 7 January 1984[33] in an atmosphere of Soviet–American recrimination.

Not surprisingly, 1983, the year of Pershing 2 and Cruise, produced an intensification of France's participation in the game of nuclear diplomacy. This was the result of a variety of new developments. The new Soviet leader, Yuri Andropov, reacting to the unquestioning support for NATO which was forthcoming from France under Mitterrand, proposed that a solution to the stalled INF talks in Geneva would be for the USSR to reduce its intermediate range nuclear missiles to the level of the combined French and British totals, in exchange, of course, for non-deployment of Cruise and Pershing 2. Mitterrand's 'independence bluff' had been called. In January, former President Giscard broke his self-imposed silence and openly criticized the Socialist Government for its public support for NATO military decisions. He was quick to spot the Achilles heel of the Socialist stance and warned that France was in the process of destroying her own case for not having her nuclear arsenal discussed at Geneva. Two days later, one of Giscard's former senior diplomatic advisers, Gabriel Robin, pressed the attack on the Government by arguing that the SS-20 had hardly affected the balance of forces in Europe since the Soviets, with their SS-4 and SS-5, had for years possessed the capacity to destroy the continent several times over. What, asked Robin somewhat disingenuously,[34] did the SS-20 add to that capability? Quite apart from the internal political capital that the Giscardians stood to gain from entering the controversy in this way (the Mitterrand line was becoming increasingly controversial, both with the general public and with the PCF) the ex-President's low-profile approach to arms control contrasted sharply with that of Mitterrand.[35] Moreover, sensing that Reagan's 'zero option' was increasingly perceived in the West as an unrealistic starting-point for arms control negotiations, Giscard pressed home his attack in February 1983 by suggesting that it should be reformulated as 'objective zero' and by arguing in favour of a compromise which would generate a process leading to gradual disarmament.[36]

But François Mitterrand was not deterred. On 20 January 1983, he addressed a specially convened session of the German Parliament and urged the German people to welcome Pershing 2 on to their soil as the only way of establishing a nuclear balance in Europe. To enthusiastic applause from Christian Democratic benches, and mortified silence from his fellow Socialists of the SPD (including his personal friends, Willy Brandt and Helmut Schmidt), Mitterrand put the entire weight of his authority behind the NATO '2-track' decision which was, to some extent, at the heart of the forthcoming German election campaign.[37] The right-wing Bavarian leader, Franz-Josef Strauss, later estimated that Mitterrand's speech had been worth an extra 3 per cent of the votes for the right-wing candidates.[38] Yet so great was Mitterrand's fear lest an SPD victory at the German polls break what he considered to be the ongoing dynamic of nuclear diplomacy, that the *politics* of his speech was clearly the last thing on his mind. There is an element of self-fulfilling prophecy in nuclear diplomacy which involves the players in getting more and more deeply involved the longer they play. The Williamsburg summit brought this lesson home to the French President in no uncertain terms.

In May 1983, Mitterrand allowed himself to be manoeuvred by Mrs Thatcher and President Reagan into signing a joint communiqué on the security of the Western World.[39] The anomaly of the Williamsburg communiqué derived not only from the fact that this was the first time an economic summit had given rise to a defence statement, but also from the fact that the presence at the conference of Mr Nakasone implied an extension of the Atlantic Alliance to include Japan. The French protested energetically against any such interpretation.[40] Moreover, it is clear that Reagan and Thatcher had hoped to use the statement as a reassertion of the non-negotiability of the 'zero option', and it was due to resistance from both Mitterrand and German Chancellor Helmut Kohl that a sentence was included in the statement to the effect that 'the negotiations will determine the level of deployment' of any new missiles. This turned out to be a highly significant development in more ways than one.

In the first place, it represented the first occasion on which Mitterrand had openly departed from the official 'zero option' position on Geneva. By the summer of 1983, it had become clear that the rigidity of that position was merely an obstacle to progress. In this sense, the Williamsburg statement can be seen as a united Western move in the direction of flexibility. In the following weeks, Mitterrand was to stress on numerous occasions that he found both the American starting position ('zero option') and the Soviet starting position (slight reductions in the SS-20 levels in exchange for non-deployment of the NATO missiles) unacceptable. After a series of discussions with German leaders, he began to promote with some degree of energy the 'walk-in-the-woods' compromise solution which had been elaborated by the US and Soviet negotiators in the summer of 1982 (no deployment of Pershing, and reduction of cruise levels to around 300, with corresponding reductions in the SS-20 to about 100 missiles).[41] This was in fact a tacit admission that time was running short and that if nuclear diplomacy were to produce any result at all, the West would have to change its negotiating stance.

But that shift in position after Williamsburg also produced a new line from the French Communist Party. They interpreted the joint communiqué as a *hardening* of Western resolve, since not only was this the first time France had signed a statement to the effect that 'the security of our countries is indivisible', but also the reference to the negotiations deciding the level of missile deployments was seen as acceptance of the fact that *some* Western missiles *would* be deployed. Therefore, on 31 May 1983, the political bureau of the PCF, in an important statement critical of the French position at Williamsburg, argued that since the various governments had taken this line on Geneva, the INF (Intermediate Nuclear Forces) talks should be opened up to all European countries.[42] From all sides the criticism of Mitterrand began to pour in. The Gaullists[43] and the Soviet Union[44] joined forces in denouncing his return to 'Atlanticism'.

In the summer of 1983, the diplomatic battle over the euromissiles saw France at the centre of the controversy in various ways. First, the Soviet proposal that France's arsenal should be put on the table at Geneva became a major sticking-point in the INF negotiations. Second, the decision of the French Government to break a seventeen-year isolation and act as host to the NATO Council meeting, which was held in Paris in June, gave rise to predictable criticism from Gaullists and Communists, not to mention the Kremlin.[45] Third, in his speech to the NATO meeting, Mitterrand came out openly in favour of the 'walk-in-the-woods compromise', which had recently found favour with the SPD,[46] and formulated the hope that Geneva would fix the INF 'balance' at 'the lowest level possible'. This may well have been in part an attempt to stave off a mounting challenge to the French position from a combination of the PCF, the peace movement and the Soviet Union. For the fourth development was precisely such a challenge.

On 19 June 1983, the PCF-inspired Appel des Cent held a highly successful 'peace picnic' in the forest of Vincennes, which many commentators interpreted as the moment of take-off for the French peace movement.[47] Although the slogans for this demonstration remained as vague as ever, the position of the PCF itself had shifted quite markedly since the Williamsburg declaration. With increasing regularity, the PCF was beginning to agitate for France to accept the Andropov proposals that the French nuclear arsenal should, together with the British, be 'balanced' against the SS-20s.[48] These proposals were made quite explicit after a surprise visit by Georges Marchais to Moscow on 12 July. Despite a public relations exercise which consisted of conjuring up a false 'quarrel' between Marchais and Andropov, it rapidly transpired that what was afoot was an agreement between the PCF and the CPSU on taking the French weapons 'into consideration' at Geneva.[49] Despite PCF reassurances to the contrary,[50] this possibly reinforced the grievances which caused the Communists to leave the Government in France. The ambiguities in the defence policies of the various components of the 'presidential majority' finally burst out into the open in the summer of 1983 when the CERES joined in the chorus of criticism.[51]

At this stage, one can only speculate as to why Mitterrand has chosen to give such unswerving public support to Pershing and Cruise. Quite apart from his conviction that nuclear diplomacy is an appropriate occupation for a country like France, he is clearly convinced that there exists a danger of Soviet supremacy in Europe from the mid-1980s. He greatly fears the potential impact of such an imbalance on the attitude of Germany towards the Soviet Union, and is determined to do everything in his power to continue to weld Germany to the West. However, his initial faith in the bargaining process has worn rather thin, and there are signs that his irritation with Washington has become as severe as his posturing towards Moscow. The political price of unswerving support for Reagan has begun to prove rather high, and it has exposed the conflicts and contradictions not only as between the PS and the PCF, but also within the governing PS. It seems clear that, before Williamsburg, he felt that, whatever the impact of his position on the Russians, he was building up a stock of credit in the White House which he presumably felt he would later be able to cash in on other issues. But his total failure to persuade the US administration to alter its monetary and fiscal policies has destroyed that illusion as well.[52] In order to understand fully the direction of French defence policy in the years to come, we must now look at the item which, as we go to press, remains at the heart of the euromissile debates: the French independent 'deterrent'.

## THE FRENCH 'DETERRENT'

If all the signs had suggested that Giscard d'Estaing had subtly been restructuring France's entire defence panoply, including her nuclear arsenal, with a view to *rapprochement* with the NATO doctrine of 'flexible response', there have been many indications that Mitterrand wished to be seen as trying to reverse that trend. The first defence budget, published in October 1981, was the occasion for confirmation that France would construct a seventh nuclear missile-launching submarine (of a completely new type), would develop a new, mobile, surface-to-surface strategic missile (the SX), with which to replace the vulnerable fixed-silo S-3, and would replace the ageing Pluton tactical missile with the longer-range Hades. While the first two decisions confirmed the Government's stated intentions of affording absolute priority to strategic systems, the decision on Hades came as something of a shock to many Socialist deputies who had been under the impression that tactical weapons might be phased out.

The fact that they are not being phased out is significant. Senior politicians and military leaders have repeatedly stressed, in recent months, that the 'all-or-nothing' strategic approach to 'deterrence' lacks credibility. France, they insist, needs an intermediary stage in the strategy of *du faible au fort* which will allow her to make clear her intentions. Under the Socialist Administration, there has been an unequivocal public return to the doctrine first theorized under the Gaullists, by General Lucien Poirier, of the 'test' or 'ultimatum' shot. Under this theory, the tactical missile is to be used, under the political authority of the president, only in the event of an enemy advance which seems to be threatening France's 'vital interests'. The very act of firing it is intended as an unambiguous statement that the enemy must now stop its advance or else the strategic weapon will be fired almost immediately. In speech after speech, beginning with Pierre Mauroy's first lecture to the IHEDN on 14 September 1981, this interpretation of the tactical weapon has been driven home time and again.[53] Moreover, the same spokesmen have insisted that the Giscardian notion of tactical missiles as part of a war-fighting or battlefield panoply within the strategic context of 'flexible response' is anathema. In this respect, therefore, there appears to have been a very clear break with the direction Giscard seemed to be taking France under his presidency.[54]

But strategic nuclear weapons cost money, and at the height of the economic crisis that particular commodity was beginning to be in short supply. As early as January 1982, Pierre Mauroy had ordered the Defence Minister to freeze approximately 25 per cent of his expenditure, and in the summer came a general wages and prices freeze, together with deep cuts in government spending. More than ever, it was incumbent on the Socialists to make clear their defence priorities. When the 1983 defence budget was made public before the parliamentary defence commission on 30 September 1982, those priorities were unequivocal. Top priority was given to the strategic arsenal, with substantial resources being channelled into R & D for the mobile SX missile, the seventh nuclear submarine and plans for the new 'mirved' M-5 submarine missile with which it was to be equipped.[55] But if such absolute priority was being afforded the strategic nuclear arsenal, what role was left, within a constantly decreasing level of resources, for France's conventional weaponry?

## THE LAND ARMY

The question of the conventional armed forces was important, not only internally, where it had implications for military service as well as for the career structure of the professional soldier, but also, perhaps even more significantly, externally, where it had direct bearing on France's role in the defence of Europe. As early as 1974, the Socialist Party had made public its proposals for a radical restructuring of the land army, involving two main thrusts: a 'popular defence force' composed of locally-based territorial militias; and a more professional, highly-trained, permanent 'rapid deployment force' for use in the European theatre or overseas.[56] The overall aim had been to reduce the size of the army, to phase out conscription (which would be replaced by regular retraining sessions for the territorials) and to make maximum use of the new defence technologies in order to secure France's integrity through a combination of the rapid deployment force and the strategic nuclear arsenal. By 1982, in the heat of the economic crisis, it had become more than ever necessary to reduce the army budget. The officer corps began to hum with rumours. Their fears were increased when Pierre Mauroy addressed the IHEDN in September 1982 and spoke of the imminent organization of a 'new model army' with fewer men and more sophisticated equipment.[57] During the long interval between this speech and the publication of the Government's defence white paper in May 1983, a vigorous controversy raged throughout the defence establishment as to the most appropriate and desirable type of reform for the army, a controversy which may well have done irreparable harm to the Socialist ambition of reconciling the army with the nation.[58]

Before the precise reforms in the army were made public, however, a completely new strategic context began to emerge. On the very day when Hernu made clear his intentions to afford absolute priority to strategic nuclear weapons (30 September 1982) it so happened that General Bernard Rogers, Supreme Allied Commander in Europe, made a speech in Brussels to launch what was rapidly interpreted in France as a new war-fighting scenario for NATO, in line with the new American strategy of the 'Air–Land Battle',[59] which had been formulated a month previously in the USA, without any consultation with NATO. If France and her NATO allies appear united on deployment of Pershing 2 and Cruise as an element of nuclear diplomacy, the new American proposals for the defence of Europe seem liable to create very serious disruptions in Franco–NATO relations. There are two somewhat separate wings to what has increasingly come to be known as the 'Rogers doctrine'. The first is the desire to increase conventional defence capability in Europe so as to be able to 'raise the nuclear threshold' and possibly make a 'no early use' (of nuclear weapons) declaration. The second, which is much more closely associated with the notion of 'Air–Land Battle', is the prospect of abandoning thirty years of defensive posture on the part of NATO and preparing consciously to adopt an offensive strategy which would, in the early stages of conflict, carry the war into socialist-bloc territory using, if necessary, a combination of conventional, chemical and nuclear weapons. The two separate wings of this strategic theory are, of course, contradictory rather than complementary, and it is the case that while General Rogers himself gave regular publicity, throughout 1983, to the question of raising the nuclear threshold and increasing conventional defences, the more aggressive, war-fighting aspects of the Air–Land Battle scenario have remained confined to the specialist military journals.

Publicly Charles Hernu rejects both aspects of the new American theory. One month after the initial Rogers speech in Brussels, Hernu addressed the delegates to the Western European Union and denounced the first part of the Rogers plan in ringing terms, criticizing the attempts to raise the nuclear threshold as a covert effort to withdraw the American nuclear umbrella from Europe and as a misguided gamble which would in fact make war more likely. Moreover, Hernu sensed that there was much more behind the Rogers speech which had not been made public in Europe: 'I have the impression that General Rogers has only told us half the story. If he doesn't tell us the other half, there is every reason to be very concerned'.[60] Hernu continued, on many subsequent occasions, to offer public (and increasingly negative) criticism of the 'Rogers doctrine', stressing above all its incoherence and the considerable degree of uncertainty which surrounded it,[61] although he has so far (April 1984) refused to make any public statement on the Air–Land Battle scenario.

The strategic doctrine implicit in either aspect of the new American approach to the defence of Europe conflicts on a number of major points with the professed strategic thinking of the Socialist Administration in France. This conflict may appear to be masked on the surface by the resemblances between French and NATO military modernization plans at the conventional level. These changes were introduced in France with the important *loi de programmation militaire* which was finally passed by the National Assembly in May 1983. During a much publicized visit to the military camp at Canjuers on 15 October 1982, Mitterrand tried to allay the fears of many army officers by insisting that the land army *would* continue to play a major role in French defence policy.[62] But he made it clear that that role was to be one of 'global deterrence' in which conventional defence, like the tactical nuclear missiles, is considered to be one element in an overall defence policy whose key is the strategic nuclear arsenal.[63] The basic argument is that all three elements are considered to be part of the 'global deterrent'. The 'deterrent' operates against any threat to France's 'vital interests' (which, in order to increase the level of uncertainty, are never defined). Since it is vital to know whether an enemy, by engaging in a certain form of military action, is seriously intending to threaten those 'vital interests' (as opposed to merely manoeuvring in the hope of gaining some minor advantage), it is necessary, according to French military strategy, to force that enemy to make his intentions crystal clear. If the conventional defence forces are sufficiently well organized, trained and equipped, then only a major attack from an enemy could hope to defeat them. A major attack would immediately be interpreted as a threat to the nation's 'vital interests', and would therefore introduce at once the prospect of recourse to the strategic nuclear arsenal. The tactical nuclear missile might come in at an intermediate stage in this process, but the main point is that every aspect of French defence policy is geared to preventing war from breaking out rather than to actually fighting it. If it were to break out despite these precautions, then the doctrine is clear: escalation to the level of strategic nuclear fire would be almost immediate. Such is the theory behind the French notion of 'global deterrence'. It is a very different theory from that of 'flexible response'.

Of course, the distinction lies essentially at the level of the political usage of the available systems. And since the systems are essentially the same whatever the government in power, it is quite conceivable that their political usage can vary quite considerably from administration to administration. This aspect of the question no doubt helps to explain why the Mitterrand Administration has seemed so genuinely shocked by Soviet suggestions that the French nuclear arsenal should be included in the Geneva talks. Mitterrand, Hernu and Cheysson argue that France's nuclear strategy (global deterrence) is quite distinct from that of NATO (flexible response). Therefore, the French argument goes, because the strategic doctrine governing these different systems is so distinct, the systems themselves cannot be lumped together for arms control purposes. By the same token, Giscard's belief that France's strategic posture is (and should be) no different from that of NATO means that his only hope of keeping the French nuclear arsenal out of the Geneva negotiations is by keeping a very low profile on NATO. In actual fact, it becomes more and more obvious that Mitterrand and Hernu are about to carry out the very policy which, when openly proposed by Giscard in 1976, brought down around his ears the combined wrath of the Gaullists, the Socialists and the Communists: they are preparing, for the first time ever, to deploy French divisions on the front line in any future 'forward battle' in Europe. The only difference is that, whereas Giscard felt that, politically, he could weather the storm created by such a proposal, and therefore did not hesitate to make the proposal openly, the Socialists know that, politically, they could not survive open admission of such plans, and therefore dress them up as something else (global deterrence). All this is very confusing and it is hardly surprising that the opinion polls indicate almost universal ignorance about the strategic theories underlying France's weapons systems.

That ignorance and that confusion were hardly dispelled by the publication of the Socialists' military white paper, the *loi de programmation militaire 1984–1988*.[64] For it was less the strategic theory underlying the use of the new armed forces which was given prominence in the press coverage of the bill, than the actual weapons systems themselves.

The LPM involves military expenditure rising to 830,000 million francs (£72,000 million) over a five-year period. It contains very few surprises and, for the most part, merely gives programmatic form to a variety of decisions which had already been taken. The priority to strategic nuclear deterrence is reasserted, 30 per cent of the overall equipment budget going to nuclear hardware. The land army is scheduled for massive restructuring, the main feature being the planned creation of a rapid deployment force for use either in Europe or overseas. The reduction in officer personnel, which so many professionals had feared, is to be kept down to 35,000 men, with natural wastage accounting for the totality of this figure.

The most significant feature of the bill is the projected rapid deployment force (FAR). Details of the composition of this force were fleshed out in mid-June 1983 when the new Supreme Commander of the land army, General Imbot,[65] addressed a gathering of the military top brass in Paris. The FAR is composed of 47,000 men and involves five separate divisions: the 11th parachute division: the 9th marine infantry division; the 27th Alpine division, the 6th light armoured division; and the 4th airborne division — all under one unified command. There are three main thrusts to this reorganization: polyvalence, mobility and firepower. Polyvalence because the FAR embraces a variety of elite and highly trained units; mobility because it will be armed with the lightest equipment and based on new helicopter gunships or light tanks; firepower owing to its massive armoury of anti-tank PGMs and other 'fire and forget' self-targeting munitions. The airborne division alone will have at its disposal almost 600 anti-tank weapons, ranging from the most sophisticated missile-firing helicopter to modern artillery pieces.[66]

At one level, there are remarkable similarities between this type of modernization and the rapid deployment preparations being made by NATO in the context of the Air–Land Battle. The emphasis is on speed and the ability to carry the war rapidly into enemy territory. In presenting the new force, Charles Hernu specifically indicated that discussions would take place with the NATO allies as to how and under what circumstances it might be deployed in conjunction with other allied forces. And under questioning from the parliamentary defence commission on 21 June 1983, he admitted that deployment could only take place with the agreement of the NATO Supreme Commander, since the FAR would be dependent on NATO for air and logistical support.[67] These developments began to look extremely suspicious in various quarters. The PCF issued a strong criticism of any plans to use the FAR in Europe,[68] and similar worries were expressed by the dean of post-Gaullist defence strategy, General Poirier.[69]

But both Hernu and the Supreme Commander of the French armed forces, General Lacaze, have publicly insisted that the FAR will not be used automatically in the event of hostilities in Europe, still less will it be used to cover a section of the West's defences along the 'Iron Curtain'. Moreover, they have repeatedly stressed that FAR is a war-prevention force rather than a war-fighting force. It will be under the political authority of the President of the Republic and his decision to deploy would symbolize the determination of the state to go to the ultimate extreme if hostilities do not cease immediately.[70] Thus the three legs of the French strategic 'deterrent' are structurally linked in a cohesive unit.

That, at any rate, is the professed theory behind the FAR. There is likely to be vigorous debate in the coming years over several aspects of the doctrine. First, whether the stated usage is in fact the real one. Second, whether the FAR could be put to different strategic usages (it is clear that it could easily be adapted to fit in perfectly with current NATO strategy). Third, whether the theory itself is viable, whether there is any meaningful correlation between the theory and the practice: could such a political and indeed cerebral approach to 'deterrence' have any real meaning, let alone any chance of success in the heat of battle between the superpowers?[71] The pages of the specialist journals will no doubt address these issues over the coming years. At the heart of them, of course, is the fundamental question of the relationship between the defence of France and the defence of Europe.

THE FUNDAMENTAL DILEMMA OF FRENCH DEFENCE POLICY

The political and diplomatic constraints under which the Mitterrand Government is functioning in the field of defence policy all boil down, in one way or another, to the key *problématique* of knowing (and saying) whether the defence of France begins with her geographical or with her political frontiers. The threefold set of constraints outlined at the beginning of this chapter (left politics, domestic politics and international politics) all situate that basic dilemma at the heart of the debate. There is an irreconcilable tension between the need to formulate public policy on defence in a clear and precise manner and, on the other hand, the triple political impossibility of either clarity or precision.

Within the political spectrum covered by the 'presidential majority', the left is evenly split on the dilemma of an 'integrated' or an 'independent' defence. It was largely because of the old SFIO's uncritical Atlanticism that the party withered and died. When it was reborn in 1971 on a programme of left-unity with the Communists, the foreign affairs counterpart of 'rupture with the capitalist system' was a form of neutralism (dissolution of the blocs). The *texts* of 1971 were the only way of allowing the party to live. But they did not conceal the fact that a majority of Socialists remained (and still remain) committed to some form of supranational defence structure and doctrine. But there's the rub. Who are to be France's military partners, with which weapons systems, and with what objective in view?

While there no doubt remain, in the PS, large numbers of 'pure' Atlanticists, it is still politically impossible for them to speak out openly because that option is anathema to the CERES, the PCF and most of the extreme left. Without the active or passive support of at least the first two of these elements no left-wing government is conceivable. Moreover, at the second level of constraint, that of French domestic politics, the heritage of Gaullism is so strong that the Atlanticist option is too dangerous to espouse directly (as Giscard d'Estaing found). Since the other pole — 'total independence', based on the French strategic deterrent alone — is no longer a viable project either, then clearly the only channel left is some form of *European* defence system. But this is precisely where the political debate becomes complex, subtle and, ultimately, blurred.

Within the PS, there is a deep split between those, like Mitterrand, Mauroy and Hernu, who see such a European project as part of a broader 'Atlantic' defence system, and those, whose numbers extend beyond the CERES (and who are joined by the rest of the left parties) who would wish it to be totally independent of the USA. These lines of division are very profound and effectively prevent the Socialist Government from entering into the details of its defence policy. On this subject, the same constraints exist at the level of national politics. Many centrists would tend to see an integrated European defence system as involving some nuclear understanding between France and Great Britain; but it is recognized that this option is merely a roundabout way of promoting Atlanticism without pronouncing the word. Paradoxically, the Socialists, among whom there is a deep-rooted current of anglophilia going back to the 1930s, would be happy to have a genuine *European* understanding with the British, but recognize that this is Utopian and so look elsewhere. Elsewhere, in effect, means Germany.

The German option is the most complex of them all. Most political parties in France, whether of the right or of the left, consider that it is essential to maintain the status quo in Germany. There is a widespread suspicion of anything tending towards unification, from which even Brandt's *Ostpolitik* was not exempt. For the right-wing parties, the preservation of West Germany in the Atlantic camp kills two birds with one stone. But for the left-wing parties, the price of German division is reinforcement of Atlanticism. It was precisely that paradox which tore the SFIO apart over the European Defence Community project in the early 1950s. Nevertheless, as the defence stakes in

Europe have grown higher and the need to solve the dilemma of 'integration' versus 'independence' has grown more urgent, the German card has seemed to be the only available one. It has, in any case, been the one which Mitterrand has chosen to play. In the nine months following Helmut Kohl's accession to the chancellorship, he and Mitterrand met specifically for Franco-German 'summitry' on no fewer than six occasions (not counting other international meetings). After only the second of those meetings, they took the initiative of establishing a permanent Franco-German defence commission which meets regularly every three months. To what end? It is here that the international perspective brings in a new set of constraints.

It is clear that any Franco-German initiative which sought openly to distance Europe from the USA would run into considerable opposition from Washington. At the same time, any such initiative which was openly drawing France more closely into NATO's web would fall foul of at least 50 per cent of the French political class (including approximately the same proportion of the Government's own left-wing support). It is hardly surprising, therefore, that the specifics of Franco-German military cooperation are impossible to pin down.

Even at a theoretical level, Franco-German cooperation is fraught with contradiction and obstacles. The 'Atlanticist' right wing of the Socialist Party clearly has no *desire* to attempt to construct a problematic European defence system based on a Franco-German project. The 'anti-Atlanticist' elements in the party have every theoretical reason in the world to wish to do so, but unfortunately cannot even start to find a formula which might be attractive to the Germans, let alone the Americans. Why would the Germans be interested in exchanging a relatively committed American 'nuclear umbrella' for a far more hypothetical French one which continues to proclaim high and low its national specificity? The one fundamental principle on which opinion in France is unanimous (at least in public) is that there can be no *sharing* of France's nuclear arsenal. And yet any meaningful European defence project which did not involve unilateral abandonment of nuclear weapons inevitably involves 'integration' of the French 'deterrent'.

Thus the politics of France's role in the defence of Europe presents the strange spectacle of an endless round of shadow-boxing. The nuclear arsenal is consistently stated to be totally autonomous, yet part of it is destined for use in a European war, without there ever being any clear doctrine behind its use. France continues to insist that she is not a member of the integrated military command of NATO, and yet all her pronouncements on NATO nuclear policy are as wholeheartedly (if not more wholeheartedly) in support of that policy as those of any other member state. At the conventional level, France is developing a rapid deployment force which seems a mirror image of similar developments in NATO; yet, officially, this force is presented as part of France's independent 'global deterrence' strategy. Negotiations on a project (as yet unspecified) for Franco-German military cooperation continue with a government in Bonn which is as close to Washington as any in the last twenty years; yet these negotiations are presented as part of a *European* defence project. All the external signs —the *things* and the *facts* — point to greater and greater alignment with NATO. Yet all the speeches — the *words* and the *ideas* — proclaim autonomy and independence. Such is the price Mitterrand must pay for trying to reconcile the conflicting ideals of Atlanticism, Gaullism and 'Nuclear Neutralism'. But to choose between them is as impossible as to reconcile them . . .

NOTES

1. See Jolyon Howorth, *Édouard Vaillant et la création de l'unité socialiste en France* (Paris: EDI/ Syros, 1982).
2. Jean Jaurès, the French Socialists' most famous theoretician, whose work, *L'Armée nouvelle*, first published in 1911, is still seen by many as the most solid foundation for a French Socialist defence policy.
3. Lucien Poirier, *Des Stratégies nucléaires* (Paris: Hachette, 1977), p. 178.
4. Pascal Krop, *Les Socialistes et l'armée* (Paris: PUF, 1983), pp. 35–45 and 93–4. Pontillon nevertheless succeeded in reconciling the Atlanticists with the French nuclear arsenal.
5. The old SFIO, which had been completely discredited under the Fourth Republic, had eventually been disbanded and was replaced, in 1971, by a new Socialist Party committed to left unity with the PCF and a common programme of government.
6. See Jolyon Howorth, 'Defence and the Mitterrand Government', in Jolyon Howorth and Patricia Chilton, eds, *Defence and Dissent in Contemporary France* (London: Croom Helm, 1984), p. 101.
7. The adoption of flexible response was seen as an abandonment of the US commitment to the nuclear 'umbrella' over Europe. On the debate unleashed in France, see Lothar Ruehl, *La Politique militaire de la $V^e$ République* (Paris: FNSP, 1976), Chs. 9 and 10, especially pp. 168ff.
8. Hernu was an animator of the Club des Jacobins. His gradual emergence as the PS's leading defence authority is recounted in his book, *Soldat-citoyen: essai sur la défense et la sécurité en France* (Paris: Flammarion, 1975).
9. The CERES (the Centre d'Études, des Recherches et de l'Education Socialistes) is a left-wing, Marxist pressure group within the PS. For its military thinking, see Jean-Pierre Chevènement et Pierre Messmer, *Le Service militaire* (Paris: Baland, 1977).
10. Mitterrand had been opposed to nuclear weapons throughout the 1960s, but gradually moved closer to the position of Charles Hernu. See, on this, Jolyon Howorth, 'Defence and the Mitterrand Government' op. cit.
11. The final resolution is published in *Le Poing et la rose*, supplement to No. 73, 'Textes de référence', pp. 32–5.
12. *Projet socialiste pour la France des années 1980* (Paris: Club socialiste du Livre, 1980), pp. 346–50.
13. Mitterrand promised to build two more (bringing the total to eight). Chirac accused Giscard of having tried to reduce the total to five, and proposed, on behalf of the RPR, to increase the fleet to fifteen by the year 2000.
14. Georges Sarre, 'Une initiative européene pour le désarmement', *Le Monde*, 17 April 1981; Jean-Pierre Chevènement, 'Le pourrissement de la doctrine militaire', ibid., 5 May 1981.
15. The Larzac decision cost the Government nothing since the camp had been intended as a tank base and the PS had long ago decided to regard tanks as a very low priority. On the other hand, the promised reduction of military service to six months did not take place, and the nuclear tests were resumed at Mururoa shortly after the general elections in June. See on these early decisions, *Le Monde*, 11 July 1981.
16. Interview with Hernu in ibid.
17. *Stern*, 8 July 1981.
18. Previously, in the book published to launch Mitterrand's presidential campaign, *Ici et maintenant* (Paris: Fayard, 1980), he had expressed basic agreement with the equation: withdrawal of SS-20/non-deployment of Pershing 2 and Cruise (p. 244).
19. Charles Hernu, *Nous . . . les grands* (Lyon: Boursier, 1980), pp. 47–51.
20. It was the bookseller at the PS headquarters who informed me, in June 1981, that this book existed. After trying to order one in vain through various channels for over a year, I finally obtained a copy from a member of Hernu's staff.
21. *Stern*, 8 July 1981.
22. This idea forms the basis of official Socialist thinking on disarmament since the national convention of January 1978. The USSR has traditionally demanded that the French and British nuclear arsenals be included in disarmament discussions, but during the SALT talks the Americans had persuaded them to accept the notion that these arsenals were 'intermediate' rather than strategic. Once Mitterrand began openly to side with the US, the Soviets launched an avalanche of demands for inclusion of the French and British weapons in the Western 'arithmetic': *Pravda*, 9 July 1981; *Izvestia*, 13 July 1981; *Temps Nouveaux*, 20 July 1981. In December 1982, the new Soviet leader, Yuri Andropov, made inclusion of the French and British arsenals the principal Soviet demand at the Geneva talks.
23. In an interview with the author on 4 August 1983, the CERES leader, Didier Motchane,

argued that the tenor of socialist diplomacy in the early months was conditioned to a very large extent by the necessity 'not to enter into head-on collision with the Americans' and by the 'need to buy a certain amount of peace from the right-wing'.

24.   Mitterrand: 'My personal conclusion is that in fact a genuine strategic balance will be maintained until 1984–85, but that after 1985 it may swing in favour of greater power to the Soviet Union.' *Le Monde*, 26 September 1981, p. 6. Hernu: 'It is quite useful, as regards the degree of balance between the superpowers, to speak, as the Soviets do, of a "global correlation of forces", but we foresee a potential serious risk that this balance may be broken in favour of the Soviets in the middle of the decade.' *Défense Nationale* (December 1981), p. 7. However, Hernu argued that the potential new destabilizing factor was not so much the SS-20 as the new Soviet *tactical* weapons, the SS-21, SS-22 and SSX-23.

25.   TV interview with François Mitterrand, transcript published in *Le Monde*, 1 December 1981. In *Ici et maintenant*, op. cit., p. 245, Mitterrand had stated that, for the Soviets, Pershing 2 missiles were 'an intolerable imbalance'.

26.   *Défense Nationale* (December 1981), p. 8.

27.   Ronald Reagan had caused a considerable stir in Europe in October 1981 by stating that he could imagine circumstances under which the USA would engage in a limited nuclear war in Europe without having recourse to the American strategic weapons.

28.   Most French leaders have argued that the main aim of the SS-20 is to 'decouple' the USA from Europe, since the Soviet missile does not threaten American territory. However, for every commentator who has seen Pershing 2 as a way of 'recoupling' the two halves of the Alliance, there is another who interprets it as further evidence of 'decoupling' since the Pershing 2 will actually be fired from Europe. On 'recoupling', see *The Modernization of NATO's Long-Range Theatre Nuclear Forces* (Washington, D.C., 1981). For the response to this, see Mary Kaldor, 'Nuclear Weapons and the Atlantic Alliance', *Democracy* (January 1982), pp. 9–23.

29.   Complete text of Cheysson interview in *Le Monde*, 2 December 1981. For a general study, see Wilfrid L. Kohl, *French Nuclear Diplomacy* (Princeton, N.J.: Princeton University Press, 1971).

30.   In his first interview as President, Mitterrand had stated pointedly that 'one cannot both hope for greater political and military homogeneity within the Alliance and, at the same time, put up with "everyman-for-himself" in economic matters'. *Le Monde*, 2 July 1981.

31.   See, for analyses of the Mitterrand visit, *Le Nouvel Observateur*, 13 March 1982; *Le Point*, 15 March 1982; and *L'Express*, 19 March 1982.

32.   PS, *Déclaration sur la paix, la sécurité et le désarmement* (Paris, 1982), 20 pages.

33.   Thierry Maliniak, 'Enfin un accord entre l'Est et l'Ouest', *Le Monde*, 17–18 July 1983.

34.   G. Robin, 'Hors des Pershing, point de salut', *Le Monde*, 18 January 1983.

35.   Mitterrand had been one of the most scathing in his attack on Giscard after the latter, by visiting Brezhnev in Warsaw in May 1980, had broken the diplomatic blockade of the Soviet Union which the West had imposed after the invasion of Afghanistan. For an overview of Giscard's diplomacy, see P.M. de la Gorce, 'Bilan d'un septennat: la politique extérieure française', *Politique étrangère*, 1 (1981), pp. 89–104.

36.   V. Giscard d'Estaing, 'Une occasion historique pour l'Europe', *Le Monde*, 19 February 1983.

37.   See *The Guardian*, 21 January 1983, and *Le Monde*, 22, 23 and 24 January 1983.

38.   See André Fontaine, quoting *Die Welt*, 'Entre la "Suite" et le "Requiem" ', *Le Monde*, 26 January 1983.

39.   The text of this communiqué, and a long analysis of the circumstances under which it came into being, is in *Le Monde*, 31 May 1983.

40.   Claude Cheysson, in addressing the press at the same meeting at which the communiqué was read out was categorical in stating that under no circumstances was France prepared even to entertain an extension of the Atlantic Alliance 'geographically or functionally', ibid., 31 May 1983, p. 6. However, it would seem that Cheysson's protests were mainly for the public back home.

41.   Helmut Schmidt spent two days (2–3 June 1983) at Mitterrand's country house at Latche, and, on 19 July, Chancellor Kohl had an informal meeting with Mitterrand at Dabo (Moselle). In an article published in the *Washington Post*, 22 May 1983, Schmidt has already expressed his opinion that the 'walk-in-the-woods' compromise was 'totally acceptable'.

42.   *L'Humanité*, 1 June 1983, and *Le Monde*, 2 June 1983.

43.   Philippe Séguin, RPR deputy for the Vosges, stated on France-Inter that Mitterrand had made 'a major concession' to Reagan by signing the communiqué (*Le Monde*, 1 June 1983, p. 2); and the former Foreign Trade Minister Michel Jobert, speaking on RTL on 5 June,

referred to France's 'good faith' having been 'caught napping' and regretted that France had now placed herself 'under the wing of the American broody hen', *Le Monde*, 7 June 1983.

44. *Pravda*, on 1 June 1983, spoke of 'substantial shifts in French deterrence theory' after the Williamsburg communiqué.
45. Details in *Le Monde*, 10 June 1983.
46. Text of his speech and details of the 'walk-in-the-woods' formula in ibid., p. 8.
47. *L'Humanité*, 20 June 1983. See André Fontaine, 'Quelles armes contre la guerre?', *Le Monde*, 18 June 1983, and J.-M. Colombani, 'Le pacifisme peut-il prendre en France?', ibid., 19–20 June 1983.
48. Maxime Gremetz had been the first to make this proposal in a little-noticed speech on 20 May, and this had been followed up by a speech by Georges Marchais on 26 May which had caused rather more of a stir. Michel Tatu analyses the issues in 'La France et les euromissiles', *Le Monde*, 23 June 1983.
49. See, on the manoeuvring which surrounded Marchais's visit, M. Tatu, 'Ou sont les "désaccords" entre M. Marchais et M. Andropov?', ibid., 19 July 1983.
50. Appearing on the TV programme 'L'Heure de Vérité' on 9 June 1983, Charles Fiterman, the senior Communist minister, categorically denied that the euromissile issue would ever be responsible for the Communists leaving government (*Le Monde*, 11 June 1983). But the fact remains that, once the PCF feels it has the masses behind it on this issue, it is unlikely to relinquish its pressure on Mitterrand.
51. Didier Motchane had already been highly critical of Williamsburg (*Le Monde*, 3 June 1983). Then, in an article in the pro-CERES monthly, *Enjeu* (July–August 1983), Motchane extended the range of his disagreement with the Government to cover France's position on the euromissiles, the strategic implications behind the new defence white paper and the entire attitude of France's leaders towards the Alliance in general and the USA in particular. In an interview with the author on 4 August 1983, he said he was now more or less convinced that the PS leaders had embraced Atlanticism and that the rest was mere window-dressing.
52. Philippe Bauchard, in an article in *Témoignage chrétien*, 11–17 July 1983, revealed that, in a series of private conversations with journalists, Mitterrand had confessed that he no longer expected anything from Reagan.
53. The most recent and most categorical statement of this case was in General Lacaze's speech to the IHEDN, published in *Défense Nationale* (June 1983); 'Politique de défense et stratégie militaire de la France', pp. 16–18.
54. For an analysis of the theory of the tactical 'ultimatum' shot, and of Giscard's attempts to alter that theory, see General Lucien Poirier, *Essais de stratégie théorique* (Paris, 1982), pp. 287–311.
55. See Hernu's presentation of his budget in *Le Monde*, 1 October 1982, p. 15. Unfortunately for him, between the time he presented his budget to Parliament and the debate in the Assembly several weeks later, Mauroy imposed severe cutbacks on all spending departments and the M-5 missile was one of the victims of the cuts.
56. See the 'Fiche de Synthèse' in Hernu, *Soldat-citoyen*, op. cit., pp. 131–40 and 236–42.
57. P. Mauroy, 'Vers un nouveau modèle d'armée', *Défense Nationale* (November 1982), pp. 9–28.
58. By allowing wild rumours to circulate without having firm proposals with which to scotch them, the PS helped generate a great deal of suspicion about its real intentions. See the scandal which broke when private letters critical of the Government written by the Chief of the General Staff (Army) to the Supreme Commander were published in *Le Matin*, 6 December 1982. The disillusionment of the officer corps, a majority of whom had voted for the Mitterrand experiment in May 1981, is expressed in 'L'Armée et la gauche, un rendez-vous manqué', *Armée Nouvelle*, No. 8 (1983), p. 11 — article by a serving officer close to Charles Hernu himself.
59. On Air–Land Battle, see 'Une nouvelle stratégie atlantique?', *Le Monde*, 5 October 1982; Konrad Ege and Martha Wenger, 'La nouvelle doctrine "Air Land Battle"', *Le Monde Diplomatique* (February 1983); A.M. Thomas, 'L'Air Land Battle et l'engagement américain en Europe', *Défense Nationale* (April 1983).
60. Hernu's speech was analysed in *Défense Nationale* (January 1983), pp. 167–8 and reported in *Le Monde*, 2 December 1982.
61. Hernu had already cast doubt on the Rogers plan in his speech to the IHEDN on 16 November 1982, *Défense Nationale* (December 1982), p. 13. During a trip to the USA in January 1983, he made a point of publicly demanding further information about the new

strategy, *Le Monde*, 20 January 1983. In his closing speech to the colloquium on Science and Defence on 27 April 1983, he overtly dismissed the Rogers plan as misguided and in any case incapable of making France change her strategic plans, ibid., 30 April 1983. Claude Cheysson, during the meeting of the NATO Council in Paris in June, also made a point of rejecting the logic behind the Rogers plan, ibid., 9 June 1983. See also on this subject, Claude Le Borgne, 'Le Général Rogers, l'Amérique et l'Europe', *Défense Nationale* (February 1983), pp. 25–32.

62.  *Le Monde*, 17–18 October 1982.

63.  On 'global deterrence' see Hernu's and Lacaze's speeches to the IHEDN, in *Défense Nationale* (December 1982 and June 1983).

64.  *Journal Officiel*, Assemblée Nationale, No. 1452, 'Projet de loi portant approbation de la programmation militaire pour les années 1984–1988', 22 pages.

65.  General René Imbot replaced General Delaunay after the latter announced his early retirement in March 1983.

66.  See Jacques Isnard's interview with Hernu when the details of the FAR were released, *Le Monde*, 18 June 1983.

67.  *Le Monde*, 24 June 1983.

68.  See Louis Baillot's comments, on behalf of the central committee's defence commission, in *L'Humanité*, 8 June 1983.

69.  Lucien Poirier, 'La greffe', *Défense Nationale* (April 1983). Poirier admitted that he hoped the explanations given by Hernu were the correct ones, but added that the FAR remained very much an unknown quantity. In an interview with the author on 6 August 1983, Admiral Sanguinetti expressed the view that the FAR *was* intended to be used as part of NATO's panoply.

70.  Jean-Yves Le Drian, *Le Monde*, 20 May 1983; Hernu, ibid., 18 June 1983; Lacaze, *Défense Nationale* (June 1983), p. 21.

71.  Michel Pinton, then General Secretary of the UDF, ridiculed this overly theoretical aspect of the deterrent in his highly provocative article in *Le Monde* on 16 June 1983. Pinton's personal attack on the theory of deterrence has been formally disavowed not only by the RPR, but also by his own party (ibid., 24 June 1983).

# II THE LEFT AND THE STATE

## 6 The Socialist Elite, 'les Gros,' and the State*

*Pierre Birnbaum*

The slogan of the left in 1981 was *'changer la vie'* — to change the way of life of the French people for the better. In order to achieve this, the parties of the left in France have long believed it indispensable to *'changer l'État'* — to reform the state, which has played such an essential role in France since the distant Age of Absolutism. Thus when the left came to power in 1981, it was confronted with the central problem which all would-be reformers face in France: how to transform a state structure which had over time become more and more differentiated from the rest of the social forces in French civil society through its ever-increasing institutionalization. It seemed like a head-on collision of two powerful forces — that of the state, based on its civil and military apparatuses, and that of the social forces of the left, which appeared, at least in the beginning, to want to set in motion a process of *de-differentiation* of a state which they felt they should fear.

### I. A NEW SOCIALIST GOVERNING ELITE?

This confrontation between an *État fort* and the new Socialist elite was marked, firstly, by the socio-professional characteristics of this new governing elite: whether in the National Assembly, or in the Government, or, even more markedly, in ministerial *cabinets*, the higher civil servants — such a crucial element in the classic functioning of the French state — seemed to take more or less a back seat to the teachers and professionals who have traditionally predominated among the party regulars and elected officials of the major parties of the left.[1] In the Assembly elected in 1981, to be sure, civil servants *as a general category* saw their numbers increase once again; but this time, previous trends were reversed *within* that category as teachers and professors [classified as civil servants in France, unlike Britain or the United States — Eds.] far outdistanced the higher civil servants whose growing strength had been such a notable characteristic of earlier phases of the Fifth Republic. Indeed, 48 percent of the PS deputies were teachers or professors and only 10.5 percent higher civil servants; in contrast, in the UDF for example, fully 16 percent of the deputies were higher civil servants (a high figure given the small absolute numbers of civil servants) and only 9.6 percent teachers and professors; furthermore, UDF deputies in this category were mainly professors in higher education, while PS teachers came mainly from secondary schools.[2]

The Government itself was headed this time by Pierre Mauroy, a former

* Translated and adapted by the Editors

**Table 6.1**   The occupational composition of the National Assembly in June 1981 by party group

| | PS | | RPR | | UDF | | PC | | No party | | Total | |
|---|---|---|---|---|---|---|---|---|---|---|---|---|
| | No. | (%) | No. | (%) | No. | (%) | No. | (%) | No. | (%) | No. | (%) |
| Farmers | 1 ( | 0.4) | 2 ( | 2.3) | 4 ( | 6.4) | 3 ( | 6.8) | 0 | | 10 ( | 2 ) |
| Industrialists and owners of large commercial establishments | 1 ( | 0.4) | 8 ( | 9.1) | 2 ( | 3.2) | 0 | | 0 | | 11 ( | 2.2) |
| Liberal professions | 40 ( | 14 ) | 14 ( | 16 ) | 14 ( | 22 ) | 1 | | 1 ( | 8.3) | 70 ( | 14.2) |
| doctors | 19 | | 6 | | 5 | | 1 | | | | 31 | |
| lawyers | 15 | | 4 | | 6 | | | | | | 25 | |
| Civil Servants (including judges and army personnel) | 30 ( | 10.5) | 19 ( | 21.5) | 12 ( | 19.3) | 0 | | 3 ( | 24.9) | 64 ( | 13.2) |
| Central Administration | 22 ( | 7.7) | 16 ( | 18.2) | 10 ( | 16 ) | | | 2 ( | 16.6) | 50 ( | 10.3) |
| Inspection des finances | 1 | | 1 | | 1 | | | | | | 3 | |
| Cour des Comptes | 1 | | 3 | | 3 | | | | | | 7 | |
| Conseil d'État | 8 | | 3 | | | | | | | | 11 | |
| diplomats | 1 | | 3 | | | | | | | | 4 | |
| prefectoral corps | | | 2 | | 1 | | | | | | 3 | |
| civil admin. | 5 | | 1 | | 4 | | | | | | 10 | |
| state engineers | 2 | | 3 | | 1 | | | | 1 | | 7 | |
| other central admin. | 4 | | | | | | | | 1 | | 5 | |
| External administration | 7 ( | 2.4) | | | | | | | 1 ( | 8.3) | 8 ( | 1.7) |
| administrative cadres | 4 | | | | | | | | 1 | | 5 | |
| technical cadres | 3 | | | | | | | | | | 3 | |
| Teachers | 137 ( | 48 ) | 6 ( | 6.8) | 6 ( | 9.6) | 13 ( | 29.5) | 5 ( | 41.7) | 167 ( | 34 ) |
| primary school | 19 | | 1 | | | | 6 | | 1 | | 27 | |
| secondary school | 77 | | 2 | | 2 | | 7 | | 4 | | 92 | |
| higher education | 41 | | 3 | | 4 | | | | | | 48 | |
| Blue-collar Workers | 6 ( | 2.1) | 0 | | 0 | | 15 ( | 34 ) | 0 | | 21 ( | 4.3) |
| White-collar Workers | 4 ( | 1.4) | 0 | | 0 | | 5 ( | 11.4) | 0 | | 9 ( | 1.8) |
| Middle managers | 17 ( | 5.9) | 4 ( | 4.5) | 1 ( | 1.6) | 2 ( | 4.5) | 0 | | 24 ( | 4.8) |
| Engineers and higher management | 19 ( | 6.6) | 16 ( | 17 ) | 12 ( | 19.3) | 0 | | 1 ( | 8.4) | 48 ( | 9.5) |
| Journalists | 7 ( | 2.5) | 3 ( | 3.4) | 1 ( | 1.6) | 2 ( | 4.5) | 0 | | 13 ( | 2.6) |
| Others | 23 ( | 8.1) | 16 ( | 18.2) | 10 ( | 16 ) | 3 ( | 6.8) | 2 ( | 16.8) | 54 ( | 11 ) |
| Total | 285 ( | 100 ) | 88 ( | 100 ) | 62 ( | 100 ) | 44 ( | 100 ) | 12 ( | 100 ) | 491 ( | 100 ) |

teacher who had also long been a trade-union militant in the technical section. Thus while all of the former Prime Ministers of the Fifth Republic had come from the higher civil service, this change alone testifies to the new orientations of the Socialist leadership. Similarly, it is important to emphasize the wholesale turnaround in the respective representation of teachers and of higher civil servants in ministerial posts compared with previous governments: between 1974 and 1980, there were, for example, 40.2 percent higher civil servants; but in the first two Mauroy Governments they held only 25.5 percent of ministerial posts. On the other hand, the percentage of teachers increased from 8.7 percent to 34 percent from the one period to the other. Similarly, *énarques* (graduates of the École Nationale d'Administration) represented only 14 percent of the members of these Socialist governments, whereas they had provided as much as 30 percent of ministerial personnel during certain periods in the Fifth Republic. Thus while the PS controls the highest positions in the state, it has not given higher civil servants a predominant role. Rather it has been the teachers, and particularly the highest-level secondary-school teachers (*agrégés du secondaire*), who have so heavily dominated the ranks of traditional political professionals among the mass parties, who are once again playing an essential role — as they had done in the Third Republic.[3]

**Table 6.2**  Occupations of government ministers in three Republics*

| | Third Republic | Fourth Republic | | Fifth Republic | |
|---|---|---|---|---|---|
| | 1870-1914 (%) | 1945-58 (%) | 1959-80 (%) | 1974-80 (%) | 1981-82 (%) |
| Civil servants | 29 | 28.5 | 50 | 48.9 | 63.8 |
| higher civil servants | 6 | 11.8 | 34.1 | 40.2 | 25.5 |
| teachers | 10 | 11 | 11 | 8.7 | 34 |
| Industrialists | 5 | 14 | 9.3 | 13 | |
| High management | | 0.9 | 13.6 | 6.5 | 6.4 |
| Shopkeepers/artisans | 1 | 2.6 | 2.6 | 2.1 | |
| Farm owners | 2 | 0.8 | 0.8 | 1.1 | 2.1 |
| Blue-collar workers | | 3 | 0.8 | 1.1 | 4.3 |
| Journalists/writers | 7 | 8.3 | 7.7 | 3.2 | 6.4 |
| Liberal professions | | | 13.5 | 14.1 | 14.9 |
| lawyers | 41 | 23.3 | 9.3 | | 8.5 |
| doctors | 6 | 6.6 | 1.7 | | 4.3 |
| Officers | 14 | 1.7 | | | |
| No profession | | | 0.8 | 2.1 | |

* The data for this table are derived from the following sources: Pascal Antoni and Jean-Dominique Antoni, *Les Ministres de la 5ᵉ République* (Paris: PUF, 1976); Jean Estèbe, *Les Ministres de la République (1870-1914)*) (Paris: Presses de la Fondation Nationale des Sciences Politiques, 1983); Jean Gabay, *Les Ministres du gouvernement Mauroy*, Mémoire de DEA, Université de Paris II (1982); E.G. Lewis 'Social background of French Ministers,' *Western Political Quarterly* (September 1970); M. Nouge-Sans, *Les Ministres de la 5ᵉ République sous la Présidence de Valéry Giscard d'Estaing*, Mémoire de DEA, Université de Paris II (1980).

Now although this conclusion is valid for the Socialist leadership as a whole, there are nevertheless certain nuances within the governmental pattern which must be analyzed. It is almost as if the PS, confronted by the logic of an '*État fort*,' has, in spite of its ideology and its desire to give fuller representation to the social forces of civil society, begun none the less, especially in the last Mauroy Government, to favor the presence of higher civil servants — a trend which culminated in the appointment of the *énarque* Laurent Fabius as Prime Minister in July 1984. From the second Mauroy Government (appointed in June 1981) to the third (appointed in March 1983), the proportion of all civil servants grew only slightly, from 50 percent to 55.8 percent. However, if we look at the category of higher civil servants, we see that they came to comprise 36.4 percent of those of full ministerial rank in the third Mauroy Government, up from 21.4 percent in its predecessor. On the other hand, we do not find a single higher civil servant among the numerous secretaries of state (junior ministers), even though the proportion of *all* civil servants among these junior ministers effectively doubled as the result of the drastic slimming of the government as a whole in March 1983 (the number of full ministers was nearly halved), making it higher than the proportion among full ministers. By comparison, 40 percent of this relatively larger category of secretaries of state in the third Mauroy government came from the teaching profession, compared with only 9.09 percent of the full ministers. By distinguishing between these categories, and then by comparing the last Mauroy Government with its predecessor, we can see that the relative position of teachers — as compared with higher civil servants, the privileged agents of the state — has declined at one of the most essential levels of power. Thus the Socialist elite has become somewhat more heterogeneous, to the benefit of the pre-existing sources of recruitment to the state elite.

The composition of the ministerial *cabinets* (ministers' advisory staffs) has also been profoundly transformed. It would appear at first glance that things did not change a great deal after May 1981. From 1958 to 1981, higher civil servants comprised between 87 and 91 percent of the members of ministerial *cabinets*; this proportion is slightly smaller in the Socialist ministerial *cabinets*, where higher civil servants make up only about 75 percent of the total members. However, this small decline masks an important modification in the composition of this category (of higher civil servants in ministerial *cabinets*). The arrival of the left in power was the revenge of the corps of civil administrators, a relatively new and somewhat less prestigious body than the old *grands corps*. The Inspection des Finances, for example, which has constantly held all of the most essential posts, was practically evicted; none of its members was appointed to presidential or prime ministerial *cabinets*. Members of the Conseil d'État, the Inspection des Finances and the Cour des Comptes, who together comprised 27 percent of the advisors of previous Fifth Republic Prime Ministers from the former right-wing majority, constituted only 6 percent of the members of the entourage of Pierre Mauroy. The *grands corps* as a whole (including the diplomatic and prefectoral corps) made up more than 60 percent of the advisors of the former Presidents of the Republic, but they hold only 19 percent of the posts in the entourage of François Mitterrand. On the other hand, members of the lower levels of the higher civil service — who often come from a more modest social milieu, even if they have also been students at the École Nationale d'Administration — this time play an essential role.

Furthermore, the general importance of higher civil servants has diminished significantly to the benefit of professional politicians who have made their careers through political organizations — teachers or, to an even greater extent, the representatives of trade unions and associations who have penetrated the world of the state, formerly closed to them, for the first time. Next to competence, political commitment has become once again an essential element for recruitment of new political personnel for the ministerial *cabinets* of the Socialist Government; they often belong to political organizations themselves, and almost always belong to the same internal political current of the Socialist Party as their minister.[4]

## II. SOCIAL CONTRADICTIONS OF SOCIALIST DISCOURSE

Composed above all of secondary school teachers, the Socialist majority

Table 6.3 Socioprofessional origins of the members of the second and third Mauroy Governments

| | Second Mauroy Government (MII) (June 1981) (%) | | | Third Mauroy Government (MIII) (March 1983) (%) | | |
|---|---|---|---|---|---|---|
| Civil servants | 57.1 | 25.0 | 45.5 | 66.6 | 50.0 | 28.6 |
| Higher c.s. | 21.4 | | 36.4 | 33.3 | 30.0 | |
| Higher education | 14.3 | 25.0 | 9.1 | 33.3 | 10.0 | 28.6 |
| Secondary education | 17.9 | | | | | |
| Primary education | 3.6 | | | | | |
| Other | | | | | 10.0 | |
| Higher management (public sector) | 10.7 | 12.5 | 9.1 | | 10.0 | 14.3 |
| Higher management (private sector) | 3.6 | 12.5 | 9.1 | | 10.0 | 14.3 |
| Middle management and white-collar (private sector) | 7.2 | | | | | |
| Blue-collar workers | 3.6 | | 9.1 | | | |
| Liberal professions | 10.7 | 25.0 | 18.2 | 16.7 | 10.0 | 28.6 |
| Lawyers | 7.1 | 12.5 | | | 10.0 | 14.3 |
| Notaries | 3.6 | 12.5 | 18.2 | | | |
| Doctors | | 12.5 | | 16.7 | 10.0 | |
| Journalists | 7.1 | | | | | |
| No profession | | 12.5 | 9.1 | | 10.0 | 14.3 |
| Total | 100.0 | 100.0 | 100.0 | 100.0 | 100.0 | 100.0 |

tends to conform to the sort of universalist and edifying behavior and world vision that can easily be reconciled with a mechanistic and often simplistic Marxism. Thus they exhibit a certain reserve toward the counter-culture and express a distrust in numerous dialogues about 'Anglo-Saxon' theoretical contributions. For this reason a part of the Parisian intelligentsia, which with its habitual delay has only recently discovered Popper and Feyerabend, systems analysis, relativism, or utilitarian philosophy, has moved away from the socialists.[5] Even when it was in opposition, the PS was unable to develop a truly coherent theory of society, and in its programs and its schools often adopted the vocabulary used by the Communist Party. This helps to explain the struggle that the Socialists led during this period against *les gros* — the fat cats — and the weakness of the theory of the state that this kind of campaign presupposes.[6] Between the two world wars, for example, or under the Fifth Republic before 1981, the PS took on certain formulas from the PCF, but with a far more moderate tone. After May 1981, it even appeared as if the opposite was true; not only did the PS once again adopt the approach proposed by its ally, but it used it more aggressively. During April 1981, François Mitterrand denounced the danger which resulted from the power of the 'wall of money.'[7] And between the two rounds of the presidential election, Mitterrand's language was curiously close to that of Georges Marchais:

I wish to remind M. Giscard d'Estaing [Mitterrand said] that it was the people who conquered liberty almost two centuries ago against the old feudal order. It has been the people who have defended it, often with the price of their blood, against the feudality of money. and it is the people who still fight for it today, against the narrow caste which is incarnated by Giscard d'Estaing.[8]

After the victory, Pierre Mauroy concluded that 'the men of the château have departed,'[9] and the PS in its turn took over the slogan of the PCF: 'Let us make the rich pay.' We can see how far these expressions (the 'wall of money,' the 'château,' 'the rich,' the 'caste,' etc.) not only derive from Marxism and return to a precapitalist language, but also lead to strategies which are poorly adapted to the social and economic realities of modern France. These expressions, however, began increasingly to fill the discourse of the Socialist leaders. In his press conference of 24 September 1981, François Mitterrand declared: 'One of you asked me a question about the wall of money. Do you think, he asked, that there is a wall of money? I did not tell him, but nevertheless I believe there is.'[10] At the time of the Socialist Congress of Valence the following month, Claude Estier made accusations against the 'internal *émigrés*,' and the PS newspaper *L'Unité* attacked those who 'grew rich for so long,'[11] while the final motion of the Congress retained this language, so embedded in contemporary French ideology, by pointing the vengeful finger at 'the cosmopolitanism of the worldwide bourgeoisie,'[12] in which the privileged French *gros* are the active agents. It is known that during the Congress a kind of revolutionary exaltation, well formed by a precapitalist vocabulary and conforming to the myth analyzed here, prevailed.

For Pierre Mauroy,

If the opposition reacts with such surliness, it is because we have touched what for them is the supreme value — money. Certain bankers have even rediscovered the mentality of the *émigrés* of Koblenz, and do not hesitate to act against the country . . . My dear comrades, the time of the masters is over.[13]

From 1936 to 1981, the formulas look the same, haunted by the conflicts of the prerevolutionary period.[14] And although Jean-Pierre Chevènement confesses that he has no taste for dancing around the guillotine, Paul Quilès is more unmerciful even than Robespierre: 'We must not be content to say in an evasive manner — like Robespierre at the Convention — [that] heads will roll. We must say which ones, and say it quickly.'

So dramatic a time, when the united people confront a handful of new feudal reactionaries, imposes an unorthodox class struggle. For Louis Mermaz, there is 'an internal and an external class struggle.'[15] The Deputy Jean-Paul Planchon calls it 'the arm-wrestling match between the financial circles, cosmopolitan by definition, and the democratically elected government.' And *L'Unité*, rediscovering the period of great caricatures of class warfare, shows two fat capitalists smoking cigars, supporting — sponge in hand — the opposition as it engages in heavy combat.[16]

After the setback in the local elections in 1983, *L'Unité* only partly altered its sociological analysis of the social categories making up the opposition. The newspaper still denounced the 'wall of money' — but also discovered even more anachronistic symbols. 'Who owns these snakes that hiss on our heads?' they asked. They again presented, as those responsible for the severe electoral setback, three fat capitalists dressed in black, smoking enormous cigars[17] — a caricature from another age that shows a poor sociological imagination. François Mitterrand, as vehement as Georges Marchais in his condemnation of money, recalled that in his Catholic family money 'was the enemy, the corruptor with which we did not negotiate.'[18] For him,

the real enemy, I would say the only enemy, because everything is related to it, the one that holds the key, is monopoly, a broad term used to indicate all of the powers of money — money that corrupts, money that buys, money that crushes, money that kills.[19]

With a morality as anticapitalist as this, Mitterrand even criticizes social democracy, since it has not destroyed 'capitalism and its masters.'[20] By constantly opposing Valéry Giscard d'Estaing to 'the people,' and money to the workers; by constantly denouncing the 'money lenders,' 'the castes,' 'the possessors,' 'the masters of money,' 'the lords of money,' 'the debauchery of money,' 'King Money,' and 'the men of the right' who have placed themselvs in the service of 'a handful of monopolies;' by arguing that 'big capital is an ogre, it devours us, picks at our bones, even eats our bones, because it is hungry;' by accusing 'the barons' of Gaullism or arguing over their 'disinherited fiefdoms;' by caricaturing Valéry Giscard d'Estaing as a 'baron of unemployment, marquis of inequality, count of price increases, duke of technocracy, prince of electoralism and king of anaesthesia,' François Mitterrand clings to the myth of 'the people' against the '*gros*,' and, at the instigation of the Communist leaders, perpetuates the moralizing, pre-capitalist metaphorical style. This approach is even more astonishing since, as with the spokesmen of the PCF, it places the analysis in the Manichaean perspective of a foreign Marxism, even though Marxism itself, at least at the end of the nineteenth century, recognized the merits of capitalism and of capitalists, whom it saw as true revolutionaries.

The revolutionary perspective is even more surprising when we recognize the constant attachment of François Mitterrand to the virtues of the land, as opposed to the evils of capitalism. 'I am and I remain,' he has said, 'a man of

my region.' Born 'of old stock,' his 'genealogy' goes back to the 'mists of the
middle ages.' That is why, he emphasizes, 'I have an instinctive consciousness
deeply rooted in France.'

I have a passion for her geography, for her living body. There my roots grew. I have no
need to search for the soul of France. It lives in me just as it lives in all of our people. A
people that sticks to its land is no longer separable from it.[21]

From this emerges images that are more Barrèsian than Socialist, more
antimodernist and anticapitalist than Marxist — images which were used
during the presidential election campaign around its central slogan, '*la force
tranquille.*' We are very far from class struggle and from industrial conflict, but
close to an accusatory moralism, one which focuses on money as the
corruptor of the values of our sweet and profound France. Commenting on
the poster in which he apears against the background of a village near his
home in the rugged Morvan region, with its church at the bottom, Mitterrand
noted: 'I saw nothing inconvenient, and even saw many advantages, in
symbolizing this vision of a fading rural France. There are many city people
who still think about it, and who would very much like to find it again.'[22]

While this sort of imagery quite naturally opens the door to a rejection of
cosmopolitan Anglo-Saxon culture, it probably does not further a strategy of
uniting the people of the left. They consist mainly of big-city workers who are
usually dechristianized, deprived of roots going back to the 'mists of the
middle ages,' who take more pleasure in listening to the noise of the city than
to the 'silence' of the country, who sometimes feel closer to those outside of
France sharing identical working conditions, who do not reject the pleasures
of money or the means by which they earn it, and who do not always feel that
it is essentially corrupting.

Under these circumstances, the ambiguities are apparent in a strategy of
unity in the context of a 'class front' that aims to exclude only 'those of the
château' while advocating the constitution of 'a new social bloc around the
working class.' How can they presume to represent the 'sociological majority'
— of the cities, the offices and the factories — while, at the same time, making
themselves the quasi-exclusive spokesmen for '*la France profonde*'? Such a
contradiction is clearly demonstrated through the constant usage of
moralizing or precapitalist metaphors. How can they wish to incarnate, at
one and the same time, the values of 'profound France' — the parochial
values of the provinces — those of the 'profound left' — of the 'popular
electorate, constituted essentially of the majority of wage-earning workers'[23]
— and those, finally, of the other groups supposed to make up the class front
— and uniting 'around the blue-collar and white-collar workers' sections of
the managers, the artisans and the shopkeepers. Such a coalition is not
supposed to be 'a coalition of malcontents,' nor a simple 'addition of different
corporate interests,' but is supposed to be based on a 'class choice' favorable
to socialism, even if it is torn, like the wage-earning workers themselves, by
strong internal divisions.[24] Indeed, for François Mitterrand,

It is strange that in this difficult world of free enterprise, of the struggle to become the
strongest and most powerful, the small and medium enterprises always identify with
the very largest, and the same is often true in agriculture. They do not understand that
it is the largest enterprises which exploit them and devour them . . . Logically, they
should support me.[25]

Before the beginning of the 1981 presidential campaign, the Socialist Party was not concerned with the values of *la France profonde*. The only contradiction with which the Socialists, like the Communists, had to deal was their desire to represent a broad 'class front' that only excluded a minority of the *gros*, while appearing to be the only true spokesmen of the workers. This contradiction has not been completely resolved. Since the PS was committed to a policy of social transformation and income redistribution which would permit an appreciable increase of the lowest wages, of old-age pensions and of various other types of welfare benefits, it felt an obligation to 'make the rich pay' by imposing taxes on excess incomes and on wealth. However, they were also obliged to impose higher taxes on managers and white-collar workers — and, indeed, on a large number of blue-collar workers who felt their incomes stagnate or decline during the wages freeze of the summer and autumn of 1982.[26] The managers and the middle class generally reacted strongly to the currency limits on holidays abroad, while the Auroux Laws stimulated negative reactions among the owners of small and medium enterprises who, together with certain higher executives, according to the PS, should have been part of the class front.[27] The sirens of protectionism and the charms of 'radicalization,[28] which alone would make the demands of the 'social base' possible, also frightened the modernist middle class. The doctors, notaries and lawyers demonstrated in the streets of Paris, protesting against the economic policies of the Government, together with many merchants who joined *'le déçus du socialisme'* — those who had voted for Mitterrand but changed their minds in March 1983.

By proclaiming, as does André Laignel, National Secretary of the Socialist Party, that 'finally class conflict has entered parliament;' by affirming, as does Pierre Joxe, that 'Socialist nationalization is an act of class;'[29] by stressing that 'the class front' is not like 'a sea front,' since it 'depends upon a class choice;'[30] by claiming that 'the live wire, today as yesterday, is the confrontation of classes' against the bosses and their allies in the state technostructure who 'would, in their own way, make a Chilean-style *coup d'état* if they could.'[31] — the different components of the 'macho'[32] left reveal the ideological and strategic contradictions within the PS, which navigates between *la France profonde*, the catch-all perspective of the class front, and the class struggle itself, through which it catches fewer votes each time as the results of the 1983 municipal elections and the 1984 European elections demonstrate.

The PS no longer seems to know how to retain its electoral support. This leads to the ambiguous tactics proposed by Jean-Pierre Chevènement, according to whom 'it is the people both of the left and of the right who must be made to rise above themselves simultaneously. The coalition must not be made from the center . . . It can only be made from its most advanced elements.'[33] For Jean Poperen, 'The left can only win with the cooperation of what are called the margins . . . We win with the *cooperation* of the margins, but we do not win by *aligning* ourselves with the margins.'[34] It is not hard to understand why, given a role with such low prestige, the marginal categories of the class front have turned away from the 'deep left' and hardly participate in the 'forward coalition.' It seems rather doubtful whether the virtues of better 'social communication' will be successful in retaining them at the side of the 'people of the left.'[35]

At the time of the Congress of Valence, when in the euphoria of victory it was possible to think that from now on a France of the left would continue to vote for the left, and that the left would gradually come to attract the support of the immense majority of the French except for the very small minority of *les gros* and their allies, Louis Mermaz declared: 'The right is by necessity the expression of a set of social groups created by historical evolution. Well, I think that these social groups are to some extent in the process of drying up.'[36] In the municipal elections of 1983, a considerable number of 'small people' returned to the side of the *gros*, increasing the ranks of a right that the PS or the PCF often confused with 'those of the château,' the 'masters' and the monopolies. Not only did the shopkeepers reinforce their attachment to the right, but numerous white-collar workers, technicians and managers of 'modernist' France joined them.[37]

The right can therefore, wholly legitimately, refuse to be assimilated into the *gros*, the feudal lords, the masters of money, with whom it is frequently identified by the PS as well as the PCF. Reversing the shock formulas of the left, the spokesmen of the right have fully indulged themselves. In the 1983 municipal elections, according to Louis Pauwels, 'it is not the right that won; rather it is that the sociological majority no longer coincides with those in political authority.'[38] Jean d'Ormesson observes cruelly:

If the 'right' and the 'château' were really the only ones to oppose the Government, as the Prime Minister would have it, then the French would now be right-wing supporters of the château . . . [But] this is an abuse of language . . . it is [rather] the center, it is the moderates, it is the mass of the French people [who are now in opposition].[39]

Because they have adopted such a caricatured vision of the right, the parties of the left have provided an easy target for opposition polemicists. After citing the celebrated statement of François Mitterrand identifying the left with the sociological majority, the editor of *Minute*, François Brigneau, declared after the municipal elections:

Thus it was not only a political alliance which won the [1981] elections, it was a social class which henceforth would reduce and dominate the others. Now there we have a seditious idea, an anti-constitutional idea, and an anti-national idea — one that is essentially anti-French. But it is the idea of the President of the Republic, and he wants, by all means, to bring down the château, as Mauroy calls it, as well as the notables, the owners, the managers, the artisans, the bosses, the independent workers, and those who work sixty hours a week.[40]

Whether a good prince or a bad sociologist, Brigneau should have been able to add to this 'class front in reverse' a part of the blue-collar workers and of the conservative white-collar workers.

### III. THE SHORTCOMINGS OF SOCIALIST ANALYSIS AND REFORMS

By adopting this coalition strategy, and by assuming this 'catch-all,' cross-class perspective, the PS neglects both the enduring reality of the organization of social classes in French society, which makes it extremely fragile, and the existence of a highly differentiated and institutionalized state that has in no way been dominated by *les gros* in recent times. In these conditions, we can see why the PS has often utilized the model of 'state monopoly capitalism' proposed by the PCF, and which has played such an essential role in the Communist movement since the Third International. This model, while giving the structure of the state more importance than in certain 'vulgar Marxist' interpretations, in fact denies the state any real autonomy from the economic base, considering it simply as an instrument of the monopolies; thus it is in reality particularly poorly adapted for analyzing the nature of the French state, which has been built through history through a constant process of differentiation — a process which has been dominated by the relationship of the political center with the problem of boundaries and border regions and with integrating groups peripheral to society. It is equally wrong to consider the state bureaucracy, in the Althusserian perspective, as a simple tool of the capitalist state, for this is to neglect the institutionalization of the state, which is particularly advanced in the French case.

The model of the people against *les gros* and the model of monopoly capitalism reveal that, at least on the programmatic level, the parties of the left have wanted to 'change the state' in order to 'change life' — that is rapidly to transform a state that seems to them to be the pure and simple instrument of *les gros*. The *Projet socialiste* already puts forward the idea of the necessity of 'rapidly democratizing the high administration through the transformation of the modes of recruitment, remuneration and the reorganization of posts.' In the same spirit, Anicet Le Pors, until July 1984 the Secretary of State for the Civil Service (a full minister until March 1983), and a member of the PCF, felt it indispensable to transform the ENA in order to open up the administrative apparatus — which 'must be the social reflection of the nation' — to local elected officials, trade-union officials and leaders of various voluntary assocations.[41] These proposals were supposed to have the consequence of challenging the universalism of the French state, by introducing a sort of *proporzdemokratie* founded on meritocracy. This theory of 'social reflection' also partially brings into question the principle of differentiation.

In reality, the civil service has not experienced a shake-up comparable with other major administrative reforms undertaken since the nineteenth century. Even though directors of ministerial *cabinets* have increasingly been appointed using partisan criteria, there are still many directors who were already in office before May 1981. And with the exception of certain posts which have long been profoundly politicized, such as those of the regional directors of the state education system (rectors), and of a significant percentage of political nominations to diplomatic posts, the civil service itself has not experienced changes in any way comparable to the introduction of a spoils system.[42] The most important changes will probably emerge from the reforms of ENA, which are important because this *grande école* has played a key role in recent decades in the reinforcement of the institutionalization of the state.[43] The decrees of September and October 1982 established a rule of parity between students and lower civil servants among candidates for admission to the school, prevented students from other *grandes écoles* from claiming that they were already civil servants when they apply to ENA, reduced the element in the entrance examination for 'general culture,' which had given an advantage to applicants from the upper classes, raised the age limit to make it possible for less favored candidates to catch up on career advancement, and so on.

The objective of all of these measures has been to diminish the very selective character of the traditional recruitment of *énarques* from the standpoint of social origins. Moreover, the Law of 19 January 1983 created a third route of access to ENA, reserved for those who for at least eight years have had important posts in trade unions, voluntary associations and mutual aid societies, and extends this opportunity to certain local elected officials.

These reforms are far from negligible, and they can in the long run modify the recruitment of higher civil servants by democratizing the process somewhat.[44] However, they present the risk of undermining the universalist principles upon which are based both the universalization and the institutionalization of the state administration by introducing a particularist dimension into the recruitment of higher civil servants. However, we should emphasize that they do not for the moment really shake up the higher civil service, which continues to recruit through *grande école* competitive entrance examinations — which the civil service branch of the CFDT wanted profoundly transformed and which the PCF in its program wanted to abolish.[45]

CONCLUSIONS

The evolution of the Socialist Party in government since May 1981 has been characterized by the tensions inherent in its approach to both the nature of the state and the class character of French society. In terms of its own composition, the Government was already diluting its 'new elite' of schoolteachers and lower civil servants, and turning once again to higher civil servants for its more essential positions, by the time the third Mauroy Government was appointed in March 1983 — a trend which would seem to be continuing or even accelerating with the appointment of the Fabius Government and the withdrawal of the Communist ministers. Secondly, since 1983 the language of the dominant Socialist leaders, especially that of the President of the Republic and his now Prime Minister, Laurent Fabius, has begun to praise rather than to attack entrepreneurs and the profit motive, hoping to pave the way for a recapturing of the *déçus du socialisme* in 1986, but at the time of writing it still seems too little and too late. And finally, government attempts to change the state from the inside, especially through the reform of the admissions procedure for ENA, have not had, and are not likely to have, any profound effect upon the internal functioning of the state. With the appointment of the Fabius Government, there would seem to be a more open reassertion of another important subculture within both the PS and the higher civil service — a kind of *énarchie socialiste*, technocratic and *étatiste* — but the real power of this group will have to be assessed over the longer term as the party's rhetoric and coalition strategy for 1986 become more clearly defined. On the whole, however, the Socialist movement seems eventually — despite a number of specific exceptions — to have adapted to the logic of a state which it has in fact only moderately questioned.

NOTES

1.  On the traditional role of higher civil servants within the French political elite in earlier periods, see Pierre Birnbaum,*The Heights of Power* (Chicago: University of Chicago Press, 1983).
2.  For an analysis of the relationship between teachers and professors (*enseignants*) and higher civil servants within the French political elite in earlier eras, see Véronique Aubert and Jean-Luc Parodi, 'Le personnel politique français,' *Projet* (July–August 1980). Cf. A. di Stefano, *La Participation des fonctionnaires civil à la vie politique* (Paris: Librairie Générale de Droit et de Jurisprudence, 1979).
3.  For a comparison with earlier periods, see Francis de Baecque and Jean-Louis Quermonne, eds, *Administration et politique sous la Cinquième République* (Paris: Presses de la Fondation Nationale des Sciences Politiques, 2nd edn., 1982).
4.  See Monique Dagnaud and Dominique Mehl, *L'Élite rose: Qui gouverne?* (Paris: Éditions

Ramsay, 1982), and also Samy Cohen, 'Les hommes de l'Élysée,' *Pouvoirs*, No. 20 (1982). For a comparison with the members of earlier *cabinets*, see René Rémond, Aline Coutrot and Isabel Boussard, *Quarante ans de cabinets ministeriels* (Paris: Presses de la FNSP, 1982).

5. Diana Pinto, 'Le socialisme et les intellectuels: le conflit caché,' *Le Débat* (January 1982). For a more recent comment (by the Government's official spokesman) on the distance which the intellectuals have been keeping between themselves and the Governent, see Max Gallo, 'Les intellectuels, la politique et la modernité,' *Le Monde*, 26 July 1983.

6. Pierre Birnbaum, *Le Peuple et les gros: Histoire d'un mythe* (Paris: Grasset, 1979).

7. *Le Monde*, 7 April 1981.

8. *L'Unité*, 2 May 1981.

9. *Le Monde*, 17 July 1981. This same theme often reappears in the speeches of Pierre Mauroy. See, for example, *Le Monde*, 12 February 1983.

10. *Le Monde*, 26 September 1981.

11. *L'Unité*, 31 October and 6 November 1981.

12. *Le Poing et la rose*, November 1981, p. 10.

13. Ibid., pp. 22–3.

14. Arno Mayer has shown how values associated with, and references to, the *ancien régime* still had great influence in France at the beginning of this century, in *La Persistance de l'Ancien Régime* (Paris: Flammarion, 1983).

15. *Le Poing et la rose*, op. cit., pp. 20–1.

16. *L'Unité*, 31 October 1981.

17. *L'Unité*, 25 March 1983.

18. François Mitterrand, *Politique* (Paris: Fayard, 1977), p. 510.

19. Ibid., p. 536.

20. Quoted by Paul Valadier in 'François Mitterrand: Des idées politiques pour prendre le pouvoir,' *Projet* (December 1982).

21. See Dominique Labbé, *François Mitterrand: Essai sur le discours* (Grenoble: La Pensée Sauvage, 1983), pp. 51, 77, 112, 118 and 133.

22. Ibid., pp. 122, 124 and 127.

23. In the words of Jean Poperen. *Le Monde*, 27/28 March 1983.

24. See *Non!*, September/October 1981 and May/June 1982, and also Jacques Mandrin, *Le Socialisme de la France* (Paris: Le Sycomore, 1983), p. 100.

25. François Mitterrand, *Politique 2* (Paris: Fayard, 1981), p. 293.

26. According to the study by the Centre d'Études des Revenus et des Coûts (CERC). See *Le Monde*, 19 March 1983.

27. For François Mitterrand, 'small shopkeepers, artisans and small and medium-sized businesses (PME) have everything to gain from change, if they will only listen to me. It is the same for those smaller industrial firms (PMI) which refuse to accept the control of the CNPF' (the employers' confederation). [Mitterrand is here partially referring to the conflict between the more traditional small business trade assocation, the CGPME, and its newer and more radical rival, the SNPMI — Eds.] *Le Monde*, 5 May 1981.

28. See Serge July, 'Le gâchis de Louis Mermaz,' *Libération*, 10 March 1983.

29. *Le Monde*, 3 February 1982.

30. Mandrin, op. cit., pp. 99–100.

31. Jean Poperen, in *Le Monde*, 28 April 1983. Likewise see the statement by Georges Sarre (leader of the CERES faction in Paris), who denounces the comeback in force of 'the collaborationist right' motivated by a 'rampant fascism' which is at the service of 'a class front the wrong way round,' *Le Monde*, 26 May 1983. According to the friends of Pierre Joxe, 'It is more than ever important to find out whether we consider that French society is still composed of antagonistic classes; nothing in present circumstances allows us to say the opposite ... It is now time to enter into a real strategy of rupture [with capitalism],' extract from a contribution submitted to the PS Congress at Bourg-en-Bresse in October 1983, which followed on from the now famous Congress of Valence, *Le Monde*, 10 May 1983.

32. *Le Monde*, 13 February 1983.

33. *Le Monde*, 10 March 1983.

34. *Le Monde*, 22 March 1983. For Jean Poperen, 'it is not the "programme" which attracts the *marais* [Literally the 'swamp', this term is used in French to lump together those voters who are inattentive,undecided, floating, prone to abstain, etc. — Eds], it is the steepest slope.' *Le Monde*, 27/28 March 1983.

35. After having affirmed week after week in *L'Unité* that the PS's most fundamental problem was how to improve the diffusion of its message, Max Gallo was appointed the Minister of Social Communication shortly after the setback of the 1983 municipal elections.

36. Quoted in Bernard Chapuis, *Le moulage* (Paris: Fayard, 1983), pp. 114–15.
37. See the dossier published by *Libération*, 'Qui sont les déçus de la gauche? Le cas de Grenoble,' 11 March 1983.
38. *Le Figaro Magazine*, 12 March 1983.
39. Ibid.
40. *Minute*, 14–20 May 1983.
41. *Le Monde*, 22 September 1981.
42. François Bardos shows that the purge was extremely limited: 'Les fonctionnaires et le pouvoir politique,' *Pouvoirs*, No. 20 (1982).
43. See Patrick Viveret, 'La gauche piégée par l'État,' *Projet* (June 1982).
44. It is also intended to create more Institutes of Political Studies, modelled on the famous establishment in Paris, in the provinces in order to diversify the social recruitment of civil servants. Furthermore, several measures have been taken to reinforce the rights of civil servants and to allow them to become 'citizen civil servants' (*fonctionnaires-citoyens*).
45. The PCF has even gone so far as to alter its conception of the state — a state which, however, has hardly changed at all. For the Communists, strange as it may seem, the simple coming to power of the left transformed the very character of the state, which 'since the 10th of May has been organized as a function of political objectives which are no longer determined by the general structures of state monopoly capitalism (CME);' from Gilles Masson,'Sur quelques aspects contradictoires de l'État aujourd'hui,' *Cahiers du Communisme* (April 1982), p. 48. For the PCF, since May 1981,'the superior part of the state' has been taken away from the right; see J.-C. Poulain, 'Persévérance de la stratégie du grand capital,' *Cahiers du Communisme* (January 1983), p. 23. The same is true, finally, for Anicet Le Pors: '. . . our quality of being a party both in and of government today calls for a much more elaborate appreciation of the state,' *Le Monde*, 5 July 1983. According to the extreme left, on the other hand, '. . . this is a government of the bourgeoisie, because the Ministers — these so-called Socialists, these so-called Communists — are just the vulgar servants of the bourgeoisie:' Arlette Laguiller in *Luttes Ouvrières*, 5 June 1982.

# 7 'L'Alternance' and the Higher Civil Service*

*Anne Stevens*

In the autumn of 1982 I interviewed a long-serving and fairly senior civil servant in the French Ministry of Finance. We talked about changes since the coming to office of President Mitterrand in May 1981 and I suggested that after all, minister, organizational structures, even some policies, had changed before. The civil servant replied in terms that made it clear that the post-May 1981 changes were perceived as being fundamentally different in quality. Previous changes had not sought to undo and upset and alter everything, he said.

This perception, and it seems to be widespread (although civil servants of a different outlook would describe the impact of the new Government in a more positive way), may seem surprising, for two contradictory reasons. On the one hand, my interlocutor had seen the change of regime in 1958, a change that was more than mere *alternance*. Yet it can be argued that despite, eventually, considerable alteration in the environment in which civil servants worked, as far as the Administration was concerned the changes in 1958 were questions of degree, not of nature. Certainly civil servants then acquired a greater degree of freedom of action and noticed the escape from some parliamentary considerations and constraints. The President's influence became steadily more important. However, de Gaulle's first cabinet, when he was Prime Minister, contained only two declared Gaullists, the other ministers being either the leaders of the traditional parties with governmental experience or themselves former officials, while Debré's first Government, after the installation of the Fifth Republic, while distinctive in also containing nine non-parliamentarians out of its total of twenty-four ministers, included twelve from the traditional parties. These ministers were concerned to order things better than had been possible under the previous regime, but were not from the beginning committed to ordering them very *differently*.

On the other hand, it may seem surprising that a political change should be felt to have impinged upon the administration, if only because some historians argue that political changes very rarely in fact do so. As Catherine and Thuillier point out:

the historian has always noted that the administration, living within its own time-scales, ignores political changes ... This remains true: one has only to wander down the corridors of certain ministries to see files labelled 1935–1955: the administrative

* This chapter is based in part upon the chapter 'The French Higher Civil Service and Economic Policy-Making' in P.G. Cerny and M.A. Schain, *French Politics and Public Policy* (London and New York: Frances Pinter, St. Martin's Press and Methuen University Paperbacks, 1980). I am very grateful to Dr Siân Reynolds and Handley Stevens who read this chapter in draft. Other discussions of some of the issues raised here are to be found in J.-L. Bodiguel and J.-L. Quermonne, *La Haute Fonction publique sous la V*ᵉ *République* (Paris: Presses Universitaires de France, 1983), *passim*, and in 'Postface à Deux Voix' in F. de Baecque and J.-L. Quermonne, *Administration et politique sous la Cinquième République* (Paris: Presses de la Fondation Nationale des Sciences Politiques, 2nd edn. 1982), pp. 361–86.

world ignores breaks and crises and the administrator who retires today may have entered the ministry around 1935. He has lived through the Laval decrees, the Popular Front, Vichy, the Liberation, the Fourth Republic, De Gaulle and the Fifth Republic . . . Events slide over the administration and leave almost no traces . . . [1]

It is undoubtedly too soon to arrive at any conclusion about the extent of change since 1981 which a long-term perspective will reveal. It seems likely that the effect of *alternance* on the higher civil service will prove to be a matter of shifts of emphasis, a matter of degree, and in no sense an abrupt rupture. My interlocutor probably felt, however, that almost all change stemming from *alternance* was to be deplored. After all, the French Administration is frequently perceived, not least by those who belong to it, as the embodiment of a state which, being itself the expression of the nation, endures and persists when governments and even regimes shift and change. However, the relationship between a changing government and the higher civil service is complex, and the nature of the civil service not so straightforward as such a perception implies. Four aspects of the higher civil service seem especially relevant to a consideration of the effects of a change of government for they condition the nature of the relationship between politicians and administrators. They are the legitimacy of the higher civil service in policy-making; the effect of the administrative environment on policy-making; the civil service response to political change; and the structures available to the incoming government for the enforcement of its political direction.

## THE LEGITIMACY OF THE HIGHER CIVIL SERVICE

In France the belief persists that civil servants are well qualified to intervene in policy-making —especially, perhaps, in economic policy-making — and that it is important and right that they should do so. Public servants, as the guarantors of the general interest, themselves serving no particular or partial interest, are alone able to perceive the true nature of this general interest and pursue it. This belief rests upon certain key assertions: that the administration is the embodiment of a durable and benevolent state in its guardianship of the general interest; that public servants are associated with a rational and dynamic approach to policy-making, especially economic policy-making; and that the higher civil service system of recruitment and training ensures the presence in top posts of people whose educational prowess allows them to claim pre-eminence.

In part the claim of the higher civil service to embody the impartial role of the state and guard the general interest is based simply on the durability of the administration, which sees itself, because of its tradition and its guaranteed permanence, as capable of making measured and rational assessments of the longer term. The notion of the general interest, however, is also based upon a certain conception of the state. This conception sees the state as the agent through which the polity is held together and ordered; without which the nation would be divided, indeed atomized.[2] Associated with this concept are a cluster of notions, described by Dyson as characteristic of a 'state' society, which 'find their coherence in a rationalist conception of the technical requirements of an "ordered" society'.[3] They include the view that the public interest is not simply the sum of private interests, an emphasis on legalism and codification, and on the unitary character of 'public power' and an active conception of the administrator's role. Although not specifically attributed by Dyson to the French administrative system, all these features are characteristic of its ethos and working practices. Claims to permanence, to a monopoly of the sense of the general interest, to neutrality, are strongly expressed or implied within the French civil service, and in so far as they fashion not only the higher civil servant's own perception of his role, but also the image he presents to outsiders, they are a basis for the legitimacy accorded to this role.[4]

The notion of the 'general interest' constitutes an important support for the claims of the civil service to a major role in the public life of France, a claim that has fashioned, and continues to fashion, relationships between politicians and administrators.The notion, however, is neither clear nor unambiguous and does not by itself provide an adequate basis for a description of the relationship. The claim of the civil service to a particular competence, especially in the management of the economy, also plays an important role in the determination of political–administrative relationships.

The claim of French higher civil servants to a pre-eminent place in the management of public affairs, and especially the economy, is supported by a tradition which associates public servants with a rational and dynamic approach. This tradition, however, provided the civil service with most support during periods when the political environment was particularly receptive to it. It was amongst the former students of the École Polytechnique that Saint-Simonian ideas about the importance of the rational guidance of the state by experts in the economic and industrial fields spread particularly rapidly in the 1840s. Something of the same current of ideas was to be found in the movements which, prompted by the experience of the First World War, the economic crisis of the inter-war years and the failure of the governments of the 1930s to cope with economic problems, began to study the possibilities of economic forecasting and planning. These 'technocratic' groups, one of the most important of which centred round the *polytechnicien* Jean Coutrot, and which included a number of officials (the liberal Jacques Rueff as well as the future planning commissioner Pierre Massé), saw themselves as providing a dynamic progressive element in national economic life. However, only in the changed atmosphere of post-war France could their ideas begin to make headway. As Kuisel points out, the 'technocratic' groups emerged from the war unscathed, into an atmosphere of widespread support for economic renovation and state action, 'armed with new governmental organs, granted autonomy by de Gaulle and backed by the public's desire for structural reforms, the technocrats had come to stay'.[5]

The attitude that had been found in these groups was also to be found after 1945 amongst the students of the newly created École Nationale d'Administration (ENA). The founders of the ENA and its staff (a great many of whom were serving civil servants) emphasized the contribution which the higher civil servant could and should make to the reconstruction and growth of the post-war French economy. The School was, in the eyes of its creators, to produce an active and dynamic civil service which would be prepared to take responsibility for the economic development of France. The training which was provided at the ENA in Keynesian economic ideas — lecture courses given in the early 1950s by Jean Marchal on Keynesian theories and by Pierre Mendès France on the problems of the reconstruction of France were particularly influential — possibly helped to instil confidence in an interventionist approach. A study of the topics chosen for the report which students were, until 1971, required to produce at the end of their year of practical attachments within the administration (*mémoire de stage*) shows a clear preference for themes with some economic aspects. Throughout the 1950s and 1960s, most former students aver, the ENA's training had as one of its central guiding themes the idea that the reconstruction and growth of the economy could not be left to individuals or enterprises. It depended upon the state, and thus, essentially, upon the state's most senior servants:

We were clear that the renewal and growth of the country depended upon us.

The training at the ENA ... presented the top administration as the 'active force' in French society.

It would, however, be wrong to convey the impression that it is the former students of the ENA alone who have been responsible for the attitude of the higher civil service. As Kuisel points out, certain senior officials in the Ministry of Finance had, at the period of the Liberation, already adopted a more dynamic outlook, and they were supported by many of the younger generation of officials.[6] This brought them into conflict with those who maintained a traditional non-interventionist approach, and who did not inspire or even support many of the major economic reforms of the period, but even the traditionalists eventually found themselves obliged to work within a new pattern of economic responsibilities, and under strong-willed Prime Ministers or Ministers of Finance (Kuisel instances Pinay, Mayer, Edgar Faure, Mendès France) so they were gradually converted to a more dynamic approach to managing economic growth. Suleiman, considering the attitudes of the top civil service to the economy, traces the progress of the modernizing approach under the Fifth Republic and also emphasizes the role of political impulsion as well as elite strategies.[7]

### THE LEGITIMACY OF THE HIGHER CIVIL SERVICE: RECRUITMENT AND TRAINING

The claim of the higher civil service to an active role within the management of public affairs stems from a particular tradition reinforced whenever the political climate has been particularly receptive to it. It stems also from a system of recruitment and training which, while operating in a way which reinforces the claims of civil servants to intellectual and educational prowess, is also, in important ways, dependent upon the political climate.

Ezra Suleiman, examining the nature of the higher civil servant's role, quotes one *grands corps* member.

It is that members of the *grands corps* are something of an aristocracy in French society. But why? Simply because they are superior to others. They are the most brilliant. They are the top graduates of their schools and they have been very carefully selected. Put in a nutshell: they are the ones who have performed the best.[8]

The system of recruitment allows higher civil servants to claim a unique competence. Most senior officials are recruited through one of two main channels: the École Polytechnique, through which members of the Corps des Ponts et Chaussées and the Corps des Mines are recruited; and the École Nationale d'Administration, which provides members of the non-technical *grand corps* and also senior general administrators. Selection takes place at several levels. The École Polytechnique takes in about 300 students a year who prepare for the highly competitive entry examination in special classes attached to certain *lycées*, after having passed the *baccalauréat*. Entry into these classes is in itself highly competitive. At the end of the students' period at the École Polytechnique they are ranked in order of merit on the basis of examinations, and choose their careers on the basis of their rank. Those ranked highest invariably choose the *grands corps*.

The École Nationale d'Administration does not recruit directly from the *lycées*, but has, up to now, been open to university graduates and to officials who have spent at least five years in the public service. In practice, success in its fiercely competitive examinations requires a period of specialized preparation. Most of the successful graduate candidates undertake this at the Institut d'Études Politiques in Paris. A measure of selection operates within the IEP. Bodiguel's figures suggest that only just over 20 per cent of those who are candidates for entry into the first year of the IEP diploma course emerge after three years with the diploma.[9] And finally, as at the École Polytechnique, a second stage selection operates at the ENA, in that those who achieve the highest rank in the final assessment examination have the widest choice of jobs and invariably choose the *grands corps*.[10] Membership of the *grands corps* thus reflects repeated success in negotiating a series of intellectual hurdles and it is hardly surprising if this produces cases like those cited by *Le Point* in 1974: that of the 40-year-old head of a department in a large electronics firm in the Paris area with a brilliant career behind him who knows he will go no higher, and explains 'to go higher you have to come from [the École Polytechnique]. It's the unwritten rule';[11] and that of the executive of the semi-public petrol company who knows that 'I shall always have an *énarque* (a former student of the ENA) above me. It is inconceivable that I, with only my IEP diploma, should be in charge of a former student of the ENA.'[12]

The part played by the higher civil service in policy-making is thus important, at least in part, because it is expected to be important, and this expectation has had practical consequences. Civil servants themselves have taken an exalted view of their role, and this view has been widely accepted,[13] both outside the Administration, and even abroad, as the admiring glances cast from Britain at French recruitment and training demonstrate. Certainly, the success of the strategies of the *corps* as they have adapted themselves to new situations, giving priority to their own survival and the furtherance of their *corps* interest has had its part to play in the acceptance by society of the *grands corps*' own image of themselves.

Since the nature of their recruitment and training plays such an important part in determining the status and claims of senior civil servants, it is hardly surprising that refashioning the system to accord with the principles of a changed situation has often been accorded a high priority. After the 1848 Revolution, Hippolyte Carnot set out with great speed to create an École Nationale d'Administration. Emile Boutmy found much support for his École Libre des Sciences Politiques in 1872 coming from those who wished to reshape the political and administrative elites in response to the trauma of defeat. Michel Debré's École Nationale d'Administration opened its doors less than two years after the Liberation of Paris, and was explicitly designed to produce senior civil servants who would respond in a new way to the needs of the country.

For President Mitterrand's incoming Socialist Government the existence of the École Nationale d'Administration posed a dilemma. The School was indisputably elitist. It had developed an ethos which, while more a matter of style than of content, and by no means affecting all students equally, had accorded particularly well with the aspirations of the governing majority of the first twenty years of the Fifth Republic. Catherine Lalumière, briefly herself the ENA's minister *de tutelle*, summed up the dilemma on the occasion of the School's thirtieth anniversary: 'Should a professional training school be destroyed because its pupils have become too able workers?'[14] while for Jean-Pierre Chevènement of CERES, product as well as critic of the School and a Socialist minister, writing in 1980, the profound social changes which a government of the left would eventually produce would themselves destroy it.[15] In the meantime certain reforms would be useful. The Socialist Government has found that it requires able servants, capable of operating within a mixed economy and within an international system. It has decided to reform, not to abolish. The Communist Anicet le Pors, Minister for the Civil Service until July 1984 and hence the School's minister *de tutelle*, who was himself for many years a civil servant in a senior grade, although not a graduate of the ENA, said in March 1983 that he had come to believe in elitism, but an elitism *de masse*.[16] The most important reform proposed has been the opening up of a third method of recruitment, which would take into the School people who had been engaged for a certain period of time in the activities of voluntary bodies, associations, trade unions, and local politics in elective posts. Those who had contributed to the life of the nation in a non-official capacity should be given the opportunity to make this contribution also in official posts.

This proposal has proved controversial. The opposition referred it to the Constitutional Council on the grounds that it infringed the constitutional rights of all citizens to equal access to official posts. It also poses the difficult problems of the nature of the selection process for such candidates. Will a special preparation be required for the entry competitions? Such entrants will follow a particular training course of their own which will be separate and different from those for other entrants. A certain proportion of the top jobs will be reserved for them — but will they nevertheless become more or less a B stream? The proponents of the reforms maintain that, in conjunction with other measures such as the raising of some age limits for entry, a more democratized and less socially exclusive entry will result and will in time be reflected within the administration. But even should such changes occur — and if they do they will be very slow — the politicians will continue to find themselves working with administrators with formidable claims to technical excellence and intellectual prowess.

## THE ADMINISTRATIVE ENVIRONMENT

The environment within which the civil servants whose claims to a powerful role in policy-making have been examined above operate is complex and fashioned by extraneous pressures and internal blockages and conflicts. The administration is neither monololithic nor dominant. The point is important, for it implies that the senior civil service cannot be regarded as operating as a relatively autonomous political force in its own right. In their recent book, Bodiguel and Quermonne discuss the role of the *haute fonction publique* as a political force:

Let us admit that the higher civil service is composed of a series of groups which . . . are fashioned simultaneously both by the corps to which the higher civil servants are individually attached, and by the structures to which they are posted. We may agree that if we wanted to establish a parallel between the higher civil service and recognised political forces, it would most resemble a system of groups rather than a single coherent unified force.[17]

The higher civil service cannot and does not react to change in the political complexion of government in a coherent way. It cannot advance a political vision of its own.

Firstly, the old barriers and divisions within the Administration persist. In the late 1920s Walter Rice Sharp described the rigidly hierarchical structure of most ministries, and stressed the lack of horizontal communication which resulted. In 1945 this excessive 'compartmentalization' (*cloisonnement*) was one of the failures of the French Administration which Debré hoped a common recruitment and training would remedy. Nevertheless, the concept of authority as strictly located within an area marked out by the texts which define a ministry's or a division's jurisdiction persists. A division which has been in existence over a long period can trace its evolution through a series of legislative texts. The influence of a division may depend upon its standing and longevity, and some — the Budget and Treasury divisions are the most outstanding examples — are regarded as *nobles*. The result of this compartmentalization is the *batailles des compétences* vividly described by Suleiman. He reports:

I once heard two Directors in the Ministry engage in a heated discussion over a sentence that threatened to shift an element of control over a minor domain from one *direction* to another . . . Power, for them, is strictly definable: it does not emerge from complex relationships. It is to be located, as the quarrel between the two Directors suggested, in the list of jurisdictions That there is no necessary connection between the legally defined jurisdiction of a *direction* and the influence that a Director actually exerts is not evident to most of the Directors.[18]

This mentality —'when I go to a meeting my task is to defend the interests of my division'[19] — tends to lead on to the adoption of the ideas and approach of that particular division or ministry.

Each division has its own patterns of thought and is used to arguing within its own intellectual framework which is often based on a view confined to the management of its own services. . . 'In the light of the matters with which I am concerned . . .' thus a *directeur* of the Treasury division often prefaced his remarks . . . The divisions of the Ministry [of Finance] are often reluctant to pass on the information required to carry out their respective tasks. Each branch prefers to work within a closed circuit.[20]

An example of just such a situation was reported by *Le Nouvel Observateur* in July 1982. At the general meeting of the newly nationalized Compagnie Générale d'Électricité, senior officials of the Ministries of Industry and of Finance were in evident dispute, the former wanting to reduce the distribution of dividends to provide finance for reinvestment, and the latter wishing for as large as possible a distribution of profit, which could then be used for general state expenditure.

Secondly, the policy-making process is further complicated by the relationships between the different *corps* of which the higher civil service is composed. The *corps* system has effects which go beyond merely structural problems and seem to extend into policy-making areas.

A higher civil servant's *corps* membership results from his performance in the assessment examinations of the ENA or the École Polytechnique. Membership of one of the *grands corps* provides the sense of belonging to a small and exclusive club; it conveys a certain social status; it offers opportunities for interesting and remunerative occupation both within the Administration and outside it; it allows a certain freedom in the organization of one's time and activities. However, the maintenance of this status requires that each *corps* should retain its claim to expertise in certain areas and should if possible seek to extend the area which it dominates.

The desire of the *corps* to maintain their positions may have policy consequences. Jean-Claude Thoenig, for the Corps des Ponts et Chaussées, and Ezra Suleiman, for the Corps des Mines, have shown how the *corps* tend to approach policy in terms of the opportunity which it offers for the maintenance of the power and position of the *corps*. Suleiman says:

It would be difficult to pinpoint a coherent set of policies that the Inspection des Finances or the Corps des Mines are committed to within the areas of the economy or energy. It is not difficult to find examples where policies have been embraced, sometimes smoothly, sometimes after a difficult adjustment period. But the important point is that it is not the policies *per se* that matter, for policies are judged according to their impact on the power and the position of the elite.[21]

and adds: The commitment of the elite is to the health and well-being of its corporate organization, rather than to a set of policies. Policies are looked upon as a means of enlarging a *corps'* domain, of leaving it unchanged or of reducing it.'[22] Jean-Claude Thoenig cites the motorway building programme as an example of such a policy. The Corps des Ponts et Chaussées opposed the extension of the motorway network largely on the grounds that the projects were too large to be handled by their traditional autonomous basic local units.[23]

Thirdly, the attitudes of higher civil servants within the policy-making process may also vary according to their role. The conflicts which arise between the members of a minister's private office — themselves usually higher civil servants — and the divisions of the ministry are a particularly clear example of this type. Membership of the staff of a private office (*cabinet*) has not in the past necessarily implied a close political identification with the minister; rather it is for many a necessary step in a successful career. The division does not only represent a separation between 'political' and 'technical' spheres. It is characterized by what Jean-Luc Bodiguel describes as *un climat de défiance*. There is a division between those who seek to coordinate and resolve conflicts — and this is in part the *cabinet's* role — and those who seek to maintain their own point of view. There is equally a division between the *cabinet* that seeks to ensure the implementation of the minister's policy against what may seem to be the hidebound reaction of the divisions, and the heads of the divisions who feel that the *cabinet* does not take sufficient account of 'reality'.

If the ministers and their entourage concern themselves with the implementations of policy and check the details, it is because they are wary of the *directeurs*.[24]

It is not in fact unusual for the *cabinet* to devise the principles of a new policy virtually without consultation, and even for it to take on almost unaided the drafting of the texts which embody this policy.[25]

Changes have, however, come to the administration since 1945. While the common background of the higher civil servants has probably not had a major effect upon their behaviour, it has certainly affected the ease and speed of communication between them. 'I remember the old days, how slow and rigid everything was, all on paper. Now I telephone a fellow former student of the ENA.'[26] Diana Green found that great use was made within the budget division of informal contacts, often on the basis of membership of the same graduating class at the ENA.[27] While most ENA students seem to retain a close working relationship with only a handful of contemporaries, the relative ease they feel in any dealing with a fellow former student is important.

Secondly, higher civil servants can no longer be confined for their entire working career within one division. If they are to be eligible for appointment to the most senior posts they must have spent at least two years outside their ministry of first posting. The institution of this obligation was seen as a means of breaking down some of the barriers between ministries, and of making the *corps* of *administrateurs civils* a more genuinely interministerial *corps*.

The effects of the ENA training should not, however, be exaggerated. Competition exists at the top between *énarques* and *polytechniciens*. It also exists between *énarques* whose *corps* membership may have been determined by a very small margin in the final assessment examination. The desire to achieve the necessary marks led, in the early years of the School, to intense rivalry. If such fierce competition now affects only about a third of the students each year, a certain bitterness can still sour those who see prospects blocked and interesting posts permanently occupied by members of the *grands corps*.

The conformity and similarity which the ENA training induces is essentially a conformity in style, but not necessarily in content. There is no doubt that style plays a vital part in success both in the entrance examinations to the ENA and in the assessment examinations. In their advice to candidates the examining boards stress the importance of structure and clarity of expression. Much of the training, especially in the two core subjects — administrative texts and documents, and fiscal and budgetary problems — has the effect of teaching the student to express himself and present his work in an acceptable, and fairly uniform way. Stress upon style is not, of course, unique to the ENA — the student only reaches the ENA after an educational process in which he has consistently been more successful than most of his colleagues in presenting his work in an articulate and acceptable way. Uniformity of style, however, does not imply uniformity of ideas.

The policy-making process within the administration is, thus, subject to both conforming and contradictory pressures. One of the effects of the training provided by the ENA since 1945 has been to provide officials with some economic competence and understanding for most of the ministries and administrations. This may, at least in recent years, have had the effect of enlarging the scope for conflict over economic questions, and of making more acute the need for political direction. The administrative environment is not divorced from the political structure — indeed, the two overlap closely, both in institutions such as the *cabinets*, and in personnel. As Saint-Geours points out,

Some years ago, a continuous and homogeneous politico-administrative line, based on the Finance Inspectorate, linked the Prime Minister to the young desk officer in the Treasury Division, through the Minister of Finance, his *directeur du cabinet*, the *directeur* of the Treasury division, and the appropriate *sous-directeur*.[28]

Paradoxically, however, the effects of links may have been to increase the scope for political action and direction. Another Finance Inspector recognized this:

Twenty years ago it was relatively easy for a *directeur* to impose his wishes, disguised as technical necessities, upon a well-meaning veterinary surgeon [i.e. a minister from a very different background]. Nowadays, even if he says 'tu' to his boss, who may have been a member of the same promotion, his relationship is actually one of strict subordination.[29]

The French State . . . has the structural potential for autonomous action, but structure does not determine how or whether that potential is used. A political explanation will always be required to explain the direction of State activity.[30]

Thus John Zysman insists upon the necessity of political direction for economic policy-making. It is to the attitudes, structures and personnel upon which the political direction of all policy-making depends that the next sections of this chapter turn.

## THE RESPONSE OF THE HIGHER CIVIL SERVICE TO POLITICAL CHANGE

The scope for the effective exercise of political control over the civil service is in part determined by the nature of the attitudes towards political direction and control that an incoming government encounters. The attitude of many civil servants to political change is fashioned partly by the concept of the general interest, but while this produces a language which is very persuasive within the higher civil service, of separation between politics and administration, and of neutrality, this language is not in fact used to defend a certain overall vision of the future of society. Certainly, although the higher civil service may from time to time have been swayed by common enthusiasms (for Mendèsism in the 1950s, for example), there has never been any unanimity around a specific platform or programme. So the language of the general interest can be used, for example, as a mask for the natural conservatism of large bureaucratic structures. Arguments which claim to be founded on a superior perception of an overall situation may well emphasize moderation, caution, practicality. The 'general interest' becomes defined in terms of what already exists: 'Concerned above all for order, regularity, continuity, they emphasise static, not dynamic values; the cult of tradition and precedent means that they only conceive of the future as a projection and reproduction of the past.'[31] Proposals for reform often appear to represent threats and the civil servant's task becomes that of limiting the damage.[32]

The existing situation which the language of 'the general interest' may serve to protect will quite largely be concerned with the position and privileges and field of activity of any particular group of civil servants. It may be significant that a senior French civil servant invited in 1979 to instance circumstances which had involved opposition between ministers and their staff on policy matters cited only conflicts which concerned the organization and activities of certain corps, notably that between the *ingénieurs des ponts et chaussées* and

Albin Chalandon in the late 1960s. The ability of the prefectoral corps to ensure that the title 'Prefect' has not disappeared with the Mitterrand Government's decentralization reforms, but has simply been supplemented by the new title 'Commissaire de la République', may also be significant.[33]

Lacking, as it does, any programme or specific content, the notion of the general interest becomes ambiguous in its application. Seen from the point of view of the long-standing orthodoxy of the budget division of the Ministry of Finance, the general interest involved the limitation of expenditure and the maintenance of a balanced budget. Spending ministries accorded the social needs of the population a rather different priority. Such ambiguities are related to those which allowed wide and reformist objectives on social policy to be written into the Seventh Plan which never materialized.[34] Even more clearly, a language of the 'general interest' provides the civil servants with no guidance as to where (or indeed whether) to site a nuclear power station or route a motorway. All that such an approach can do is to stress harmony, conciliation, negotiation:

This is, above all, the mediatory role of the prefectoral corps, but also of other corps (Labour inspectorate, central administrative services of the Ministries of Industry, Health, Young People, etc.) who have many private interests in their care. Settling disputes, taking the heat out of issues, flattering and threatening turn by turn, negotiating, persuading . . . .[35]

The notion of the general interest tends to shape a particular style, rather than a specific content, in administrative action. The third aspect of the ambiguities to which it gives rise is the question of the relationship between politician and administrator.

On the one hand, the civil servant asserts a traditional independence from the political sphere:

Inherited from the French Revolution, the distinction between 'representatives' and 'agents' was for a long time one of the unwritten rules of the Republic. It produced, in France, the separation between administration and politics. Myth or reality, this separation was the basis for the policy towards the civil service carried on under the Third and Fourth Republics. In the eyes of many officials it retains today the status of an ethical principle.[36]

On the other hand, this principle became increasingly difficult to maintain as the making of policy moved, under the Fourth Republic, and even more markedly under the Fifth Republic, from Parliament to the executive. It became harder for the administrator to define a specific, technical, separate sphere where the 'general interest' operates, as the ministries, rather than parliamentary committees, became, with ministers, the leading actors in the making of policy.[37] And the civil servants found that they needed the political contribution of the minister to fill out the content of the policy and ensure its adoption. They might also need some support from the minister to advance a career. 'The administrator too must in fact learn to sell what he does, to make himself known and appreciated. . . Thus the administrator is at one and the same time detached from and dependent upon the political sphere . . . '[38]

If the civil servant is both detached from and dependent upon the political sphere, then in what sense can he be said to be neutral? Clearly, the nature of the claim by the civil service to neutrality is of great importance to a government facing an administration which has served its predecessors of a markedly different political complexion. Formally, the French civil servant's obligation of neutrality requires him to abstain from doing anything which might call his neutrality into question. It is an obligation to restrain professional behaviour, not private actions or beliefs and tends to be interpreted narrowly — as relating to policy in a particular sector.[39] Civil servants do feel free to dissent publicly from the overall policy of the government. Nevertheless, civil servants make use of a language of neutrality and impartiality which insists upon their 'sense of the state' which enables them to resist pressures that outside groups, including political parties, attempt to exert upon the process of decision-making. It is a language which emphasizes a degree of distance and separation between politics and administration.

It is interesting to note that this bears, for example, little relationship to the British concept of neutrality as it is traditionally formulated. The British concept has never involved detachment from the political goals of the incumbent government, nor a search for objectively correct solutions. Rather it has required a chameleon-like ability to evince enthusiasm for and political sensitivity in the cause of the policies of any government. French observers are inclined to regard such an attitude as involving either cynical careerism or unendurable violation of any individual's integrity. An approach which stresses the technical sphere of administrative action is part of the French civil servant's solution to the problem of a permanent administration and a politically changing government.

This approach is assisted by the legal background to much discussion of and comment on public administration. Most senior administrators have a background training in administrative 'sciences' and administrative law, but the academic development of these subjects has also been dominated by lawyers.[40] Such an approach is further assisted by recruitment and training processes which judge candidates on the basis of objective academic examinations in relevant subjects. Such an examination system tends to reinforce the feeling that to any given political/administrative problem there must be a technically correct answer — the answer that will receive the highest marks. There is also a tendency to narrow down problems in a way which may ignore the possibly complicating interconnections with other problems. A French civil servant may maintain that 'it would be perverse to try to take into account the interests of one group (e.g. the shopkeeper) in a measure designed to promote the interests of another (e.g. the consumer).'[41]

Undoubtedly, the degree of policy continuity which France has experienced at least since 1945 has also assisted the development of feeling for administrative specificity and technicality. The solutions to administrative problems put to examination candidates are required to be 'realistic'; as Riemer has pointed out, this has essentially involved assuming the continuation of the main lines of policy of the government in power.[42] This is not to suggest that there have not been policy changes, some of them sharp, abrupt and often opposed by civil servants.[43] On the whole, however, as Helen Wallace pointed out as long ago as 1973 in connection with French policy towards the EEC, French officials had, until May 1981, been able to operate from their training days onward with a degree of autonomy within well-understood and fairly unchanging parameters.[44]

The immediate response of the administration to the electoral success of the former opposition certainly emphasized the absence of a well-defined administrative routine for handling such eventualities. In contrast to the practised British system, which ensures the advance preparation of at least two sets of briefing papers before any general election[45] and manages to contrive that the outgoing Prime Minister's private secretary accompanies him to the Palace to tender his resignation and is also ready to greet his successor at the doorway of No. 10, there was a certain air of confusion about the handover of power after 10 May 1981. Not only was there some doubt about the exact date upon which it should occur, but incoming ministers in some cases found either no office, and were obliged to engage in rapid manoeuvres to ensure suitable accommodation, or found their predecessor's offices bereft of everything except a paper-knife.[46] Additional incinerators had been hastily acquired and used, especially in the Ministry of the Interior, and several lorry-loads of papers were apparently also despatched to the municipal incinerator outside Paris at Issy-les-Moulineaux.[47] There were, however, reportedly a number of notable exceptions to this general pattern of disarray. The Foreign Ministry, and particularly the General Secretary of the Government, M. Marceau Long, and the Governor of the Bank of France, M. Renaud de la Genière, were said to have responded rapidly and helpfully to the task of setting a new government and new policies in place.

### STRUCTURES OF POLITICAL CONTROL OF THE CIVIL SERVICE

The incoming Government found itself obliged to put to the test the nature of the concept of neutrality and loyalty held by most civil servants. Its initial pronouncements were cautious: *Le Nouvel Observateur* quoted one of President Mitterrand's staff: 'We shall define a policy and give them the means to implement it. If the officials responsible do their job loyally, there's no problem. If they sabotage the policies they will suffer the consequences, rapidly and hard.' A French government, however, also has a number of institutional structures upon which it can rely to enforce its political purposes. They include its rights concerning the appointment of senior officials, the operation of the *cabinet* system, the commissioning of special studies or reports and the creation of administrative units outside the normal structure. It is with the use that the Mitterrand Government has made of these four structural resources, especially the first two, that this section is concerned.

Governments in France have long been recognized as requiring a degree of discretion in the choice of the most senior and key officials, amongst whom a more than chameleon-like attachment to the government's policies is felt to be required. The general code of civil service conditions of employment, first enacted in 1946, allows that for the most senior posts the government has total discretion in appointment. Political views may be taken into account, and previous experience within the civil service is not required, nor need the normal recruitment procedures be invoked. This totally legal power enables the government to shift and replace a number of senior administrators. President Giscard used it to ensure the presence at key points of officials sympathetic to his viewpoint. It has never, however, amounted to a systematic 'spoils system', if only because those removed from sensitive posts, provided they are, as is almost always the case, civil servants, do not necessarily leave the service, but will be redeployed elsewhere. It is clear, however, that while the consequences of such redeployment may be minimal for members of the *grands corps* they may be much more dramatic for an *administrateur civil* whose *corps* of origin can offer neither comparable pay nor adequately interesting work.[48] After May 1981, certain officials, mostly in sensitive posts concerned with internal security and police matters or particularly closely connected with the previous regime, applied for special leave or took their retirement promptly, recognizing, perhaps, the logic of their position. Other changes followed.

Change, however, is a constant feature of administrative life. Officials retire, are promoted, are moved or choose to move to other fields. The average length of stay in a post as *directeur* in the period 1958–66 was three and a half years,[49] and Bodiguel and Quermonne cite the case of the division of the Ministry of Education which experienced eight directors in the decade from 1972 to 1982. It is inevitably difficult to separate what would in any case have been normal or expected moves from what are undoubtedly politically inspired appointments. In 1978, after the general election, the Giscard Government moved twenty-six prefects, with the explanation, which was by no means generally accepted, that a normal administrative activity was all that was involved. François Bardos, writing in *Pouvoirs*, refused to accept as politically motivated most of the prefectoral movements that followed President Mitterrand's election.[50] Yves Agnès, writing somewhat later in *Le Monde*, was less sanguine.[51] He pointed out that in the year between July 1981 and June 1982, 117 prefects had been affected by movements or changes, compared with a total of 190 in the entire seven years of President Giscard's term of office. By late 1982, there had been ninety-one changes among the ninety-four *départements*.[52] Some of these changes had been caused by vacancies resulting from the voluntary departure of the former incumbents. In mid-1982, thirty-seven of those who had been prefects or sub-prefects in post in May 1981 had chosen either to follow the well-worn path for senior officials into industry or to take their chances within the newly decentralized structures on the staff of local authorities.[53] Indeed a sufficient number of former students of the ENA have taken that step for them to set up an association to represent their interests.[54] The extent to which the parties now in opposition retain control of *départements* and regions may have made this a particularly attractive proposition to those members of the prefectoral corps who are not in sympathy with the Government.

Other vacancies were, however, caused by the removal of prefects known to be Giscardian (M. Raymond François le Bris and M. Gérard Prioux were posted *hors cadre* and M Lucien Lanier placed on special leave). Blood-relationship by no means implies identity of views, but Agnès thought it worth noting that over a year after the socialist victory Mme Giscard d'Estaing's cousin was still Prefect and Commissaire of the Orne. However, few of the new appointments are of people with clear political sympathies for the left.[55] Admittedly in M. Maurice Siegel, Prefect of the Meuse, France has her first Communist prefect since the dismissal of Jean Chaintron, Prefect of the Haute-Vienne, in the autumn of 1947.[56] His is an isolated case, and even amongst those few identified with the Socialist Party political allegiance may not have been the sole criterion. Mme Chassagne's gender may, for example, have played as important a part as her Socialism in her appointment as the first female prefect.

The difficulty of distinguishing between normal administrative career movements and political promotions does not, however, apply to all appointments. There have long been, within the French Administration, a number of administrative posts that carry a weight and autonomy that make their incumbents virtually political figures. The *Commissaire général au plan* and the director general of the regional planning body DATAR are two such officials, and the Director of the Budget division of the Ministry of Finance and the Director-general of the Civil Service, while perhaps less exposed to public attention, should probably also be considered within this category. All these posts have new incumbents. There are new directors at the state research institute, the CNRS, the Caisse des Dépôts et Consignations and a number of other major public and para-public bodies. Some key posts were, however, in mid-1982, still occupied by their previous incumbents — the Governor of the Bank of France (M. Renaud de Genière) and the Director of Local Government in the Ministry of the Interior (M. Pierre Richard) were, for example, still in place.

Two areas in which important changes were made quickly and much discussed were in educational administration and in broadcasting. The left had criticized President Giscard and his Minister for Universities, Alice Saunier-Seïté, for their political appointments to the senior posts in regional educational administration, the *recteurs d'académie*. Of twenty-seven *recteurs*, one has been moved, eight retained in post, and eighteen replaced. Broadcasting was a particularly sensitive area for an opposition which had long complained of bias. Almost all the heads (chairmen and directors-general) of the various radio stations and television channels were replaced, as were the directors of the television news services 'including the well-known Socialist *bêtes noires*, Jean Pierre Elkabbach, director of news at Antenne 2 and Patrice Roland, news editor at TF1'. They were largely replaced by journalists sympathetic to the left. These moves preceded the restructuring of the broadcasting system, which took effect at the beginning of 1983.[57]

Within the central ministries there have been considerable variations.[58] Some ministries have changed all their directors (Trade, Civil Service, Health, Transport) or most of them (Agriculture, National Solidarity, Justice, Education). Others (Environment) have hardly changed any directors at all (as in the case of the Ministries of Finance, the Interior, Defence) or left more than half in post. Of the new incumbents Agnès reckoned that about one-quarter (occupying 14 per cent of the total number of posts as director) were directly involved with left-wing politics either through the parties of the Government (Socialist or Communist) or through the trade unions (CFDT and CGT). One interesting and unusual appointment has been the choice of a former businessman, without either political or previous civil service connections, M. Claude Jouven, as Director of the Ministry of Finance's division of competition and prices.[59] While it is common enough for civil servants to move out into industry it is virtually unheard of for businessmen without previous civil service experience to move into administrative posts.

The fact that the Communist ministers (of Health, Transport and the Civil Service) were particularly active in replacing their *directeurs* raises the question of the activities of Communist ministers in civil service appointments. It is sometimes said that when Communists held official office between 1945 and 1947 they took advantage of this systematically to place their nominees in key posts. Certainly when they left the Government a number of steps were taken. The dismissal of Jean Chaintron has already been referred to. Dismissals also occurred in the Broadcasting Service, and a hundred or so army officers, who were thought to have links with the extreme left were placed in posts where they could do no harm.[60] Within the central Administration the *cabinets* of the Communist ministers might be expected to have been important areas for the appointment of party militants. The most comprehensive and well-documented study of ministerial *cabinets* concluded, on the basis of precise information about twelve out of the thirty *cabinets* of communist ministers in the 1940s, that in only one were all the members (three out of three) Communists.[61] In all the others, including that of Maurice Thorez, the party leader, there were some non-Communists as well as party members and fellow-travellers. One man, a former member of the Resistance and inmate of Dachau, a non-Communist, served as *Directeur de Cabinet* for two Communist ministers and went on after 1947 to be a member of the *cabinets* of two independent ministers whom he had known through the Resistance.[62]

This evidence suggests that even the places that Communist ministers could, in the 1940s, easily have filled with their party members were not monopolized by them. However, the leader of the left-wing but anti-Communist union Force Ouvrière attacked the Communist ministers in November 1981 on the grounds that 'wherever they can the Communists put their people into politics, as they have always done, including just after the war'.[63] It should be noted that his union is particularly strong amongst health and civil service employees, both after May 1981 subject to Communist ministers. He subsequently modified his statements, suggesting that all he had wanted was to ensure proper treatment of his union members.

The Communist ministers of the Mauroy Government did not differ from their Socialist colleagues in surrounding themselves by those who were politically sympathetic. Anicet le Pors, Minister for the Civil Service, looked to his former colleagues in the Ministry of Finance and to those whose experience in the CGT has made them familiar with civil service problems from the union side. In the *cabinet* of Charles Fiterman, Minister of Transport, in mid-1982, thirteen out of seventeen members were attached to the Communist Party. The *cabinet* had been carefully put together by Guy Braibant, Fiterman's personal adviser, who was both a member of a *grand corps*, the Council of State, and a long-standing Communist.[64]

*Cabinets* are highly politicized institutions. There is no evidence of systematic attempts by Communist ministers to infiltrate their supporters into higher civil service posts. Indeed, it remains hard to see how this could occur, given the relatively small pool of people upon whom it is possible for the Government to draw in making top appointments. Those within the civil service who preferred left-wing sentiments, whether genuine or opportunist, have seen their hour come, but precisely because of the difficulty of appointing to top posts from outside the small elite, many French observers resist the idea that a spoils system exists in France while accepting that the French Government, like other European governments, does and should enjoy extensive powers of discretionary patronage. An incoming Socialist government faces particular difficulties in its use of these powers. A comparison of experience since 1981 with that of the Blum Government of 1936, whose problems in this area have been so well and extensively described by Irwin Wall, is illuminating. Wall points out that Blum had legalistic scruples about laying his Government open to the same charges of politicization and discrimination which he had previously been levying against the governments of the right. This did not prevent his Government coming under bitter criticism from its own supporters.

The failure of the Blum Government to 'democratize' the French administration appears almost certainly to have been the most critical single source of disillusionment with the experiment among the militants of M. Blum's own party, if not for supporters of the Popular Front as a whole.[65]

President Mitterrand's Government has faced similar criticism. A motion at the Valence Congress of the Socialist Party in the aftermath of victory noted that nearly twenty-five years of the dominance of one governing coalition had transformed certain parts of the Administration into adherents of a particular policy, and at that congress M. Paul Quilès hit the headlines with his demand that heads should roll rapidly. The storm of protest that this aroused did not prevent the voicing of further criticism. M. Michel Jobert, admittedly no Socialist himself and occupying a ministerial post with a particularly precarious administrative base, said in November 1981 that he saw still in posts people whom he wondered why they continued to enjoy the Government's indulgence; and other Socialist parliamentarians, though not ministers, subsequently repeated the charge that the difficulties experienced by the Government in 1982 would at least have been less serious had the Government been more determined to put into key posts officials who would genuinely support its policies.[66] Even M. Mauroy, then the Prime Minister, recognized that the Administration did not like to have long-standing habits and methods upset.[67] However, just as some of Blum's ministers, at least, were prepared to recognize the loyal cooperation they had received from their officials, so President Mitterrand acknowledged at the end of 1981 the loyal behaviour of the mass of officials which had eased the handover of power.

In so far as ministers and government supporters are inclined to blame the Administration for unwillingness to cooperate, this in part reflects a conflict which is institutionalized within French administrative structures — that between the divisions of the ministries and ministerial *cabinets*, discussed briefly above. The nature of the *cabinets* that the new ministers formed around themselves, and the characteristics of the five hundred or more individuals who found themselves in post within them have already been the subject of a full-length study.[68] Its authors have been able to demonstrate the extent to which the arrival in power of a left-wing government has meant an almost complete change in the personnel of the *cabinets*. This has produced the occasional irony. Anicet le Pors, the Minister for the Civil Service, found himself negotiating with the civil service unions backed by a *cabinet* team which included several people formerly active on the staff of the unions whom they confronted. There are elements both of continuity and of change in the make-up of the new *cabinets*. In the first place, it is clear that a larger number of *cabinet* members have been politically active. Only 31 per cent of those studied were not members of a political party and 61 per cent of those studied were classified as politically active, as opposed to being merely members, sympathizers, or non-political. This contrasts with Dr Ella Searls's finding, in her study of Giscardian *cabinets*, that many *cabinet* members were not politically active before their entry into a *cabinet* and that the number of party activists working within *cabinets* was small.[69] It also seems that the coming of the new dispensation has greatly diminished the numbers of those who have been able to 'flit between *cabinets*, for fifteen years or more'.[70] It is certainly true that certain members of the Mauroy Government's *cabinets* found themselves in post because of the recommendation of their own *corps* or administration. However, although the *cabinet* of Laurent Fabius, Budget Minister from 1981 until March 1983, included a tax specialist who had also served in his predecessor's *cabinet*, this appears to be very much an exception, and the authors of *L'Élite rose* estimate that only some 8 per cent of 122 *cabinet* members interviewed owed their posts chiefly to technical competence alone.

There have been changes, too, in the professional background of *cabinet* members. Dr Searls estimated that 90 per cent of the members of the *cabinets* she studied were civil servants.[71] In 1980 about half the *cabinet* members were graduates of the ENA, and over the period 1958–76 a total of 13 per cent of *cabinet* members were members of one of the three main non-technical *grands corps*.[72] After 1981, although 65 per cent of *cabinet* members were civil servants, only 29 per cent were graduates of the ENA and only 7 per cent members of a non-technical *grands corps*.[73]

It is important to be cautious about the interpretation of these facts. Sweeping change was to be expected, and in terms of personnel has occurred. A number of people such as former academics and former staff of political parties and trade unions who certainly were not previously part of the network of those who dispose of key positions now find themselves at very central points of the governmental process.[74] But half of them come from families described as belonging to the elite,[75] and over 40 per cent have previously formed part of the administrative services of the ministry in whose minister's *cabinet* they serve. Ella Searls points out that 'In order for governments to implement programmes on which they were elected they need to build effective bridges of communication between the political and administrative worlds.[76] The need for an incoming government to reinforce its political control over its administration, especially in the implementation of change, has probably exacerbated the inevitable tension between *cabinets* and divisions, and the selection of personnel, while reinforcing ministers' political backing, may also have contributed to problems and misunder-standings.[77]

Where ministers desire to give particular impulsion to a certain policy, and to some extent to force the hands of the administrative divisions, judicious appointments at senior level and *cabinet* oversight may be adequate. Other techniques also exist, however. They are not specific to the Mitterrand Government, but both have been used by it. One is the commissioning of a special report upon a policy problem area, which may then be published. There is a sense in which such reports fulfil the functions of the white and green papers of the British Government; indeed, their scope goes wider and relatively minor policy changes may benefit from public presentation in the form of reports. They are none the less also a useful means of reinforcing a particular policy line within an administration.

Another technique which has also been adopted is the setting up of administrative units outside the normal structures with the task of forwarding a particular development. Such *administrations de mission* were known under previous regimes. A well-regarded and highly placed leader, who may gather a small team about him, is charged with ensuring that all the necessary branches of the perhaps more rigid administrative structures cooperate towards the achievement of the government's aims. The appointment of Pierre Lalumière as *Délégué-Général à la Décentralisation*, with a particular brief to consider the medium-term problems of decentralization especially the financial aspects, was one such action. Lalumière had, however, left the post by the beginning of 1982. In the vital field of employment the Prime Minister, Pierre Mauroy, appointed in 1982 a special mission under Jean Saint-Geours, a very senior and distinguished *Inspecteur des Finances* with long experience both in banking and administration.

CONCLUSION

The coming into power of a government based upon an organized, coherent and politically self-conscious party has greatly affected relationships between the Government and the senior civil service. The relationships between ministers and the political parties between 1958 and 1981 had been complex, but in general the role of the parties had been seen very much as providing the necessary political and legislative support to a government, or perhaps even more to a President. Ministers, from this point of view, had become increasingly the 'technicians' or 'officials' of politics. President Giscard abandoned the attempt to include the leaders of the main political forces that made up the coalition that supported him as members of the Government. Civil servants, whether in the divisions of the ministries or in the *cabinets*, had to reckon only with the political direction which emanated ultimately from the President and from ministers working in close collaboration with him. 'On the pretext of depoliticising the exercise of the governmental function and of associating with it the higher civil service, the *République gaullienne* in fact brought politics and administration closer together and "officialized" the politicians.'[78]

The politicians who have come into power since May 1981 have not, however, been so 'officialized'. They have firmly retained their links with their parties. Mitterrand has been anxious to ensure continuing close contact with the Socialist Party both within and outside the National Assembly. Ministers too have recognized the importance of the Party, and the joint seminar held at Maisons-Laffitte in July 1982 between Socialist Party members and elected representatives and ministers was a sign that the Government did not intend that the party should be cut off from the policy-making process. To some observers steeped in the habits and rhetoric of the earlier years of the Fifth Republic this seemed little less than shocking. Yet certainly it is this close association between ministers and their party that explains the somewhat changed nature and greatly increased weight of the *cabinets* in the policy-making process within ministries.

The response to so changed a situation has been, in many cases, slowness and uncertainty, and this too has caused an increase in political surveillance of civil service activities. There is, however, relatively little evidence of intentional sabotage or even of excessive obstruction. The Government, on its side, has refrained from calling into question the main structures of the civil service. Moreover, the presence within the civil service of a number of officials who had already been active within the party provided a reservoir from which ministers have been able to draw candidates for appointments in *cabinets* and in senior posts. The application of the austerity policies in the autumn of 1982 , and especially the decision that civil servants should pay unemployment insurance contributions, produced a great deal of restlessness within the civil service. Certain groups had hoped for rapid action to improve their position and have so far been disappointed. So far, however, serious confrontation has been avoided.

At the centre of the French system of government there exists a powerful tension. It is the tension between the legitimacy of the democratically elected representative, returned on the strength of a specific, and now usually partisan, programme, on the one hand, and the power of the state, seeking the general interest, on the other. Bodiguel and Quermonne characterize it as the tension between *les Français* and *la France*.[79] Of the factors discussed above, the strength of the legitimacy of the civil service, and the nature of its response to political change have proved to be sources of stability. The effects of the administrative environment, however, and, most of all, of the Government's use of the means at its disposal to enforce its own political direction have been forces for change. *L'alternance* has reinforced political control over the Administration.

## NOTES

1. Robert Catherine and Guy Thuillier, *L'Être administratif et l'imaginaire* (Paris: Economica, 1982), p. 13. All translations, unless otherwise acknowledged, are by the author.
2. Jacques Chevallier, 'Un nouveau sens de l'État et du Service Public', in de Baecque and Quermonne, *Administration et politique*, op. cit., p. 170.
3. Kenneth Dyson, *The State Tradition in Western Europe* (Oxford: Martin Robertson, 1980), pp. 51–2.
4. Catherine and Thuillier, *L'Être administratif*, op. cit., p. 9. The choice of the masculine pronoun throughout this chapter to refer to higher civil servants is not entirely based on traditional usage. Very few senior civil servants in France are women; in the first thirty years of its existence, the École Nationale d'Administration produced just over one hundred female graduates and some two and a half thousand male graduates. In the past decade the proportion of women graduating annually had risen to 10–15 per cent.
5. R.F. Kuisel, 'Technocrats and Public Economic Policy: From the Third to the Fourth Republic', *Journal of European Economic History*, vol. 2, No. 1 (Spring 1973), p. 83.
6. R.F. Kuisel, *Capitalism and the State in Modern France* (Cambridge: Cambridge University Press, 1981), p. 255. See also Jean Saint-Geours, *Pouvoir et finance* (Paris: Fayard, 1979), pp. 47–9.
7. Ezra Suleiman, *Elites in French Society* (Princeton: Princeton University Press, 1978), p. 262.
8. Suleiman, ibid., p. 113.
9. Jean-Luc Bodiguel, *L'École Nationale d'Administration: les anciens élèves de l'ENA* (Paris: Presses Universitaires de France, 1978), p. 207.
10. With the sole and isolated exception of the students of *promotion* 'Charles de Gaulle' in 1972.
11. *Le Point*, 21 May 1974.
12. Ibid.
13. Catherine and Thuillier, *L'Être administratif*, op. cit., p. 9.
14. Catherine Lalumière in *L'Unité*, October 1975, quoted in Institut Français des Sciences Administratives, *L'Administration vue par les politiques* (Paris: Cujas, 1978), p. 154.
15. Jacques Mandrin, *L'Énarchie ou les mandarins de la société bourgeoise* (Paris: La Table Ronde de Combat, 2<sup>e</sup> edn. 1980), pp. 159–60.
16. *Le Monde*, 22–23 March 1983.
17. J.-L. Bodiguel and J.-L. Quermonne, *La Haute Fonction publique sous la V<sup>e</sup> République* (Paris: Presses Universitaires de France, 1983), pp. 251–2.
18. Ezra Suleiman, *Politics, Power and Bureaucracy in France: The Administrative Elite* (Princeton: Princeton University Press, 1974), p. 263.
19. Interview, Ministry of Finance, October 1977.
20. Saint-Geours, *Pouvoir et finance*, op. cit., pp. 55–6.
21. Suleiman, *Élites* . . . , op. cit., p. 242.
22. Ibid., p. 247.

23. Jean-Claude Thoenig, *L'Ère des technocrates: le cas des ponts et chaussées* (Paris: Les Éditions d'Organisation, 1973), p. 61.
24. Jean-Luc Bodiguel and Marie-Christine Kessler, 'La Haute Fonction publique en France', unpublished note prepared for the Groupe d'Études Comparatives sur la Fonction Publique (February 1979), p. 88.
25. Francis de Baecque, *L'Administration centrale de la France* (Paris: Armand Colin, 1973), p. 189.
26. Interview with former ENA student, internal entrant with previous experience in the Administration, graduated 1954, October 1977.
27. Diana Green, *Economic and Financial Decision Making in the Fifth French Republic* (unpublished doctoral thesis, London School of Economics and Political Science, 1976), p. 237.
28. Saint-Geours, *Pouvoir et finance*, op. cit., p. 206.
29. Jean-René Bernard in *Le Monde*, 29 December 1976.
30. John Zysman, *Political Strategies for Industrial Order: State, Market and Industry in France* (Berkeley and Los Angeles: University of California Press, 1977), p. 195.
31. J. Chevallier, 'Un nouveau sens de L'État . . . ', op. cit., p. 31.
32. Catherine and Thuillier, *L'Être administratif . . .*, op. cit., p. 31.
33. Thus 'M. le Préfet, Commissaire de le République . . .'. See John Frears, 'The Decentralisation Reforms in France', *Parliamentary Affairs*, vol. 36, No. 1 (Winter 1983), p. 60.
34. Saul Estrin and Peter Holmes, *French Planning in Theory and Practice* (London: George Allen & Unwin, 1983), p. 108.
35. Catherine and Thuillier, *L'Être administratif . . .*, op. cit., p. 19.
36. De Baecque and Quermonne, *Administration et politique . . .*, op. cit., p. 14
37. R. Kuisel, *Capitalism and the State . . .*, op. cit., p. 254.
38. Catherine and Thuillier, *L'Être administratif . . .*, op. cit., p. 15.
39. Bodiguel and Quermonne, *La Haute Fonction publique . . .*, op. cit., p. 77.
40. There have been a few notable contributions by sociologists, for example, Catherine Grémion, *Profession: décideurs* (Paris:Gauthier-Villars, 1979), but these have been few and far between.
41. Sir Kenneth Clucas, 'Parliament and the Civil Service', in Royal Institute of Public Administration, *Parliament and the Executive* (London: Royal Institute of Public Administration, 1982), p. 40.
42. R. Riemer, *The National School of Administration: Selection and Preparation of an Elite in Post War France* (unpublished doctoral thesis, Johns Hopkins University, 1976), p. 309.
43. For example, Vincent Wright quotes the French withdrawal from the military side of NATO. Vincent Wright, *The Government and Politics of France* (London: Hutchinson, 2nd edn., 1983), pp. 113–14.
44. Helen Wallace, *National Governments and the European Communities* (London: Chatham House PEP, 1973), pp. 86–7.
45. In 1983 three sets of briefing papers were prepared. And there are sometimes further ramifications. On the papers prepared in the Department of Energy in 1974 for an incoming Labour minister (if *not* Mr. Benn), see Tony Benn, 'Manifestos and Mandarins', in Royal Institute of Public Administration, *Policy and Practice: the Experience of Government* (London: Royal Institute of Public Administration, 1980), p. 67.
46. *Le Nouvel Observateur*, 6 June 1981.
47. *Le Nouvel Observateur*, 18 May 1981.
48. Bodiguel and Quermonne, *La Haute Fonction publique . . .*, op. cit., p. 111.
49. Jeanne Siwek-Pouydesseau, *Le Personnel de direction des ministères* (Paris: Armand Colin, 1969), p. 7.
50. François Bardos, 'Chasse aux Sorcières?', '81: la gauche au pouvoir', *Pouvoirs*, No. 20, (1982), p. 101.
51. *Le Monde*, 26 June 1982.
52. Douglas Ashford, 'Decentralising France: Opportunities and Risks of the *loi Defferre*', in John Ambler, ed., *Mitterrand's Republic* (New York: forthcoming).
53. They included MM. Charles-Noël Hardy, Jacques Perillat and Jean Anciaud. Yves Agnès in *Le Monde*, 29 June 1982.
54. *Le Monde*, 7 October 1982.
55. Personal communication from Dr Howard Machin.
56. Paul-Marie de la Gorce, *L'Après-Guerre* (Paris: Grasset, 1978), p. 326.
57. Raymond Kuhn, 'Broadcasting and Politics in France', *Parliamentary Affairs*, 36, No. 1 (Winter 1983), p. 71.

58. Yves Agnès, in *Le Monde*, 29 June 1982.
59. *Nouvel Observateur*, October 1982.
60. Paul-Marie de la Gorce, *L'Après-Guerre*, op. cit., p. 326.
61. René Remond, Aline Coutrot and Isabel Boussard, *Quarante ans de cabinets ministériels* (Paris: Presses de la FNSP, 1982), pp. 224–5.
62. Ibid., p. 221.
63. *Le Monde*, 13 November 1981.
64. Monique Dagnaud and Dominique Mehl, *L'Élite rose: qui gouverne?* (Paris: Éditions Ramsay, 1982), pp. 308 and 296.
65. Irwin M. Wall, 'Socialists and Bureaucrats: The Blum Government and the French Administration 1936–7', *International Review of Social History*, XIX (1974), p. 326.
66. *Le Monde*, 30 June 1982.
67. *Le Monde*, 15 October 1981.
68. Dagnaud and Mehl, *L'Élite rose . . .*, op. cit.
69. Ella Searls, 'Ministerial *Cabinets* and Elite Theory', in Jolyon Howorth and Philip G. Cerny, eds, *Elites in France: Origins, Reproduction and Power* (London and New York: Frances Pinter and St. Martin's Press, 1981), p. 174.
70. Ibid.
71. Ibid., p. 173.
72. Rémond *et al.*, *Quarante ans . . .* , op. cit., p. 87.
73. Dagnaud and Mehl, *L'Élite rose . . .* , op. cit., p. 328.
74. Mauroy's *cabinet* in 1981–2 contained several people (Alduy, Corbin, Rollet) who had previously been members of the rather marginalized 'confraternité de la planification', on which see Estrin and Holmes, *French Planning . . .*, op. cit., p. 95.
75. Dagnaud and Mehl, *L'Élite rose . . .*, op. cit., p. 326. They define elite (p. 342) as 'senior official, liberal professions, industrialist, large-scale commerce, senior executive in private sector, high rank in armed forces'.
76. Ella Searls, 'Ministerial *Cabinets . . .*', op. cit., p. 178.
77. Interview, Ministry of Finance, November 1982. In an article in *Le Monde* (3 November 1982), J.-P. Soisson, a Giscardian former minister, described the current state of relationships between *cabinets* and their ministries as 'une immense pagaille' (a huge mess).
78. De Baecque and Quermonne, *Administration et politique . . .*, op. cit., p. 361.
79. Bodiguel and Quermonne, *La Haute Fonction publique . . .*, op. cit., p. 79.

# 8. The Tranquil Revolution at Clochemerle: Socialist Decentralization in France*

*Mark Kesselman*

After being consigned to the opposition for the first two decades of the Fifth Republic, the Socialist Party's 1981 sweep brought it control of every major political office in France. Yet, rather than enjoying the fruits of the most centralized political system of any capitalist democracy, the Socialist Government immediately proposed a substantial transfer of power from the national bureaucracy to sub-national governments. Within a year, the *loi Defferre* was enacted, followed soon after by two major additional decent- ralization laws and a host of other laws and administrative decrees. To what extent does this vast reform represent a rupture with past trends and to what extent does it merely codify them? What is the rationale for the Socialist Government's decentralization reform and how does decentralization relate to the left's overall project? These are among the issues suggested by the Government's surprising initiative that will be examined in this chapter.

The Socialist Party's attachment to decentralization initially developed during the period when it was excluded from national office and gained a strong local base. The party's commitment to increase the power of sub- national government is understandable in light of the large number of local officeholders who are Socialist militants. The PS gained local primacy years before it captured national office. Yet the left's fidelity to decentralization has deeper causes: decentralization is a central ingredient in the overall Socialist project, which seeks to rationalize the state, revitalize civil society, and alter the balance between the two. Within this project, vibrant local governments serve as a buckle (to use Bagehot's metaphor) linking state and civil society. The decentralization reforms aim to strengthen the regulatory capacity of local government and civil society, thereby relieving the state of primary responsibility for regulating local socioeconomic and political conflicts.

When Socialist electoral platforms in the 1970s and 1980s pledged a commitment to decentralization, scholars of French local politics under- standably assumed that this was no more than an out-party's attempt to capitalize on popular opposition to the cumbersome French bureaucracy. Peter Gourevitch discerns 'the following decision-making rule among French politicians: when in the opposition, support decentralization; when in power

* Earlier drafts of this paper were presented at the conference on Local Institutions in National Development: Strategies and Consequences of Local-National Linkages in the Industrial Democracies, sponsored by the Social Science Research Council, Bellagio, Italy, 15-18 March 1982, and at the 79th annual meeting of the American Political Science Association, Chicago, 1-4 September 1983. I am grateful for suggestions from conference participants and other colleagues, including Michael Aiken, Douglas Ashford, Edmond Preteceille, and Martin Schain. I am particularly grateful for the generous cooperation of French political party activists, local elected representatives, and government administrators. Financial assistance was provided by a Rockefeller Foundation Humanities Fellowship in 1981-2. A condensed version of this paper was published in *Contemporary French Civilization*, VIII, Nos. 1-2 (Fall- Winter, 1983-4).

hang on to all the instruments centralization provides.'[1] Gourevitch predicted that a left victory would not bring a 'massive reshuffling of the redistribution of power among [levels of government institutions] . . .' Writing in 1980, he suggested, 'Over the next ten years, one can predict little dramatic change in the territorial distribution of power in France . . .'[2]

Vincent Wright agreed: 'zeal for decentralization varies in inverse proportion to the prospects and realities of holding office.'[3] Ezra Suleiman asserts, 'Precisely because decentralization whittles away the power of the major administrative corps, it has been, and will continue to be, resisted and sabotaged all the way.'[4] At the very moment that Douglas Ashford's extraordinary comparison of French and British policy-making was in press, events belied his observation that '. . . France cannot engage in massive structural change of the subnational system.'[5] Sidney Tarrow provided a thorough analysis of the constraints on local government reform in France — but ignored the possibility that they might be overcome.[6] These astute observers correctly emphasized that intergovernmental relations in France have demonstrated incredible resiliency, durability, and resistance to change.

While local governmental reform has been widely discussed, decades of abortive reform efforts suggest how difficult it is to achieve. Save for the Vichy regime, the only previous comparably ambitious attempt to reform sub-national government in this century was Charles de Gaulle's 1969 referendum organizing regional government and weakening the Senate — and local notables responded by closing ranks to force de Gaulle from office. Subsequent reform efforts were modest and piecemeal . . . until 1981. An additional anomaly is that decentralization has been sponsored by the left, usually viewed as Jacobin.[7] And yet there is a powerful rationale for the rapid timing and sweeping character of the decentralization reform.

## BACKGROUND TO DECENTRALIZATION

The Socialist decentralization reforms are a response to widespread demands for additional autonomy by energetic local elected officials. In some respects, the trend of past decades was quite opposite, as a corporate rationalizing state tore asunder the traditional web of relationships linking local elected officials to state administrators, especially the prefect.[8] In recent years, the state imposed increasingly stringent technical and financial procedures on local activities, a practice informally designated as the technical and financial *tutelle* (tutelage) as opposed to traditional prefectoral oversight. Although local officials loudly proclaimed their opposition to prefectoral supervision, in fact it was not only not unpopular but often positively welcomed.

At the same time that local governments were subject to increasing technical supervision, their financial burdens increased. Between 1959 and 1970, the proportion of local governmental expenditures for capital investments as a proportion of all public investment increased from 56 percent to 68 percent, and by 1980 it had risen to 75 percent.[9] Further, despite their narrow and inelastic tax base, local governments were forced to finance an increasing share of public investments. Between 1962 and 1977, state subsidies fell from 28 to 12 percent of local investments. Between 1975 and 1979, local taxes rose 30 percent in constant francs; moreover, local taxes increased from 24 to 35 percent of all direct taxes.[10]

Alain Richard, National Assembly floor manager for the *loi Defferre*, suggested that a major cause of Giscard's defeat was citizen disgust with the increasing weight of the state bureaucracy. He argued that decentralization will encourage local governments to fashion their own solutions to social and economic problems.[11] The model for this approach was provided by Socialists who led local governments while in opposition. Both Prime Minister Pierre Mauroy and Interior Minister Gaston Defferre were mayors of large cities and presidents of regional councils for many years. (Thanks to the *cumul*, both continued to serve as mayor after joining the Government.) During the Giscard regime, they attempted, with considerable success, to circumvent state restrictions on local government activity. At Marseille, under Defferre's leadership, the city government purchased factories and equipment from bankrupt firms and made them available to new entrepreneurs, in an attempt to salvage jobs. The Provence regional council, which Defferre chaired, organized an agency to promote tourism in Provence. In the North, Mauroy's regional council developed regional transportation facilities. These innovations stretched — or exceeded — state regulations. One of the newly elected Socialist Government's first actions was to rescind a ministerial circular issued by the previous Government that limited regional council initiatives.[12]

The impetus for the reform could be traced to modernizing forces within the Socialist Party, including big-city mayors (the PS was the leading party among urban mayors — and continues to be despite the party's setback in the 1983 municipal elections). Support for decentralization derived from local party activists who joined the PS in the period after 1968, when the party sought to embrace the May 1968 call for *autogestion*. The PCF also threw its support behind decentralization; it had long criticized the administrative framework which limited local autonomy. This coalition overcame the tacit yet durable alliance of state administrators and traditional local notables that had blocked previous reform efforts. State administrators had derived extensive benefits from the status quo; many local politicians also preferred the existing situation, in which they served as privileged intermediaries with the national bureaucracy and could evade accountability by using the state as a scapegoat. In 1981, armed with a fresh electoral mandate and firm command of France's centralized political institutions, the Socialist Government was in an excellent position to break this logjam.

Interior Minister Defferre (whose position was redesignated Minister of Interior and Decentralization) devised an ingenious strategy to overcome the difficulties encountered in past reform efforts.[13] (For example, the last comprehensive decentralization proposal had become mired in interminable parliamentary debate, not surprising given the scope and complexity of the issues addressed.) Defferre initiated the decentralization reform in stages, rather than combining all aspects of decentralization in a single omnibus bill. The first phase of decentralization was launched before reform energies began to dissipate and newly appointed cabinet ministers came to share their departments' aversion to relinquishing power.[14] The first bill was mostly confined to reorganizing interrelations between sub-national governments and the state. By initially granting local officials greater autonomy within their existing areas of competence, Defferre correctly calculated that they would soon mobilize to seek enlarged powers.

The procedure succeeded brilliantly. Initially, attitudes toward decentralization divided along partisan lines (although, within the Socialist party itself, there was some resistance, for example, from the statist CERES faction). However, many opposition politicians, especially local officeholders, quickly recognized the value of decentralization and began to demand additional power. Support for decentralization outside the left increased when opposition parties outpolled the left in 1982 cantonal and 1983 municipal elections. Whereas in 1981-2 the opposition vociferously criticized the Government's decentralization plan as a devious plot to consolidate left control, by 1983 it vociferously criticized the Government's delay in implementing decentralization!

The Government initially projected three phases of the decentralization reforms: the first proposal, introduced in the National Assembly weeks after the 1981 Socialist victory and enacted 2 March 1982, restructured intergovernmental relations by reducing state supervision of local governments. The *loi Defferre* did not much alter local governmental political functions: that was the object of laws passed 7 January 1983 and 7 July 1983. The third projected phase of the reform package was to involve increasing the local tax base. After a transitional period, when the Government promised to transfer sufficient funds to finance local governments' enlarged political responsibilities, a comprehensive reform was to rationalize thoroughly the cumbersome, antiquated, and inequitable system of local taxes. If the Government were to enact and implement these reforms, the result would amply justify former Prime Minister Mauroy's characterization of decentralization as 'la grande affaire du septennat' (the major reform of President Mitterrand's seven-year term). To what extent has this occurred? What is the Socialist Party's motivation for sponsoring the reform? What is the character of the reforms and their relationship to the overall Socialist project?

## INTERGOVERNMENTAL RELATIONS: THE END OF THE *TUTELLE*

The basic principle regulating intergovernmental relations in France has been that, although local governments enjoy a constitutional right to exist, they exercise only those powers delegated by the state, in a manner prescribed by the state, under tight administrative control (prior state approval was required for virtually all local governmental activities), and with state bureaucrats directly administering many local governmental activities. Actual practice differed sharply from this legal model. For example, local politicians forged alliances with state administrative officials and gained direct access to the center by simultaneously holding national political office (the *cumul*). Informal networks were at variance with juridical description. Big cities enjoyed considerable autonomy, thanks to their technical staffs, financial resources, and the political clout of their mayors. Yet these developments, described in ample detail by decades of 'revisionist' scholarship on French local government, did not alter the fact that the state possessed a near-monopoly of most governmental functions.

While the Socialist decentralization measures do not modify constitutional principles — France remains a unitary state — they substantially increase local governments' legal autonomy. Henceforth, local governments are no longer considered, in effect, administrative arms of the national bureaucracy but autonomous institutions possessing their own democratic legitimacy and proper powers. They are granted specific areas of responsibility formerly the prerogative of the national government, and state supervision has been sharply reduced. Within their enlarged areas of competence, local governments are effectively autonomous; the previous system of supervision, consisting of prior clearance by administrative officials, has been replaced by *ex post* quasi-judicial scrutiny by administrative and financial tribunals. State administrators are now charged with tending the state's business rather than supervising and administering local governmental affairs.

This summary, however, must be qualified in several respects. First, it accentuates the contrast between past and present, minimizing important continuities and past trends. Second, it implicitly assumes that the decentralization reforms will be completed and implemented as announced, which is far from certain. Third, it reflects official descriptions; the reality is more complex. These issues will be examined after details of the reforms have been enumerated.

1. The administrative *tutelle* — the system of prior approval exercised by the prefect over local governmental decisions, and widely regarded as the linchpin of French intergovernmental relations — was abolished by the *loi Defferre*. Local decisions are now self-executory after a brief period. The prefect (renamed the state's representative in the department or region) can no longer veto local decisions. If the prefect judges a local decision to be illegal, he or she is merely authorized to sue in an administrative tribunal following its promulgation.

    The *tutelle* had already lost much of its bite. A 1970 law limited the number of local decisions which required authorization, the *tutelle* had been transformed into a system of tacit approval, and, in recent years, local decisions could be vetoed only on grounds of illegality, not because the prefect judged them to be unwise. None the less, the *tutelle* continued to be a symbol of state prerogatives, a threat to be brandished, and a sheer nuisance. One scholar characterized its abolition as 'a profound modification of the traditional conception of intergovernmental relations ...'[15]

    The *loi Defferre* mandated substantial changes in the financial and technical features of state supervision. First, the power to order the disbursement of expenditures voted by local governments has been transferred from agents of the Ministry of Finance to the elected executives of local governments. Formerly, centrally appointed financial officers could refuse to make local expenditures if they considered them illegal. Henceforth, local officials order payments, although their actions can be challenged in newly created regional financial tribunals whose mandate also includes conducting an annual audit of local expenditures. The new procedure considerably reduces state controls, especially since parliamentary pressure forced the Government to modify its initial plan to impose substantial sanctions on local officials for financial irregularities.

    The *loi Defferre* mandated the state bureaucracy to rationalize and simplify the technical regulations which local governments must observe in sponsoring local investments. Through the years, state technical ministries, including housing, urbanism and construction, specified innumerable procedures for local projects (a senatorial commission estimated the number to exceed 10,000). These procedures were an indirect method of subordinating local governments to the state bureaucracy. Local officials objected far more to the 'technical *tutelle*' than to the prefect's administrative *tutelle*. The *loi Defferre* specified that mandatory procedures can be imposed only by a law or implementing decree and must be included in a code of technical procedures.

2. Transferring the executive power of departmental and regional governments. Until 1982, local governmental subordination to the state was epitomized by the fact that the prefect acted as the executive of departmental and regional government. The prefect was responsible for convening the council, deciding its agenda, preparing the dossiers to be examined, proposing the local budget, executing council decisions, and supervising the prefectorial bureaucracy. The elected president of the council was a figurehead who presided over council meetings but had few independent powers.

The *loi Defferre* transferred all responsibility for local executive functions from the prefect to the local council's elected president. Hence, the president became the hierarchical superior of the departmental and regional bureaucracy, which were formerly integrated into the state administration. The shift necessitated dividing prefectoral personnel between those within the departmental or regional jurisdiction as opposed to those who remained part of the state field administration. In a transitional period, the prefect, council president and civil servants' union representatives negotiated agreements in each department and region dividing prefectoral services. However, prefectoral civil servants often resisted transfer to the less prestigious, less privileged and less secure sector of sub-national governments. The Government devised a compromise in which, during the transitional period, those civil servants transferred to departmental or regional governments would retain national civil servant status. The Government meanwhile proposed civil service reform in the fall of 1983 to create comparable rights and benefits for administrative personnel of sub-national governments to those enjoyed by national civil servants. Within several years, a definitive division will be decided.

The elected presidents of departmental and regional councils are the major beneficiaries of the decentralization reform and have been catapulted to a position of major importance within the French political system, especially given departmental regional governments' new powers reviewed below. Conversely, prefects lost substantial power by the reforms. They no longer exercise prior clearance over local decisions, act as executive of the department or region, or direct the administrative services attached to departmental or regional government. However, the former prefects are granted new supervisory powers over state field administrators, partially offsetting their loss of power over local government. Prior to 1982, they represented the Ministry of the Interior in the department or region, and were authorized merely to *coordinate* the other field services of the state in their locality. Henceforth, they are the official representative of the entire Government and (with certain exceptions) are empowered to *direct* all state field services. Further, they have been delegated new responsibility for administrative activities formerly conducted within Paris ministries, additional control over allocating state investment subsidies, and are authorized to participate in preparing and executing the national plan as well as coordinating regional and national plans. These changes aim to separate levels of government, increase the autonomy of sub-national governments and rationalize the state administration.

3. The *loi Defferre* contained two provisions for enlarging the powers of local governments. First, the department is authorized to create a technical agency to assist local governments that cannot afford technical staffs and that request its services. This is intended to reduce local dependence on state technical officials (especially those in the powerful Department of Civil Engineering (DDE)).

Second, the *loi Defferre* authorizes local governments to facilitate economic development and protect the economic and social interests of their constituents. Local governments can henceforth provide direct subsidies, loans or loan guarantees, as well as purchase building and equipment for private businesses and producers' cooperatives. (Local governments have subsidized non-profit community associations in the past; the new measure extends this approach to the economic sphere.) Certain restrictions apply: local governments must not infringe free trade, must ensure equality of citizens before the law, and act in conformity with the national and regional plans. They may not purchase stock in a profit-making firm, save where the firm provides a municipal service. And local governments must balance their budgets and limit loan guarantees. (These restrictions are relaxed when a local government intervenes to protect a firm threatened with bankruptcy.) This measure was among the most controversial in the *loi Defferre* and was modelled on past practice by activist Socialist mayors. Opposition politicians charged that it would encourage waste and would distort market forces. Although one cannot yet evaluate the extent of local economic intervention, some village governments have already purchased buildings and equipment for local commerce (grocery stores, bakeries, etc.) which they have leased at subsidized rates to ensure provision of local services. Although the *loi Defferre* creates broad latitude for local intervention, the economic crisis severely limits possibilities.

4. With regard to regional government, previously the region had the limited status of a specialized agency, comparable to a port authority or other quasi-public organization. The *loi Defferre* transformed regions into full-fledged local governments, identical in law to municipal and departmental governments. Regional governments are granted new powers of coordinating public investments in the region, supervising vocational training programs, and (most importantly) developing regional plans for economic, social, and cultural development. The regional institutional structure now parallels the municipal and departmental model. In the past, most regional councillors were elected by mayors and departmental councillors; the remaining members were deputies and senators from the region who sat ex officio. Henceforth, the *loi Defferre* specified that regional councillors will be directly elected by universal suffrage. Further, as noted above, the council's elected president has become the regional executive. In an interim period, before regional council elections are held, the regional government exercises restricted powers.

The *loi Defferre* is the most important reorganization of French local government in decades. However, because it did not much alter the jurisdiction of local government — and the Government had not announced its plans in this regard when the law was debated — the opposition dismissed it as an 'empty shell'. The situation changed with the two laws on transfer of political powers that were passed in 1983.

TRANSFERRING POLITICAL POWERS

Although economic and political factors led the Government to reduce the scope of its initial proposals, the powers transferred by the two laws passed in 1983 range across the spectrum of state activity. The Government announced that three principles guided its actions. First, as far as possible, the Government sought to transfer complete responsibility for a given function to a single level of government, thus promoting specialization. The broad division announced by the Government was that regional governments are responsible for planning overall development, departmental governments are responsible for administering services, as well as reducing financial disparities among localities (*péréquation*), and municipal governments for urban planning, citizen participation, and regulating daily political life. However, it quickly realized that, as generations of scholars analyzing American intergovernmental relations have argued, political functions simply cannot be divided by levels of government.

Second, the Government sought to prevent hierarchical relations among sub-national governments by prohibiting them from exercising supervisory powers over each other. While sub-national governments are encouraged to negotiate cooperative arrangements with one another, only the state can impose rules and regulations on other governmental levels. Pierre Grémion aptly terms this the Government's non-decision regarding whether the department or region would be accorded priority.[16] By dodging the issue, the Government tried to forestall conflicts between partisans of the department — primarily traditional notables — and partisans of regional government — more 'modernist' elements among politicians, trade union leaders, and local associations. A related principle was that powers were transferred from the center to sub-national governments, not from one level of sub-national government to another. Further, the Government decided not to consolidate municipal governments — whose number exceeds that of all other countries in Western Europe combined. This decision was defended on the grounds that citizens were attached to their local government; the Government thus avoided a major political battle which would have alienated many of the Socialist Government's own militants (who include many local officeholders).

Third, the Government promised that, until it carries out a comprehensive local tax reform, it would provide sufficient subsidies and tax transfers to finance the new political responsibilities being decentralized. The principle was to ensure that local governments would not be compelled to raise local taxes to finance their new activities.

The powers transferred by the two laws of 1983 (with the actual transfers to be phased over three years beginning in 1983) include:

1. Regional planning, regional economic development, and coordination of public investments. The regional government participates in elaborating the national plan and the development of national guidelines for regional development (*aménagement du territoire*). The regional council develops and approves a regional plan that runs concurrently with the four-year national plan. The national planning reform authorized the national planning agency to negotiate planning contracts with the regional government and other groups, in which state assistance is provided for projects which further national planning objectives. At the

departmental level, the president of the general council and the departmental prefect jointly sponsor an annual conference to coordinate public investments in the department; a similar conference is held twice yearly at the regional level.

2. Urbanism. The most important transfer to municipal governments concerns the power to develop local zoning regulations (and, at the level of urban agglomerations, a metropolitan plan) and to issue building permits in conformity with the local plan. This shift is of major importance, for it transfers responsibility for orienting land use from the Ministry of Urbanism to local elected officials. If localities choose not to develop a land-use plan, they have sharply restricted powers to issue building permits. Localities lacking the technical staff to prepare a land-use plan can request the assistance of state agencies in preparing a draft plan.

3. Housing. Although the Government initially intended to transfer responsibility for public housing construction to sub-national governments, it reversed itself on the grounds that there was a need for a crash program of housing construction, given the acute housing shortage and the Barre Government's refusal to sponsor public housing construction. In addition, public housing construction was to serve as a chief instrument in counter-cyclical macroeconomic policy to stimulate economic growth. Whereas all levels of sub-national governments gained a role in developing housing priorities, with the regional government authorized partially to subsidize public housing construction, the national government retained major responsibility in this sphere. Further, the economic crisis forced a scaling down of the Government's ambitious public housing program.

4. Vocational training and apprenticeship programs. Major responsibility is transferred from the national to regional governments, who will allocate funds for vocational training from a business tax of 1.1 percent and from funds obtained by transfer of motor vehicle taxes to regional governments.

The Government initially introduced legislation in the Senate in the fall of 1982 which included the above measures and other proposals. However, the crush of parliamentary business led to an abrupt change in procedure. The Government postponed consideration of additional measures, which were not scheduled to be transferred until 1984 and 1985, for a second bill on transferring political powers that was introduced in early 1983 and passed in July 1983. It included:

5. Transport. Decentralization measures, included in a separate reform of transportation facilities, delegated to regional governments major responsibility for establishing a regional transportation plan, with departmental governments responsible for coordinating and administering public transportation facilities. Local governments were delegated new responsibilities for ports and navigable waterways.

6. Education. Municipal governments were empowered to sponsor elementary school construction. On the basis of a program developed by departmental and regional governments, the regional prefect establishes a construction program for secondary schools; departmental and regional governments direct construction. Local governments will assume the costs of construction and upkeep of schools, while the

national government remains responsible for training, hiring, and paying teachers, curriculum development, and all aspects of higher education.

7. Public health and social welfare. Most public health and social welfare programs are transferred to the departmental level, with the state setting minimum payment levels.

8. Financing the cost of decentralization. The Government financed the costs of responsibilities transferred to local governments by two procedures: a transfer of tax resources and a direct grant (*dotation générale de décentralisation*). The Government also maintained a bloc grant initiated by the previous Government for underwriting current expenses of sub-national governments (*dotation globale de fonctionnement*) as well as creating a new bloc grant for investments (*dotation globale d'équipement*) which was to be a first step toward consolidating the previous system of categorical grants. An additional grant was created for subsidizing local cultural activities and projects.

The Government initially promised to sponsor a comprehensive reform of local taxes. However, as the legislative timetable became clogged, the crisis deepened, and a new phase of economic *rigeur* began, it decided to postpone the reform. Moreover, it became clear that such a reform would require the most intricate calculations and would doubtless engender fierce resistance. The Government decided to analyze the effects of the partial financial transfers accompanying the first decentralization reforms before proceeding further. A member of Defferre's *cabinet* estimated that local tax reform was potentially the key aspect of the decentralization reform — and the most complex. Moreover, if the problem of local finances was not eventually resolved, it could become a nightmare. Rather than being remembered for decentralizing, the Government would be remembered for emptying local governments of their substance.

9. Additional measures. A number of other proposed reforms relate to decentralization:

Professionalizing local elected office. The Government sponsored legislation to provide substantial increases in salary for local elected officials, pension rights, the right to 15–35 hours a month released time from regular employment, and subsidized training.[17] However, the Government rejected a recommendation to limit the *cumul*, made by a commission it appointed to study the question, after the measure provoked opposition from most politicians while attracting little support. Instead, the Government proposed limiting the total compensation that an elected official can derive from cumulating mandates to 1.5 times the salary of a deputy. This indirect method aims to accomplish the same goal of enlarging the ranks of French local officeholders and demarcating responsibilities more clearly. However, by failing to confront the issue squarely, the Government tacitly accepted one of the most anomalous features of French political life.

The Government created a number of local agencies for specific purposes. For example, local employment committees bring together local elected, union and business officials in an attempt to boost local employment opportunities. The national Government provided regional governments with funds to provide grants for firms making investments to create jobs and foster regional economic development. Underdeveloped regions are given additional funds for grants to firms locating in these regions. Nationalized firms are encouraged to have local plant managers sponsor an annual conference, chaired by the plant manager in an area, with union r presentatives, local elected officials, subcontractors, and others to discuss the firm's local impact.

The Government modified the existing municipal electoral law which made it difficult for opposition candidates to gain representation on the municipal council. A new electoral law adopted for the 1983 municipal elections provided for a modified form of proportional representation in communes over 3,500, with the winning slate allotted half of all council seats plus a share of the remaining seats commensurate with its popular vote. The other seats are allocated to rival slates by proportional representation. In many cities, opposition forces gained representation on municipal councils for the first time. The Government argued that this should foster greater dialogue and democracy within local politics.

Despite the substantial extent of changes that were legislated, the Government retreated from several of its initial goals, including limiting the *cumul*, reforming local finances and decentralizing several functions. It asserted that these issues proved more complex than anticipated, the legislative agenda was overburdened and the economic crisis dictated increased caution. The left's setback in 1982 and 1983 local elections probably further restrained its will to decentralize. (This was doubtless the reason why the Government postponed elections for regional councils, thereby curtailing the power and legitimacy of the councils.) Increasing the power of institutions that the left did not fully control to the detriment of institutions that it did would have been incomprehensible. And the Government's retrenchment should not obscure how sweeping were the changes that were legislated.

THE IMPACT OF DECENTRALIZATION

What changes might be unleashed by the decentralization reform? How might it change the rules of the local political game in France? At this early stage, one can merely speculate on future tendencies. To begin with, several cautionary notes. Although the decentralization reform appears to represent a substantial break with the past, this impression must be qualified. First, in certain respects, the reforms merely may reinforce or confirm previous trends toward decentralization; in other cases, they may even reverse decentralizing tendencies. The Barre Government had proposed many of the innovations legislated by the Socialist Government. Further, big cities, which had already achieved substantial autonomy, may be subject to new constraints.[18] Second, the decentralization reforms will, to a considerable extent, remain parchment promises (to borrow from the lexicon of the American Constitutional Founders) unless the political powers that were transferred are matched by adequate fiscal transfers, which is far from certain. The global investment grant was substantially reduced from its initial optimistic projections (decided before the economic crisis imposed a new policy of 'rigueur'). Third, although the reforms promise much on paper, the national bureaucracy may devise ways to safeguard its prerogatives, relying on little-noticed features of legislative texts. For example, the fact that local fiscal officers continue to be named by the Ministry of Finance may count as much as the fact of formal subordination to local elected officials. Further, many areas of government remain untouched by the decentralization reforms, notably police, educational curriculum, and welfare eligibility requirements and benefit levels. Some areas not formally included within the decentralization reforms may become subject to more centralized direction, for example, the unification of the public and private educational system, abandoned (temporarily?) in July 1984.

There may well be unanticipated consequences which help to produce the 'centralization of decentralization' through certain forces (notably bureaucrats, departmental presidents and political parties) accumulating concentrated power. And yet the decentralization reforms will certainly produce substantial changes in the French political and administrative system.

First, many medium-size cities are likely to develop the kind of independent base that, in the past, only large cities were able to achieve thanks to their more ample resources. This means a further dissolution of the clientelist web of complicity between notables and state administrators, as well as a decline in the more recent technocratic statist domination. A report to the 1983 Congress of the French Mayors Association asserted: 'In place of the former system, which emphasized individual appeals to the state, and with grants-in-aid distributed in a unilateral fashion by the state, a system will develop founded on negotiation and contractual relations among local governments at different levels.'[19]

Yet new forms of inequality and clientelism will surely develop as local governments rush to fill the vacuum created by the state's retrenchment. Scholars have warned of the substitution of 'one dependence for another,' the risk of clientelism, a 'new vassalage,' and the 'centralization of decentralization.'[20] A major shift is toward increased power for departmental governments, especially their elected presidents. Mayors continue to journey to the prefecture (renamed *hôtel du département*). But they now seek appointments with the president of the departmental council, not the prefect. (The department finances about one-third of communes' public investments.) Thus, the web of complicity between *le préfet et ses notables* is being replaced by *le président du conseil général et ses notables.* [21]

Departmental presidents have gained control over a substantial portion of the prefectoral personnel, the symbols of power (for example, official limousines) and other prerogatives. They have appointed personal advisers to supervise departmental administration, usually — in a revealing symbol of changed power relations — from among members of the prefectoral corps. (Many of the 'migrants' are personally opposed to the Government and have joined the staff of opposition politicians.)

There is a certain *naïveté* in criticizing the decentralization reform for buttressing the power of local politicians. On the one hand, such criticism implies that the traditional system was apolitical; it evokes the myth of an impersonal, objective administration above the partisan fray. On the other hand, the form is designed precisely to remove the veil of administrative neutrality, as well as to prevent local politicians from evading responsibility for their action (or inaction).

A more accurate interpretation of the reform was suggested in an interview with a subprefect appointed to direct the departmental bureaucracy by an opposition general council president. Although critical of the left on a partisan level, the subprefect enthusiastically supported the Government's decentralization reform because, he asserted, it would promote a greater sense of responsibility among local elected representatives. This was preferable to the previous situation which accorded major weight to Paris technocrats, who lacked concrete knowledge of local problems and who stifled local initiatives. However, he admitted, the reform might provoke a scramble for influence among local politicians, with decisions made wholly on the basis of power relations rather than equitable criteria.

The decentralization reform is likely to involve a substantial transfer of power among bureaucracies: from Parisian ministries to field agencies and local governmental bureaucracies. Indeed, bureaucracies at all levels will probably derive major benefits from the reform: Parkinson's law would lead one to predict that the Parisian ministries which have been shorn of their functions will not wither away, whereas bureaucracies at sub-national governmental levels will proliferate.

Political parties will probably also benefit from the reform through the increased patronage and influence gained by local governments. This would strengthen a trend toward the politicization of local governments. National political parties had been playing an increasing role in organizing local slates, as evidenced by purges of local politicans who violated party directives regarding alliance strategy in recent local elections. Whereas party influence had mainly been confined to municipal elections, parties will doubtless now seek to penetrate the departmental and regional councils. (If elections to regional councils are by proportional representation, as the Government has announced, parties would gain an especially powerful role.)

Although the decentralization reform will thus provide important material benefits for French political parties, which are notoriously weak in members and resources, it may also strengthen intraparty divisions. Local officeholders already represent a large proportion of French party membership. Especially if the increased demands of local office and the new financial disincentives to cumulate office lead to a specialization of officeholding, parties are apt to be fractured by conflicts among officials representing different levels of government.

As local governments become more politicized, this will increase diversity, conflicts and competition among localities. For example, leftist governments will be more likely to sponsor quasi-public agencies to administer local services, assist local firms and promote producers' cooperatives.

Partisan differences have already become more evident in local political life. Following the 1983 municipal elections, newly elected rightist governments renamed streets and public squares to conform to their political predilections (with, for example, *rue Salvador Allende* rebaptized *rue Thiers*). Some conservative governments fired local administrators of cultural and medical centers or (as at Suresnes and Tourcoing) closed these facilities. These actions are part of the right's overall strategy of trying to reshape French culture. Several organizations were formed after the 1983 municipal elections, with representatives from conservative city governments, to promote more 'appropriate' forms of contemporary culture.[22] These examples suggest that, even in the short run, a Trotskyist analysis of the decentralization reform underestimates its significance:

The real meaning of decentralization thus seems to be a subtle transfer: the prefects will gain a share of the ministers' power and the local elected councils a part of the prefects' power. For political notables, all this will provide new perquisites and occasions for maneuvers. For the general population, the changes will hardly be visible.[23]

Longer-run changes may even be greater. First, the changed electoral system for municipal elections means that opposition elements have gained representation on most municipal councils. Second, there will doubtless be growing awareness that the municipal governments are responsible for zoning and granting building permits, departmental governments for public health and welfare, and regional governments for vocational training. Citizens may increasingly redirect demands from the state to local governments, a shift of paramount importance (see below).

It is especially noteworthy that local governments are empowered to sponsor measures to promote economic development, reduce unemployment, and bail out failing firms. French citizens will doubtless expect their local government to act in a crisis. For example, since 1968, French workers routinely occupy their factory when it threatens to close. (The contrast is striking between the reactions of French and American steelworkers to lay-offs and shut-downs in the late 1970s.) Henceforth, demands will be addressed to local governments as well as the state. There will certainly be local attempts to counteract the crisis, although possibilities are sharply limited. These shifts are hardly visible as yet, but they may eventually alter fundamental patterns of French political culture first described by Tocqueville. Given the lack of adequate means of regulating conflict locally, the French state has traditionally exercised major responsibility for conflict management. But this, in turn, has intensified national conflicts by making the state the sole prize worth capturing.

However, rather than reducing conflict the decentralization reforms may exacerbate it by overlaying partisan and class cleavages with conflicts among sub-national governments of different partisan persuasions. Take the issue of the future relationship between the department and region. The Government aims to strengthen the capacity of both levels of government to manage conflicts without recourse to the state. And, by seeking to prevent a hierarchy among them, it aims to promote pluralist vitality. Critics fail to appreciate this goal. 'One can be a "regionalist" or a "departmentalist" but certainly not both at the same time.'[24] This seems unduly formalistic; why cannot *both* the department and region gain power? Similarly, 'The project apparently assumes that a strong region, strong department, and strong commune can coexist without difficulties. This refusal to choose is illogical.'[25] And another Cartesian viewpoint: 'To decentralize only has meaning in the framework of an overall project, hierarchically articulated from a functional and geographic point of view. One cannot decentralize in a serious manner without choosing.'[26] In these views, conflict is regarded as undesirable; integration, order, and hierarchy are prized — the very values on which the previous system was ostensibly based. By contrast, the decentralization reforms aim to promote conflicts at lower levels in order to foster resiliency throughout the entire political fabric.

This does not mean that the goal will be achieved. Precisely because conflict is so extensive in France, and the inability to resolve conflicts locally has invited state intervention in the past, there is the likelihood of extensive conflicts among departmental and regional governments, especially if they are controlled by opposing partisan forces. Such a situation would, ironically, create fresh impetus for state intervention.

Moreover, the Government itself was unduly formalistic when it proposed legislation forbidding different levels of government from exercising supervision over one another: it seems inconceivable that inequalities will not occur. Given the regions' small budgets and delay in holding regional elections, departments have gained a head start in organizing power that will be hard to overcome.

## SOCIALIST MOTIVATIONS AND GOALS

The Socialist Government's motives for undertaking decentralization may shed further light on the character of the reforms. Opposition critics were doubtless correct that the Socialist Party's decentralizing zeal partially derived from the party's strong base in local government. But the argument could be reversed with equal cogency. Given the absence of political alternation in France at the national level for over two decades and the regime's lack of responsiveness to the opposition, the Socialist Party's only chance of gaining a share of power was at local levels. It pursued this objective with enormous tenacity. The Socialist Party came to appreciate the value of sub-national governments when it was confined to these levels. Indeed, the party survived largely in the early years of the Fifth Republic because many Socialist militants were local officeholders and functionaries. During the 1970s, the Socialist Party considerably increased its local electoral base and by the end of the decade was the most powerful party at all levels of sub-national government. One reason why conservative governments in the 1970s were reluctant to decentralize was the bonus that this would provide the Socialist Party.

The importance of the Socialist Party's urban base cannot be emphasized enough (and three-quarters of the French now live in cities). Virtually all party leaders occupy local elected offices. Socialist leaders too young to have officeholding experience in the Fourth Republic gained their political spurs in municipal elections in the Fifth Republic. Following the 1977 municipal elections, when leftist alliances won control of two-thirds of the 220 largest cities, the Socialist Party ranked first in urban France. The Socialist Party became devoted to local governments when they served as oases during the party's exile in the political desert nationally.

The reverse process began to occur after 1981. Soundly thrashed in the 1981 national elections, and with no immediate prospect of reversing this situation, the right concentrated on winning the only elections in sight. Its notable success in 1982 and 1983, the product of a combination of Socialist government errors, the economic crisis, and a typical mid-term backlash, enhanced the value of local government for the right. Its share of the 220 cities over 30,000 went from sixty-four to ninety-three in 1983. While leftist mayors continue to outnumber rightist mayors, the municipal elections signified a substantial shift in the right's favor and helped ease the sting of the 1981 electoral defeat. As a member of Defferre's *cabinet* humourously remarked, nothing could have been more helpful for establishing a wider consensus for decentralization!

And yet, albeit with diminished ardor, the left has remained committed to decentralization. Why?

The timing of the decentralization reform provides one clue: it was the first major reform sponsored by the newly elected Socialist Government and was introduced immediately after the election of a parliamentary majority. One reason may be that the Socialist Party had prepared a counterproposal in

1979 to a decentralization reform proposed by the Barre Government. The party was not prepared to introduce other reforms and needed to demonstrate its reformist commitments. Defferre observed: 'We reached power thanks to a veritable wave of popularity. If we allow enthusiasm to fade without acting, we risk compromise and a downhill slide. On the contrary, if we act rapidly, we will create a favorable political and social climate.'[27]

The decentralization reforms are an overdue response to the top-heavy and often unpopular French bureaucracy. In many respects, the Socialist measures echo proposals by liberal reformers in the 1960s, including Michel Crozier and the Club Jean Moulin, who asserted that decentralization and participation were needed to modernize the stalled society. Following monopoly capitalist industrialization and the resulting social dislocations of the 1960s, as well as the economic crisis of the 1970s, it became even more apparent that France lacked political shock absorbers to cushion conflict and reduce demands on the state. Whereas in other capitalist democracies, local government played this role by regulating local conflicts and partially shielding the state from demands, French local governments acted as a conduit for channelling demands to the center. Ashford observes: 'The French local government system tends to compound national political conflict and tensions rather than reflect them . . .'[28]

Thus, the rationale for decentralization can be traced back to Tocqueville, who unfavourably compared the French situation, where the bureaucracy absorbed much of society's vital substance, with the decentralized American system, which fragmented conflict and resolved disputes locally. By attempting to regulate every detail of French life, the state overreached itself and became the focal point for all political struggles.

The prefectoral system symbolized the tendency for the state to exercise total responsibility. The prefect simultaneously embodied the state's hierarchical authority and (as executive of the department and regional councils) the locally based representative principle. As a result, the prefect naturally served as the keystone of local political life — and the object of continual contestation. (Most local demonstrations ritually march to the public square opposite the prefecture.)

The left sponsored decentralization to alter this situation. Elected officials promise to replace the prefect as arbiter of local political life, thus acting as a buffer to protect the state. Moreover, thanks to measures which increase prefectoral authority over activities within the state's jurisdiction, the Government expects its local representatives to serve as an additional shield. Prime Minister Mauroy instructed prefects to 'prevent dossiers from being sent to Paris by insisting that they be handled locally.'[29]

When the opposition charged that the Socialists were dismantling the state, a Socialist deputy cogently rejoined: 'Decentralization is not synonymous with weakening the state. Quite the contrary. By intervening only in those sectors that are key for the nation's future, and relying on powerful and democratic local governments, the efficacy of state intervention cannot fail to grow.'[30] Attempting less will mean that the state can 'devote itself to the essential tasks.'[31] By freeing itself from a plethora of demands, the state can concentrate on the primary challenges of developing overall regulatory mechanisms, arbitrating among social classes, and strengthening France's productive apparatus to compete better in international markets. Thus, rather than a zero-sum logic, in which local governments gain power at the state's expense, the Socialist reform aims to promote a positive-sum logic in which the powers of all levels of government are increased.

The decentralization reforms seek to combine pluralist mechanisms of local self-regulation with rationalized, selective state intervention. The Socialist project looks to a new political formula to restructure the state, civil society, and their mutual relations in an era of capitalist crisis.[32] This is especially difficult given the high degree of class conflict in France.

Although social stability has become frayed throughout the advanced capitalist world during the present crisis, it may be exceptionally weak in France. The Socialist project attempts to achieve social cohesion in a society that never enjoyed a durable class truce in the post-war period. During the economic expansion of the 1960s and early 1970s, the Gaullist regime was able to purchase social peace through economic redistribution. However, the accumulation of capital also provoked the accumulation of social costs. The fragility of consensus based on charismatic leadership and material distribution became dramatically evident in May 1968. None the less, following de Gaulle's abortive attempt to find a new solution stressing participation, the regime responded by renewed efforts to accumulate. This in turn became increasingly difficult with the onset of the economic crisis in the mid-1970s.

The Giscard regime reversed de Gaulle's and especially Pompidou's emphasis on large, centralized, 'heavy' public and private investments, which concentrated industrial development and public investments in the largest cities. Giscard sought to stress the qualitative and social aspects of urban life, the value of small and medium-sized cities, and historic preservation and restoration rather than gigantic new housing complexes. This both made a virtue of a necessity, given economic stagnation, and was a response to the social and political dangers posed for a conservative regime from large-scale concentrations of workers and accumulating discontent.[33]

Giscard initially sought to liberalize the blocked society through consultation and reform. But, a prisoner of conservative forces, he soon adopted an opposite stance — what Poulantzas termed authoritarian statism — which was the antithesis of decentralization.[34] The Socialist Party's eventual victory over both the Communist Party and the right was due in part to the party's sensitivity to the aspirations of the rising middle stratum. Decentralization is an integral part of the Socialist Party's larger project, which seeks to achieve a liberalized, pluralist civil society along with a rationalized state divested of responsibility for social regulation so that it can directly organize key industries and plan the entire economy.

This represents a tendency toward merging the economy and polity, whose separation is a distinctive feature of capitalism. The merger would be democratic and decentralized, rather than coercive and centralized, as in Soviet societies. Much societal regulation would be carried on by voluntary associations and local governments. The aim is local initiative and diversity, not programmed uniformity. The new approach would create a network of planning, participation and consultation throughout the society. It would extend the public sphere as well as mobilize private energies for economic and social renewal. These arrangements represent a step beyond Keynesian welfare statism, which presupposed economic growth, centralized corporatist arrangements and redistribution. Instead, the Socialist project emphasizes qualitative values, including participation and local identities. The new social movements and middle stratum spawned by advanced capitalism would provide the motor force for the Socialist project.[35]

Decentralization assumes its fullest significance in the current period of economic crisis and severe international economic competition. By decentralization facilitating social peace and self-regulation, the state is better equipped (especially after the nationalization reforms) to modernize the productive apparatus and improve France's position in the international division of labor. The decentralization reforms seek to decrease class and partisan conflicts, in order better to mobilize social forces in the current crisis. During the National Assembly debate on decentralization, Jean-Pierre Worms, Socialist floor manager for the proposal, declared:

During the crisis, there is a risk of groups directing enormous demands toward the state . . . It is crucial for the state to find allies in the crisis; this is the aim of decentralization, which also aims to create a new field of intervention and experimentation . . . Some members of the majority ask whether it is wise to give the opposition additional strength by decentralization. I say it is, for the reform will oblige the opposition to accept the need for 'rigueur' and force it to assume its responsibilities . . .[36]

Without working-class support, such a project is doomed. The Auroux laws, which reorganize industrial relations and strengthen union organizations, provide incentives. Unions have also seen possibilities for defending their interests within the decentralization reforms. The CFDT has been a foremost proponent of decentralization. In a special issue of its theoretical journal devoted to decentralization, contributors emphasized the possibility of trade-union participation.[37] Decentralization is also linked to increasing worker and union participation within the firm, as well as developing new forms of a mixed economy. 'If the desired evolution consists in encouraging more extensive and better participation by workers in the life of the firm, if the firm must henceforth shoulder social costs, then it follows that public agencies should also assume and share economic risks.'[38]

While the working class might derive some benefit from the new project, the middle stratum would gain more.[39] An article in the Socialist Party theoretical journal argued that decentralization is part of a triptych whose two other elements are planning and nationalization. While they 'guarantee a global and coordinated orientation of the ensemble of national activity, decentralization reduces the risk of a top-heavy, monolithic state. A nation both revitalized in each locality and rationally organized as a whole: this is the emerging picture of a socialist France.'[40]

## SOCIALISM FOR THE MIDDLE STRATUM

What is socialist about this project? Why does decentralization reflect socialist principles? When Socialist party officials and militants were asked these questions, most replied that decentralization strengthened socialist tendencies by promoting greater citizen participation in local affairs. While this may be progressive in France, in contrast to bureaucratic dominance, it is hardly radical or innovative compared to the practice of other capitalist democracies.

Further, the major group that has gained power thus far is local officeholders. No provision has yet been made for greater direct citizen participation. The Socialist call for *autogestion*, so prominent in the 1970s, has disappeared from the party's program.

In these circumstances, the Socialist project potentially promises more benefits to the mdidle stratum than to the broad majority of manual and white-collar workers. Take the triptych of decentralization, planning and nationalization. As presently implemented, they will create new opportunities for members of the middle stratum — professionals, managers, experts — but few benefits for workers. The reforms do not seem likely to erode the division of labor; on the contrary, by further organizing society along meritocratic lines, they will enhance the middle stratum's position.

It should be apparent why, rather than a minor element in the Socialist program, decentralization is one of its key features. The decentralization reforms represent a bold attempt to modernize the left's Jacobin legacy and reduce political and class conflict in France. As President Mitterrand remarked, whereas centralization was necessary at one stage in French history to assure national unity, in the present era decentralization is necessary to accomplish the same goal. What are the prospects that decentralization will help the Socialists to realize their goals?

While there would be immense obstacles to achieving the Socialist project under any circumstances, the severity of the economic crisis further diminishes its chances. The Government's turn to *rigeur* in mid-1982 meant that local governments are being given smaller grants for new initiatives. Overall, conflict has increased as numerous interests have launched protests to defend their privileges. The present situation does not lend itself to reducing tensions or mobilizing on behalf of a new project. Thus, it is clear that the decentralization reform, as well as the Socialist Government's overall project, will not be fully or smoothly achieved. Instead, the reforms provide new terrain on which socioeconomic and political contests will occur. But, although it would be fruitless to predict the shape or outcome of these struggles, it should be apparent that the implications of the tranquil revolution at Clochemerle reach far beyond parish-pump politics.

## NOTES

1. Peter Alexis Gourevitch, *Paris and the Provinces: The Politics of Local Government in France* (Berkeley: University of California Press, 1980), p. 49, emphasis removed. My own previous research has also stressed the immobility of French local politics.
2. Ibid., p. 234.
3. Vincent Wright, 'Regionalization under the Fifth Republic: The Triumph of the Functional Approach,' in L.J. Sharpe, ed., *Decentralist Trends in Western Democracies* (London and Beverly Hills: Sage Publications, 1979), p. 3.
4. Ezra N. Suleiman, 'Administrative Reform and the Problem of Decentralization,' in William G. Andrews and Stanley Hoffmann, eds, *The Impact of the Fifth Republic on France* (Albany: State University of New York Press, 1981), p. 77.
5. Douglas E. Ashford, *British Dogmatism and French Pragmatism: Central-Local Policymaking in the Welfare State* (London: Allen & Unwin, 1982), p. 362.
6. Sidney Tarrow, 'Local Constraints on Regional Reform: A Comparison of Italy and France,' *Comparative Politics*, 7, No. 1 (October 1974), pp. 1-36.
7. For an interpretation along these lines, see Pierre Rosanvallon and Patrick Viveret, *Pour une nouvelle culture politique* (Paris: Seuil, 1977).
8. For the definitive work on the traditional model of French intergovernmental relations and recent changes, which described both the greater degree of local autonomy than was commonly realized and how this was being undermined by technocratic rationalization,

see Pierre Gremion, *Le Pouvoir périphérique: bureaucrates et notables dans le système politique français* (Paris: Seuil, 1977).

9.   Commission du Bilan, *La France en Mai 1968*, Vol. 5, *L'Etat et les citoyens* (Paris: La Documentation Française, 1981), p. 270.

10.  Max Querrier, 'Collectivités libres ou corrois de transmission?,' *Projet*, No. 142 (February 1980), p. 166; Odon Vallet, 'D'abord, entrer dans la vie des communes,' *Projet*, No. 142 (February 1980), p. 152.

11.  Alain Richard, 'Une grande ambition, la responsabilité locale,' *Nouvelle Revue Socialiste*, No. 54 (September-October 1981), pp. 34-40.

12.  See Pierre Sadran, 'Les Socialistes et la région,' *Pouvoirs*, No. 19 (1981), pp. 139-47.

13.  Interview with Gaston Defferre, *Nouvel Observateur*, 18 July 1981, p. 24. I have also benefited from interviews with participants. For analyses of the reform proposals by those involved, see Defferre's speeches to the French Mayors' Association, *Départements et Communes*, December 1981 and December 1982, as well as the Government's introduction to its various decentralization bills. For unofficial Socialist Party analyses, see *La Nouvelle Revue Socialiste*, special issue on decentralization, No. 54 (September-October 1981); and Michel Philipponneau, *Décentralisation et régionalisation* (Paris: Calmann-Levy, 1981). Critiques of the decentralization reform include Bela Farago, 'De la décentralisation,' *Commentaire*, No. 21 (Spring 1983), pp. 38-48; Jean-Pierre Garnier, 'Liberté, urbanité, sécurité,' *Non!*, No. 13 (May-June 1982), pp. 62-77; Garnier, 'Le Local, le central, et ... le capital,' *Metropolis*, No. 51 (Spring 1982), pp. 22-7; Hubert Haenel, 'Les dangers de la décentralisation,' *Projet*, No. 173 (March 1983), pp. 199-204; Emile Montorsier, 'La Disparition de la tutelle administrative: vers une nouvelle féodalité,' *Economie et Humanisme*, No. 265 (May-June 1982), pp. 69-73; Jean-Emile Vié, *La Décentralisation sans illusion* (Paris: Presses Universitaires de France, 1981). Other analyses of the Socialist decentralization reforms include Douglas E. Ashford, 'Questions sans réponses sur la loi Defferre,' in *Annuaire des Collectivités Locales*, Vol. 2 (Paris: Librairies Techniques, 1982), pp. 19-31; Ashford, 'The Socialist Reorganization of French Local Government — Another Jacobin Reform?' *Government and Policy*, 1, No. 1 (1983), pp. 29-44; Paul Bernard, *L'Etat et la décentralisation: Du préfet au commissaire de la République* (Paris: La Documentation Française, 1983); Jacques Caroux, 'The End of Administrative Centralization?' *Telos*, No. 55 (Spring 1983), pp. 105-14; Jacques Chevallier, 'La Réforme régionale,' in Jacques Chevallier, François Rangeon and Michèle Sellier, *Le Pouvoir régional* (Paris: Presses Universitaires de France, 1982), pp. 109-85; Bertrand Eveno, 'Démocratiser la décentralisation,' *Le Débat*, No. 16 (November 1981) pp. 16-27; Paul J. Godt, 'Decentralization in Socialist France: A Strategy for Change', *The Tocqueville Review*, 5, No. 1 (Spring-Summer 1983), pp. 215-30; Georges Gontcharoff and Serge Milano, *La Décentralisation: nouveaux pouvoirs, nouveaux enjeux* (Paris: Syros, 1983); Pierre Grémion, 'Régionalisation, régionalisme, et municipalisation,' *Le Débat*, No. 16 (November 1981), pp. 5-15; Grémion, 'Région ou département? Les raisons d'un non-choix,' *Intervention*, No. 3 (March-April 1983), pp. 18-25; Daniel Kaisergruber, 'Donner le pouvoir aux élus,' *CFDT Aujourd'hui*, No. 59 (January-February 1983), pp. 41-50; Philippe de Lara, 'De Nouvelles règles du jeu pour la démocratie,' *Intervention*, No. 3 (March-April 1983), pp. 7-13; Gary G. Meyers, 'After Jacobinism? Center–Periphery Relations in Socialist France,' unpublished paper presented to the 79th annual meeting of the American Political Science Association, Chicago, 1-4 September 1983; Franck Moderne, ed., *La Nouvelle décentralisation* (Paris: Sirey, 1983); Claude Reynoird, 'La Décentralisation, un pari ambitieux,' *Projet*, No. 166 (June 1982), pp. 675-86.

14.  In order to expedite the reform, Defferre relied on the full panoply of powers that the Constitution provides the Government. The opposition immediately pointed to the anomaly of promoting decentralization by centralized means. However, the decentralization reform still took far longer to elaborate, pass, and implement than the Government initially planned. Thus, eight months were required to pass the *loi Defferre*, and several provisions were nullified by the Constitutional Council, which necessitated an additional law. The second major bill, involving the transfer of national functions to local governments, was delayed and, as the Senate was reviewing the bill, the Government decided to postpone consideration of one part in order to expedite other parliamentary matters. The whole measure was eventually passed in 1983.

15.  Chevallier, op. cit., p. 135.

16.  Grémion, 'Région ou département?' op. cit.

17.  *Le Monde*, 30 July 1983.

18.  Meyers, 'After Jacobinism?' op. cit.

The Tranquil Revolut

19. George Lemoine, 'Rapport Moral,' delivered to 66th annual Congr
Maires de France, *Départements et Communes*, **31** (September-Octo
20. Haenel, op. cit.; Reynoird, op. cit.; Montorsier, op. cit.; de Lara, op.
21. The phrase comes from Jean-Pierre Worms's seminal 'Le Préfet et ses m
*du Travail*, **8** (1966), pp. 249-75.
22. *Le Monde*, 3 November 1983. This is not intended to suggest that the right has
vice, the left a monopoly of virtue. However, the shift to the right meant that
rightist mayors replaced leftist incumbents than the reverse. Beyond this, there ha
evidence of comparable leftist discrimination of this kind, for example, following
1977 municipal gains. It is generally agreed that mayors of all political persuasio
partisan criteria in filling at least some offices.
23. *Lutte Ouvrière*, 8 August 1981.
24. Chevallier, op. cit., p. 175.
25. Ibid.
26. Eveno, op. cit., p. 18.
27. Defferre interview, op. cit., p. 24.
28. Ashford, *British Dogmatism . . .*, op. cit., p. 146.
29. Pierre Mauroy, 'Transfert et répartition des compétences', speech reprinted in Parti Socialiste, Société d'Études et de Documentation Municipale, No. 19, Paris, 1982.
30. André Laignel, 'Une Révolution tranquille,' *Nouvelle Revue Socialiste*, September-October 1981, p. 22.
31. Cited from Government's explanation for its bill redistributing political powers, Senate document no. 409 (Annexe au procès verbal, *Journal Officiel*, 22 June 1982).
32. For fuller analyses, see my 'Socialism without the Workers: The Case of France,' *Kapitalistate*, No. 10/11 (1983), pp. 11-41; 'Socialist Possibilities and Capitalist Realities: All's Quiet on the French Leftist Front,' in Paul Zarembka, ed., *Research in Political Economy*, Vol. 6 (Greenwich: JAI Press, 1983).
33. Guy Loinger, 'Esquisse d'analyse de l'évolution de la politique urbaine en France depuis la Libération,' *Espaces et Sociétés*, Nos. 36-37 (January-June 1981), pp. 91-109; Jacques Ion and Andre Micoud, 'La commune entre l'État et le quartier,' *Espaces et Sociétés*, Nos. 34-35 (July-December 1980), pp. 83-96.
34. Nicos Poulantzas, *State, Power, Socialism* (London: New Left Books, 1978).
35. For critical leftist analyses, see Jean-Pierre Garnier and Denis Goldschmidt, *Le 'Socialisme' à visage urbain, essai sur la 'local-démocratie'* (Paris: Éditions Rupture, 1978); Alain Bihr and Jean-Marie Heinrich, *La néo-social-démocratie ou le capitalisme autogéré* (Paris: Éditions Sociales, 1981).
36. Remarks in National Assembly, 24 June 1983.
37. Special issue of *CFDT Aujourd'hui*, No. 59 (January-February 1983).
38. Josée Landrieu, 'Décentralisation, développement local, mutations économiques,' *CFDT Aujourd'hui*, No. 59 (January-February 1983), p. 39. This captures well the aim of the CFDT and Rocard faction of the Socialist Party. Many on the left are opposed to this rather extreme form of class compromise.
39. Dominique Mehl, 'Les voies de la contestation urbaine', *Les Annales de la recherche urbaine*, No. 6 (January 1980), pp. 26-62. Also see Hugues Portelli, *Le Socialisme français tel qu'il est* (Paris: Presses Universitaires de France, 1980).
40. Alain Meyer, 'Décentralisation à la française,' *Nouvelle Revue Socialiste* (September-October 1981), p. 18.

...on at Clochemerle
...ss of the Association des
...ber 1983). P. 18.
...it., respectively.
...otables', Sociologie
... monopoly of
... many more
... s not been
... he left's
... s use

...ily an activity of government which is concerned ...and and the use of buildings. The roots of the activity are very ...ch tied up with the process of urbanization and the notion of egalitarianism. As a greater proportion of a country's population moves to live in towns and cities, the pressures on land increase. Planning policies and proposals as laid down in statutorily approved plans seek to control or to intervene in the market forces of land use in an effort to create access, safety and some measure of a visually pleasing environment for the greatest number of people. The degree of control or intervention is, of course, largely dependent on the political ideology and the extent of urbanization.

In France, in contrast with many of her neighbour states in Europe which urbanized in the late nineteenth century, the process of urbanization took place much later, well into the twentieth century.[1] Although successive French governments provided the necessary legislation for the production of plans from 1919 onwards,[2] few local authorities who were charged with the responsibility for their preparation seemed either able or willing to commit themselves to such a statutory control document. The ability of these local authorities — the communes — to do so was limited because they had no technically or professionally qualified staff of their own to produce plans. Their willingness to commit themselves to a legally binding land-use document was tempered by at least three considerations. Firstly, no action was taken against them by central government if they did not provide plans; secondly, political flexibility to arrive at agreements locally with developers was an important aspect of re-election; and thirdly, there was little electoral mileage in plan preparation since no planning lobby of any significance existed at local or even central level. By the start of the Fifth Republic in 1958, then, successive central governments in France had paid lip-service to the notion of statutory land-use control, but, in practice, the planning system as operated at the local level was very much the prerogative of the communal mayor.

During the de Gaulle Administration, the planning system in France changed dramatically with the introduction of the *Loi d'orientation foncière* (LOF) in 1967.[3] This act laid down a comprehensive system of land-use plans at both strategic and local levels. The former, the *schémas d'aménagement et urbanisme* (SDAU) or structure plans, were to provide broad guidelines for physical development in the context of projected socioeconomic change, while the latter, called *plans d'occupation des sols* (POS) or local plans, were to provide clear guidelines for building or land-use control.[4] Although there has been criticism of the slow rate of production of these plans since 1967,[5] the record of plan preparation in France has clearly improved in comparison to the earlier decades of the century. However, rates of plan preparation apart, what has been interesting in urban planning since 1967 has been that formalized procedural mechanisms have been created for plan preparation, that staff and finance have been made available for plan-making, and that urban planning has become a much more important electoral issue — initially at the local level and more recently at the national level.[6]

Of particular significance in French urban planning, as in many other areas of public administration in France, is the relationship between central government and the local communes. Plan-making is organized as a joint state/local activity, but it is clear from investigation of the plan-making process that the joint partners are not always equal partners. Indeed, for the majority of communal mayors, plan-making may place them at a considerable disadvantage in the central/local power struggle. At the same time, however, it is also clear that many communal mayors, who claim that they want full decision-making powers in planning free from central government involvement, are content to be only joint partners — particularly when electorally unpopular planning decisions come to be made. Clearly state/local relations in this process are both subtle and complex.[7]

Recent legislation to decentralize decision-making in planning to communal mayors has been an important political platform of the current Mitterrand Administration. On the face of it, the legislation certainly gives the impression that plan-making and decisions over planning applications will now become the responsibility of the mayor. However, closer examination of the two acts issued to date[8] reveals that what power is given to communes by one hand is often taken away by the other. In other words, the legislation itself reveals sufficient loopholes for continuity in the power of the center over the communes. Moreover, consideration of the legal texts apart, of more immediate and direct concern for the practice of urban planning are questions of how this legislation can be made operational, whether or not the willingness and ability of mayors to intervene in land-use control will actually be made *more difficult*, and finally, in a technical sense, whether those longer-term improvements in planning which have developed under the Fifth Republic since de Gaulle can withstand a period of discontinuity of the sort which may result from the difficulties of putting this new legislation into practice.

The Mitterrand Government has taken advantage of a political window, a situation where the majority in power at both central and local levels was to their advantage between May 1981 and the local elections of March 1983. In this period, they have introduced a series of sequential acts, rather than a single legislative text, for the purpose of reorganizing the general distribution of power between central government and communes. Thus far only the first two decentralization acts in the sequence have emerged, and one might wonder whether a single act (as we saw in British local government reorganization in 1972) might not have been more politically advantageous — advantageous, that is, before the window is possibly bricked up by the opposition — as well as being more administratively efficient and smooth to implement.

This chapter will explore some of the issues mentioned above. It will be divided into three sections. The first section will discuss the process of preparation of local plans (POS) as an example of centre–periphery relations before the new decentralization legislation, and will focus on the 'working group' (*groupe de travail*), the institutional locus in which they were elaborated;[9] this section is based on observations made during *groupe de travail* meetings and on interviews with mayors and planning officials.[10] Three sorts of conclusions emerge from this material: firstly, that informal contacts between centre and periphery — in other words between state civil servants (*fonctionnaires*) and mayors — are as important as, if not more important than, the formal process of contact during the *groupe de travail*; secondly, and more generally, that the model of cross-functioning controls put forward by J.-C. Thoenig[11] provides a useful explanation of the process; and, thirdly, that the technical limitations on the POS itself — representing as it does only one element of urban policy — mean that it is insufficiently sensitive or flexible to define future urban land use effectively. The second section will briefly consider the main provisions of the second Decentraliza-tion Act (January 1983) in respect of planning and the POS. The transfer of responsibility for planning to the commune occupies a large proportion of this act, and this transfer is intended to have considerable consequences in the broader shift of power from center to periphery. The final section will discuss the nature of this shift in power by identifying those factors which are likely to be influential in the decentralization or transfer of planning responsibility to the commune and consider the ambiguities and even potential contradictions which they contain. This analysis, while somewhat preliminary,[12] is based not only on the two Decentralization Acts to date, but also on the *avant-projet* for the next act[13] and on the current views, policies and practice of mayors and planning officials as these have emerged in recent fieldwork.[14]

POS PREPARATION

The preparation of the POS had a clearly defined administrative procedure which involved a priori control by the departmental prefect (now renamed the Commissioner of the Republic) and a number of sequential stages of preparation centring on the *groupe de travail*.[15] It has been at these meetings of the *groupe de travail* — comprising representatives of the state's 'field services' in the *département* (DDE and DDA[16]), the mayor of the commune, municipal councillors and representatives of the Chambers of Commerce and Agriculture — that the plan is, in theory, prepared jointly by the participants. Such meetings are of particular interest since they represent one of the few areas of local administration in France where the state and local communes sit down together in the same room to achieve a joint purpose. Thus they are one of the very few settings where a researcher can directly observe the nature of these subtle and complex relationships.[17] Although the purpose of the *groupe de travail* is clear, however, what is not clear at this stage is the range of expectations, motivations, knowledge of planning, and power bases of the participants; these can of course vary considerably, and we shall consider the contribution of each of the participants below.

As a general guideline to the conduct of the *groupe de travail*, we could expect that, since it is a joint state/commune function, the traditional division of labour between officials and politicians would be relevant; in other words, officials of the DDE, and in particular the GEP section (*Groupe d'études et programmation*),[18] would carry out technical investigations before the meetings, report on their findings at the meetings, and make professional recommendations. In turn, we could expect that the politicians and other members of the group would consider these findings and recommendations and, on the basis of the planning issues and the various elements of public interest within the commune, arrive at decisions. In practice, of course, the picture is rather more complex.

The conduct of these meetings, as we have observed it, demonstrates the importance of two individuals in particular, namely, the mayor and the senior civil servant of the GEP. Indeed, the meetings are more of a dialogue between these two participants than a discussion for the remaining participants — who will only intervene if asked by either of the two principal participants. Those participants unconnected with the municipal council or the DDE may make contributions but their role is much more peripheral to decision-making. Clearly, it would appear that there are important status differentials between the participants, both within the two main groups — the mayor and municipal councillors on one side and the staff of the DDE on the other — and between these groups and the rest. The mayor, as chairperson, in the absence of a formal agenda, orchestrates the proceedings. Without exception, mayors observed in this study devoted much more time to procedural rather than substantive issues. Such substantive issues as were discussed tended to relate to detailed issues concerning land use within certain land-use zones, and, most importantly, to future public developments such as swimming pools or sports stadiums and to future land for private housing. At no time, however, were planning problems/issues clearly identified and discussed with a view to resolution. Moreover, a lack of prepared technical investigation, other than a simple survey of existing land use, was evident.

By and large, the senior civil servant of the GEP was content to follow the mayor's lead in the discussion of procedure and minutiae. This is hardly surprising given that neither of the two main participants, mayors or civil servants, have any training in planning and generally have little experience.[19] Indeed, the only participants with any experience or training in planning are the lower professional contracted staff of the GEP.[20] However, their participation during the *groupe de travail* is minimal and is tightly controlled by their civil servant superiors. It tended to concentrate on the verification of existing uses or land-use conditions or the provision of information about zone namings or building regulations. Of the remaining participants, municipal councillors tended to intervene only to defend possible decisions concerning their own land interests. The representatives of the Direction Départementale d'Agriculture would intervene if good agricultural land seemed threatened by decisions, but their interventions were often ignored, especially by the DDE who regard them as an inferior 'field service'.

Tensions are evident during these meetings between a number of participants. Between mayors and senior civil servants of the GEP, tension develops when discussion focuses on public developments. In fact, these are issues upon which any compromise necessary for the completion of the plan must be based. On the one hand, mayors hope to secure from the plan electorally advantageous public developments funded, in part, through loans and grants from the state. Civil servants, for their part, wish to secure supervision of public works projects within the commune for which they receive honorariums.[21] In other words, they can gain personal benefits from projects concerning which they were a party to the decision. In turn, they have to present arguments for such projects through the channel of the prefect to the various ministries involved in funding. Of course, it is hard to say whether the tension between mayors and civil servants is real or contrived. Clearly there is, as witnessed, considerable collusion both before and after the actual meetings of the *groupe de travail*. Vincent Wright has put the general picture well: 'Paris bureaucrats and their provincial agents, prefects and local elected politicians, are condemned to live together in a chaos of surreptitious bargaining, illicit agreements, hidden collusion, unspoken complicity, simulated tension and often genuine conflict.'[22]

There is also tension evident between senior civil servants of the GEP and the lower professional contractual staff of the GEP. In particular, the latter object to many judgements of the former which have no technical basis whatsoever. Moreover, many expressed concern that the issues discussed at the *groupe de travail* bore no relationship whatsoever to the planning problems of the communes. By virtue of their inferior status position and, in particular, because of their limited-term contracts of employment, they are obliged to remain quiet yet present during what they regard as extremely frustrating dialogues. Tension is heightened between them and their superiors if there is any indication that they have a rapport with a mayor. Such situations tend to arise more frequently during the pre- and post-*groupe* meetings over the customary aperitif.

Thus a consideration of the contributions of the two main participants and their relations with other participants at the *groupe de travail* would suggest that the process of POS preparation does not conform to the formal model outlined earlier in this section. In the first place, there is no clearcut political/technical division of labour. Secondly, it is clear that meetings are orchestrated outside of the *groupe de travail*: the group does not meet frequently, and there are generally no more than an average of six meetings for the elaboration of a particular POS; and there is little exploration of the issue behind the decision. And thirdly, the decisions reached are generally compromises between the two main participants. Naturally, we would expect decisions reached by a joint state/local body to be compromises, but what we might not expect is that these compromises are overtly skewed in favour of the personal interests of those whose power base is strongest. Analysis of this process of POS preparation as an example of centre–periphery relations can be made in the context of Thoenig's model of 'cross-regulation', where the centre is represented by the civil servants of the DDE and the periphery by the mayor. Thoenig suggests that there is considerable interrelationship and interdependence of centre and periphery, that neither is able to take decisions without recourse to higher authority (the cross-functioning controls), that the system is inefficient and insensitive, that there is a mistrust of public debate, and that decisions are taken in secret.[23] Let us look at some of these issues more closely.

The factors which will weaken the degree of interdependence and interrelationship between mayors and civil servants — factors to the mayor's advantage — will to a large extent depend on the status of the mayor, the nature of the commune, the extent to which he understands the planning process and its associated terminology, and the extent to which he is able to penetrate the local administration. Mayors of large communes or mayors of communes which form part of a *communauté urbaine* or *syndicat intercommunal* (joint bodies set up by groups of communes to perform specific common functions) with a planning function may have a planning agency of their own to produce the POS. In such cases — and they are limited[24] — the mayor will have much less intervention by the DDE in the content of his plan, although the crucial negotiations of funds for public developments will still involve the interrelationship with the DDE. However, if the mayor has accumulated public offices at different levels — what is known in French politics as the *cumul des mandats* — whether or not he has his own planning agency, then this will assist in his direct contact with the centre, thus bypassing the local DDE. The nature of the commune itself may assist the mayor in weakening the DDE's control, especially if his commune requires the type of public works which the DDE can supervise, giving him extra bargaining chips in the negotiating process. During meetings of the *groupe de travail*, the mayor's position will be much stronger if he has been able to understand and effectively use the planning jargon. This is not an easy task since the jargon comprises acronyms describing each of the land-use zones and subdivisions within them.[25] The final factor which may be used by the mayor to his advantage in reducing his dependence on the civil servants of the DDE is his ability to exploit the internal tensions between civil servants and contractual staff. In particular, a skilful mayor will be able to develop his own contacts amongst the contractual staff who may assist his understanding of the projects which are likely to be given financial assistance. It follows, of course, that the less that a mayor possesses such bargaining resources — or is able to manipulate them skilfully — the more the civil servants of the DDE, with their more direct institutional links with the structures which control the disbursement of central government funds, with their professional prestige, and with control of technical information, can turn the bargaining process in their favour.

Of course, to suggest that all mayors are intent on independence and conflict with the DDE would be an exaggeration. The administrative mechanism, however, is such that they are prisoners of this system. Some mayors are certainly willing prisoners, because they are able to use the state services as a scapegoat when unpopular decisions are made. The criticisms of the system — inefficiency, mistrust of public debate and insensitivity — seem justified with regard to the POS, but in varying degrees. Furthermore, the POS takes a long time to produce, on average about six years in those *départements* studied, although this slowness is due not only to the bargaining process but also to the fact that there are a large number of communes and only a small number of staff at DDE level to do the work.[26] The remaining two criticisms are much more valid. The POS is legally described as being 'opposable aux tiers'; in other words, it is a legally binding document which in turn is supposed to provide third parties with certain rights of information and objection in order to protect their own land interests. However, this is only partially true in practice. The plan is prepared in the absence of public participation save token *post hoc* gestures, notably public exhibitions of the final plan. The system of *enquête publique* (public inquiries or hearings) is not democratic and the originators of the plan are judge and jury in cases of objection.

The insensitivity of the POS is often evident in terms of the detailed and rigid land zonings and building regulations which it contains, especially because these regulations imply that existing land use will be incapable of changing to meet the needs of wider social and economic change. Of even greater concern in respect of the insensitivity of these plans is the fact that they are often prepared in the absence of other planning documents which extend beyond the area of the commune itself. In particular, the upper tier structure plans (as defined in the 1967 LOF), the SDAUs, are few, and even where one does exist, its content tends to be of the 'blueprint' variety — somewhat abstract and loosely connected with problems on the ground — and it has all too often been overly optimistic in its assumptions of future population growth. In other words, there is generally little or no link between strategic and local plans. This is particularly important in terms of urban policy. The POS effectively treats the commune as a planning island; the problems of one commune may be exactly those of a neighbouring commune, but there is no account taken of this in the plan. Or, alternatively, proposals made in the POS may have consequences for a neighbouring commune but these are ignored. Even in cases where loose groupings of communes have come together to negotiate a joint plan — only a small minority of cases — close examination of the resulting document demonstrates that the only commonality amongst the constituent communes is the dossier of land and building regulations. No effort is made to reconcile problems and issues across communes or indeed to achieve economies of scale in public investment through joint projects. Consequently the POS, in its present form and with its current process of preparation, cannot be regarded as an adequate basis for framing urban policy.

### DECENTRALIZATION AND THE TRANSFER OF RESPONSIBILITY

Into this situation the Mitterrand/Mauroy Government, under the impulsion of the Minister of the Interior, Gaston Defferre, has brought the Decentralization Acts. The Government's main aims relative to the decentralization process are articulated as, first, providing greater local democracy, secondly, clarifying responsibilities of elected members to provide for ease of administration, and, finally, relieving the state of the management of certain local affairs which will permit more efficient handling of national issues.[27] Essentially, through a series of acts, these aims will lead to the establishment of a system of 'local government' in France rather than a system of 'local administration', to use a distinction which has become a classic in the literature. The first of these acts, dealing with the rights and freedoms of *communes, départements* and *régions*, has laid down the two fundamental principles of the new system: suppression of *la tutelle* (central government supervision of the actions of local authorities) and its replacement by a posteriori intervention of the new *Commissaire de la République* and the transfer of executive power of the prefect — the principal channel of centre-periphery relations since the Napoleonic era — to the elected officers at each level. At commune level, the recipient of this new formal responsibility is, of course, the mayor. The second act relative to the transfer of responsibilities within these three levels begins the process of operationalizing these principles specifying the competence of each level for particular policy areas. The two acts together have been described as a process of 'robbing Peter to pay Paul' and as 'a sort of administrative Yalta'.[28] Both the state and the municipal councils, for example, will have their own services, buildings and agents. But, more importantly, the extent to which the local authorities will be truly autonomous and independent of state control can be questioned, and even at this early stage interventions by central government are evident in law.

The transfer has, in and of itself, certain guiding principles, in particular:

(i)   the acts do not provide for a redistribution of responsibilities, but merely for a transfer;
(ii)  the transfer to communes is made as they exist at present, and there is no obligation for them to regroup or rationalize their boundaries;
(iii) the transfer does not imply any executive or administrative hierarchy in the discharging of responsibilities;
(iv)  transfer of responsibilities is paralleled by transfer of resources; and
(v)   different local authorities will have different specializations.[29]

In other words, then, the transfer is not vertical but local between locally based state services and the three sorts of councils.

Turning to the provisions which concern planning, three general and important changes can be identified. First, the responsibility for the preparation of POS and the granting of planning permission (for development, land use changes, etc.) pass to the commune[30] with only a posteriori control by the *Commissaire de la République*. However, the latter still has the right to intervene in the content of local plans to ensure that national planning regulations are adhered to.[31] Naturally, with such provisions, one wonders if what is given by one hand is taken away by the other. Secondly, the services of the state, the DDE and the DRE (Direction Régionale de l'Équipement), are *mis à la disposition* (placed at the disposal) of the commune.[32] In other words, even before the preparation of the subsequent decrees provided for in the Second Decentralization Act (the *décrets d'application*, a crucial legal step in the implementation of legislation in France) and the appearance of the sequential legislation (on administrative reorganization), it is clear that the state's 'field service' apparatus will remain at least in some recognizable form. Thirdly, the finance for planning studies and for infrastructure costs will revert to the commune[33] through the *dotation globale de l'équipement* (a specific kind of central government revenue-sharing or rate support grant for infrastructure) progressively over the next three years, releasing the communes entirely from their dependence on the DDE in respect of finance for planning projects and finance for infrastructure.[34] Indeed, of these three general changes, the last is perhaps legally the most clear-cut in clarifying the new distribution of responsibilities between state and local authorities — although doubts have been expressed about the inadequate amounts of money to be redistributed in a period of economic recession, and, in addition, it is not yet clear how the grants will be allocated.

Of the more specific changes in statutory planning, the most important is found in the now infamous Article 38 of the Second Act.[35] This lays down the principle that if a commune does not have an approved POS, then the mayor will not be allowed to hold the executive power over planning applications. In view of the statistics of POS approval, given in Table 9.1, then the majority of mayors will be denied this power.

Moreover, given the long time involved in producing a POS, then it would not be unreasonable to assume that the majority of mayors will be denied this power over the period of the present Administration.[36] A further specific change in statutory planning at the local level is that the previous obligation

**Table 9.1**   Progress in POS preparation (as of July 1982)

| Stage of preparation | Number of plans |
|---|---|
| Started | 10,357 |
| Published | 6,260 |
| *Approved* | *4,487* |
| Total started or completed | (21,104 |
| (Total number of communes) | (36,371) |

*Source:*   *Receuil des statistiques sur l'urbanisme,* Ministère de l'Urbanisme et du Logement, 1983, p. 46.

for communes of up to 10,000 population to prepare a local plan has been removed. This means that if a commune decides not to produce a local plan then the mayor will never have the right to decide on the specific applications for planning permission which would follow. In this set of circumstances, and the circumstances mentioned earlier where a plan has been started but not yet approved, central government field services — the DDEs — maintain their former control over planning permission.

In a strict legal sense, then, the first two of the Decentralization Acts have transferred executive powers to elected officers of municipal, departmental and regional councils, and this transfer is clearly set out in formal terms in specific sections of the acts. However, close examination of the texts suggests that other sections of the same acts make provision for the continued right of state intervention in plan-making, as the title of a recent article suggests: 'L'Urbanisme en décentralisation surveillée; chassez la tutelle, elle revient au galop!' ('Urbanism under supervised decentralization: having got rid of the formal tutelage system, it just bounces right back!').[37] Danan and others,[38] for example, have argued that not only do the legal texts contain elements which contradict the principles of power transfer, but so also does a consideration of the future implementation and practice of the new legislation. In particular, the inequality and impracticality of the legislation for small communes has been mentioned as one important feature amongst others. This and other issues related to the future implementation of the legislation will be considered in the next section.

CENTRE-PERIPHERY RELATIONS: A SHIFT IN POWER?

One important way to help in identifying some of the factors which may generally affect the power distribution between centre and periphery at this transitional point in time is to analyse the views of politicians and state and local officials concerning the Decentralization Acts and their consequences for urban planning. During the summer of 1983 we interviewed, among others, a range of politicians and officials in the Nord/Pas de Calais Region.[39]

All of the politicians interviewed in the Nord/Pas de Calais were positively in favour of the transfer of planning powers and, in particular, of the right to make executive decisions concerning planning applications. The question of POS preparation was not regarded as a high priority, although the belief was widespread that those communes without an approved plan would simply have to ensure that one would be prepared in the near future. None of the politicians interviewed expressed concern or displeasure to be given these new powers, although non-Socialist politicians were rather more critical of the resources which would be made available to implement the powers. In particular, they felt that small- to medium-sized communes (approximately up to 10,000 population) would find it difficult financially to employ technical staff of their own to assist with planning decisions. Socialist politicians, by contrast, felt that resources would be both forthcoming and sufficient for this purpose and that some form of technical service department responsible to the departmental council would be developed to assist mayors of these small communes. Also, the Socialist politicians viewed the transfer of responsibilities in planning and the new financial arrangements for planning as a method of crushing the power of the DDE. Concern was expressed by many, however, that since the publication of the legislation, the DDE had been attempting to take on a new role as political educators. This was evidenced by numerous publications for mayors and various series of seminars which had been held by the DDEs in the two departments studied. Clearly the DDEs were attempting to establish their position as 'experts' who would continue to prepare plans and deal with planning applications.

The question of moving towards more *regroupements* (functional groupings) of communes was discussed at length because it seemed reasonable to assume that in cases of small- to medium-sized communes, technical planning assistance might be sought on a shared basis. This view did not seem to have been actively considered, however. Those who were already a part of a communal grouping with a planning function had considered the possibility that some communes would wish in fact to withdraw, but the majority view was that they were likely to remain within the grouping for the purposes of plan-making but not for the treatment of planning applications. In other words, the status quo would remain. However, given the political changes which have taken place within communal groupings in the Nord/Pas de Calais Region as the result of the municipal elections of March 1983, the view was widely expressed that in those councils in which the right-wing national opposition had gained control, the new majority coalitions, once they had gained some political experience with the new system, might put the future of such functional groupings in doubt.

A small but significant minority of the politicians interviewed made the even more problematic point that many mayors might not be happy to have these new responsibilities, not only because of the problems of technical assistance attached to them, but also because the decisions arrived at would be directly accountable to the mayor. In other words, no longer could mayors hide behind the DDE.

In general, the interviews with politicians suggested that there had been very little forward planning of how they would implement the legislation apart from some vague ideas which had not really been thought through. No clear-cut decisions or documented approaches had been produced or arrived at even by the Socialist Party, although they had two committees working on the issue.[40] It seemed that the party, at the regional level in Nord/Pas de Calais, was making no directives or suggestions to mayors in the area although there was a general view held that the DDE would no longer maintain its former role. Given that the legislation was to be implemented only two months after this investigation, this finding was surprising.

Planning officials interviewed comprised both contractual staff and civil servants. Given their very different roles, backgrounds and views of planning, as discussed earlier, then it was hardly surprising to find that their views in respect of decentralization would cover different aspects of the implications of the process. Civil servants (officials of the central government hierarchy) took the view that the legislation was too rushed and too complex for the average mayor to understand let alone implement. In addition, they felt that their role as planning 'experts' would continue as before simply because there was insufficient money available for the majority of communes to employ their own staff. It was clear that they felt threatened by the legislation, but none the less it did provide for the continuity of their organizational role and structure — at whatever size and in whatever capacity — and, given the absence of further operational legislation, they saw some future for themselves. Uncertainty and lack of staff motivation did seem to be a problem, but they were devoting their efforts towards political education. Interestingly, neither of the two DDEs seemed to have had any difficulties with their new administrative masters — the respective *Comissaires de la République* — despite the fact that traditionally the Ministries of the Interior (the hierarchical superior of the prefects and later of the commissioners, whose functional responsibility widened with decentralization) and of *Équipement* (the ministry charged with public works and development, which formerly controlled its own field services — the DDEs) had had overt differences of opinion. (This was an issue mentioned by both contractual staff and politicians as likely to lead to difficulties in the future should the role of the DDE be substantially modified and threatened by the establishment of technical departments accountable to elected members.)

Contractual staff viewed the transfer of power more as an issue with specific implications for planning administration and practice. Although most contracted staff viewed the transfers positively and likely to lead to greater democracy, many believed that the determination of planning applications would become much more *laissez-faire* than in the past. Largely this view derived from the impossibility of technical service departments being in place at the enactment date (October 1983), and the view that if mayors with executive powers did refuse to use the DDE's technical services meantime, then little action could be taken to prevent decisions being taken which might be to the mayor's electoral or even personal advantage — perhaps not in the best interests of the community.

Many contracted staff, however, were optimistic that, even in the medium term, they might find employment opportunities outside the state service and in the local authorities. Moreover, given the small number of communes with an approved POS, and given that these plans are now the key to the powers to rule on planning applications, they saw a consequent need for early and speedy progress on the preparation of these plans — but, like many civil servants, they were sceptical of sufficient financial resources being available for this to take place. Connected to this issue was a further concern mentioned by contracted staff. This was that even though they were better equipped professionally to provide technical assistance to politicians than were the civil servants of the DDE, many still felt that no significant improvement would take place in the quality of technical work provided. Moreover, they felt that analysis of survey information — which is, at present, minimal in plans — might become even more limited as communes became even more insular than before and even less inclined to form the sort of groupings which would be necessary to tackle many urban planning problems.

Clearly, then, the planners, whether contractual staff or civil servants, viewed the outcome and implications of this transfer of power as one which depended heavily upon the evolving relations between the state services (the DDEs), whose future role was uncertain, and the willingness and capacity of mayors to strike out on an independent path. That path, in turn, could lead either to a neglect of technical expertise (and a further increase in the influence of political and personal considerations) or to the development of independent local planning staffs, whose make-up, local role, and links with the state and/or other localities have as yet hardly begun to be considered. Indeed, all of these possibilities will crucially depend upon financial resources for which no details are available at the present time.

CONCLUSIONS

We can now venture some preliminary observations and conclusions about the planning system in France as an example of centre–periphery relations — and as a system in change. In the first place, Thoenig's model of cross-functioning controls, which seemed adequately to explain the relationship between the state and the communes prior to decentralization, is unlikely to provide such an adequate framework for future analysis. In those communes without executive powers over planning applications, there will be continued technical control by the DDE until these communes have prepared and have approved a POS. This latter process is not likely to happen quickly. In those communes with an approved POS and therefore with executive powers over planning applications — by and large the bigger, more powerful communes — the degree of relationship between municipal councils and the DDE will very much depend on the extent to which a 'tutelle technique' will be exercised *de facto*, and, in particular, the extent to which they are likely to use their a posteriori controls under article 36 of the Second Decentralization Act on the transfer of responsibilities.[41]

Secondly, little thought seems to have been devoted to the operational aspects of the decentralization legislation, and especially the extent to which local authorities will employ their own technical assistance. This would seem to be a logical priority for mayors who wish to take up their new responsibilities at the present time. The DDEs are working to maintain a technical superiority over communal mayors for reasons of self-preservation, and therefore if mayors are willing to continue to use this 'field service' as it still exists then there might be little likelihood of their establishing their own technical services in the future. Not only does this question involve the relative allocation of as yet unspecified financial resources, but it also touches on the availability of central government funding in general in a period in which the Mitterrand Administration has turned towards the imposition of a far-reaching general austerity programme.[42]

Thirdly, mayors are now under considerable political pressure to be seen to take up their responsibilities. There will be little mercy from any quarter for a mayor who is seen not to be using his new powers. This is clearly iniquitous in the context of the planning system, where a layman is expected to take responsibility for the execution of complex technical decisions. Whether or not mayors have their own technical assistance to do this, or even if they continue to use the DDE services, one thing is clear: they will require education not only in respect of the new legislation but also in the technical aspects of planning. Urban planning may have been used by the Government as a way of smashing the *corps des ponts et chaussées* in the DDEs, but it will be the mayor of a commune who might have to pay a heavy political price for this — not an insignificant issue given the strength of the Socialist Party at the local government level.

Fourthly, urban planning is unlikely to be made any more democratic by the new legislation. Indeed, quite the opposite could happen; municipal councils can now generate and approve their own plans, or, alternatively, they can refuse to produce plans altogether. This situation would seem to be inconsistent with Socialist planning ideology, which normally seeks a greater degree of intervention, control and public accountability. In practice in France, what could conceivably happen is quite the opposite; the personal interests of local decision-makers could become even more influential in the plan-making process than before.

Fifthly, the practice of urban planning in general is unlikely to make progress over the next few years since too many people with technical planning skills are waiting for future legislation to emerge. The system of planning introduced by de Gaulle was in no way exempt from criticisms, but at least it led to significant improvements in planning practice. It is unlikely that there has been sufficient technical progress for the system to be able to withstand the period of discontinuity that the process of sequential legislative change is necessitating.

Finally, and related to the method of legislating through a sequence of acts rather than a single decentralization bill, it may be that the Mitterrand Administration saw political advantages in the former. After all, the principle of decentralization has long been espoused by many on the centre and right of French politics — who also stood to gain from any erosion of Socialist dominance at local level — and the Government's 'salami tactics', starting with the principle and gradually filling in the details, was clearly an attempt to undermine opposition and construct a broad consensus on the principle, leaving divisive details till last. However, the tactic may well backfire as the state and the newly-empowered lower levels become bogged down in the inconsistencies of successive measures. Furthermore, if the political tide turns against the Socialists and no further legislation emerges, those loopholes in the existing texts which allow central intervention could simply be emphasized in practice by a non-Socialist government. Alternatively, the French left is not without a certain *étatiste* tradition which could reassert itself if efficient state economic management, for example, were to meet with local resistance. Under such circumstances, decentralization legislation would remain on the statute books, but recentralization would take place in daily administrative practice.

NOTES

1. Britain and Germany, for example, had more than 50 per cent of their populations living in towns by 1890. The percentage of town dwellers in France was still only 54 per cent in 1950, rising to 73 per cent in 1975.
2. Apart from legislation referring to plan production in 1919, further legislation was passed in 1924, 1943 (under the Vichy Regime) and 1958.
3. A *loi d'orientation* establishes principles and structures for the future development of particular sectors (major measures of this sort under the Fifth Republic have included

agriculture and education), and *foncière* refers to the use of land; it is usually translated here as the Outline Planning and Land Act.

4. Within the context of the POS, decisions on development are made through individual planning applications known as *permis de construire*.

5. See H. Lena, 'Le régime contentieux des "plans d'occupation des sols" ', *Urbanisme*, No. 172 (1979), pp. 39-43.

6. Planning became a major political platform in the municipal elections of 1977, and the present Government has used planning powers as a central feature of the new decentralization legislation.

7. Vincent Wright, *The Government and Politics of France* (London: Hutchinson, 1979), p. 200.

8. Loi N° 82-213, *Les droits et les libertés des régions, départements et communes*, 2 March 1982.
Loi N° 83-88, *La répartition des compétences entre les communes, les départements, les régions et l'État*, 7 January 1983.

9. *Groupe de travail*: this is the group comprising the mayor of a commune, officials of the 'field services' of *Équipement* and Agriculture, municipal councillors, and representatives of the Chambers of Commerce and Agriculture, who meet to elaborate the POS. On average, there are about six such meetings for the preparation of a plan.

10. During 1981, the author conducted research in four French *départements*, Bouches du Rhône, Loire, Essonne and Pas de Calais. More than sixty interviews were conducted with mayors and planning officials.

11. See J.-C. Thoenig, *L'Ère des technocrates* (Paris: Éditions d'Organisation, 1973; 'La relation entre le centre et la périphérie en France', *Bulletin de l'Institut International d'Administration Publique*, No. 36 (1975); and 'Local Government Institutions and the Contemporary Evolution of French Society', in J. LaGroye and V. Wright, eds, *Local Government in Britain and France* (London and Winchester, Mass.: Allen & Unwin, 1979), Ch. 5.

12. Decentralization is proceeding by a series of acts which have begun with those mentioned in note 2, and which will continue with legislation relating to finance and local taxation, the election of council representatives and officers, a new statute for local administrative staff (possibly creating a local civil service with some of the advantages of tenure, classification, promotion, etc., characteristic of the central state's administrative hierarchy), and the status of Paris. These would all be necessary for a full and detailed evaluation of the shift in power — as would, of course, be some *post hoc* analysis of practice.

13. The Mitterrand Administration introduced for general comment what, in Britain, is called a white paper, or, in other words, a detailed report giving the main provisions of a bill which it is intended to introduce into the legislature. The French term is *avant-projet*.

14. The author has completed more than thirty interviews with mayors and planning officials (July/August 1983) in Paris and the Nord/Pas de Calais Region.

15. For a full explanation, see I.B. Wilson, 'Preparation of Local Plans in France', *Town Planning Review*, 54, No. 2 (1983), pp. 155-73.

16. DDE (Direction Départementale de l'Équipement): a field service of the Ministry of Urban Planning and Housing (formerly the Ministère de l'Équipement), which is concerned with planning documents, planning permissions (building permits), infrastructure and services, transport planning, and construction of public buildings.
DDA (Direction Départementale d'Agriculture): a field service of the Ministry of Agriculture, which is involved in urban planning in the interest of protecting good or high-quality agricultural land and afforested areas.

17. The author was permitted to attend *groupe de travail* meetings in the four *départements* studied, but these meetings are not open to the public.

18. The Groupe d'études et de programmation (GEP) is one of the sections of the DDE and is the section responsible for carrying out planning studies and plans.

19. See, for example, F. d'Arcy and B. Jobert, 'Urban Planning in France', in J. Hayward and M. Watson, eds, *Planning, Politics and Public Policy* (Cambridge: Cambridge University Press, 1975), where they comment that senior civil servants of the DDE are '. . . ill prepared intellectually for the task' (of plan-making), p. 308.

20. By and large, senior civil servants of the DDE have trained as engineers in the *grandes écoles* system, especially in the École Polytechnique and the École des Ponts et Chaussées; they are generally members of the Corps des Ponts et Chaussées, one of the oldest *corps* (a traditional corporate body with a privileged role in recruitment, promotions, etc.) in the French civil service. The lower professional staff have multidisciplinary university backgrounds and often have postgraduate qualifications and/or experience in planning.

21. Honorariums for supervisory work in communes can amount to anything up to 50 per cent of the total salary of a DDE civil servant. This is mentioned, for example, by Y. Mény, in 'Relations Between Central and Local Government in France', SSRC/IPSA Conference on International Relations, Brasenose College, Oxford (September 1980), p. 17.
22. V. Wright, op. cit.
23. Howard Machin, commenting on Thoenig's thesis, outlines these points, in 'Centre and Periphery', in P.G. Cerny and M.A. Schain, eds, *French Politics and Public Policy* (London and New York: Frances Pinter, St. Martin's Press and Methuen University Paperbacks, 1980), p. 140.
24. Planning agencies exist in Paris and some provincial cities. The Paris agency (Atelier Parisien d'Urbanisme or APUR) is an agency for both the city and the department of Paris. The agencies set up in large towns include: Troyes, Marseille, Aix, Brest, Toulouse, Bordeaux, Rennes, Tours, Grenoble, Saint-Étienne, Nantes, Metz, Dunkerque, Mauberge, Saint-Omer, Strasbourg, Lyon, Paris, Rouen, Le Havre and Belfort. For a full discussion of urban planning agencies, see Y.M. Danan, *Les Agences d'urbanisme d'agglomération* (Paris: CRU, 1976).
25. For example, all urban zones are denoted by 'U' and open space/agriculture by 'N'. Subdivisions of 'U' and 'N' are used to describe different zone types within these two categories, e.g., Uab, Uac, Nab, Nac, etc.
26. From current statistics produced by the Planning Ministry (*Recueil d'informations statistiques sur l'urbanisme*, Ministère de l'Urbanisme et du Logement, 1982) there are 36,371 communes in France. There are 660 civil servants and contracted staff working in DDEs.
27. J.-P. Worms, 'La décentralisation: une stratégie du changement social', *Revue pour le pouvoir local*, No. 238 (1983),pp. 4-5.
28. J.-C. Thoenig and F. Dupuy, 'Les conventions entre l'État et le département', CNRS/Ministère de l'Environnement et Cadre de Vie.
29. G. Gontchatoff, 'Les principes généraux du transfert des compétences', *Revue pour le pouvoir local*, No. 238 (1983), pp. 5-12.
30. Article 35 (Loi 83-88).
31. Article 36 (Loi 83-88).
32. Article 50 (on POS) and Article 61 (on *permis de construire*), ibid.
33. Article 40, ibid.
34. The progressive transfer of funds will take place thus: 1st year — 20 per cent; 2nd year — 60 per cent; 3rd year — 100 per cent. The distribution of the DGE amongst communes will be calculated as follows: 40 per cent will relate to levels of investment already made in infrastructure; 15 per cent will relate to each of (a) the number of schoolchildren, (b) fiscal potential, and (c) housing built in the past three years; and 15 per cent will relate to the tax-receiving potential, i.e. if the low level of business implantation or activity reduces the potential base for the local transaction tax. C. Braillon, 'Les transferts des compétences issus de la loi du 7 janvier 1983: l'urbanisme et les moyens financiers', *Revue pour le pouvoir local*, No. 238 (1983), pp. 13-20.
35. Article 38 (Loi 83-88). For a full discussion of Article 38 and other articles mentioned in this text, see Y.M. Danan, ed., *Décentralisation et urbanisme* (Paris: Direction de l'Urbanisme et des Paysages, 1983).
36. Previous research conducted by the author indicates typical preparation timescales as shown in Table 9.2.

Table 9.2  POS timescales

| Département | No. of communes | No. of POS approved (1967–81) | Average time between start of POS and approval | |
|---|---|---|---|---|
| Bouches du Rhône | 119 | 14 (at 1 Jan. 1981) | 6 yrs | 3 ms |
| Loire | 327 | 72 (at 1 Feb. 1981) | 5 yrs | 8 ms |
| Pas de Calais | 909 | 25 (at 31 Dec. 1981) | 6 yrs | 8 ms |

*Source:*  Periodic returns for the *Receuil d'information statistiques sur l'urbanisme*, Ministère de l'Environnement et Cadre de Vie.

37. Y.M. Danan, 'L'urbanisme en décentralisation surveillée: chassez la tutelle, elle revient au galop!', *Le Moniteur* (18 March 1983).
38. See Y.M. Danan, 'La décentralization de l'urbanisme existe, je l'ai rencontré', *Le Moniteur* (27

February 1981), or V. Renard, 'Décentralisation des compétences d'urbanisme', *Études foncières*, No. 18 (1983), pp. 50-2.

39. See note 14. Also note that the Nord/Pas de Calais Region comprises the two *départements* of Nord and Pas de Calais.
40. The two committees related to *Urbanisme* and to *Décentralisation*.
41. See note 31.
42. See Chapters 4 and 10.

# III STRUCTURAL CONSTRAINTS AND POLICY ARENAS

## 10 State Capitalism in France and Britain and the International Economic Order *

*Philip G. Cerny*

The experiences of capitalist mixed economies with nationalized industries have created an ambiguous legacy, a legacy within which tensions and contradictions have emerged in a new stark light in the world recession of the 1970s and 1980s. Nowhere does the contrast seem clearer than between Britain and France under the Thatcher and Mitterrand Governments respectively. And yet, in both Britain and France, things have been happening to the public sector which go beyond the bounds not only of mainstream analysis — neo-classical economics and the Keynesian/social democratic approaches — but also of contemporary Marxist interpretations. In this context, the neo-Marxist 'state derivation' debate seems all too often to be merely an attempt to translate into Marxist terminology, and then chiefly to explain away, Keynesian and social democratic approaches to the mixed economy during the long boom cycle from the Second World War to the early 1970s; the crisis then becomes simply a logical conclusion to the contradictions of capitalism in spite of the efforts of a 'relatively autonomous' state to counteract the general tendency of the rate of profit to fall. But new developments in Britain and France, under highly problematic conditions, suggest that things are not so simple, for any of the existing schools of thought.

In this chapter it is my intention to explore some recent developments in 'state capitalism', narrowly defined, and to suggest that the autonomy of the state, and the complex and increasing constraints upon it in the international economic context, are in certain circumstances closely and directly related. Thus what we may see as contrasting experiences in Britain and France in the 1980s may be analysed as different modes of a very specific state capitalist phenomenon linked to recessionary conditions. In doing this I will first attempt to distinguish between state capitalism and the 'capitalist state' in different theoretical traditions, and to characterize state capitalism in broad context *and* as a special type of interventionism, qualitatively different from the others, within liberal–democratic mixed economies. This particular form of state capitalism will then be located in the specific context of Britain and France as 'intermediate economies,' and its recent — and potential future — role will be evaluated by both continuing recessionary and possible incipient expansionary conditions.

* An earlier version of this chapter was presented at the Conference of Europeanists, Council for European Studies, Washington D.C., and to the Inter-University Seminar on the State, Columbia University, during October 1983.

I. STATE CAPITALISM AND THE CAPITALIST STATE

Most theorizing about the role of the state in advanced capitalist society is simultaneously concerned with, on the one hand, the growing *power* of the state in the regulation of economic activity and, on the other, the inherent or necessary *limitations* on the nature and scope of state activity. There are clear conflicts between three approaches: the neo-classical approach, which emphasizes the long-term counterproductive effects of growing state intervention in terms which stress dysfunctional increases in the amount of extra-economic coercion inherently bound up in such developments and their distorting effects on efficient market allocation of resources; the Keynesian/social democratic approach, which emphasizes the role which 'fine-tuning' and aggregate demand management can play in counteracting cyclical distortions in the markets themselves while also increasing the welfare of the working class; and the neo-Marxist notion of the state as 'collective capitalist,' ensuring the general conditions of capitalist production and building functional class alliances, which may go against the interests of particular fractions of capital but which cannot go so far as to undermine the systemic necessity for the continued private accumulation of capital. The neo-classicists oppose growing state interventionism; the Keynesian social democrats approve growing *relative* state intervention (that functional to fine-tuning and social peace); and neo-Marxists approve it in so far as it reinforces the long-term tendency toward the socialization of production and the well-being and political consciousness of the working class, but oppose it in so far as it props up capital and delays the onset of crisis conditions.

It is clear, however, that each of these approaches contains within it a theory of the *limitations* of state interventionism. Indeed, the nature of those limitations is highlighted much more strongly in recessionary conditions, when capitalist societies are seen to bump firmly up against those bounds. Here, even for the neo-Marxist and the Keynesian, the need for the state to create general conditions of profitability for the private sector demands austerity to combat stagflation. *How much* austerity, rather than its necessity, becomes the central question, along with that of *who* should or can most functionally be squeezed (with the implications of this for class alliances and political stability). In neo-classical economics, firstly, the limitations are in some ways less automatic in purely political terms; indeed, state regulation of the economy is seen to be no different in principle in advanced capitalist society than it was in pre-capitalist or mercantile societies, i.e. dysfunctional to the self-sustaining creation of wealth, but politically perfectly capable of imposing non-capitalist structures of the authoritative allocation of value (bureaucratic and/or coercive allocation). The 'invisible hand' operates efficiently only when it is politically freed to do so. People accustomed to, and aware of, the longer-term benefits of free market conditions (and aware of their implications for individual and political freedom in the furthering of historical progress) will thus act rationally by resisting the return of dysfunctional non-economic forms of allocation; the need for it will be self-evident. However, they may act irrationally if those benefits are mis-represented or hidden — by indoctrination, by personal greed (especially the collective greed of the working class, whose growing wage demands can price their labor out of the market), *or* because a long boom with its attendant 'growing pie' can given the impression that market distortions can be lived with if they lead to an increase in the general welfare through either demand management or social justice.

Thus while limitations on state activity are not reached in any automatic way, the necessity to re-establish even stricter limits in a period of recession becomes self-evident to anyone who understands the natural laws of market economics. In this perspective, two main kinds of interlocking constraints can be seen to operate. On the one hand, the expanding role of the state is directly dysfunctional for the operation of the major markets which regulate economic activity in a capitalist economy, and this dysfunctionality becomes critical to the regeneration of economic activity in a recession. In the operation of capital markets, the state's deficit financing, which becomes necessary for both the maintenance of existing programs and the adoption of any reflationary programs, soaks up private capital, 'crowding out' new (and existing) private investment — whose expansion is the most critical factor in creating new growth tendencies in a mixed economy — and, in doing so, raising interest rates in such a way as to channel funds away from risky investment in industry towards safe investment in money markets. In the operation of labor markets, state programs of demand maintenance and non-market 'corporatist' intervention in the settling of norm-setting wage levels in both the public sector and 'tripartite' forms of government–industry–union bargaining make it difficult to readjust real wage levels downward to reflect the requirements of profitability. And in the operation of consumer markets, the combination of the two above factors both leads to demand-pull inflation, as continued consumer spending chases too few goods in a context where domestic demand is still insufficient (given constraints on profitability) to counteract investment decline and the cost of labor, and (in an open international economy) exacerbates the vulnerability of the national economy to import penetration. Thus the state is tempted (or forced) to expand the money supply in an authoritative (rather than market-led) fashion, further reducing the real return on investment and permitting inflated wage claims, leading to a vicious inflationary spiral rather than a virtuous inflationary circle, exacerbating existing distortions in the other markets.

On the other hand, the state is seen as inherently parasitic, with a bureaucratic dynamic of its own — dependent on its capacity to extract resources from society in a coercive manner (through its fiscal and monetary powers) — which provides a permanent temptation to attempt to counteract the market by increasing the range of its activities and the size of its structures (the tendency toward a 'command economy'). If the state is freed to expand in this way, a widening process of market distortion will lead to a tendency for the rate of profit in the private sector to fall and therefore for the mixed economy to move toward one increasingly dominated by the public sector, which is inherently incapable of acting in a market-rational manner — or, at least, is increasingly incapable of so acting as market distortions, themselves the product of expanding state activities, incrementally reduce whatever market constraints do operate on the public sector in a mixed economy where the private sector is profitable. Thus, in a recession, when market distortions cannot be hidden behind private sector profitability, a dual process takes place. On the one hand, private sector profitability is increasingly undermined; and on the other, the public sector increasingly allocates value in an authoritative manner. These processes together both prevent the return of self-sustaining growth fuelled by the profit incentive — the basic driving force of economic expansion — and reduce the political freedom which has been the historical product and condition of efficient private resource allocation. The bureaucratic state inevitably leads to political repression. Political democracy, however, given public awareness of the dangers and resolute leadership, can act as a barrier to such developments if people can be convinced to defer gratification (one-third of the unemployed voted Conservative in the June 1983 general elections in Britain) until profitability is restored and capital reconversion sufficiently advanced to lead to a new boom. And if constraints in the internal political system are insufficient — as with the 1981 Socialist victories in France — then international market constraints will reinforce internal market constraints and make such an experiment counterproductive even for the workers in the longer run. Ultimately, however, the adoption of a Soviet-style autarchic command economy remains a political alternative if ideological vigilance is not maintained. Thus the autonomy of the state to regulate economic activity is inherently counterproductive in economic terms, and the contradictions embodied in such activity — and the dangers inherent in the alternative — become starkly obvious in a recession.

Keynesian/social democratic approaches also embody functional limitations to state autonomy, limitations which share several of the features of the neo-classical model despite the modifications which they brought to it and which were so important in the long boom following the Second World War in influencing economic policies of both right and left in the advanced capitalist nations. These modifications rested on the premise that even free markets became distorted of their own accord for a number of reasons because of tendency of competitive pressures to lead to the development of overcapacity, and the limited adaptability of fixed capital (which tied up investment needed for reconversion). In such contexts, fixed capital too often tended to become idle capital in the event of a slump, with the resulting rise in unemployment further reducing the consumer demand required to generate an upturn. Thus a division of labor was envisaged between private capital, which continued to be the basic source of investment and dynamism in the economy's productive structure, and state intervention, which took on three types of tasks: firstly, it would, through its general level of spending (and especially through welfare spending), maintain demand at a level which could sustain production and allow a breathing space for capital to readjust its investment structure; secondly, it would, through fiscal and monetary controls directly aimed at business and finance, 'fine-tune' the economy to reward efficient investment and to punish 'overheating;' and, thirdly, it would guarantee the maintenance (directly or indirectly, through subsidies or nationalization) of production and services which, though chronically unprofitable, none the less provided crucial infrastructure for economic growth and the profitability of private capital in general. The new equilibrium point at which such tasks were aimed was full employment. Such measures also had the side-effect of allowing the creation of class alliances around certain traditional welfare and trade-union demands, giving a new democratic legitimacy to the more pragmatic, group bargaining-oriented political process which would be necessary for achieving some of these goals.

This division of labor was meant to prevent the recurrence of serious slumps; it was not meant to substitute state management and/or ownership for private capital which, as in the classical model which it criticized, still provided the fundamental dynamic mechanism for self-sustaining economic growth and development. The fundamental thrust of governmental measures is thus to influence the evolution of demand and its impact on industry and to provide basic energy resources, intermediate goods, some transportation, communication and other services, and basic regulatory frameworks necessary to counteract dysfunctional tendencies in markets, not to replace those markets. Therefore there arises a crude distinction between the 'supply-side' or 'production functions' of the economy, which are the arena proper to private capital, and the 'demand-side' or 'consumption functions,' in which the state oversees the basic conditions for the first to continue efficiently to operate. None the less, slumps have not been fully eliminated, and even Keynesians and social democrats, in somewhat differing ways, have seen such developments as resulting partly from new rigidities built into governmental measures themselves, preventing capital from playing its role in its proper sphere. The combination of stagnation and inflation seen in the 1970s has been considered to be relatively impervious to reflationary measures, and the need for reconversion involved in the so-called 'Third Industrial Revolution' based on electronics and related new technology to be beyond the capacity of private investment to fuel. Thus state intervention in this approach, too, finds its limitations in the structural rigidities constraining its conjunctural measures, although the result is not seen to lie in the emergence of a repressive 'command economy' so much as in a lumbering, muddling, 'overloaded' state.

The 'overloaded' state is seen to bump up against three main types of constraint, similar in some ways to the limitations found in the neo-classical model though without the extreme consequences. In the first place, chronic deficit financing by governments in a slump period is seen, once again, to soak up private investment and raise interest rates in ways which crowd out private investment and channel resources into non-productive financial outlets. Secondly, we once again find nationalized industry and tripartite wage bargaining blamed for maintaining 'wage-push' inflation and preventing rises in productivity and/or the shedding of newly redundant labor (given the obsolescence of such fixed capital and the pressing need for reconversion), lowering profitability through labor market rigidities. Thirdly, attempts to maintain overall levels of economic activity — to maintain demand and infrastructure, and to prevent unemployment — is seen to lock state interventionism into a 'lame duck' syndrome in which the state takes responsibility for more and more unprofitable sectors of the economy. All three of these constraints interact in recessionary conditions to restrict the capacity of private capital to perform its supply-side or productive function. The state itself is capable only of more *ad hoc* regulation which demonstrates not so much the repression as the inefficiencies of bureaucratic overplanning. Thus the challenge for the Keynesian/social democratic state is to realize its limitations and to combine a measure of austerity with the retention of a minimal welfare net to sustain some degree of consensus, while occasionally making forays into 'industrial policy' to help restructure old industry and encourage the new in particular, targeted 'growth sectors;' ability to carry out the latter, however, will depend upon success in putting across the former without destroying the class alliance upon which control of the state's political apparatus is based. Many false starts and internal conflicts are built into such a problematic strategy (or set of new tactics). For the limits to state autonomy are again set by the inappropriateness of bureaucratic management to self-sustaining economic growth based in the private, sector-led productive sphere.

Marxist theories about the role of the state were originally directed against classical economic theories, too, but they attributed certain crisis tendencies to the general underlying structure of capitalism — its class antagonisms — rather than to market distortions; thus the role of the state was constrained primarily by its class nature. As in the classical model, the advent of capitalism was characterized by a reduction of the role of the state to its 'night watchman' functions — maintaining a stable currency, defense, and law and order — with the nature of its interventions stemming from the needs of the 'bourgeoisie as a whole' to maintain its dominant position and to accumulate capital efficiently (once again, the main motor force of capitalist expansion). A number of factors made this characterization more problematic in the twentieth century — the popularity of liberal democracy, the rise of fascism with its corporatist appeals to large sections of the masses, and the post-war dominance of the Keynesian/social democratic approach in actual policy-making structures and decisions along with its element of popular consensus. Neo-Marxist theory of the state, given new ideological impetus by the radicalizing experiences of the 1960s, sought first to demystify the capitalist state[1] and then to re-evaluate its role in maintaining the *general* material conditions for the accumulation of capital — often involving state opposition to the demands of *particular* fractions of capital, building class alliances with the working class which created 'real gains' in welfare terms for that class, and pursuing the interests of the capitalist nation-state as a whole in an international capitalist economy characterized by competing national capitals and by structures of multinational capital and peripheral 'dependency' on the industrial 'core.' Thus, in different ways, the state was seen to have, in 'advanced capitalist' or 'late capitalist' society, a new 'relative autonomy'[2] which could be traced back to the establishment of a 'capitalist world-system' even before the advent of full industrial capitalism,[3] or to the real power of the bureaucratic state apparatus in creating capitalism itself,[4] or to the political and economic power of the organized working class in the corporate state, or to the relative autonomy of ideology and culture in sustaining capitalist hegemony,[5] or, ultimately, to the possibility for the state to take measures to counteract the long-term tendency for the rate of profit to fall,[6] etc., or to some combination of these.

This autonomy of the state, however, was still only relative. Its tasks were ultimately circumscribed by the class nature of capitalism itself — by the interlocking imperatives within capitalism to allow the private ownership of the means of production to dominate (this, after all, is the defining characteristic of the capitalist mode of production), and efficiently to provide for the accumulation of capital despite crisis tendencies (this being the dynamic force behind capitalist expansion, which gives it its historical force and significance). As neo-Marxist theories grappled with the recession, wondering whether this could be the sign of a final crisis of capitalism, the growing concern with the limits to the autonomy of the state demonstrated a remarkable similarity in content — if not ideological imperative — to the limitations asserted by the neo-classical approach or grudgingly admitted by the Keynesian/social democratic approach.

The need to maintain the position of the ruling class while also maintaining worker compliance creates a double constraint. The right is forced to bargain with labor, or to appeal to labor, to a minimum extent, and therefore cannot impose repressive or extensive labor-shedding policies directly through the state, but must find a way for private industry to do so; thus it must try to mollify labor while removing the barriers to increasing unemployment, encouraging labor 'realistically' to accept a higher level of unemployment. At the same time, the left is forced to bargain with capital (or with different capitals), and cannot take over its very functions, i.e. capital accumulation and investment, without undermining its own *raison d'être*. State structures, too, have expanded their intervention in response to *ad hoc* exigencies and demands, and (as with other theories of bureaucratic rigidity) are characterized by the form of 'primitive accumulation;'[7] therefore they lack sufficient coordinating and strategy-developing capacity to replace private capital accumulation in a self-sustaining growth process, and cannot deal with serious recessionary challenges in an autonomous fashion except by authoritarian repression of the working class. Thus the need for symbiosis between the private sector and the public sector if the state is to have any autonomy at all means that the public sector loses whatever autonomy it has in crisis periods. Despite the differences in language, underlying these considerations is the assertion that the state can only operate autonomously at all if it is, in the process, sustaining or re-establishing, directly or indirectly, the profitability of private capital, an assertion which is not exactly incompatible with the neo-classical and Keynesian/social democratic approaches as outlined above.

Thus in an open, liberal–democratic mixed economy, the capitalist state is limited to a role which forecloses the possibility that the state itself, particularly in recessionary conditions, can act in a truly autonomous fashion, which might mean challenging or replacing private capital in creating self-sustaining economic growth. The consequence is that the capitalist state in a recession must readjust its priorities. Its first task is to restore the profitability of private capital. Its other tasks in advanced capitalist society — market regulation, welfare, maintenance of employment, demand management, infrastructural support, provision of public services, etc. — are downgraded if not excluded. And the most problematic of these activities must be direct state control of profitable industries — 'state capitalism' in its strict sense. In this case, the role of private capital *is* replaced. Now where such state capitalism has been observed and analysed, its historical forms tend to comprise a set of exceptions which prove the rule. None the less, I shall argue later in the chapter, there may be circumstances in which state capitalism is beginning to take on the appearance of a more permanent phenomenon. For the moment, however, I would simply like to look at some of the main guises in which state capitalism has normally been seen to appear. In all cases, two interrelated conditions are present. Firstly, private capital is unable to operate profitably. Secondly, bureaucratic drawbacks are not a great handicap. The balance between these two elements operates in various different ways and at different levels of the economic structure, but together they lead to the emergence of some form of state capitalism.

The most controversial use of the term is in relation to bureaucratic, authoritarian and autarchic state structures where surplus is extracted by state-owned and managed industries from a wage labor force and then reinvested through these industries themselves or through an equally state-controlled credit system in an expansionary cycle analogous to that found in private sector-based capitalism. The element of autarchy (the exclusion of market exchanges with the outside world, and the condition of self-sufficiency in raw materials, capital goods and market outlets) prevents the competitive effects of other capitalist systems from undermining the circuit of capital. The main difference, of course, is that the motor force of the system is some form of public rather than private incentive structure to fuel the accumulation process — ranging from the internalized (patriotism, social consciousness, etc.) to the imposed (coercion, etc.). In this way, some theorists still label the Soviet Union as state capitalist, although this is widely contested. None the less, the possibility of the state itself engendering and structuring a self-sustaining process of capital accumulation and economic growth would be an important pointer as to whether other 'capitalist' states might eventually so act autonomously. Criticisms of this model include the assertion — widely held in the West — that private incentive is far more efficient than such public incentive (a matter of kind and not merely of degree) and that therefore such systems would involve an inherent tendency towards either growing dysfunctionalism and recurrent crises (possibly leading to overload and breakdown), or towards increasing use of coercive measures as in the traditional critique of bureaucracy, reducing the element of internalized public incentive and thus undermining the system's capacity to accumulate, reverting eventually to non-capitalist modes of surplus extraction in any definition. Also the need for impermeability to foreign competition would eliminate not only the negative effects of such competition (under-cutting of home prices by imports, etc.), but also the positive spur to efficient production and technological adaptability — for example, comparative advantages could not be efficiently exploited. But, as we have said, the very significance of the application of the label 'state capitalist' in such circumstances lies in its implications for the scope of state autonomy to transcend the limitations inherent in our three approaches in a consistent and self-sustaining fashion.

The second use of the term refers to the historical perspective which asserts that between the sixteenth and the nineteenth centuries capitalism itself as an economic and social phenomenon was in fact an epiphenomenon deriving originally from processes of state formation which were not themselves capitalist in character; in consequence, it remains dependent upon the state. In other words, self-sustaining capital accumulation could never exist in a vacuum, guided by an invisible hand, operating according to the efficient dictates of a free market. Rather, it was — and still is — the product of the goals of states themselves whether to power, or to legal personality, or to some set of substantive goals embodied in an ideology of the common good. Thus emerging state structures were not essentially or primarily capitalist in nature, but they did, in some direct or indirect process, deriving from the need for growing sources of wealth to maintain their expanding military and administrative bureaucracies and legal systems, support the incorporation of more and more groups of people into some form of association with the state. Hence these structures assimilated wider political publics which demanded a form of contractual recognition of their status, either in terms of the generalized protection of their new forms of property or by way of a say in the running of the state apparatus. Thus the state created the bourgeoisie — at least in terms of its legal ownership of the means and products of production — and therefore has the potential, in theory at least, of creating alternative modes of production.[8] The realization of that potential depends upon the conjunction of old-fashioned 'extra-economic power' with more powerful ideas and substantive goals about the establishment of more efficient and more just forms of production and distribution. Therefore the very *étatiste* nature of 'original' capitalism provides the conceptual breakthrough to the transcending of that capitalism through the state's potential for genuine autonomy. Again, we find a transcendence of the limitations of our three approaches.

A third form of state capitalism, perhaps foreshadowed to some extent in the discussion above, is of course the use of state-led development strategies in the Third World in order to compensate for either the lack, or the exploitative nature, of foreign and domestic private investment (and thus the lack of sufficient fuel for a 'take-off' into self-sustained capitalist economic growth). This can either be part of an avowedly capitalist development strategy, designed to insert the developing nation into the world capitalist system at a level at which it can fend for itself and profit from whatever comparative advantages it possesses, or merely a transitional strategy to some form of socialism (as evidenced by the popularity of Maoist-derived socialism in just such conditions). It may involve a greater or lesser degree of 'delinkage' or autarchy — in fact, a radical form of delinkage is sometimes considered to be the only alternative to dependency — and it will probably involve cooperation with a 'national bourgeoisie' through state-led planning and investment. It is thus analogous to the second type, with two differences. In the first place, its source is to be found in an already capitalist world system characterized by dependency and neo-colonialism — and not by any real extant state autonomy. And, in the second place, it may have as its goal its own self-liquidation — i.e., it may be consciously transitional — and regard the state as only having real autonomy for a limited period under exceptional circumstances. On the other hand, it may not, and may seek to associate the state permanently with the role of leading capitalist in a world in which the only alternative is a relapse into dependency, again contrasting with our three approaches.

The fourth mode of state capitalism only partially fits our basic definition, and we have already dealt with it to some extent. This is found in the view that certain kinds of activities in developed capitalist societies, *whether or not they are profitable*, comprise 'public goods' which by their very nature can (if the state so decides) be produced as well as allocated by the state itself without danger to the mixed nature of the economy. We are accustomed to public and social services being included in such a category, as well as (potentially) defense[9] or energy. Direct state management still tends to be the rule primarily where such activities are unprofitable — the 'lame duck' syndrome — but the state otherwise normally limits its interventions to consumption and/or allocation, leaving production to the private sector. However, the debate over where any such dividing line should be drawn is at the heart of public policy conflicts between social democrats and center–right parties in Western liberal democracies. As we pointed out in the earlier discussion of Keynesian/social democratic approaches, the resolution of such conflicts may take a different form in general conditions of prosperity than in a recession, and a variety of attempts have been made to transcend such a cleavage through the recognition of 'social limits to growth'[10] or of the true public character of economic activity generally.[11] If such a dividing line could be transcended or displaced, and if this were to remain effective or even progress further in recessionary conditions — as some democratic socialists think that it must, given the exacerbation of inequalities — then, once again, state autonomy might develop beyond the limits of our three approaches. None the less, while this form is the most common application of the notion of state capitalism, its limitations are the most directly subject to the kinds of considerations developed in the three approaches, which see the eventual result of a slump involving the displacement of the 'dividing line' *not* towards greater state autonomy, despite occasional attempts to reverse the process (as, it is often claimed, in Mitterrand's France), but away from such autonomy and back towards the reaffirmation of the primacy of the private sector.

Each of these four types of 'state capitalism' can, however, be characterized as the exception which proves the rule. The first type — Soviet-style 'state capitalism' — involves the abolition of the private sector and the adoption of extreme protectionism, and thus violates our conditions of an open, mixed economy (not to mention the assumption of liberal democracy, which is less central to the logic of the argument). The second can be seen as a kind of 'original sin' which capitalists can recognize but which has been transcended by subsequent history that has seen the emergence of capitalism in a form which has outgrown its filial dependency on the state. Indeed, the Maoist example becomes more problematic here given the evolution of the Chinese state after the death of Mao Zedong. The third can be characterized as a form of the second, as merely a transitional stage to insertion or take-off, with any genuine delinkage leading either to dependency upon the Soviet Union (i.e. Cuba) or a lack of development characteristic of a feudal rather than an advanced society (e.g. Albania). And the fourth, as we have mentioned, is highly problematic and tends to revert to the rule in recessionary conditions in order to restore profitability on as wide a basis as possible within the national economy. None the less developments in the structure of state capitalism in Britain and France over the past three to four years raise the question as to whether we are not seeing the rise of a fifth type, dependent on particular conditions, and providing a potential paradigm for future structural development reflecting the contradictory nature of the autonomy of the state in the contemporary world economy. The second part of this paper will be devoted to exploring some of the possible ramifications of such a phenomenon for the limitations which have traditionally been attributed to the interventions of the capitalist state and for the potential of the state to act as an autonomous, capital-accumulating entrepreneur.

## II. STATE CAPITALISM IN INTERMEDIATE ECONOMIES IN THE RECESSION

Recessions and depressions vary greatly, both in different historical periods and across different types of national (and international) economic structures, in the extent and complexity of the adaptation and reconstitution of capital which may be required to restore profitability and competitiveness (or, at the very least, the capacity to avoid continued losses). In some cases, the rationalization of existing capital structures, for example, through labor-shedding or the reorganization of management or marketing structures, may be sufficient. In other cases, complete conversion to new productive technologies may be required, with a consequent destruction and replacement of existing fixed capital — where, for example, amortization of existing fixed capital provides an insufficient margin in the face of productivity gains and/ or the competition of new, more efficient and technologically more complex product lines. Each of these sets of cases, taken in isolation, may present challenges that can be overcome within the bounds of existing capital structures, especially where the state can provide support facilities, including temporary employment subsidies, relocation grants, investment allowances, and the like. Here private capital and relative state autonomy can be mutually supportive. Here, too, the role of the state is likely to be limited in the ways suggested in our treatment of the neo-classical, Keynesian/social democratic and neo-Marxist approaches. (It must be recognized, of course, in passing, that the role of the state in wartime is frequently extended beyond these limits, but that is beyond the scope of the paper except in terms of a problematic analogy.)

However, when these two sets of cases occur together, this symbiosis may be harder to achieve. For Western industrial countries the so-called 'Second Industrial Revolution' can be seen, in retrospect, to have involved a reconversion process over the space of two generations, the general outcome of which involved labor-shedding in many industrial sectors, but which, taken as a whole, led to the possibility of actually increasing employment in both capital and consumer goods industries, as well as to a growing extent in services; the 'lesson' of this period has generally been taken to be that the efficient division of labor between private capital and the state in open, mixed economies was not only possible but essential in generating and sustaining an expansionary dynamic. In contrast, the capitalization of agriculture in Britain in the sixteenth–eighteenth centuries created a mass of landless agricultural workers, and the 'First Industrial Revolution' not only seemed to require a large 'reserve army' of labor which could not be fully absorbed but also led, for example, Germany, France and the United States, in varying ways, to go through long periods of extensive tariff protection, cartelization, concentration of industrial and finance capital, and state-led imperial expansion in order to develop a sufficiently strong capital structure to compete on the world market previously dominated by the free-trading British. The 'Third Industrial Revolution' presents a distinct configuration, too, and may have special consequences not only for international economic change but also for differing types of national capitalist economies.

The Third Industrial Revolution, in so far as its broad outlines can be dimly perceived in its early stages thus far, combines our two sets of cases. Not only is a huge effort required to re-tool the productive capacities of industry in general, but that very re-tooling further involves extensive processes of labor-shedding at a number of levels. In the first place, the capital-intensive productive processes require much less labor (and indeed much of their rationale is labor-saving and quantum leaps in productivity). And, in the second place, the core industries of the Third Industrial Revolution — small electronics firms engaged in research and development — do not take on large amounts of new labor. Furthermore, those countries with a strong capital structure and an existing pattern of investment in such industries and processes, such as the United States, Japan or Germany, are in a position to absorb and incorporate even those technological breakthroughs pioneered in other countries more effectively than the latter countries themselves can do. At the same time, multinational firms based in those structurally advanced countries are in a position to relocate their labor-intensive productive processes in the Third World where labor costs are lower. Where such significant advantages do not already exist in the structures of capital markets or labor markets, there may develop severe rigidities which combine the worst effects of both labor-shedding and 'disinvestment.' In these countries, the state is *forced* to tinker, overtly or covertly, in ways which range between disguised and *ad hoc* state capitalist interventions (which can even run directly counter to the stated aims of the government in power, as in Barre's France or Thatcher's Britain) to attempts to develop an avowed public policy strategy across a wide range of industries (as in Mitterrand's France). As Mitterrand stated a few months after coming to power, in his view the only alternative to extensive nationalization was to allow increasing multi-nationalization of French industry, with the implicit premise that such multinationalization would further squeeze the French national economy between disinvestment (as assets and profits were drained abroad) and unemployment. Thus those national economic systems which have been labelled as 'intermediate economies' faced a threat which inevitably would draw the state — even in pursuing its minimal definitions of national interest and general welfare — into a new economic role. Let us look, first, more closely at the wider processes at work,[12] and then consider the possible consequences of these developments for state autonomy and state capitalism.

France has, in effect, been an 'intermediate economy' since the mid-nineteenth century,[13] while Britain's movement into such a category is, on the whole, more recent — although its origins have been traced back to the mid- or late nineteenth century, too.[14] In the context of the world economy, an intermediate economy is one which is structurally less advanced than the most advanced economies and more advanced than the great majority of less developed ones. This does not simply refer to growth rates[15] — which are relative to existing levels of output and income — nor to macroeconomic indices — which can conceal a wide range of contrasting trends and performances in different sectors and subsectors. Rather it refers to the types of goods which are produced and exchanged with (and received in exchange from) structurally different categories of national economies. It means than in those sectors which are economically most advanced in terms of both technological sophistication and productive efficiency (particularly the productivity of capital), there is a structural gap between an intermediate economy and those of the most advanced countries, a gap reflected in the composition and terms of trade not only between those countries themselves but also between each of them and third countries. An intermediate economy is thus structurally underdeveloped in such sectors. At the same time, an intermediate economy is considerably more advanced — not only in those sectors but also in a number of other, generally technologically more traditional and more labor-intensive — than less developed economies.

In the former relationship, the growing structural deficit in French trade with both the United States and West Germany in a number of crucial sectors (industrial capital goods, electronics, more advanced consumer durables, etc.) is seen as a vicious circle, relatively unresponsive to short-term price changes, as patterns of specialization — with experience of production techniques, marketing networks, economies of scale, etc., reinforcing the market position of those countries already advantaged — are consolidated in investment patterns and purchasing habits.[16] Sectors of British production have conformed to this pattern for some time, too,[17] and the beginnings of the present crisis in the 1960s reflected the gradual spread of such a syndrome to large areas of traditionally profitable industries such as machine tools in spite of Prime Minister Harold Wilson's call in 1964 for Britain to forge a new industry 'in the white heat of the technological revolution.' One key component of this pattern is technological exchange (licencing, patents, etc.), which reflects and reinforces the wider technological deficit.[18] In contrast, however, the *relative* advance of these countries in just such areas, in addition to certain more traditional sectors, over the underdeveloped world, gives France and Britain a large structural surplus in such exchanges.

However, the growing deficit with the most advanced countries reflects a growing competitiveness of the latter in terms of both price and capacity, with intermediate economies such as the French and British having to rely more and more on governmental and intergovernmental supports —export credits, special agreements (such as that between France and Algeria over natural gas) at non-market prices, technical assistance and subsidies — to counter the erosion of their competitive positions in these very markets and to open up new markets (such as the current French trade offensive in India, and French and British attempts to widen trade with the countries of the Middle East). In some cases, such measures simply reflect the decreasing rate of profit inherent in such ventures in a context of declining competitiveness, although they do maintain vital trade patterns which might otherwise atrophy, provide crucial infrastructural resources, maintain employment in socially or economically critical sectors, and hold down the overall balance of trade deficit. But they are dependent upon a wide variety of factors which are difficult to control and coordinate, including the state of political relations between the countries involved.[19] At another level, however — arms sales are a particularly critical example, but industrial capital goods can be another in many circumstances — the maintenance and favoring of such patterns can have a multiplier effect on the rest of the economy by providing an alternative to protectionism in the nurturing of sectors which need restructuring or which can provide the source of technological and productive spillover.

In reacting to the policy problems embedded in the 'intermediate economy' structural position, national policy-makers have a range of responses with which to work. Each one of these responses has potential benefits for the national economy, but each can also have severe disadvantages in the context of the world economy. The most obvious is straightforward trade protectionism, the drawbacks to which, in terms of retaliation from those very trade partners whose competitive position is most dangerous, on the one hand, and of potential further loss of competitiveness if traditional industries are 'featherbedded' or new industries nurtured in conditions inappropriate to market conditions crucial to future export potential, are well known. While France and Britain have both tinkered with certain highly selective trade controls — those in France having achieved, for political reasons, a high degree of visibility — few politicians or other policy-makers would consider wholesale protectionism other than on the model of 'voluntary' agreements such as those between the EEC and Japan over automobiles or the Multifiber

Agreement. Other forms of what is often called 'hidden protectionism' — government procurement, tax advantages, difficult import regulations, subsidies, financial and political support for exports, etc. — can have the same effects, but are more widely used in an *ad hoc* manner.[20]

Broader measures of Keynesian fiscal and monetary policy are also important elements of any policy response, but any consideration of these quickly reveals the bind they can create. Reflation may increase demand; however, in the current world context, given the competitive advantages of the most advanced countries in the most 'upmarket' consumer goods and the advantages of the low-wage, newly industrializing countries in 'downmarket' consumer goods, the result is often a greater relative increase in demand for imports than for home-produced products, fuelling the political call for greater traditional protectionism. Problems are thus merely exacerbated. On the other hand, deflation may well hold down imports, as has happened in both Britain and France, but it will also hit home demand and undermine investment, leading to falling output. In terms of exchange rate policy, devaluation may have the desired effect of reducing imports and increasing exports, but it will also increase costs and cause a flight of capital, reversing the positive effects in the longer term; revaluation will reduce costs, but make exports more expensive, also hitting sales and investment. Countries in a strong structural position, such as the United States, can, as 1983 and 1984 have shown, sustain a demand-led boom despite a worsening balance of trade deficit, in part because of an inflow of capital from abroad and in part because an overvalued currency helps keep inflation low. Germany, too, under the Social Democrats, was able for some time, by combining revaluation with a measure of domestic reflation, to perform the same feat, thanks to her strong structural export position (with demand again relatively resistant to price increases).

Countries in a weak structural trade position have less room to maneuver. Policy-makers are continually having to navigate between policy combinations which, in particular conjunctural conditions, may prove not only to be ineffective and internally incompatible, but also to be counterproductive and to involve significant opportunity costs. 'Stop-go' policies in Britain in the 1960s are archetypical. France avoided such problems during the long boom before 1974 because, starting from a lower economic base than Britain after the Second World War, its economy adapted better to the post-war world market, modernizing and expanding at the same time. The state played a crucial role in this process both before and after the coming to power of General de Gaulle in 1958.[21] Of course, in a boom period, such questions are not of the same degree of centrality. Not only is there more money in the kitty with the international economic 'engine' pulling the weaker economies along behind, but in fact the very 'intermediate' position can be an asset. Production can not only add fuel to the 'engine' — complementing its productive repertoire and increasing trade in general — but also provide the essential linkage mechanism to articulate the expansion of the 'core' industrial economies with those of the underdeveloped world, as the Yaoundé Convention did, connecting global capitalist development with the rising expectations of the Third World in a neo-colonial manner, avoiding the more brutal interventionism of the two 'superpowers.' Thus the engine is seen to pull an ever longer train behind it.

Needless to say, such structural complementarity, in a way which is perhaps analogous, at the world level, to the role of Keynesian policies at the domestic level, becomes a factor of rigidity in the more competitive, zero-sum world of an international recession. What had appeared to be a division of labor turns into competition over stagnant or declining markets. The intermediate economies, as we have said earlier, find their positions eroded on both the upmarket and downmarket sides: growth sectors elude them, and 'captive markets' are no longer secure. Trading partners and currency markets pull in opposite directions, as currency speculation follows interest rates. Tight monetary policies, which reduce inflation and costs (in the long run), also hit both investment and exports, thus reducing output and creating more unemployment; looser monetary policies and reflation increase inflation and costs in a way which also reduces profitability, thus hitting investments and exports, but also propping up uncompetitive enterprises. The question becomes one of which is the necessary evil: high unemployment and a reduction in output and capacity, in the hope that improving market conditions abroad will pull investment into new, more competitive firms and sectors once the uncompetitive ones have fallen by the wayside; or the maintenance of a large uncompetitive sector, in the hope (again) that improving market conditions abroad will increase overall demand sufficiently that they can find markets anyway and be starting from a broader industrial base, too. Experience of the 1970s shows that the second approach, based as it is on the Keynesian principles which sustained the long antecedent boom, tends to be adopted first; this was true in Britain in 1974, with the Labour Government's Social Contract, and in France, too, under the Chirac Government. Its failure leads to the adoption of some version of the first approach, painfully at first under the Wilson and Callaghan Governments after 1975, with their union-supported and enforced incomes policies up to 1978, but more abruptly under the Thatcher Government, and the other way around in France, with the early austerity of the Barre Government incrementally giving way to a more pragmatic policy of assisted 'redeployment.'[22] Of course, such efforts are constrained not only by external forces but by political and social coalition-building.[23]

A third possible approach, but one which also comes up against serious constraints at all of these levels, would be to try to get the state to act not simply in response to exogenous conditions (market conditions on the one hand, political conditions on the other) but rather as an efficient, capital-accumulating entrepreneur, as we have discussed earlier in the paper. Liberal–democratic states with open, mixed economies are not accustomed to acting in this fashion, where economic/structural and political/social constraints have confined governments for the most part to manipulating 'distributive' or 'demand-side' policies in a Keynesian/social democratic fashion. Just what such a 'structural' or 'state supply-side' approach might consist of is, as we have seen, highly problematic. For example, in responding to the condition of an 'intermediate economy,' it would have to relate a repertoire of 'carrot-and-stick' policies to a series of strategically coherent choices about what sectors to restructure and how. Should the effort be directed to the 'downmarket' side, emphasizing, say, 'appropriate technology' for the Third World? China has made a success in recent years of such an approach, but the difficulties are obvious, especially in a world where the newly industrializing countries are setting the competitive pace. On the other hand, an 'upmarket' strategy, in a period of tight costs and a position of having to catch up with more advanced rivals, has its obvious pitfalls; for a social democratic government, in particular, with its popular constituency based on just those social strata which would be most affected by 'socialist rigor,' the counterproductive impact of reflationary policies and labor indiscipline is a clear danger. Building a policy response would require a sufficiently strong internal power base, with the capability of ignoring or manipulating the pressures brought by loyal supporters as well as by disinvesting capitalists and currency speculators. The 'winter of discontent' in Britain in 1978–9 is a clear warning that even three years of success in doing just that can fall apart. The French Government's recent success up to the end of 1983 in eliciting cooperation from the CGT was as remarkable as it was fragile. In any case, we shall argue, both the Thatcher Government, in an ideologically counterintuitive fashion, and the Mauroy and Fabius Governments, in a strategic fashion which has survived a number of early setbacks to reflationary parts of its original economic policy package, have been pursuing industrial policies in which state capitalism as defined here has been playing a crucial and unprecedented role in the 1980s, extending our understanding of the role of the state.

At first, the contrast between the two approaches seems dominant. By extending the nationalized sector to include the country's main industrial groups and the remainder of the non-nationalized banking sector, the French Government has sought precisely to make the state sector the spearhead of any new boom through greater access to long-term, high-risk capital investment, growing and energetic government-backed efforts in research and development in the high technology field, government support through planning agreements for the targeting of specific growth sectors, and the restructuring of firms in the public sector (as well as certain traditional industries still in the private sector), to reconcile the sometimes conflicting requirements of competitiveness at both national and international levels with those of product specialization and more effective organizational integration. The complexity of the task is exemplified by the problem of arranging for nationalized firms to swap subsidiaries in such a way as to avoid the inefficiencies of dependency upon a monopoly supplier in the domestic market, while still integrating and streamlining the firms sufficiently to increase their international competitiveness, a dilemma illustrated by the recent controversial decisions (after nearly two years) about how to restructure the telecommunications industry,[24] or the desire of the main state chemical firms to avoid taking on each others' loss-making subsidiaries. None the less, government commitment to this effort has continued despite some changes in emphasis with changes in the holder of the office of Minister for Research and Industry (especially in March 1983), despite the requirement for heavy additional compensation to the previous owners of newly nationalized firms and unanticipated losses by those firms in 1981 and 1982, and despite the conversion of the Government as a whole to a strong austerity plan in three phases (June 1982, March 1983 and April 1984) which will reduce the overall level of real expenditure in the Government's general budget for 1984 below that of 1983.

The Thatcher Government has been just as fully committed, on the other hand, to a broad and deep reduction in the size of the public sector, returning as much of it as possible to private ownership. This goal has gone hand in hand with a strong austerity plan virtually since coming into power in May

218 Philip G. Cerny

1979 (with the exception of the three months before the June 1983 election, when a government-engineered expansion of the money supply created a short-lived pre-election boomlet), involving the setting of firm cash limits to the expenditure of public sector industries. Some public firms, including the British Oil Corporation, have been fully or partly sold off to the private sector, and the Government's 1983 election campaign highlighted promises to return parts of the British Gas Corporation, British Telecom, British Airways and other public firms to the private sector and even to open up parts of the social and public services to competitive private subcontracting (provision of laundry and cleaning services to the National Health Service hospitals, local refuse collection, etc.). Those public sector industries and services which are too deeply dependent on the state to be sold off — steel, coal, the railways, British Leyland (for the time being, at least) — have been, or will be, drastically rationalized, modernized and reduced in size by firm management, labor-shedding and expenditure ceilings. Even where a public service has already been restructured and rationalized, as with local-government-controlled water supply, the central government has set a firm face against even productivity-based wage rises (only narrowly avoiding trouble for itself when the water workers won an arbitrated wage claim in February 1983), further eroding the historically restricted scope of local government autonomy.[25]

None the less, the Thatcher Government's approach, like that of the French Socialist Government, has reflected — in a covert way — the state capitalist imperative which we identified earlier. For the British private sector has been no less resistant to the lure of domestic investment and expansion than the French. The rush to purchase shares in British Shipbuilders on the London Stock Exchange was not an indicator of a new vitality of British capital, but, like the vertiginous rise of trading in nationalization compensation bonds on the Bourse in the months preceding the French nationalizations in early 1982, private capital was taking an Olsonian free ride.[26] If anything, the Thatcher Government has been far more effective than the French, up to now, in making state capitalism work. It has made many loss-making industries profitable — British Telecom is one of the most profitable in the country now — and, in doing so, it has reconstituted capital far more effectively than the private sector itself has done. Unlike the bureaucratic model so disliked by the neo-classicists who control the policy-making process in Britain, it has demonstrated that the state can take the lead as an autonomous, efficient, capital-accumulating entrepreneur in a structurally vulnerable intermediate economy. In doing this, of course, the Thatcher Government has created widespread unemployment and real hardship, which the French Government had sought to avoid prior to late 1983; one of the results of this has been a persistent differential in inflation rates, with the British rate falling as low as 3.4 percent in June 1983 and the French rate sticking at 9 percent in 1983 despite rapidly improving trade figures.[27]

In looking a little more closely at our restricted sample, let us compare certain dimensions of the British and French 'modes' of state capitalism in the 1980s. The purpose of such a comparison is to show that (1) a number of contrasting political choices can inform the relatively autonomous state as to the way it pursues a state capitalist policy — prioritizing certain values over others — and (2) there are nevertheless certain parameters set by the fact that these are both open, mixed economies in a constrained world which makes some form of state capitalism necessary to counteract their structural vulnerability. In the first place, the underlying constraint is to make the industries involved competitive. This requires extensive rationalization and restructuring to an extent which, given the scarcity of private capital, would lead otherwise to an *ad hoc* process of mergers and bankruptcies which might or might not lead to a strengthening of the structure of the national economy as a whole. None the less, there is a wide range of choice of how to go about this restructuring. In the British case, it involves a systematic slimming down of industry in order to make more efficient use of the reduced and closely controlled state subsidies which were still maintained despite severe ideological opposition from within the Conservative Government. (It was said that the supposed hardliner Sir Keith Joseph was shuffled off from being Secretary of State for Industry because he was seen as being too generous in his subsidies to British Leyland and other public sector firms, which some wanted to see bankrupted, but his policies were none the less maintained.) In the French case, it also involves reduction in capacity (as in the steel industry), but it is much more directed along the lines of management restructuring, market streamlining, subsidiary swapping, and the planning of new long-term investment (partly from the new controls on the nationalized banking sector) with state supervision. The British approach has worked much more quickly than the French, but with a severe drop in industrial output which, in the late Spring and early Summer of 1983, meant that for the first time since the Industrial Revolution Britain was importing more industrial goods than it was exporting. The long-run comparison of the consequences of these contrasting approaches must, of course, wait until it is possible to see how each country's industry responds to a hypothetical recovery.

A second dimension of comparison is employment policy. In the British case, the rationalization and restructuring discussed above led to a dramatic process of labor-shedding in the public sector. The unemployment rate for the United Kingdom rose to 14 percent, with certain blackspots — generally characterized by the dominance of traditional and frequently public-sector industries like steel and shipbuilding — going well over the 50 percent level. In the Netherlands, a government with a similar approach achieved a 17 percent unemployment rate in mid-1983. In France, despite a steady rise through the 1970s into early 1982, the unemployment rate stabilized for over a year at just around the 8.5 percent level (just over 2 million), although under the 1983-4 austerity plan it has risen to 2.4 million and will continue to rise in 1985. French employment policy has in fact passed through two phases. In the first phase, an increase in civil service employment was decreed, and attempts were made through planning agreements (*contrats de progrès*) with both the public and private sectors to make government restructuring aid dependent upon additional marginal hiring. This was quickly reduced to a requirement not to lay off any further workers, and in the second phase the requirement is that government subsidies will be granted only if any further redundancies are clearly linked with a restructuring plan. Crises in the declining industries (steel, shipbuilding, coal), however, have proved more intractable. Thus state capitalism, while unable to reverse the general increase in unemployment consequent upon the current crisis, can attempt to influence the extent of that increase in certain cases. Incidentally, both the British and French Governments have introduced remarkably similar youth temporary employment and training schemes and are promoting the idea of job-sharing and a general increase in part-time working, along with various early retirement schemes either in general or in particular sectors, as ways to cushion the unemployment problem; these schemes are also linked to subsidies, in France through the planning agreements.

A third dimension, again linked with the first two, is the attempt to regulate wages and conditions, with a concentration upon the public sector in order to reverse the tendency which developed during the previous boom for nationalized industries to become the special target for wage claims because they were financed out of (confiscatory) taxes rather than from profits. Indeed, in Britain, the effectiveness of government cash limits and labor-shedding policies in the public sector made it possible, especially after the failure of the steel strike in 1980, for the Thatcher Government, despite their free-market claims that no government could set a market-efficient wage level and that free collective bargaining should rule, to decree in effect maximum percentage wage rises in the public sector well below previous going rates and to make them stick. This was brought about simply by declaring that a particular rate was the Government's preference, and then establishing it as a new going rate through a well-publicized confrontation with a vulnerable sector of public service workers (the most significant being the health service workers' dispute in 1982, broken partly by the threat to privatize certain of the tasks mentioned earlier). The water workers' victory was an exception which only proved the rule. A main factor until 1984 was the failure of the new, radicalized leadership of the National Union of Mineworkers, under the former Communist Arthur Scargill, to convince his members to strike to prevent the closure of a number of marginal pits — pits which the National Coal Board covertly planned to close, although they strenuously denied such intentions — in a number of defeated national strike ballots, but a bitter strike in 1984 has lasted nearly eight months by November 1984. It was Stanley Baldwin who said that a Conservative government must never confront the miners; the Thatcher Government is doing so in a very determined fashion so far. The French method was for a long time a more traditional, social-democratic form of 'consensual wage restraint,' in which, through direct bargaining between the Government and the unions (especially the CGT, the Mauroy Government's privileged partner), a trade-off seemed to have been broadly achieved between wage restraint, on the one hand, and the reduction of the working week and the introduction of new shop-floor union rights and participation in advisory administrative councils (the 'Auroux Laws'), on the other. The limits of such a trade-off are more obvious in 1984; none the less, it has had one demonstrable result — limiting the scope for the Government to reduce the rate of inflation to British levels. Thus, within the broad, common British and French recognition of the need for public-sector wage restraint, different methods have created somewhat different results. It remains to be seen whether the higher rate of inflation in France will hinder recovery any more than, once again, the reduction in output consequent upon the British approach.

A fourth dimension, in which the contrasts are rather greater, is public-sector support for high-technology research and development. Lead time is important in evaluating this dimension, and it is once again too soon to reach conclusions. The British approach is not particularly 'state capitalist,' but depends on a number of microeconomic measures such as advice and subsidies for the setting up of small businesses (also attempted by the French). The French approach is to integrate direct public support for R & D into its nationalization policies through the combined Ministry for Research and Industry, whose planning agreements attempt to ensure the expansion of R & D through direct subsidies and restructuring, and to maintain its original commitment to expand the research budget at a rate faster than the general increase in industrial policy expenditure throughout the five-year life of the current National Assembly. The contrast can be seen in the two Governments' approaches to the setting up of cable television. The British Government is seeking to balance traditional demands for the maintenance of a high standard of 'public service broadcasting' as embodied in the charters of the British Broadcasting Corporation and the independent television companies (ITV) with an opening up of market opportunities for private cable operators. The French Government, on the other hand, is attempting to coordinate the development of cable television through its control of the nationalized telecommunications and electronics industries, providing public facilities such as the computerization of a number of experimental local telephone directories, requiring the wiring of each house with a telephone to receive cable transmissions and the provision of a monitor. At the same time, part of its subsidy for research and development to the electronics and tele-communications industries is intended to speed up development of fiber-optic technology and to gain a world market position in the field. Despite Zysman's scepticism over the potential effectiveness of state interventionism in the electronics field,[28] recent developments in the United States — the renewed success of IBM in competing with the previously leading small, engineering-based advanced technology companies in the personal computer field — might seem to indicate that large firms with extensive bureaucratic and economic resources as well as sufficient capitalization for extensive research and development, i.e. the sort of firms which French electronics policy since the 1960s has sought to encourage and which it is currently hoped Thomson-Brandt might yet become, can still play a crucial role in the Third Industrial Revolution. Cable television may, indeed, be especially suited to such an approach because of its need for extensive communications networks which must be capitalized. In any case, it once again remains to be seen whether the future rests in the hands of the Thomsons and Bulls of this world or to the Sir Clive Sinclairs and Iann Barrons.

The final dimension is, of course, the future structure of a state capitalist sector of the kind which we have been examining. The French approach is to see it as a permanent fixture in the face of growing vulnerability of the intermediate economies — Mitterrand's 'multinationalization.' Thus self-sustaining economic development and growth in the future are seen to be dependent upon the health and strength of the new state structure. We are witnessing, it is suggested, a new phase of capitalism in which only the state can provide the requirements for long-term viability. In contrast, the British approach is to see the goal as privatization, in a world where the profitability and competitiveness of the private sector has been restored through the effectiveness of government policies. Of course, the Labour Party would wish to renationalize those sectors sold off by the Conservatives; and Jacques Chirac, emulating Mrs Thatcher and President Reagan, promises to sell off the recently nationalized firms if he returns to power. The key factor in any of these calculations, however, will be the condition of the intermediate economy in the international economic conjuncture. If the private sector in Britain continues to be sluggish, then privatization may be counterproductive and renationalization a far more credible political prospect; a general revitalization of British private capital, however, fuelled by a combination of privatization and an international recovery, may make the state capitalism we have been describing a thing of the past. If French private capital can reverse its long-run tendency (observable clearly since the mid-1970s despite the Barre Plan) toward disinvestment, then a right-wing government might find privatization a credible strategy; on the other hand, if the nationalized industries become more profitable and French private capital retains the chronic weaknesses which analysts have been observing since the nineteenth century, it would not be hard for a leader like Chirac to revert to the Gaullist tradition of the 1960s and accept the wider role of the state.

It is conceivable, then, despite the limitations which all major theoretical approaches to the role of the state in open, mixed economies have placed on the role of the capitalist state, that the structural contradictions of the intermediate economies might foster a new state capitalism as a relatively stable, rational and efficient feature of the world capitalist system. Assuming that nation-states continue to play an important role — especially in liberal democracies — of representing even a minimal conception of the general or national interest, of bearing legitimacy and sovereignty in some form for the societies in which they have developed, then such a development would be logical even within a capitalist rationality. The consequences of such a developmental construct for the theory of the state, however, involve seeing it as being based on the reconciliation of an underlying contradiction. For as the autonomy of the state is ostensibly being increased on the *internal* plane, this could only be the result of increasing constraints — and, in particular, the constraints on intermediate economies — deriving from the international capitalist system. The future of state capitalism, then, will depend, paradoxically, upon the efficient adaptation of the nation-state to the imperatives of international capital and the structural conditions which the profit calculations of multinational business and finance impose. Of course, from any global historical perspective, modern nationalized industry is still in an experimental stage; we do not yet really know its limitations and possibilities, and we are still tinkering. The relationship between state and capital, or the problem of the relative autonomy of the state, is complex and — as this chapter has tried to show — historically contingent. None the less, it would see the trajectory of the British and French modes of state capitalism in the current crisis that a range of relatively new empirical possibilities have opened up, and that their theoretical potential may lead in interesting new directions in understanding the role of the state in the capitalist world.

NOTES

1.   Ralph Miliband, *The State in Capitalist Society* (London: Weidenfeld & Nicolson, 1969).
2.   Nicos Poulantzas, *Political Power and Social Classes* (London: New Left Books, 1974).
3.   E.g., Immanuel Wallerstein, *The Modern World System* (New York: Academic Press, 1974).
4.   Barrington Moore Jr., *Social Origins of Dictatorship and Democracy: Lord and Peasant in the Making of the Modern World* (Harmondsworth: Penguin, 1969).
5.   Antonio Gramsci, *Selections from Prison Notebooks* (New York: International Publishers, 1971).

6. John Holloway and Sol Picciotto, eds, *State and Capital: A Marxist Debate* (London: Edward Arnold, 1978).
7. Joachim Hirsch, 'The State Apparatus and Social Reproduction: Elements of a Theory of the Bourgeois State,' in Holloway and Picciotto, ibid., Ch. 5, and Heide Gerstenberger, 'Class Conflict, Competition and State Functions,' also in ibid., Ch. 7.
8. Consider the treatment of Maoism by Theda Skocpol in *States and Social Revolutions: A Comparative Analysis of France, Russia and China* (Cambridge: Cambridge University Press, 1979), pp. 271–80.
9. See Seymour Melman, *Profits Without Production* (New York: Knopf 1983).
10. See Fred Hirsch, *The Social Limits of Growth* (London: Routledge & Kegan Paul, 1978).
11. Robert A. Dahl, *Dilemmas of Pluralist Democracy: Autonomy vs. Control* (New Haven: Yale University Press, 1982).
12. The discussion of intermediate economies which follows is adapted from Cerny, 'Economic Policy: Crisis Management, Structural Reform and Socialist Politics,' in Stuart Williams, ed., *Socialism in France: From Jaurès to Mitterrand* (London and New York: Frances Pinter and St. Martin's Press for the Association for the Study of Modern and Contemporary France, 1982), Ch. 9.
13. See Charles P. Kindleberger, *Economic Growth in France and Britain 1851–1950* (Cambridge, Mass.: Harvard University Press, 1964).
14. See Eric J. Hobsbawm, *Industry and Empire* (Harmondsworth: Penguin, 1968), and Tom Kemp, *Industrialisation in Nineteenth Century Europe* (London: Routledge & Kegal Paul, 1969).
15. The issue treated centrally by Kindleberger, *Economic Growth . . .*, op. cit.
16. See *Le Monde*, 6 October 1981 and 18/19 October 1981; for background, see Robert Gilpin, *France in the Age of the Scientific State* (Princeton, N.J.: Princeton University Press, 1968) and John Zysman, *Political Strategies for Industrial Order: Market, State and Industry in France* (Berkeley and Los Angeles: University of California Press, 1977).
17. See the discussion of the iron and steel industry in Britain at the end of the nineteenth century in Kemp, *Industrialization . . .*, op. cit., and Colin Leys's discussion of the two structural crises of British politics in his *Politics in Britain: An Introduction* (Toronto: University of Toronto Press, 1983), Part I.
18. For France, see *Le Monde*, 10 October 1981.
19. Consider, for example, the deterioration in France's position in Franco-Soviet exchanges in the late 1970s and early 1980s: *Le Monde*, 10 October 1981.
20. Consider Zysman's argument about the *Plan Calcul* and the conditions of success in the world electronics industry, *Political Strategies . . .*, op. cit.
21. Cf. Jean Fourastié, *Les trente glorieuses: ou la Révolution invisible de 1946 à 1975* (Paris: Fayard, rev. edn. 1979); Richard F. Kuisel, *Capitalism and the State in Modern France: Renovation and Economic Management in the Twentieth Century* (Cambridge: Cambridge University Press, 1981), Chs. 7–10; and Cerny, 'Economic Policy,' op. cit.
22. Diana M. Green with P.G. Cerny, 'Economic Policy and the Governing Coalition,' in P.G. Cerny and M.A. Schain, eds, *French Politics and Public Policy* (London and New York: Frances Pinter, St. Martin's Press and Methuen University Paperbacks, 1980), Ch. 8.
23. Cerny, 'Economic Policy,' op. cit., and 'Dead Ends and New Possibilities: Mitterrand's Economic Policy Between Socialism and State Capitalism,' *Contemporary French Civilization*, special issue on France under Mitterrand, VIII, Nos. 1–2 (Fall/Winter 1983/4).
24. *Le Monde*, 22 September 1983.
25. See Douglas E. Ashford, *British Dogmatism and French Pragmatism: Central–Local Policymaking in the Welfare State* (London and Winchester, Mass.: George Allen & Unwin, 1982).
26. See Mancur Olson, *The Logic of Collective Action* (Cambridge, Mass.: Harvard University Press, rev. edn. 1971).
27. The reinforced austerity program has, however, put the French inflation rate on target for a 6–7 percent rise in 1984: *New York Times*, 2 July 1984; *Le Monde*, 12 July 1984.
28. Zysman, *Political Strategies . . .*, op. cit.

# 11 Politics and Mass Mobilization: Relations Between the CGT and the CFDT*

*Martin A. Schain*

## INTRODUCTION

Throughout most of its history, the French trade-union movement has been sharply divided into competing confederations. Although the strength and support of the rival organizations has changed over the years, except for brief periods before and after World War II, the split of 1922 over the Russian revolution has never been bridged. Indeed, with the deconfessionalization of the Confédération Française des Travailleurs Chrétiens (CFTC) in 1946, the rivalry has become more intense, as the (new) Confédération Française Democratique du Travail (CFDT) has chosen to compete directly with the CGT on the same ideological terrain, for the same working-class constituency. Inter-union rivalry has become an integral part of French industrial relations. From the very basic level of the plant sections, to the industrial federations, to the interprofessional confederations, union organizations compete constantly for members, support and control of mass action. Furthermore, competition is accentuated by the rules of the game in industrial relations, which give all of the representative organizations the right to negotiate and sign agreements at every level.

Rivalry, however, has weakened the effectiveness of all unions in collective negotiations, and appears to have reduced the attractiveness of unions to large numbers of workers. Thus, continuous ideological dialogue among and within the organizations has reflected the intensity, and defined the grounds, of union competition. Ideological dialogue, however, has reinforced the intransigence of employers, and supported their reluctance to accept — in practice — the legitimacy of the unions in bargaining.[1] Furthermore, in the process of collective negotiations, union rivalry has left employers free to choose their negotiating partners, or to refuse to negotiate altogether.

The division of the trade-union movement is also cited as a key factor in its inability to organize more than twenty percent of the workforce. While this is a complex question, there is some evidence that in so far as division is regarded as 'political,' it contributes to a lack of confidence in union organizations.[2] The reaction is strongest among workers who do not belong to unions, but is significant among unionized workers as well. Thus, in a 1970 survey, more than a third of CGT members and almost half of CFDT members agreed that unions were 'concerned too much with politics, and not

* This article is a revision of my chapter in Mark Kesselman and Guy Groux, *The French Workers' Movement: Economic Crisis and Political Change* (London and New York: Allen & Unwin, 1984). My thanks to Mark Kesselman and Georges Lavau for their comments on earlier drafts.

enough with the defense of professional interests."[3] In another survey, conducted in 1977, 30 percent of the members of both confederations agreed that *their* unions placed 'political preoccupations before the interests of the workers."[4]

Thus it would appear that union rivalry is neither advantageous nor popular. It is supported, however, by the dynamics of organizational survival, and 'union pluralism' is favored by a majority of members of both the CGT and the CFDT. Nevertheless, in an attempt to overcome at least some of the disadvantages inherent in the division of the trade-union movement — to strengthen the ability of unions to bargain and to mobilize workers — the CGT and the CFDT succeeded in negotiating a series of national agreements on joint action and strategy after 1966. These agreements were difficult to reach, and even more difficult to sustain, but they endured through 1979. The agreements survived as long as each confederation was able to conclude that its organization and its most important goals were strengthened by the alliance, even if compromise was necessary. The alliance proved impossible to sustain when both confederations concluded that their organizational survival was being eroded at the base, even as the influence of their elites was being enhanced, and that their political objectives were not likely to be attained.

This argument and this emphasis, however, are somewhat different from the more conventional argument that union relations are more or less a reflection of political party relations within the French left, and the evolution of the CGT–CFDT alliance was political in the sense that it manifested the needs of the parties rather than the union organizations themselves. It is the point of view of this chapter that the latter argument is unnecessarily simplistic, and fails to take into account the complex relationships among political parties and trade unions within the left.

POLITICS AND UNION RELATIONS

*1. Before 1968*

The political evolution of party relations within the left have often been cited as the key to understanding relations between the CGT and the CFDT.[5] While this appears to be generally true, especially for the CGT, this emphasis tends to ignore some of the important conflicts between party and trade-union strategies and concerns, as well as other dynamic forces in trade-union life that have both motivated and undermined cooperation between the CGT and the CFDT.

The period between 1964 and 1968 was marked by both a *rapprochement* of the Communists and the Socialists on the political level, and increasing collaboration between the CGT and the CFDT on the union level. An important priority for the CGT in the negotiations for the 'unity of action' pact of 1966 was the goal of the Parti Communiste Français (PCF) of a union of the forces of the left in support of a popular front-type agreement:

the union of all democratic forces, without exclusion in order to elaborate a *common program* in which demands of the working class must find a place . . . [The unity] will permit us to go together towards a real democracy and the realization of an economic and social program.[6]

However, collaboration with the CFDT on the basis of broad policy agreements 'at the summit' also strengthened the role of the CGT as an independent political force, a role sometimes disputed by the PCF.

As early as 1957, the CGT had begun to revise its orientation towards other unions. By this time, the confederation had dropped its emphasis on *unité d'action à la base* — an attempt to mobilize workers belonging to other unions, and to undermine the influence of other union organizations through unity of action committees — and, instead, stressed agreements with other unions at all levels. Increasingly, in the late 1950s, the CGT sought goals and policy objectives that were at variance with both the objectives of the PCF at the time, and with the indirect role that the CGT was supposed to play in policy development.

Although the CGT continued to emphasize 'action' goals, there were clear indications that it was edging towards linking strikes and demonstrations to broader policy. In 1957, the confederation called for nationalization of several industrial branches (two years before the PCF), and during the years of the Algerian War the CGT participated in joint anti-war actions with CFTC, UNEF and FEN. In one notable case the union was forced to withdraw its support after a demonstration was openly denounced by the PCF as 'adventurist' and 'dangerous.'[7] The tension between the more independent course being probed by the CGT, and the attempts by the PCF to impose limitations probably reached a high point in May 1962, when Maurice Thorez accused the leadership of the CGT of promoting 'inadequate and poorly thought out demands . . . of seeking unity at any price . . . and only at the summit, . . . [of] frequent violations of the rules of trade union and workers' democracy . . .'[8] After the death of Thorez in 1964, the CGT pursued its broader version of 'trade-union democracy' somewhat more easily.

Although the pact with the CFDT in 1966 was referred to as a program of common 'action' in support of workers' strike demands, it also contained references to the extension of trade-union rights, increased public investment in housing, education and health, as well as demands for guaranteed employment and tax reform.[9] Although one of the important goals of the CGT, going into the negotiations with the CFDT, was an agreement on a broad union of the left, this was dropped in favor of other goals that increased the institutional strength of the CGT.

For the CFDT, the agreement with the CGT also served political objectives, but not necessarily those of any of the political parties of the left. Summing up a discussion of 'union practice and political objectives,' in a research document published by the CFDT, Denis Segrestin stressed that the 'historic role' of the CFDT has been 'to link union practice directly to the stakes [involved] and to a *projet de société*, union action with a political dimension.' In contrast with the CGT, the action of local unions is 'impregnated with the CFDT ideology and is related to the *projet de société* defined by the whole of the CFDT.' Thus, Segrestin argues, the CFDT strives for a coherence as an independent political force.[10]

In its pursuit of an alliance with the CGT during the early 1960s, the CFDT (and before it the CFTC) sought to separate unity based on 'political' (i.e. party) objectives from unity based on agreements on 'professional' (i.e. job-related) interests. During this period, before 1968, the CFDT pursued its own political objectives, and supported a broad non-Communist left alliance. Nevertheless, in practice, the CFTC and the CFDT did participate in joint political action with the CGT.

By 1966, convinced that unity of the non-Communist left would be a long time coming, some leaders of the CFDT (notably Eugène Descamps, the general secretary of the confederation) saw an alliance with the CGT as an effective means of bypassing political parties in defining a policy of the left. 'Now, incapable of acting for political renovation — the Defferre experience and the [1965] presidential election testify to that — the CFDT, but also the FEN, are developing union action that has an evident political significance.'[11] That is, it was not the growing unity of the parties of the left that encouraged these leaders, but its failure.

Clearly, by political objectives, the leaders of the CFDT were referring to attempts by the CGT to draw them into a broad left alliance; for the CGT political objectives meant the kind of independent political program being developed and pursued by the CFDT. In their dialogue through the 1960s, each confederation resisted the 'politics' of the other, while pursuing the advantages of their alliance. The growing dialogue between the Communists and the Socialists after 1965, rather than supporting collaboration between the CGT and the CFDT, frequently became an issue of discord in itself.

For example, Georges Levard, the president of the CFDT, resigned in 1967, citing as his reason the symbolic affirmation in the 1966 agreement that the Communists were politically acceptable: 'I consider that the entire non-Communist left dishonors itself in affirming that the Communists have approached our conception of democracy in a decisive manner. I can no longer accept to cover up a policy that pretends to ignore this fact.'[12] During the following year, as the Communist–Socialist dialogue became more intense (at least until May 1968), the CGT–CFDT relationship became more tense, in part because of the attempts of the CGT to draw the CFDT into contact with the PCF. The CFDT was not at all opposed, in principle, to a left alliance, but was most distrustful of the Communist overtures: 'We are not in agreement with them,' argued the new president of the CFDT, André Jeanson. 'They are approaching democracy, but not enough.'[13] Therefore, it is not at all clear that, during the period before 1968, the growing dialogue between the parties of the left contributed to the alliance between the CGT and the CFDT. It is somewhat more evident that the tensions produced by that dialogue contributed to the growing discord between the two organizations during the months before the events of 1968.

Nevertheless, for both the CGT and the CFDT there were real benefits in unity of action, but they were less political than organizational. For the CGT, the pact of 1966 ended its national and international isolation. With the support of the CFDT, representatives of the CGT were brought into negotiations with the CNPF, and (ultimately) into the institutions of the European Community in Brussels.[14] For the CFDT, the accord also served as a means of emergence from a different kind of isolation, the Catholic ghetto, and facilitated joint action with other union organizations (notably the FEN). It also strengthened the working-class image of the CFDT as well as the internal changes signified by the deconfessionalization of 1964. These organizational advantages were certainly much more obvious than the fluid political context for understanding both the agreement of the CGT and the CFDT in 1966, as well as the strength of the agreement before 1968.

## 2. The Post-1968 Period

The period from 1970 to 1979 was marked by an intense politicization of relations between the CGT and the CFDT, a politicization that was related to, and influenced by, the successes and failures of the Communist–Socialist alliance, but that had a life of its own. In the midst of the political chaos that defined Communist–Socialist relations during the years between June 1968 and June 1971 (the Socialist Congress of Épinay), relations between the CGT and the CFDT seemed far more stable. The 1966 agreement had broken down even before the massive strikes of 1968, and for more than a year after the 'events,' the confederations went their separate ways. However, the acceptance by the CFDT, at its 1970 congress at Issy-les-Moulineaux, of the doctrine of class conflict, the condemnation by the congress of the capitalist system, and its advocacy of democratic socialism, set the stage for new negotiations with the CGT.[15] On 1 December 1970, the two confederations concluded a new accord on unity of action that, at least in its intentions, went beyond the agreement of 1966. 'This accord marks the movement from purely tactical unity of action to a strategic design that insists on the search for common objectives for the transformation of society.'[16]

During a period when the parties of the left were barely on speaking terms, the unions of the left were speaking a great deal. Six months before the December 1970 congress, CFDT leaders had initiated a long series of discussions with the CGT on common action and basic strategy. The discussions went on for two years.[17] They were also attempting to coordinate their bargaining strategies and their strike action.[18]

On the other hand, at roughly the same time that the reorganized Socialist Party and the PCF were drawing closer to an agreement on a common program for government, relations between the CGT and the CFDT were deteriorating, largely over relations with *gauchiste* militants in the plants, a conflict that accentuated the basic competition between the two organizations over the new political forces that had emerged during the 1968 events, but over party commitments as well.[19] The CGT was fully committed to the common program, while the CFDT chose to emphasize its own version of *socialisme autogestionnaire*.

Moreover, after 1970, the CFDT had its own political agenda for the left, as well as for the trade-union movement, and it was in this context that it understood relations with the CGT. If, in the early period, the main objective of the CFDT, in pursuing unity of action, was a reinforcement of both its organization and its working-class credentials, after 1970 its objectives became more frankly political, to influence the evolution of the CGT, and in this way, the entire French trade union movement. As Edmond Maire summarized this position in 1980:

Our aim is an evolution of the entire French trade union movement, in all of its component [parts]. . . . in 1974, we formulated a great strategic ambition for the union movement, resting on the development of an autonomous approach of the whole of the union movement, at least of the CFDT and the CGT.[20]

In the years after 1970, the CFDT had become an increasingly powerful component of the labor movement, and a more explicit spokesman for socialist change. Frankly committed to a political program, the CFDT sought dialogue with the CGT, not simply to work out a program for union action, but to develop a program that would link action to political change. Indeed, the great ambition of the CFDT was to draw the CGT away from the Communist Party and into an independent force of the left.[21] Therefore, political differences between the two confederations, and the conflicts and polemics engendered by these differences, were influenced not only by the evolving relationship between the parties of the left, but also by the way that the two organizations approached politics.

After the presidential elections of 1974, the parties of the left went through a period of reorganization and reassessment, marked by sharp accusations and polemics through the fall of 1975.[22] The party tensions were reflected in stronger attacks by the CGT against the CFDT. Nevertheless, in June 1974, the two confederations signed a new accord that was meant to 'reinforce the *dynamique unitaire* ... in the new situation created by the advance of the united left.' The agreement was fairly wide-ranging, once again identifying a number of common objectives, as well as methods of action and 'common principles for the participation of the workers in decisions on action.' The document was certainly a political agreement in the CFDT sense of an autonomous platform for common commitments. Indeed, it served as a basis for the common attack of the two confederations on the *Plan Chirac* and the *Plan Barre* through the spring of 1977.

### 3. The Breakdown of the Alliance

For over a decade, the CGT and the CFDT had struggled to find some common ground upon which they could build cooperation and augment their effectiveness. In the process, the CFDT had clearly moved to the left, while the CGT had moved towards supporting political objectives that were autonomous, if not divergent, from the Communist Party. The process ground to a halt just prior to the 1978 National Assembly elections, primarily because the 'strategic ambition' of the CFDT changed, a change partly related to the breakdown of the Common Program alliance of the Communist and Socialist Parties in September, 1977:

Never had the two organizations appeared closer, since the CGT no longer hesitated to declare itself *autogestionnaire*. Now the CFDT blocked the dialogue with the CGT on January 11, 1978: the accord being prepared would not be a union agreement, but, in reality, support for the orientation of the PCF.[23]

If unity among the parties of the left had raised questions about party–CGT links for the leadership of the CFDT, the breakdown of that unity presented that problem in even stronger terms.

After the failure of the elections of 1978, the CGT neither abandoned its commitment to an alliance with the CFDT, nor did it move closer to the Communist Party. For the CGT, at least initially, the lack of party unity did not preclude a trade-union alliance. During the months after the 1978 elections, when the PCF–Parti Socialiste (PS) split was becoming increasingly bitter, and when the PCF was slowly isolating the dissidents in its ranks, the CGT moved in a different direction.

A month after the elections, Georges Séguy attended the congress of the (Communist) World Federation of Trade Unions, and launched a series of attacks against the organization, as well as the East European delegates, from the podium of the congress hall in Prague. He accused the WFTU of avoiding objective and critical discussion of the situation of unions in Eastern Europe, and he expressed the hope that the international organization would be able to deal with 'pseudo-union organizations in countries where dictatorship rages.'[24] Séguy strongly defended the right to strike ('The superiority of socialism ... cannot reside in the interdiction of the right to strike ...') even in socialist countries, and, finally, withdrew the CGT candidate from the position of secretary general.[25] At the same time, in both Paris and Prague, representatives of the CGT (together with other union representatives in Paris) were meeting with dissident trade unionists from throughout Europe.[26]

In the same spirit, the 40th Congress of the CGT, and the discussion leading up to the congress, was marked by an unprecedented critical openness (as well as by invitations to other confederations to attend the congress). Séguy argued (in an *autocritique*) that indeed the CGT had played too prominent a role in the electoral campaign and 'had distanced itself from the daily preoccupations of the workers.'[27] Thus distancing the confederation from the political preoccupations and connections with the PCF of the electoral period, Séguy asked: 'Basically, the debate has posed to the congress an important question: "How to consolidate unity of action and preserve it from the disturbances of the political environment? How to elevate it to the level of the needs of the hour ... ?" '[28] The solution, argued Séguy, was a national committee of unity of action, in which all of the major confederations would be represented, would exchange views and would act in concert. The CGT overture, however, led neither to a national committee, nor to a general agreement during the next year, as it might have before 1978, principally (though not entirely) because of the political reorientation of the CFDT.

The CFDT had drawn conclusions about the period from 1974 to 1977 that were similar to those of the CGT. The CFDT had been too oriented towards political action, had been too often led 'to stake all on political change,' and had neglected social mobilization which, in the end, was the principal cause of the failure of the left. Where the CFDT parted company with the CGT was in its analysis of the importance of their alliance. Even before the elections, in January 1978, a working report written by Jacques Moreau on 'the general situation and strike activity' had been highly critical of national and centralized cooperation with the CGT that, Moreau argued, had served to demobilize, rather than mobilize, workers.[29] In April, the CFDT national council approved a *recentrage de l'action*, a re-emphasis on linking strikes and demonstrations with negotiations at different levels of decision-making, 'a search for results, even partial, which would give confidence to the workers once again.'[30] Thus, in refusing to join with the CGT in a national day of protest against increases in social security payments, Edmond Maire commented: 'the solution for problems of workers' demands is not the repetition of grand demonstrations without end, that aim above all to accumulate discontent for future elections, without bringing any real solutions for precise problems.'[31] This theme was repeated, with greater force a year later at the CFDT Congress in May, 1979: 'If we want to make of social struggles the motor of all change, then negotiation is the best way to transform conflicts and social mobilization into results.'[32]

The *recentrage* of the CFDT clearly reflected two disappointments: the shock of the electoral loss of 1978 and a disappointment with the strategy of forming an independent union front with the CGT. The leaders of the CFDT had not given up the alliance with the CGT (indeed, the new orientation was strongly criticized at the congress of May 1979), but they had clearly decided to give it lower priority. They also decided (not surprisingly) that a left political majority would not be possible in the foreseeable future. Thus, in criticizing the 'electoral strategy' of the PS in 1979, Edmond Maire noted: 'because of the breakup of the left, because of the choice of the Communist Party to weaken the P.S. before envisioning again the conquest of [government] power, it is difficult to believe the electoral logic can suffice to give a majority to the left.'[33]

The break between the CGT and the CFDT began to solidify during 1978, as the CFDT flirted with closer cooperation with the Government, and the CGT was drawn closer to the PCF. In August, in the midst of delicate negotiations with the CFDT, both the CGT and the PCF announced at the same time that they would lead a great mass movement against unemployment in September. However, the CGT leaders had failed to communicate these plans to their counterparts in the CFDT when they had met only two days before.[34] In some ways, the political break between the CGT and the CFDT was deeper than that between the PCF and the PS. In March, the two parties joined with the CGT and other unions in a march in Paris to support the steelworkers. The CFDT had declined to participate, however, and accused the Socialists of favoring the strategic themes of the CGT, of having a peculiar fascination for the Communists, and of trying to assert a Leninist hegemony of party over union.[35]

Under these circumstances, it was somewhat surprising when the two confederations reached a tentative accord on 17 September 1979 to support joint demonstrations and strike action that would favor low-salaried workers and unemployed workers' rights. The agreement was even more surprising because just a few days before negotiations between the Socialists and the Communists had broken down. The agreement proved to have been stillborn, however, since during the months that followed the confederations were unable to agree on ways of implementing it. The tensions of how to implement the September accord were augmented by conflict over the Soviet invasion of Afghanistan, and — during the following year — by disagreements on policy over Poland. In September 1980, Edmond Maire denounced the CGT as having entered a long *anti-unitaire* period, and of being totally controlled by the Communist Party — 'a complete alignment on the policy of sectarian isolationism and the ideological hardening of the PCF.'[36] Séguy responded that 'unity of action has become impossible at the confederal level.'[37] Before the summer, a CGT report on unity of action had accused the CFDT — as well as other unions — of 'using ... union activity for administering the crisis for the greatest profit of the bosses,' an accusation that was cited frequently by the CFDT as the final, unacceptable bottom line.[38]

In denouncing the CGT in sharp political terms, the CFDT had also accepted the failure of its own political strategy of the 1970s; by writing the CFDT out of the socialist community, the CGT had, in the end, aligned itself with the PCF line that marked the end of a long attempt to develop a united left bloc. For each of the confederations, the long conflictual dialogue of unity of action had had a dynamic of its own that was related to, but not always dominated by, the fate of collaboration of the left at the party level. The long-range objectives of the two confederations had always been different, but the special meaning of the breakup of unity of action in 1979–80 appeared to be the abandonment of these long-range goals.

Moreover, the relationship between the confederations appears to have been influenced little by the electoral victory of the left in May 1981. Certainly, neither the CGT nor the CFDT had seriously expected a Mitterrand victory and their long-range plans presumed his defeat.[39] The hasty Communist–Socialist *rapprochement*, the entrance of PCF ministers into government, and even attempts by the Government to encourage increased union collaboration, however, have resulted in no important change in the position of either confederation.[40]

The CFDT activity report, in preparation for its May 1982 Congress, emphasized that any alliance in the future must be built on a basis of 'precise and concrete objectives,' and no longer on 'vast common platforms. In this way, partners in collaboration will no longer be predetermined in the name of prior conditions and objectives.'[41] Edmond Maire's report to the congress reacted to the pressure of the government by stressing: 'Unity of action must not take place because the parties of the left need it or to create an illusion at the time of May Day; united union action must be deployed in full autonomy in order to place social struggles in the heart of change.'[42]

In the same spirit, Henri Krasucki, in his report for the Confederal Bureau for the June 1982 Congress, simply noted that while the alliance is more necessary than ever, the CFDT has reaffirmed its previous positions of 'recentrage.' Although the CGT will participate in a forthcoming meeting with the CFDT, 'in order to clarify things as far as possible,' the CGT is 'for unity of action with all of the representative unions of the workers.'[43]

During the two years after the victory of the left, each confederation pursued political objectives that were partially in conflict with those of the other, but that were largely different. The CFDT threw its influence behind the development of the *lois Auroux*, which emerged from a July 1981 memorandum elaborated by the confederation.[44] The new rights of expression and the rights of information for works committees in the firm were understood as expressions of the CFDT commitment to *autogestion*. The extension of union rights to firms with less than fifty employees and the creation of a legal obligation of firms to negotiate opened up new possibilities for recruitment; at the same time, the right of unions that attracted more than 50 percent of the votes in the previous works committees election to veto a collective agreement at the firm level challenged the role that FO had played in the process of collective negotiations.[45]

While the CGT basically supported the *lois Auroux*, it devoted its political energy to support for Keynesian expansion program of the Government during its first year in power. In early 1982, when Edmond Maire was calling for movement towards economic 'rigor,' the leaders of the CGT continued to support government expansionist policies. Both confederations advocated the reduction of the work week, but the CGT fought for reduction at existing pay levels (the policy adopted by the Government), while the CFDT called for salary reductions to create 'new solidarities' (increased employment). At least until the first move towards austerity in June 1982, the CGT was the most persistent supporter of the Government of the left.[46]

After the full brunt of left austerity was imposed in March 1983, the positions of the two confederations became far more critical, but divergent. The CFDT moved towards a broad sweeping 'second left' critique, and accused the Government of 'Barrism of the left'. The confederation advocated mobilization of support around a fairer, more redistributive austerity policy built on 'new solidarities' of a broad coalition of social forces. However, the real distinction of the CFDT has been its attempt to become the focal point for an alternate left political force, '... a motor of social change. The union is to be the nexus where the working class movement and the new social movements come together to formulate a new social project to revive civil society.'[47]

By contrast, the CGT proposed a more modest role for the unions in dealing with the economic crisis, a 'propositional force' for 'industrial solutions' at the firm level. On one hand, the CGT advocated 'new criteria' for investment that would go beyond profitability, that would consider 'human capital' and the expansion of jobs. The confederation also adopted the PCF positions on increased protectionism and the 'reconquest of the domestic market.'[48] Increasingly, during the past two years, the CGT has moved towards considerations of management and the development of industrial plans at the plant level.[49] '[T]he CGT thinks that participation in management will allow it to reinforce its position in the firm and, more prosaically, reinforce its apparatus. . . . What is necessary is for the CGT to proclaim itself more *autogestionnaire* than the CFDT.'[50]

Neither confederation, however, has considered the possibility that a unified position would strengthen the position of both organizations with either the Government or the private sector. During a period of austerity and growing unemployment each organization has chosen to establish its own political program, and never during the Fifth Republic have the CGT and the CFDT appeared to be further apart.

Thus, it would appear that the breakdown of 1979–80 has been reaffirmed, and that there is little possibility of the kind of understandings and united action that characterized relations between the two confederations between 1966 and 1977. As we have seen, political and strategic considerations have been important in determining the evolution of relations of the CGT and the CFDT through the years. However, we would argue that political and strategic considerations provide us with an insufficient understanding of the dynamics that have undermined solidarity between the two largest unions in France. Specifically, the final break after the 1978 elections and the surprising lack of impact of the left victory in 1981 on union solidarity cannot be understood without reference to some of the more enduring problems of the French trade-union movement — in particular, problems of membership, mobilization and control over mass action.

UNION COOPERATION AND MOBILIZATION

Despite the vehemence of their rhetoric, the CGT and the CFDT have always agreed more easily on the bargaining goals that they should pursue than on how and when to mobilize workers, and how to link mobilization to bargaining and political goals. In the French environment of weak unions, conflict over goals is perhaps less important than conflict over mobilization, because the latter touches on the power and even the survival of a union organization.

The core problem of the French trade-union movement is the difficulty unions have in maintaining a stable membership and in maintaining control over the strike weapon.

The difficulties of union action in a worker environment cannot be seen in their capacity to be officially recognized, which they won through long national struggles, but in their contact with the base, where the rate of unionization is quite weak, and, in addition, is marked by a strong current of instability.[51]

Unstable rates of unionization reduce the authority of union representatives in the bargaining process and contribute to the uncertainty of the strike process. Indeed, in France, there is a tendency to see the strike as a process with its own momentum and its own independent force, linked to an unpredictable 'social climate,' rather than as an organizational weapon.[52]

In effect, every initiative that a union takes in calling, as well as preventing, a strike becomes a test of its power to mobilize, which in turn becomes a key factor in subsequent bargaining with employers or the state. Orders at the national or regional levels for strikes or demonstrations by the confederations or federations are generally intended to be a show of strength at a particular moment, or an exercise to encourage, or to show solidarity with, 'struggles in progress.' Therefore, national mobilization in France is fundamentally different from similar action in most other industrialized countries. It neither indicates the breakdown of bargaining, nor is it a test of strength through which bargaining is continued through other means. It usually serves as a precondition for any serious bargaining. Local or plant-level strikes provide opportunities from which advantages can be extracted at many levels, but there is generally little direct connection between strike action and collective agreements. Generally less than one percent of the strikes each year are directly related to collective agreements.

In this environment, unity of action has always been marked by the uncertainties and problems of mass mobilization. A key problem for the CGT and the CFDT has always been how to link agreed-upon objectives to mobilization. A continuing conflict over the years has been whether objectives should be used as mobilizing tools, or whether mobilization based on a wide variety of demands should (indeed could) then be channeled to support agreed-upon objectives.

At the core of every accord between the two confederations has been an agreement on coordinated mobilization that both organizations have calculated would strengthen them individually and collectively — that would enable them to deal more effectively with the problem of control over mobilization. 'When an organization is too weak to act alone, engagement in action, and the means to make it effective, supposes a policy of alliances with partners in accord with the essential ends sought,'[53] argued the 'new' CFDT in 1965. Complaining that 'Since 1960, they [employers and the state] negotiate less and less,' Gilbert Declerq concluded that the 1966 agreement with the CGT would encourage mass action (i.e. local strikes) with which to challenge this obstinate resistance to bargaining.[54] For two years prior to the 1966 accord the CGT — at the confederal level, but especially at the federal level in the public services — actively sought to coordinate its objectives with the CFDT. In fact, in the autumn of 1964, both confederations had set up liaison committees to coordinate the strikes of their federations in the public services; at the same time, the metals federations had reached an agreement on the priority of strike demands (with FO joining in).[55] Therefore, by 1966, joint strike declarations by CGT and CFDT unions had become common-place, with the emphasis on stimulating and channeling strike activity towards agreed-upon objectives at every level.

The agreement in 1970 presumed that 'a high level of combativity' would serve as a firm base from which both greater organizational unity and more effective bargaining could be built. In an attempt to overcome important differences on how workers could be mobilized, the accord supported initiatives at all levels. The CGT favored national demonstrations, and the CFDT was more inclined to accentuate 'specific actions, decided by the workers themselves.' They finally agreed that the bargaining objectives that they were seeking 'can be gained only through action taken by the *syndicats*, as well as by the federations, department unions and the confederations themselves.'[56]

If there were doubts about the agreement, they were less about the objectives being sought than about process — about the possibility that bargaining would outrun mobilization. For example, a key criticism came from J. Moreau, then of the chemical workers federation of the CFDT:

Now we think that today, if we want to take the lead on 'qualitative' problems, this kind of bargaining can only be imposed to the extent that there is mobilization. And mobilization can only be organized on the basis of the problems closest to the workers. To say that we are going to act on working conditions means nothing.[57]

The last important agreement on unity of action between the two confederations in 1974 was marked by a concern not only to stimulate action at every level, but to reinforce control over mass action through direct contacts between CGT and CFDT unions, and through the establishment of 'common principles for the participation of workers in decisions on action.'[58]

Despite their divergent political strategies, what consistently drew the two confederations together from the early 1960s until 1977 were the uncertainties of control over mobilization, as well as the benefits of a common bargaining front. They presumed that in both areas they were more powerful united than separated. While they were generally able to agree on bargaining objectives, however, the uncertainties of mobilization constantly presented problems for how they would engage in action. First, the success of joint strike orders was always uncertain. Second, the uncertainties of mobilization frequently generated conflict among militants of the two organizations at the plant level. In both confederations, militants argued that the identity of the two organizations was being brought into question by unity of action. Indeed, the closer the agreement on objectives, the more important the problem of identity.

Mass mobilization is a delicate process, not easily controlled by union organizations, even when they are united in purpose and in strategy. For example, the agreement of 1966 was followed by a series of brief national strike calls that were, in general, strongly supported. Therefore, both confederations were confident that their 'invitation' to increase strike activity in the fall of 1966 would be followed, but the strike level declined. In 1967, the confederations supported national demonstrations in the public sector, but strikes increased dramatically in the private sector instead, for which the unions claimed that their national action had provided the necessary spark. A close examination of strike activity in the private sector, however, does not support this claim.[59]

Throughout the period from 1970 to 1977, when unity of action pacts were in force, they constantly broke down over conflicts over how to deal with strike activity and mass mobilization. The 1970 pact collapsed in the spring of 1972 over the decisions by the CFDT to support 'adventurist' actions by poorly organized workers. 'What is striking ... is the support that [these workers] are given by the unions of the CFDT, always available to support a movement from the base, and less inclined than the CGT to question relations of force or the political impact of the strike.'[60] The 1974 agreement collapsed slowly, but for similar reasons. The Moreau report, presented to the CFDT leadership in January 1978, stressed that, in practice, action taken together with the CGT had in fact been demobilizing, 'insufficient,' and even 'dangerous' in the sense that such actions do not favor a 'mobilization of a majority of the workers.'[61]

During the next year, the problems of mobilization emerged in a more obvious way as a key impediment to the re-establishment of union agreement. Both confederations tended to place great emphasis on the difficulties that their militants were facing at the plant level. These kinds of conflicts between the CGT and the CFDT were not new, but the emphasis given to them by each organization was indeed new.[62] Initially, the failure of the September 1979 accord was explained in terms of conflicts among militants.[63] Only later did the political rhetoric about 'class collaboration,' on the one hand, and 'party domination,' on the other, become more prominent. It appears that the final attempt to develop unity of action had failed to generate mass mobilization, and had also failed to overcome the competitive forces among the militants.

There is evidence that agreements between the CGT and the CFDT have always been a difficult problem for militants in the poorly organized union environment of France, where militants are always bidding for the membership and support of a fluid constituency. Thus, while we often think of trade-union confederations (especially the CGT and the CFDT) as organizing different working-class subcultures, the overlap is considerable, and there is movement of members and supporters between confederations. About a third of the members of the CFDT (compared with a tenth of the members of the CGT) consider themselves to be 'catholics,' and 33 percent of CFDT members (compared with 17 percent of CGT members) identify themselves as politically center or right.[64] Nevertheless, in 1970, 25 percent of the members of the CFDT once belonged to the CGT (there was not much movement the other way).[65]

As the two confederations moved closer together in their commitments to class conflict and opposition to capitalism, agreement on objectives became easier at the national level; but the task of developing mass action by militants, while maintaining the distinctiveness of their union position, became more difficult. Distinctiveness has been based less on broad programs and objectives as such, and more on strategy, style of action, and specific demands supported at the enterprise level. The confederations, far from imposing their ideological divisions on pragmatic local activists (as some commentators have argued), appear to have imposed unity on their local units, but with great difficulty, especially in the private sector. At times, both confederations have openly complained about the lack of authority of the other.[66] As one CFDT militant explained:

At the national level, the relations between the two unions do not correspond at all to the situation at the factory level. In the plants it's continuous, open warfare. And one has the impression that the union headquarters want to give an appearance of unity which is not at all felt by the base, nor even desired by the base. At the national level, the unity which seems to develop is much more political than a real desire.[67]

Although CFDT militants interviewed by W. Rand Smith agreed (in 1977) that unity of action at the plant level was associated with higher levels of controlled mobilization, less employer resistance, greater organizational effectiveness and greater strike success, and, although they felt that unity was strongly desired by the workers, they also felt that, in practice, unity was most difficult to achieve (in 1974). Although competitive tensions at the plant level have always been a factor in the relationship between the CGT and the CFDT, this factor has been accentuated by a crisis of mobilization that began to emerge in the mid-1970s, and that by 1977–8 began to have a profound impact on the orientation of both organizations.

**Table 11.1** Opinions of CFDT militants

| *Relations with the CGT* | *National level* (%) | *Plant level* (%) |
|---|---|---|
| Rather good | 53 | 23 |
| Rather strained | 30 | 66 |
| Sometimes good, sometimes strained | 13 | 9 |
| Don't know | 4 | 2 |
| Total | 100 | 100 |
| N | 47 | 47 |

*Source:* W. Rand Smith, 'Paradoxes of Plural Unionism: CGT–CFDT Relations in France,' *West European Politics*, 4, No. 1 (January 1981), p. 51.

### THE 'CRISIS OF UNIONISM' AND UNITY OF ACTION

Since 1978, it has become commonplace to refer to a 'crisis' in the French trade-union movement. The core problem has been the emergence of secular trends of membership decline, a slowdown of organizational expansion and decline in the distribution of union journals and newspapers. In a larger sense, the ability of unions to influence and control mobilization has been brought into question once again. All of this has happened during the same period that the trade-union movement has become more institutionalized, and perhaps better protected than any other time in its history. Indeed, the problem has been even further complicated by the victory of the left in May 1981, a victory which has given union leaders substantial access to political decision-making and has weakened the political and bargaining position of French employers.[68] Although it can be argued that these trends are temporary setbacks, related to the *conjoncture*, there are also structural changes that are developing in the workforce that will continue to affect the ability of unions to organize and to control events.

Since 1975, the CGT has been losing membership steadily. In six years, the confederation lost 20 percent of its members, according to official figures, and 35 percent, according to unofficial figures. For the first time since the mid-1960s, the CGT admits to fewer than 2 million members.[69] Similarly, since 1976, the claimed membership of the CFDT has declined by 11 percent, losses that are more or less confirmed in unofficial estimates.[70]

During the late 1970s, both confederations first reacted to the membership decline. Beginning in February 1976, the CGT announced a general membership drive — 'a battle of recruitment' — and emphasized recruitment among young workers in large enterprises. By the end of 1978, the confederation confirmed that more than a million new members had joined, but 'despite the important number of new adhesions, the membership of the CGT remains practically stable.' Although they claimed to have recruited more than 250,000 new members each year after 1973, they were losing at least that number each year.[71] 'We can conclude that the CGT is an *organisation passoire*,' contended one CGT report.[72] Similarly, in 1979, the CFDT noted an 'alarming evolution' of its membership — a 'rotation' of 20–25 percent of its membership each year. The confederation had become a 'leaky bathtub.' 'Until these last few years, the leaky bathtub did not empty because the faucet remained open. Today, the bathtub is still leaky, but the faucet is closed.'[73]

Both unions referred to the rise in unemployment as the cause (but not the only cause) of the growing problem. However, this presumed relationship may be exaggerated. True, there has been a decline of union presence (plant sections) in plants with more than 300 workers since 1976 (although in smaller plants, union presence continued to grow).[74] However, a detailed study, based on information supplied by the CGT in its internal publication, *Courier Confédéral*, shows that, while in some regions there has been a membership loss that corresponds to rising unemployment, in many departments where unemployment has risen there is no corresponding decline in membership; while in still others (such as the Paris region) membership losses have been far higher than the rise in unemployment.[75]

In addition to the membership decline, there are other signs of malaise in the union movement. Support for the CGT and the CFDT remains high, but it has not increased significantly in recent years, and, by some measures, it seems to be eroding. According to results released by the Ministry of Labor, for example, the 'big five' national unions (CGT, CFDT, FO, CFTC and CGC) obtained 80 percent of the vote for works committees in 1966–7; in 1978–9 support declined to 76 percent; the remainder of the vote went to smaller (often company) unions and (increasingly) to non-union candidates. The slow, if steady, decline in the share of support for the major confederations, moreover, is not evenly distributed. CGC and CFDT have maintained their share, and CFTC and FO have gained slightly. The share of support for the CGT, however, has declined steadily from about 49 percent of the total in 1966–7 to about 37 percent in 1978–9.[76] The CGT disputes these figures, but not the trend.

The trend was given added weight by the *prud'hommale* elections in December 1982. While support for the CFDT and FO remained steady (compared with 1979), CGT support declined from 42.4 to 36.8 percent among salaried workers (a decline from 50.1 to 45 percent in industry and 42.4 to 36.7 percent in commerce); support for the smaller CFTC and CGC increased significantly. A year later, the results of the first elections to social security boards in almost twenty years indicated the profound weakness of the CGT and the CFDT. Among both blue-collar and white-collar workers FO emerged stronger than CFDT, and CFTC and CGC showed surprising strength as well (see Table 11.2).

**Table 11.2**   Results of the Social security elections of 19 October 1983 (% of those who voted)

|  | CGT | CFDT | FO | CFTC | CGC | |
| --- | --- | --- | --- | --- | --- | --- |
| Blue-collar workers | 48 | 18 | 21 | 10 | 3 | 100 |
| White-collar workers | 30 | 23 | 25 | 12 | 10 | 100 |

*Source:*   Union Confédérale des Ingenieurs et Cadres, CFDT, 'Les Grandes Centrales Syndicales en France,' in *Présentation de la CFDT* (Paris: CFDT, 1984).

Another aspect of the weakness of support for the trade-union movement is indicated by a survey conducted for the CFDT in 1981. Only a bare majority of young workers, according to the survey, expressed support for any trade union at all, far fewer than their adult counterparts, while 49 percent expressed various forms of 'distance' from unions.

It is young workers, who benefit the least from collective guarantees, who indicate most often their distance from the trade union movement . . . the trainees and apprentices (64%), the temporaries and intermediaries (58%), the workers of establishments with fewer than 50 workers (55%). They are also the most disfavored: unskilled and asembly line workers (52%), workers earning less than 3,000 Fr. [per month] (53%).[77]

Another troubling aspect of the report is that adults most firmly *reject* the unions. While 23 percent of the young workers specifically reject any trade union, the figure is as high as 41 percent for the adults in private industry. Only 'disappointment after experiences with failure can explain this difference,' contends the CFDT report.

Finally, although the CGT, and especially the CFDT, have often claimed to have a special appeal for young workers, this claim is not supported by the 1981 survey. Both unions are supported by higher percentages of adults than young workers. Moreover, young workers expressed greater confidence in FO than in the CFDT. While none of this is completely new — the results of a worker survey in 1970 show similar patterns — the results were most disappointing after a decade of a massive expansion of union presence.[78]

From 1970 to 1977, the number of plants in which union sections were present more than doubled, but the unions were not able to translate this extensive expansion into intensive increases in membership. During these years, the CGT increased its plant sections by 150 percent (from 5,245 to 13,275), while its membership remained virtually stagnant and began to drop after 1977. During this same period, support for the CGT in plant elections fell steadily. Therefore, in a sense, the crisis of membership and support is worse than it appears, since it has emerged during a period when union presence has been more widespread and better protected. Indeed, the expansion of union presence may well have masked a long-term decline in the effective membership of union organizations at the plant level. While the number of plant sections of the CGT tripled from 1970 to 1977 (some plants have more than one union section) the membership per section declined by about two-thirds (from 445 per section to 176 per section), steadily declining each year.[79]

Reinforcing the problems that unions are confronting are the important changes in the workforce that eat into traditional trade-union sources of strength. Industries in which unions have been traditionally strong — steel, ship construction, textiles, chemicals — are all in the process of being restructured. At the same time, the labor force continues to change, as the proportion of clerical workers, women and immigrant workers has become more important. In addition, the role of the so-called *marché périphérique d'emploi* (temporary workers) and the underground economy has also grown. All of these structural changes in the labor force have further weakened areas of union strength, and have posed greater challenges for recruitment and mobilization.

Historically, the French trade-union movement has gained members as it has become more institutionalized. Thus, during three periods — after World War I, during the initial phases of the Popular Front, and during the period just after World War II —membership in the union movement grew as organizations gained influence and access to governmental decision-making and strength in the bargaining process. Membership began to decline (in 1920, 1937 and 1947) as the hopes raised by union power began to fade.[80]

During the last decade, neither greater protection for union presence, nor the access to government decision-making and the corresponding political weakening of the influence of French employers (after 1981) have strengthened the ability of unions to mobilize workers. For the moment, what Gérard Adam has argued appears to be true: 'I do not use the word "crisis." It seems to me that we must speak of a change in the mode of influence of the trade unions. The unions are perhaps losing members, but they are gaining in influence, even if it is a sort of influence that is more diffuse.'[81] Adam has argued elsewhere that union professionals are in effect replacing the old-style militants because of the cumulative effects of labor legislation since 1968. Released time for union militants has created '. . . close to 100 thousand full-time jobs for the enterprise unions of France,' according to Adam.[82]

However, the unions seem aware that the real problem is the gap between growing (diffuse) influence and declining support, since the effectiveness of the former is related to the growth of the latter in the long run. Therefore, both the CGT and the CFDT have turned inward and have given increased attention to the arguments and needs of the militants. Both confederations have concluded that their alliance has become a threat to their identity at the plant level, and that organizational strength at the plant level is hindered, rather than aided, by the kind of cooperation that they engaged in between 1966 and 1977.

For the CGT, this threat was expressed periodically after 1968, when they were challenged from the left by the CFDT, and more strongly at their congress of 1975 and after.[83] A sharper criticism of the alliance with the CFDT, however, appeared during the months leading up to the 41st congress in 1982, when the CGT identified its most important membership losses with a loss of identity encouraged by union cooperation. Workers turned from the CGT when they could no longer see its specificity as an organization of 'class and mass.' 'It is only when it spoke once again [argued the CGT] in its own language, when it was able to demarcate itself clearly from the unions who were seeking social consensus, that the CGT was able to find once again its audience and reverse the decline of its members.'[84] The orientation document for the 1982 congress stresses that 'union pluralism is an established fact, but not an ideal for the CGT. ... The CGT intends to work for ... one working class, one union confronting the only employers' organization.' However, 'a decisive condition' for unity is the reinforcement of the CGT: 'its action, the diffusion of its ideas, the reinforcement of its membership and organizations, the growth of its influence ...' Only by mobilizing workers itself can the CGT 'lead the CFDT and the other union organizations to adopt positions and new behavior favoring unity of action.'[85]

Similarly, the CFDT, by 1978, had begun to see cooperation with the CGT as a danger to its identity and its organizational strength. The Moreau report, which was linked to the *recentrage* of 1978–9, specifically related the alliance with the CGT to the decline of influence of the CFDT. Less categoric than the CGT, the CFDT, in 1982, viewed the importance of cooperation in a similar way. 'It is our ... action that carries the *dimension unitaire*. For we seek to unify the workers through action and for the transformation of society,' argued Edmond Maire at the 1982 CFDT congress. In responding to criticism that the alliance with the CGT was necessary for mobilizing workers, Maire responded that the capacity of the CFDT should not be underestimated, that 'it is by being itself, and by inspiring union action that corresponds to the desires of the greatest number of workers, that the CFDT can best lead its partners towards a more unitary attitude.'[86]

While denying that there is a 'crisis' of unionism as such, both the CGT and the CFDT have reacted to the problem of mobilization by turning inward, and by rejecting their alliance as a priority. Certainly, the breakdown of the alliance between the two confederations after 1978 was encouraged by the failure by each organization to attain the political objectives that it had set for itself after 1966, as well as by the tensions between the political parties of the left. However, we have argued here that the breakdown has been, primarily, a reaction to their organizational weakness, a shift of emphasis from organizational cooperation, to competitive efforts at the plant level in the name of organizational survival.

During the period between 1981 and 1984 when both parties of the left were governing, organizational survival also militated against parallel union cooperation, even for political objectives. Both confederations emphasized their specific identity and their unique image. They pursued different legislative objectives and different critical approaches to the Government of the left. Thus, the CGT developed its image around the 'struggle' for 'new criteria' for investment, while the CFDT developed a broader critical image of a 'second left,' advocating both greater rigor in economic policy, a broader distribution of the burdens of austerity and more democratic participation in economic decision-making. While these positions certainly served to differentiate the confederations from each other, they do not seem to have been very effective as positions around which workers could be mobilized and organized.

The great strike actions of the United Left period were outbursts of frustration among immigrant workers in the auto industry when the workforce was cut back in 1983, and the explosion of anger in Lorraine when yet another reorganization of the steel industry was announced in April 1984.

Although both the CGT and the CFDT have devoted considerable attention to problems of mobilization since 1978, both confederations still seem to be in the position essentially of reacting to the movements of the *climat social.* Unions made notable gains in institutionalized power during this first period of left government, but these gains in protecting union presence in an increased number of plants have not been successful in increasing the authority of union militants in worker mobilization. Indeed, there are some complaints that the distance between militants and members and workers has grown significantly because of a *fonctionnarisation des militants syndicaux* (bureaucratization of union militants).[87]

Thus, the organizational problem has encouraged each confederation to accentuate its policy differences, a trend that can only be exacerbated by the departure of the Communists from the Government in July 1984. Whatever the former success of the old alliance in maximizing union influence in bargaining and political decision-making, it is now clearly perceived by both the CGT and the CFDT as having sapped their ability to organize and mobilize workers.

## NOTES

1. Pierre Sudreau, *Rapport du comité d'étude pour la réforme de l'entreprise,* 7 February 1975 (Paris: La Documentation Française, 1975), p. 25.
2. Gérard Adam, Frédéric Bon, Jacques Capdevielle and René Mouriaux, *L'Ouvrier français en 1970* (Paris: Armand Colin, 1970), Ch. 2.
3. Adam *et al.,* ibid., p. 58.
4. Louis Harris-France, *Structure des adhérents de la C.G.T. et de la C.F.D.T.* (Paris: Louis Harris International, 1977), p. 14.
5. W. Rand Smith, 'Paradoxes of Plural Unionism: CGT–CFDT Relations in France', *West European Politics,* **4**, No. 1 (January 1981); Moss's chapter in Mark Kesselman and Guy Groux, eds, *The French Workers' Movement: Economic Crisis and Political Change* (London and New York: Allen & Unwin, 1984).
6. *Le Monde,* 20 June 1964; Gérard Adam, 'L'Unité d'action CGT–CFDT,' *Revue Française de Science Politique,* **XVII**, No. 3 (June 1967), p. 584.
7. François Fejto, *The French Communist Party and the Crisis of International Communism* (Cambridge, Mass.: MIT Press, 1966), p. 109; Serge Mallet, *La Nouvelle classe ouvrière* (Paris: Editions du Seuil, 1963), p. 248.
8. Fejto, *The French Communist Party . . . ,* op. cit., p. 139.
9. *Le Monde,* 22 June 1966.
10. BRAEC, *Mouvement ouvrier et unité d'action* (Paris: CFDT, notes et documents du BRAEC, No. 16, 1981), p. 7.
11. Adam, 'L'Unité d'action CGT–CFDT', op. cit., p. 582.
12. Georges Lefranc, *Le Mouvement syndical* (Paris: Payot, 1969), p. 195.
13. Lefranc, ibid., p. 196.
14. Adam, 'L'Unité d'action CGT–CFDT,' op. cit., pp. 584–5.
15. René Mouriaux, 'La CGT depuis 1968,' *Projet,* 49 (November 1970), p. 1089.
16. Edmond Maire, 1973, in *Liaisons Sociales,* Suppl. au No. 8237, 'Syndicats II, organisations syndicales,' April 1980, p. 147.
17. Edmond Maire, *Rapport général,* 36e congrès confédéral, 1973, *Syndicalisme,* No. 1436, 15 March 1973, pp. 82–6.
18. *Le Monde,* 28 October 1971.
19. *Le Monde,* 9 March 1972.
20. *CFDT Aujourd'hui,* November–December 1980.
21. BRAEC, *Mouvement ouvrier et unité d'action,* op. cit., pp. 49–51.
22. R.W. Johnson, *The Long March of the French Left* (New York: St. Martin's Press, 1981), pp. 171–4.
23. René Mouriaux, *La CGT* (Paris: Éditions du Seuil, 1982), p. 118; *Le Monde,* 13 September 1980.

24. *Humanité*, 18 April 1978.
25. *Humanité*, 28 April 1978.
26. *Le Monde*, 20 April 1978.
27. Johnson, *The Long March . . .*, op. cit., pp. 245–7; *Le Monde*, 28 November 1978.
28. *Le Peuple*, 16–31 December 1978.
29. *Le Monde, Dossiers et documents*, 'La C.F.D.T.,' No. 78, February 1981.
30. *Liaisons Sociales*, Suppl. au No. 8237, 'Syndicats II, organisations syndicales,' April 1980.
31. Ibid., p. 50.
32. Ibid., p. 51.
33. *Maintenant*, 2 April 1979.
34. Johnson, *The Long March . . .*, op. cit., p. 274.
35. *Maintenant*, 2 April 1979; Johnson, *The Long March . . .*, op. cit., p. 268.
36. *Le Monde*, 5 September 1980.
37. *Le Monde*, 6 September 1980.
38. *Le Monde*, 8 June 1980.
39. George Ross, 'Unions, State and Society in Mitterrand's France,' paper prepared for the Annual Meeting of the American Political Science Association, Chicago, Ill., September 1983; Joanine Roy, 'Les Syndicats après le 10 mai,' *Le Monde*, 31 December 1981.
40. *Nouvel Observateur*, 17 April 1982.
41. *Syndicalisme* (December 1981), p. 35.
42. CFDT, *Compte rendu, 39e Congrès de la CFDT*, mai 1982, p. 23.
43. *Le Monde*, 15 June 1982.
44. Ross, 'Unions, State and Society . . .,' op. cit., p. 29.
45. *Le Monde, Dossiers et documents*, op. cit.
46. Ross, 'Unions, State and Society . . .,' op. cit., pp. 33–6.
47. Richard Shryock, 'The CFDT,' *Telos*, No. 55 (Spring 1983), p. 94.
48. Ross, 'Unions, State and Society . . .,' op. cit., p. 39.
49. Michel Noblecourt, 'La lente mutation du syndicalisme,' *Le Monde*, 20 and 21 March 1984.
50. *Expansion*, 18 February 1983, in Ross, 'Unions, State and Society . . .,' op. cit., p. 40.
51. *Projet*, 1970, p. 1070.
52. Martin Schain, 'Corporatism and Industrial Relations in France,' in Philip Cerny and Martin Schain, eds, *French Politics and Public Policy* (London and New York: Frances Pinter, St. Martin's Press and Methuen University Paperbacks, 1980); Segrestin's chapter in Kesselman and Groux, *The French Workers' Movement . . .*, op. cit.
53. CFTC, *Rapport sur l'évolution et les perspectives de la CFTC*, Paris, 1964, p. 65.
54. *Nouvel Observateur*, 19 January 1966.
55. *Le Monde*, 12 January 1966, 9 February 1966.
56. Joint statement in *Projet*, 1970, pp. 1120–1.
57. Ibid., p. 1055.
58. *Liaisons Sociales*, op. cit., p. 47.
59. Schain, 'Corporatism and Industrial Relations in France,' in Cerny and Schain, *French Politics . . .*, op. cit., p. 200.
60. *Le Monde*, 10 May 1972.
61. *Le Monde, Dossiers et documents*, op. cit.
62. Eugene Descamps, 'L'Action Confédérale,' *Syndicalisme*, No. 1283 (March 1970), p. 100.
63. *Le Monde*, 2 October 1979, 31 January 1980.
64. Harris-France, *Structure des Adhérents de la C.G.T. et de la C.F.D.T.*, op. cit., pp. 5 and 8.
65. Adam *et al.*, *Ouvrier français en 1970*, op. cit., p. 137.
66. *Le Monde*, 6–7 April 1975, 2 October 1979.
67. W. Rand Smith, 'Paradoxes of Plural Unionism . . .,' op. cit., p. 45.
68. Gérard Adam, interview in *Démocratie Moderne*, 22 October 1981; *Témoignage Chrétienne*, 29 June 1981; *Quotidien de Paris*, 11 March 1982.
69. Jacques Kergoat, 'La Chute des effectifs syndiqués à la CGT,' *Le Monde*, 8 June 1982; *Le Peuple*, 24 April 1982, p. 120.
70. *Syndicalisme*, 4 February 1982; Hubert Landier, *Demain quels syndicats?* (Paris: Livres de Poche, 1982).
71. *Liaisons Sociales*, op. cit., p. 11.
72. 'La politique financière de la CGT,' *Le Peuple*, 16–30 June 1979.
73. *Liaisons Sociales*, op. cit., p. 52.
74. Ibid., p. 190.
75. Kergoat, 'La Chute des effectifs syndiqués . . .,' op. cit., p. 17.

76. Mouriaux. *La CGT* . . ., op. cit., Annex 3.
77. BRAEC. *Les Jeunes et le travail* (Paris: CFDT. notes et documents du BRAEC. No. 18. 1981 (a)), p. 56.
78. Adam *et al.*, *L'Ouvrier français en 1970*. op. cit., p. 146.
79. *Liaisons Sociales*. op. cit., p. 190.
80. Antoine Prost, *La CGT à l'époque du front populaire* (Paris: Armand Colin, 1964), p. 196; Georges Lefranc, *Les Expériences syndicales en France de 1939-1950* (Paris: Aubier, Éditions Montaigne, 1950), p. 52.
81. Adam in *Démocratie Moderne*. op. cit.
82. Noblecourt, 'La lente mutation du syndicalisme,' *Le Monde*, 20 March 1984.
83. BRAEC, *Mouvement ouvrier et unité d'action*. op. cit., pp. 40-2.
84. Kergoat, 'La Chute des effectifs syndiqués . . .,' op. cit.
85. 'Projet de la documentation d'orientation'. *Le Peuple*. 16-28 February 1982, pp. 40-2.
86. CFDT. *Compte rendu* . . ., op. cit., p. 26.
87. Noblecourt, 'La lente mutation . . ..' op. cit.

# 12 Socialism and The Farmers

*Sally Sokoloff*

INTRODUCTION

The French farming community, despite its dramatic decline in size over the last three decades, is still very important to the society and politics of France. Agriculture is an important sector of the economy, a major claimant on the state, and a vital ingredient in (some would say irritant to) the French perspective on the EEC: France has the largest agricultural sector in the whole of the EEC. Farmers have remained electorally interesting to all French political parties, on the left as well as the right, and are potentially a great source of disorder and embarrassment as well as support to any government. Furthermore, there is an especially intense relationship between the farming community and government policy generally which needs to be specified before we can ask what effect the arrival of a Socialist regime in 1981 has had on farmers and what effect the farmers have had on the Socialist governments.

The record for 1981 to 1984 is important for assessing the success or otherwise the Mitterrand presidency has had in handling a notoriously difficult social group, a group whose apparent low income and low status makes it a candidate for socialist concern and reform yet whose political profile has become increasingly anti-left since the early years of the Fifth Republic. The farming case could be a good example of how a left-wing democratic government deals with a backward-looking, politically hostile section of society which nevertheless makes legitimate claim on its compassion and support. French socialism has to be judged to be helping the poorer farmers on the smaller farms to fulfil its egalitarian aims, let alone its socialist aims.

This chapter falls into four parts. In Section 1, the economic changes experienced by agriculture since 1958 will be considered. Agriculture has undergone rapid and substantial change in the last twenty-five years, posing similar problems for the new Socialist Government as it did to the Gaullist and Giscardian Governments of the 1960s and 1970s. It is a moot point how far any government can control the process of the elimination of smaller farms from production. In Section 2, the continuing political importance of farmers will be explained: they have increasingly supported the right since the 1960s, but the left had some grounds for hope of political support among farmers. There was the basis of a venerable left-wing tradition in some rural areas, there was a small shift leftwards among farmers in the 1981 elections, and the Socialists hoped that, once in power, their policies would attract poorer farmers. It is too easy to write off farmers as naturally hostile to the left: rather, we need to understand the specific basis of their indisputably majority support for the right in the Fifth Republic.

In Section 3, relations between farmers' syndicalist organizations and government will be examined. The Mitterrand regime faced a well-established pattern of corporatist relations between the chief farming *syndicat* (the FNSEA — Fédération Nationale des Syndicats d'Exploitants Agricoles) and the state, a pattern which had moulded the character of agricultural policies since the 1960s. The strength of the FNSEA and the basis of its claim to speak for the whole of farming must be assessed before we can judge how the Socialists dealt with agricultural syndicalism. The role of the FNSEA is extremely important because farmers have traditionally expressed their politics more clearly through it than through the more direct channels of political participation. Section 4 will consider Socialist policies for farming, will assess the successes and failures of the Socialist governments in this field, and will tackle some of the general questions raised at the beginning of this introduction.

## 1. AGRICULTURAL CHANGE AND FAMILY FARMING

In the last two or three decades, the number of people working on the land in France has fallen enormously and agriculture's percentage contribution to GNP has also fallen. In 1960, 4.1 million people worked in agriculture, but by 1970 the figure was down to 2.8 million. A peak in the rate of decline was reached in the early years of the Fifth Republic, with 115,000 farmers leaving every year between 1954 and 1962. The rate slowed down to 88,000 per annum between 1962 and 1968, but rose again in the mid-1970s when about 160,000 people were leaving agriculture each year. Between 1968 and 1974 alone, farmers and agricultural labourers counted together decreased as a percentage of the male workforce from 15 to 10 per cent. The disappearance of farmers and farm labourers constitutes a large part of the staggering fall in employment in primary occupations from 27.4 per cent of the active population in 1954 to 10.1 per cent in 1975 (to the benefit of the tertiary sector which employed just over half the active workforce by 1975).[1] In 1982–3 farmers made up just over 8 per cent of the active workforce.[2]

The continued decline in the agricultural workforce in the last ten years has been partially concealed by the fact that the population resident in rural communes was stabilizing after a long period of depopulation, as the 1975 statistics showed. A million people left the rural communes between the mid-1950s and early 1960s, but a million people returned to rural communes between 1975 and 1982: those who left were mostly from farming, but those who returned were not, their return to the village concealing suburbanization and long journeys to work. Furthermore, French farmers are an ageing group: the most rural departments also have the most top-heavy age structures.[3] In 1980 there were 1,200,000 farms, and most projections agree that France will have around a million farms by the mid-1980s, most of them using only family labour.[4] It seems that there is an inexorable economic pace-setter for the elimination of small farms.

The continued fall in the number of farms has not destroyed the category of the small to medium-sized farm, although the idea of 'a small farm' has been adjusted. The vanished farms were mostly in the very small category, and they were absorbed by the next smallest category. There has been no wholesale cannibalization of many small farms into a few large ones. For all the social disruption of the rural exodus, the average size of farms has increased very soberly, from around 16 hectares in the 1960s to 23 hectares in 1976 to 25–30 hectares now (a hectare is two and a half acres). In the 1960s many experts and policy-makers acted on the supposition that the farm of over 100 hectares was the rational basis for agriculture's future: the EEC's Mansholt Report and the French Vedel Report of the late 1960s are the most notable examples of the 'giganticist' frame of mind.[5] Some agronomists continue to believe that extensive farming on units of about 200 or 300 hectares, as currently practised in the Paris Basin wheat and beet zone, is the only rational path for French agriculture.[6] One million farms is nowhere near this technical ideal.

'Small farms' are now defined as a unit of under 50 hectares capable of being run by a family with the aid of labour-saving machinery. Such farms will constitute the norm in the 1980s and onwards if current conditions continue. The rejection of giganticism had two important faces. On the one hand, governments in the 1970s decided not to force farmers to recast agriculture along large-farm lines: it would have entailed uprooting even more farmers, increasing unemployment in the industrial labour market, and adding to the financial and social costs of urbanization. On the other hand, there was a theoretical re-evaluation of the function and capacity of small farms. Rural economists and sociologists now argued ·that large-scale agriculture is curtailed by certain factors specific to farming. Capitalism *is* steadily penetrating agriculture but not by turning peasants into wage-labourers on large farms with industrial methods. Rather, surplus value can be best squeezed out of agriculture by allowing farmers to maintain small market production, while imposing all the costs and none of the benefits of land and property on them. Farmers are persuaded that their farms can survive as units of family production by way of modernization, but the mechanisms and institutions by which they modernize (credit banks, preferential agreements with agribusiness, cooperatives, etc.[7]) serve to bind them more closely into an integrated and highly exploitative system of agriculture rather than to preserve their independence.

The small-farm structure will persist on two conditions: first, that agricultural production is polycultural and intensive, thus giving the best returns to farmers who can give individual attention to the care of livestock; second, that farmers continue to regard land (a factor of production whose costs the capitalist regards with caution) as an instrument of production and also essential to their self-definition and social status. In other words, small farmers are induced to keep farming and to pay the purchase price of land at levels which any self-respecting capitalist would refuse to contemplate. The farmer's brave attempts to behave in a 'rational' economic fashion cannot succeed in a system where private property in land (at high prices) continues. The present uneconomic costs of agriculture have stopped agribusiness interests, whose intervention in the poultry and pork markets evoked much attention in the 1960s, from pursuing the full vertical integration of agriculture which would have truly proletarianized the farmer. It is cheaper to allow small polycultural farms to bear the costs of land, the costs of a rapidly evolving technology, and the poor return on labour obtained in agriculture.[8]

Opinion on the future of the small-farming systems appears to be divided into two schools of thought. One regards current small-farm agriculture as the basis for a rural renaissance towards the end of the century as population grows, ecological considerations cause decentralization of population, and as Europe rejects the irrationality of a system that builds butter mountains and denatures food.[9] The other regards the small-farm system as a temporarily finely balanced system which could soon be swept away by the deeper penetration of capitalism into the countryside.[10] Either way, farmers will never resume their earlier position as the largest occupational group, just as France will never be a peasant society again. If small farms still exist in France, peasants no longer farm them.

The French peasantry had occupied a special place in the nation and its political ideology. Ideologically, it was recognized as the social groundwork of the Third and Fourth Republics; politically, it enjoyed disproportionate electoral influence and state protection. Since 1958, however, the ideological rudiments of a land-owning Republic have been replaced rapidly by the new values of industrialization, productivity, technocracy and consumerism. Peasant society has been undermined by a potent double-binding change. Not only have the values of a peasant society been denigrated, but peasants found it well nigh impossible to join the new value system as they were urged to do. The half-way house of 'family farming' has proved a hard path for many: the farmer has been isolated 'by imposing on to the farmer the "ideology" of being and behaving like an "entrepreneur", by keeping him at the same time to the status of a "family farmer".'[11] By the 1960s rural France itself was highly conscious of the severity and irreversible nature of the change. As Edgar Morin wrote of Plodémet in southwestern Brittany, 'the peasant class is rapidly disappearing. Everyone, including the most active exponents of modernization and the most ardent unionists, is aware of living through the last days of the peasantry'.[12]

## 2. POLITICAL CHANGE AMONG FARMERS

The peasant class has been subjected to such profound economic change in the last three deades that it is now more appropriate to describe those active in farming as farmers or a farming community. That community, despite its dwindling contours, is an important influence on government and is still a potent political force.

The farming vote is undoubtedly less important than in the past simply because of the fall in the number of farmers. Obviously, it remains important in the rural parts of western and southern France, but even here the degree of ruralism and the percentage of farming workers within the rural population has fallen. It is very rare nowadays to find a rural commune where over half of the working population is in agriculture.[13] Nevertheless, all serious political parties appeal to farmers at election times, as to all substantial sectors of society. Agricultural policy and issues are frequently in the forefront of political concern, being an important component of French policy in the EEC.

As the Fifth Republic has progressed, the political margin between right and left has narrowed (finally tipping in the left's favour in 1981), giving disproportionate electoral leverage to many smaller groups in society and affecting the views of politicians towards such groups. We see a paradox of a declining social group, such as farmers, exerting increased electoral power. Suzanne Berger is the most recent observer to theorize the apparently large power of social groups which were, until recently, thought to be economically and politically marginal to the future. Although her chief concern is the traditional sector in industry and commerce in France (and Italy), she extends the general analysis to include farmers. She argues that the survival of a traditional sector is not only economically necessary to capitalism but also politically essential to the Fifth Republic, providing social stability and ideological control of the workforce, and the bedrock to the idea of individual property. In return for political support from the traditional sector, the state is expected to maintain the sector's moral right to existence and to assist its economic viability. Drawing on French and Italian examples, Berger attacks the idea that the traditional sector has been at its last gasp in recent years:

... this theory of the last gasp of the traditional sector ... has become less and less satisfactory ... considering together the hundreds of apparently unrelated skirmishes of recent decades — over the expansion of supermarkets, over agricultural subsidies for small farmers, over industrial structures, over state credit and social security systems — we see a pattern of survival that suggests that the role of the traditional sector in modern societies is far more important than we have understood.[14]

Berger's interpretation specifies a collusive political relationship between farmers and the state, as does Tarrow's scenario of political alliance-building between Gaullism and certain social groups.[15] Both are borne out by the growing smoothness of farmer–government relations in the two decades after 1958. Initially Gaullism pursued a policy of ruthless economic modernization frightening to small farmers, but this rapidly softened into a mutually supportive relationship between farmers and Gaullist and Giscardian Governments in the 1970s. The corporatist aspect of the situation will be examined later in the chapter; here the concern is its political aspects.

Before the Fifth Republic the peasantry supported all major political movements, giving support to both conservative and left-wing parties in the Third Republic, though more to the former. During the Popular Front period and between 1944 and the 1950s, left-wing parties gained substantially among the peasantry, particularly in parts of southern France and the north-west corner of the Massif Central where Communist voting seemed to be the permanent result of a left-wing tradition among peasants dating back to 1848. However, the nature of the peasantry, meant that its perception of electoral and parliamentary politics was always imperfect and its relations with parties dogged by misunderstanding and distrust. Lewis-Beck, in a recent article, argues that peasants are apolitical compared to other groups in French society, lagging behind the French average on almost any index of political participation.[16] Agricultural syndicalism certainly projects a clearer image of farming unity than does party politics.

Under the Fifth Republic, the farming community took a clear turn rightwards, within the general trend towards an ironing-out of regional political differences and the 'nationalization' of political commitment. Gaullism was the principal instrument of this change, although by the mid-1970s the farming vote could go to any strong group or party on the centre-right: at the 1978 parliamentary elections the Gaullist RPR and the Giscardian UDF were competing for an identical electorate.[17]

Gaullism made a belated appearance among farmers after 1958: relations between de Gaulle and farmers became strained and bitter as his early Ministers of Agriculture spearheaded the modernization framework through the *lois d'orientation* of 1960 and 1962. Farmers were enraged when the Government severely reduced the level of price support which farmers saw as their rightful tribute from the Republican state. In 1958, farmers and farm labourers made up a fifth of the adult population, but only 7 per cent of the

Gaullist vote came from them. The most striking examples of domestic mass political defiance to the Fifth Republic in its early years were not working-class strikes or demonstrations but farmers' demonstrations, blockades, embargoes, and violence directed against the government's agricultural policies.

By the parliamentary elections of 1962, however, farmers gave the Gaullist party 32 per cent of their vote (exactly the national average of Gaullist voting) and gave a favourable response to the referendum on direct presidential election. But in 1965, when de Gaulle and the agricultural *syndicat*, the FNSEA, were at loggerheads over the Common Agricultural Policy (CAP), farmers voted against de Gaulle in the presidential election and were held (statistically) responsible for de Gaulle suffering the indignity of a second ballot. This proved a temporary setback, and the rightward swing begun in 1962 continued in 1967 and 1968. In the parliamentary elections of June 1968 farmers gave nearly half their votes to the Gaullist party. And in the unsuccessful referendum on regional and Senate reform in 1969, farmers were the only socio-professional group apart from retired people to say 'yes' to de Gaulle's inconsistent proposals. In the presidential election of 1969, Pompidou did better among farmers than de Gaulle had done. By 1969 the Gaullist party had mopped up all support for traditional right-wing parties among farmers.[18] The Gaullists maintained their position among farmers in 1973, when they were on the wane generally: of the mere thirteen departments where the Gaullist vote increased in 1973, against the national trend, ten were rural departments of the centre and south.[19] And in 1978 **RPR** voting was greater among farmers than in any other socio-professional group: 31 per cent voted **RPR** and 27 per cent **UDF**.[20]

Explanation of the shift to the right throws much light on the political character and motivations of farmers in recent years. The first area of explanation concerns the linkages between class, religion and political commitment. Recent research has shown that the correlation between religious practice and voting is the chief constant which can explain French electoral choice over and above changes in parties, policies and Republics. Farmers, with certain regional exceptions, have been bound up in locally religious and conservative communities. Class has been growing in importance as a correlative of vote, if not as an explanation. Farmers lack a clear recognition of their own class, and weak class consciousness goes hand in hand with apolitical, right-wing or conservative attitudes. For example, 44 per cent of a sample of farmers claimed to have no feeling of belonging to any social class. Even among those who did feel they belonged to a class, consciousness was divided: 17 per cent (of the whole sample) believed they were peasants, 12 per cent working class, and 9 per cent middle class. Among the same farmers' wives, class consciousness was even weaker. Observers have always had trouble defining the class of peasants and farmers: apparently farmers themselves have the same problem. A lack of class consciousness, which may well grow as farmers feel themselves no longer peasants, favours conservative attitudes towards politics and society.[21]

A second area of explanation concerns farmers' opinion of the Fifth Republic generally. The hostility felt towards government policies diminished in the mid-1960s: many farmers involved in violent protest in the early 1960s left the land, so that the constituency for protest simply melted away, at least for that generation of farmers. Non-agricultural policies of the

Fifth Republic were attractive to farmers, notably the firm foreign policy stands taken by de Gaulle, the political stability, and the idea (if not the reality) of orderly social progress for which Gaullism stood. Farmers stood on the sidelines in May '68, supported the Government during the period of backlash, and have clearly been swayed by arguments that the ruling alliance was the only guarantee against disorder, chaos and poverty.[22] Furthermore, farmers saw an increase in their net income until the mid-1970s. Farmers still felt that they were insufficiently rewarded for their labour, but there was by the 1970s a groundswell of grudging satisfaction with improvements in real living standards among farmers. President Giscard reflected these complacent feelings in late 1977 when, in a key speech, he painted a rosy picture of French agriculture as healthily competitive, prosperous, indeed 'the oil of France' in its foreign trade.[23]

The third means of explaining the rightward trend focuses on the development of a materialist attitude to politics: farmers vote for the party or alliance which promises them most in material gains and which carries out its promises through policy. This interpretation has of course been applied to relations between farmers and governments since the days of the Third Republic. But in the Fifth Republic, it has been stretched to cover the character of all contemporary French politics, as part of a general reinterpretation of modern France as a society dominated by pragmatic assessment of interest rather than by the clash of political principles and ideals. As a recent English observer puts it, 'there was mounting evidence to suggest that the French were divided less over a fine and idealistic sensitivity about the political requirement of the country than a crude and reassuring calculation of materialistic self-interest'.[24] There is a connection between farmers' support for the majority coalition until 1981 and the easing-up of governmental pressure for modernization in the 1970s. Farmers and governments of the 1970s saw themselves as partners in a new type of trade-off: both perhaps exaggerated the power of policy to affect basic socio-economic trends. Crude assessment of self-interest and of the location of power has been observed at play in many rural constituencies, for example in the Corrèze where Gaullism had triumphed by '68, promising '. . . efficiency, growth, the stemming of the rural exodus, and the attention and concern of the political system. All that was neither of the Right nor of the Left: it was *gaullien*.'[25]

The status of the peasantry as a 'governmental class' reflects its historical role as a special ward of the French state: this relationship became even clearer in the Fifth Republic because of the transfer of power from parliament to executive. Instrumental politics simply become more obvious when they are channelled entirely through the executive rather than through the murky channels of parliamentary influence. Modernization seemed to lead away from left-wing voting towards support of 'less ideological' parties, as many theorists of modernization believed. Yet the appeal to pragmatism and personal self-interest could be dangerous shifting ground for the right to occupy, since the left could also try to occupy it, transcending ideology. Indeed, much of the appeal of the growing Socialist Party in the 1970s was its pragmatism: elections were increasingly characterized by wrangling over the detailed financial position of different classes under right or left.

While in opposition, the Communist Party diluted its concern for farmers. Between the 1930s and the 1950s, peasants made up the second largest group in the Communist clientele, second in importance to the working class, but now the new petty bourgeoisie has taken its place. The PCF's post-war solicitude for farmers was a sensible manoeuvre to acquire influence over the very small peasantry before its inevitable proletarianization took place. This pool of support has been virtually mopped up, though the PCF still keeps a syndicalist finger in the farming pie through MODEF (see Section 3 of this chapter). The Common Programme of the Left of the early 1970s devoted only two pages out of eighty to agricultural policy. There was a radical element in the left's commitment to better social benefits for small farmers, limitations on land speculation, fairer distribution of price subsidies, and more democratic methods for organizing the market. But the means by which change was to be achieved remained vague and the aim of technical modernization was similar to that of the ruling coalition. Indeed, in glibly promising to reconcile modernization with the maintenance of a prosperous small-farming sector, the tone of the left's agricultural programme was very much like that of the right, though the left was more hostile to big-farming interests.[26]

In the 1981 elections, farmers continued to give most support to the right. Yet the right's losses were greater in rural constituencies than in the big cities, where the wealthier quarters remained Gaullist and Giscardian. Outside of the cities there was a switch to Mitterrand among practising Catholics who had shown a mild disposition to the conservative camp previously. Once Mitterrand was President and the Communists shown to have been humiliated, the barrier against voting Socialist in the parliamentary election was down in these areas and a substantial leftward swing occurred. In the parliamentary elections, the right suffered a reverse in many rural departments of central and southwestern France, among them Corrèze which had swung rightwards in the 1960s.[27]

Though the constituencies which ditched the right were rural, I believe that farmers were unlikely to have switched as much to the left as did other classes in 1981. There is the usual problem of correlating electoral trends in a given constituency with the vote of a particular class, especially when that class constitutes only 8 per cent of the population as a whole. One descends to special factors, notably the influence on farmers of the FNSEA, which favoured Giscard in the presidential election, 67 per cent of farmers sampled by SOFRES supported Giscard and 33 per cent Mitterrand: in 1974, faced with the same candidates, 69 per cent of these farmers had supported Giscard and 31 per cent Mitterrand. This was a small change, still leaving farmers as the most pro-Giscardian class in 1981.[28] In the first ballot of the parliamentary elections, the SOFRES sample of farmers gave greater support to the left-wing parties than they had done to Mitterrand: left-wing parties jointly took 40 per cent of their vote (80 per cent of it going to the Socialist Party), while the UDF and RPR took 60 per cent (divided almost equally between them). So 7 per cent of the farmers questioned had shifted leftwards between the presidential and the parliamentary elections. Yet the UDF and RPR had improved their support among farmers by 1 per cent each since the 1978 parliamentary elections. It seems that farmers were susceptible to the pro-Socialist drift following Mitterrand's personal victory, but that their right-wing leanings will take a lot more shifting before they can be said to support right and left on a fifty-fifty basis. The swing towards the left among farmers in 1981 was small and hesitant: more substantial was the swing from

Communist to Socialist support in the parliamentary elections.

Since 1981, farmers have failed to make common political cause with the Socialist Governments, have regarded reforms affecting them with scepticism, and placed themselves alongside groups opposing the austerity programme in the late spring of 1983. The irony is that farmers' real income began to rise in 1981 when the Socialists came to power, that 1982 saw their biggest rise in income since the early 1970s, and that the Government intended that they should be partially exempted from austerity in 1983. Despite this, farmers deliberately embarrassed the Government by ferocious demonstrations against the EEC price negotiations. To understand this, we need to examine the syndical and political role of the farmers' professional organizations.

### 3. SYNDICALISM AND POLITICS

Agricultural interests have closer and more direct links with the state than perhaps any interest group or class in the Fifth Republic. The ideological and political priority given to the peasantry by traditional Republicanism has given way to an equally fruitful network of corporate relationships between the state and farmers' pressure groups. Qualitatively, the relations between state and farmers became increasingly institutionalized in the 1960s and 1970s so that they stood close to corporatism. The establishment of a special and exclusive world of relations between farmers and the state has occurred partly because the 'rural world' has vanished as an object of defence for farmers, leaving farmers alone at the centre of the agricultural process, with only the state to look to. Ministers of Agriculture of the Fifth Republic have also been happy to promote closer professional relations with farmers in an attempt to defuse farmers' protests and to bypass the traditional political-parliamentary channels. Furthermore, the rise of closer collaboration between interest groups and state bodies has been a general trend in the Fifth Republic, although not to the extent reached in agriculture.

Relations between agricultural syndicalism and the state have become more direct, stable and confident between 1960 and 1981: participation by syndicalist representatives in the state apparatus has become general and hierarchized. For example, there are regular meetings between leaders of the professional organizations and the Ministry of Agriculture: since 1972 an annual meeting brings together agricultural leaders and civil servants under the Prime Minister's chairmanship. Similar collaboration is found all the way down the administrative ladder, especially at the departmental level, where policies agreed are implemented. There is a multitude of organisms, of varying status, where officials and farmers' representatives work together.[29] At the local (departmental) level, there are consistently intense relations between the chief representatives of local syndicalism and officials concerned with farming: the power in the hands of the farmers' representatives is considerable, especially that of the president of the departmental Chamber of Agriculture and the president of the departmental syndicat (often one and the same person).[30] John Keeler describes how the functions and activities of the syndicalist officials overlap with those of the personnel of the local Chamber of Agriculture and of state employees involved in technical aid to farming. The humble farmer must find it hard to judge where the syndicat ends and the state begins.[31] The range of organizations of a syndicalist, professional, cooperative or interest group character is bewilderingly large, as is the range of bodies established by government initiative but counting on professional participation and advice.

Central to government–farming relations has been the FNSEA which constituted the heart of a web of interlinkages between farmers and the state. Through the FNSEA and its departmental components (FDSEAs), farmers have shown a united face to government on most occasions and issues. To do this, the FNSEA has to perform a constant balancing act between the interests of big and small farmers.[32] In the early 1960s, the FNSEA was challenged by the Young Farmer (CNJA) movement of modernization: it overcame the challenge by incorporating Young Farmer ideas without endangering professional unity.[33] The impact of the Young Farmers' movement has been assessed, depending on political standpoint, as either a sell-out whereby modernizing idealism was neutralized by contact with power, or as a movement through which the younger generation of farmers recognized the policies necessary for agricultural modernization and forced them on the archaic FNSEA.[34]

The FNSEA has achieved the remarkable feat of maintaining a rough-and-ready unity during the period of the peasantry's death throes. Whether it could have done this without support from the Gaullist and Giscardian state is a moot point. Right-wing governments gave the FNSEA a privileged position in consultations, recognized it as the corporate spokesman for farmers, and subsidized it in many different ways, thus cutting the ground from under the feet of any alternative *syndicats*, notably the Communist and Socialist ones. Keeler argues that this is another indication of corporatism — one professional, representative body more equal than the others.[35] The ideology of unity ran deep in the minds of farmers, irrespective of the monopoly position of the FNSEA. Indeed, the smaller the remnant group of farmers becomes, the more they feel the need to stick together to extract the maximum from government: all farmers, excepting a small group of large farmers, have common fears and insecurities. The three years since President Mitterrand and the Socialists came to power have been a test of unity, since one of the first things the Socialist Government did in farming policy was to open up its consultative bodies to the left-wing farming *syndicats*, putting them on an equal footing with the FNSEA for the first time.

Foremost among farmers' left-wing *syndicats* is MODEF (Mouvement de Défense des Exploitants Familiaux), under Communist influence, though this is regularly denied. By the mid-1970s, MODEF claimed 200,000 members; in the elections for the Chambers of Agriculture in 1974 it obtained 30 per cent of the vote of working farmers and 40 per cent of the vote of retired farmers.[36] The peak reached in the 1970s has since fallen away, for three reasons: first, some of its ageing small-farming support is now gone; second, Communist-influenced *syndicats* have suffered from the general decline of Communism in France; third, new farmers' *syndicats* close to the Socialist Party have sprung up since 1981 and these have drawn off some left-wing support from MODEF. In the elections for the Chambers of Agriculture which took place in late January 1983 under a new electoral system, MODEF got 10 per cent of the vote and maintained its strong position in some departments in the south-west and south-east.[37] The 10 per cent national figure is an underestimate of MODEF's real strength as in some departments it supported the candidates of other *syndicats* where their policies were compatible with MODEF's.

In the early years of the Fifth Republic, MODEF had a programme which was conservative in that it promised support and a continued existence to small farmers, even those on the most unviable farms. It opposed all government policies and was particularly hostile to the EEC. Participation in government consultative bodies was undesired and unsought, and action was thus confined to protest. Gradually, however, MODEF began to see some of the benefits of farmers' unity, cooperating with the FNSEA and other *syndicats* in protest movements to start with. In the later years of the Giscard presidency, MODEF requested entry to consultative status (this of course being refused by the Government which protected the FNSEA's monopoly), and it softened its opposition to modernization programmes and the EEC. All in all, MODEF had adapted sufficiently to make both logical and sensible its new status under the Socialist Government. Mme Cresson, the first Socialist Minister of Agriculture, was keen to hear MODEF and the other left-wing *syndicats* voicing alternative policies to those of the FNSEA. MODEF is still a tribune for the grievances of small farmers in southern France, but it does now have the attention of the Minister of Agriculture. Its new status has not brought it greater support among farmers; indeed, the FNSEA maintained its strength in the 1983 Chamber of Agriculture elections.

Two other left-wing *syndicats* could expect some benefit from the Socialist assumption of power — the CNSTP (Confédération Nationale Syndicale des Travailleurs Paysans), founded in 1981, and the FNSP (Fédération Nationale des Syndicats Paysans), founded in 1982. Both stand close to Socialist policies, the former being the successor to earlier pro-Socialist *syndicats*,[38] the latter being a radical offshoot from the FNSEA. The CNSTP polled nearly 7 per cent and the FNSP 6.5 per cent in January 1983, showing that MODEF had no monopoly of anti-FNSEA feeling among farmers.[39]

The FNSEA has, then, maintained its strength despite losing its monopoly position with government as spokesman for farmers. It took 70 per cent of the farmers' vote in 1983 at the Chambers of Agriculture election; and 70 per cent of those eligible voted, testimony to the commitment of farmers to the syndicalist movement. Under the Socialist regime, the FNSEA has continued to behave much as it did previously, though its leadership (and notably M. Guillaume, its President[40]) is anti-Socialist. Participation in the structures of cooperation with the executive has largely continued, though with some occasional friction. Growing political disagreement was in evidence between Guillaume and Cresson early in 1983 with accusations of bad faith and misrepresentation coming from both sides.[41] In February 1983 the FNSEA was the sole agricultural *syndicat* to boycott the two-day 'estates general' of agriculture, a high-powered debate on the future of French farming which drew five ministers and 2,500 representatives of 'green France'. The pretext for Guillaume's absence was that insufficient speaking time had been allowed to the FNSEA, but the real reason was clearly growing political antagonism.[42] A few days later Guillaume alleged that his telephone was being bugged by the Government: this was denied by the Prime Minister's office.[43] Not all the FNSEA leaders shared M. Guillaume's paranoia about the Socialist Government, but all were relieved to see Mme Cresson removed from the Ministry of Agriculture in the government reshuffle in March 1983 which followed the local elections. FNSEA leaders disliked her as much for her style as her Socialist policies, and their hostility may have been a contributory factor in her departure.

The methods of the FNSEA have altered little with the change from right to left in 1981, despite the occasional political fracas described above. By the mid-1960s it had come to terms with the new institutional framework of Gaullist France and had at its disposal a whole range of pressure-group channels and methods, from private consultations with ministers and officials at national and local levels, ranging through contacts with politicians in Parliament and with political parties, down to violent protest at local level. Under Presidents Pompidou and Giscard, the scale of FNSEA activity was weighted towards bureaucratic participation, that is, towards the methods and relationships which may be defined as corporatist. Yet under Mitterrand the FNSEA has shown itself willing to downgrade the corporatist ties on occasion and to revert to stronger grassroots methods. FNSEA leaders had soft words for those farmers engaged in an orgy of violent protest following the breakdown of price negotiations for the EEC in spring 1983. Farmers were hijacking refrigerated lorries containing imported meat, letting animals loose in cities, going on the rampage in country towns, ransacking official documents and roughing up officials, blocking roads and railways, closing the borders with Spain, Italy, Belgium and Luxembourg, dumping unsold fruit and vegetables, and selling surplus produce directly and cheaply to the public. In the south, protesting farmers are generally affiliated to MODEF or other small organizations and are often beyond the FNSEA's control; but in the west and Brittany the FNSEA has reacted complacently to the violence of pig farmers hit by low prices and poultry producers hit by a fall-off in the export market for frozen chickens. It is in the convenient position of being able to condone such action through its local activists while disavowing responsibility, for example, blaming Young Farmer hotheads. When it suits them, national leaders can claim to be orchestrating the protests which are really initiated by local activists and by regional issues, as in mid-May 1983 when farmers staged a series of spectacular border closures and seized food imports just as the EEC Agriculture Ministers finally made belated decisions over price increases on 17 May.[44]

Frank Wilson summarizes much recent research on French pressure groups when he argues that they conform to neither a pluralist model, nor a protest model, nor a corporatist model: rather, they keep their options open and saturate the public and official arena with their pressures, irrespective of their expectations of satisfaction from any particular channel. Agriculture in his view provides the one great exception, showing distinctly corporatist traits and leaning towards official channels rather than public demonstrations and protests. His evidence comes from fifteen leaders of agricultural syndicalism interviewed in 1979, and he himself admits that leaders are likely to overemphasize the importance and effectiveness of consultation with the executive. Furthermore, his evidence is from the period of maximum friendliness between the FNSEA and the Giscardian Government,[45] as is John Keeler's (who also regards the FNSEA as corporatist). My own view on the evidence of 1981–3 is that the FNSEA can move closer to other French *syndicats* in its behaviour and methods and that it is a pressure group with multiple activities and channels of expression, like most other pressure groups. It retains a corporatist character, however, because of the sustained quasi-unity of farmers behind the FNSEA (compared with, for example, the divided trade-union movement), and because of the extreme dependence of farmers on the French state and the CAP for their livelihood and chances of survival on the land. A 'governmental class' must keep in touch with government, but corporatism is no guarantee of social order.

## 4. AGRICULTURAL POLICY UNDER SOCIALISM

All governments of the Fifth Republic before 1981 aimed through policy to encourage agriculture towards greater productivity and efficiency, while simultaneously supporting certain smaller categories of family farm, and also attempting to reduce political discontent arising out of economic change in the countryside. These aims were incompatible in their purest forms, but each could be pursued partially through a changing policy 'mix'. Though an unstoppable pace-setting economic change was already occurring in agriculture — broadly speaking, agriculture in the 1960s and 1970s was integrated into the innovating French economy itself and into Green Europe — governmental policies aided and abetted this process while trying to control the pace and character of the rural exodus.

During de Gaulle's first presidency (1959–65), the traditional level and methods of state support to agriculture, notably the indexation of food prices achieved in 1957,[46] was shattered. Farmers were enraged by this and confused by the new laws (*lois d'orientation*) passed in 1960 and 1962 which provided the legal framework for the forms of agricultural change favoured by the Government: the FNSEA was already under threat from the Young Farmer movement and reacted by opposing de Gaulle in 1965. Another hiccup in government–farmer relations occurred in 1969 when the Vedel Report sketched out a mechanized and depopulated future for agriculture. Despite the shock of Gaullism and various ups and downs, the agreement of farmers to the new policies was eventually secured and the FNSEA resumed its place as favoured spokesman for farmers by the late 1960s. The 1970s were a less turbulent decade in the evolution of policies for agriculture: Pompidolian and Giscardian Governments contented themselves with filling in the details of policies whose outlines were established in the 1960s, and a disinclination to upset farmers was evident.

In the twenty-three years until 1981, three chief areas of policy can be estimated to have had an appreciable impact on agriculture.[47] First, the levels of price support for different products, administered and financed increasingly through the CAP, have affected the position of different sorts of farmers. Cereals and sugar-beet attracted substantial price support in the 1960s, and those farming large arable areas by 'industrial' methods still enjoy quite extraordinary rates of price support. Meat and dairy farmers were insecure and dissatisfied with their income, but they have come in for reasonable price support since the mid-1970s. Within this sector, however, specific products (like sheep-meat or pork) have experienced drastic fluctuation in price, subjecting farmers to extreme insecurity about profits and viability. The market fluctuations in both demand and price have been extremely unsettling for the producers of frozen chickens and eggs who are concentrated in Brittany. Farmers specializing in vegetable oils, fresh fruit and vegetables, and vine cultivation, have experienced great changes in market conditions, partly due to EEC competition: the lingering negotiations over Spain and Portugal's entry to the EEC will prolong their problems.

Participation in the CAP may provide a large total subsidy to French farming, but it does complicate market and price conditions and deepen the differences between the various sectors of agriculture.

Secondly, policy has helped to make the exodus of small farmers from agriculture more orderly and rather more humane than it would have been otherwise. Through the IVD (*Indemnité viagère de départ*), ageing farmers surrendering their farms receive a modest but, to them, appreciable pension. The IVD helped to lower the average age of active farmers and to improve the conditions of the handover of land from fathers to sons. By the mid-1970s it had been taken up by half a million farmers, freed 8½ million hectares, led to the formation of 95,000 farms and added land to 280,000 others. Along with the slow but steady improvement in social benefits for farmers so that the head of the farm eventually qualified for family allowances, sickness benefit, etc., on the same terms as other sorts of workers, IVD had a great impact on the living conditions of retiring farmers who otherwise might have clung on to inefficient farms: benefits and IVD pensions jointly provide an astounding 19 per cent of the total annual income of all French farmers and retired farmers. But the magnitude of these benefits in financial and humanitarian terms was not equalled by any resultant structural change in agriculture: as noted previously, the disappearance of hundreds of thousands of small farms has led to a marginal increase in the average size of farms.

Thirdly, through a whole battery of measures, policy has pushed farming cooperatives, improvement agencies and credit organizations towards certain forms of modernization which governments have regarded favourably. For example, in an attempt to guide and rationalize land sales so as to increase average farm sizes to viable levels, departmental SAFERs (Société d'Aménagement Foncier et d'Établissement Rural) were empowered to intervene in land sales. By the mid-1970s, fifteen years after their creation, these semi-public land agencies had been involved in up to 15 per cent of the total market in land, but the SAFERs themselves pointed out that they needed a 20 per cent minimum share in order to have a real impact on farm structures. Furthermore, conservative legal interpretations in contested cases has tended to muzzle the powers of SAFERs, and property rights remain resistant to modernizing trends which would logically lead to some sort of land socialization or nationalization: the CNJA had argued in 1962 that powers tantamount to socialization would be necessary to make the new agencies effective. Another policy-sponsored attempt to bypass the problem of small farms in an even more radical way is through the group farming cooperatives (GAEC) but their impact on agriculture has been much smaller than the SAFERs' impact: such group cooperatives technically pool their labour, but in practice they are a convenient legal fiction by which close relatives run a number of adjacent farms with maximum state aid.

Perhaps the semi-public agency which has had the greatest influence over farming structures, markets and technical conditions is the CAM (Crédit Agricole Mutuel). Apart from being a major banking and investment power in the French economy as a whole (20 per cent of France's savings were in the Crédit Agricole in the late 1960s), the CAM has vastly enlarged the scope of its intervention in the rural world in the Fifth Republic, now providing 80 per cent of the financial needs of farming. Its main impact on farmers is through financing land purchase, improvements and modernization by means of loans granted for up to thirty years. It also finances new food processing organizations and the commercialization of agricultural markets, working according to the criteria of the Ministry of Agriculture and the CAP. Generally it has been able to set the criteria of modernization to which farmers must conform in order to benefit from the plethora of subsidies proffered by the state and the EEC. It decides which farms survive and which founder, bringing a degree more rationality into the sifting process than the operation of entirely free market conditions would have done.

When the Socialists arrived in power in 1981, they were faced with long-established policies and institutions in the agricultural sphere. No great upheaval was to be expected immediately: most of the financial and cooperative institutions would be maintained, and reformed if necessary. One of the prime aims of Socialist agricultural policy was efficiency and greater productivity, but the productivist continuity between Giscardian and Mitterrandist policies was tempered by other Socialist aims. Egalitarianism was perhaps the strongest aim, showing itself in plans to help small farmers rather than big farmers who, it was felt, had grabbed the lion's share of state and EEC aid in the past. In projects for reforming rural education, for supplying more technical aid to farmers, and for helping landless young people to get going on viable farms, the Socialists showed their concern for the small, the poor and the relatively young in the countryside. Taken together these policies amounted to a commitment to prevent the number of farms from slipping below a million. Feminist aims were also apparent: state-supported institutions were instructed to consider women as potential heads of farms on an equal basis to men, and official encouragement was offered to syndical organizations for women workers on farms (mostly farmers' wives or daughters, in effect). The Socialists affirmed their commitment to new market structures for a wide range of products and to land reform. Finally, the Socialists wanted to alter the terms of the relationship between the state and farmers' organizations in order to reduce the power of the FNSEA, regarded as the mouthpiece of big farming interests, and to bring the smaller farmers' organizations into consultation.

The contradictions in these aims were apparent even before the Socialist Government took office. In helping small farmers, the Government might merely bolster the inefficient. In favouring MODEF and the pro-Socialist *syndicats*, it might lean too far towards the preservationist view on small farms. In curbing the power of the large-scale food processing and agro-alimentary industries, the Government might hinder the growth of food exports which was seen as essential to France's economic recovery. Land reform, with its suggestion of greater state control over property, was always a touchy subject, and market structures were so deeply entrenched in the EEC system already that change would be complicated and difficult.

No-one can accuse President Mitterrand and Prime Minister Mauroy of failing to inject some excitement into farming politics in their choice of Minister of Agriculture. Mme Édith Cresson was an unexpected choice in 1981 for a post for which staidness had often been the hallmark. As well as being the first woman Minister of Agriculture, she was young, outspoken and radical, and had a rather tenuous relationship with farming. The press and many farmers took malicious delight in her many mishaps in confrontations with protesting farmers. She gave an impression of authority and firmness in external relations, for example, during trade visits to the USA and Russia and in her typically intransigent stands at Brussels.[48] In domestic policies, she undoubtedly wished to make a rapid start on the policies outlined above. She was to be hindered in this by the difficulty of making structural reforms (usually taken to mean land and market reforms) and by the opposition of the FNSEA leadership which became increasingly hostile to her during 1982.

By the end of 1982, people were assessing the achievements and failures of agricultural policy under Cresson. The Minister herself rested a positive Socialist achievement on four points: first, farmers' incomes were rising healthily; second, consultative channels between government and farmers had been widened beyond the FNSEA; third, a reform of agricultural education and technical aid had begun; fourth, policies to assist young farmers to begin farms were succeeding. In a radio broadcast made in November 1982, she claimed that 'socialism works in agriculture'.[49] Elements within the Socialist Party and the left-wing farmers' *syndicats* expressed their satisfaction that reform was starting along the right lines, but they were concerned that the scale of change was very modest, that small farmers were not benefiting sufficiently, and that the structural reforms promised were barely begun. Less sympathetic observers pointed out that good weather rather than socialism was what had made agriculture work to farmers' advantage in 1982. The FNSEA riposted by maintaining its massive support in the Chambers of Agriculture elections in January 1983, while Guillaume engaged in mud-slinging with the Minister. By the time of the elections for municipal councils in March 1983, Cresson was clearly under pressure from both right and left, and she showed her restlessness by making changes in her personal cabinet.

By March 1983 a government reshuffle was imminent; the second Mauroy Government had been undermined by a currency crisis and the negative verdict given by voters in the local elections, and Cresson's standing was low. She was luckily redeemed by the Socialist victory in the municipal council election in Châtellerault, where she led the Socialist Party to its only gain in a major city. In the third Mauroy Government, she was given the Ministry of Foreign Trade and Tourism (another hot-seat). The verdict on her period at Agriculture was largely negative.

The new Minister of Agriculture was Michel Rocard, a much more respectable and responsible person in the eyes of farmers as well as the most popular politician in office in the Mitterrand era. It was immediately assumed that the Government wished to mend its fences with the FNSEA leadership by giving agriculture a minister (who was either a moderate socialist or barely a socialist at all, depending on your viewpoint) likely to slow down the radical policies begun by Mme Cresson and to pursue productivism. The first few weeks of Rocard's time at Agriculture certainly confirmed this interpretation. He offered soothing and flattering words to the FNSEA at its annual conference in April 1983, recognized its role as spokesman for a majority of farmers and stressed productivity as the chief aim of policy (*'l'agriculture française est condamnée à l'expansion'* was his catchphrase). He also had tacitly to condone Guillaume's speech to the conference which denounced Mme Cresson's 'ideological plans'.[50]

While it is too soon to pass a verdict on the Rocard policies for agriculture, one can speculate that both his style and his policies would be quite different to those of his predecessor. The new Minister was plunged into a long crisis over food prices in the EEC between mid-April and late May 1983; he spent what little time remained trying to calm down representatives of enraged

French farmers, by showing that the Government sympathized with their grievances and by trying to persuade them that their demands amounting to a devaluation of the green franc and increased price supports were unrealistic, given the desire for reform of the CAP within Europe and given the domestic environment of wage austerity. Rocard's conciliatory tactics were partly due to the fact that the Government could not risk farmers' joining political forces with students and small businessmen in May 1983, though most observers judged such an alliance as unlikely. In the agricultural discontents of May the FNSEA wielded its ideological hold over farmers against the Government. The insecurity of small farmers was turned against a Socialist government which had promised them security of tenure and the maintenance of real income during 1983; farmers focused on the most immediate determinant of their income (the price support levels set within the EEC) and expressed their ire in largely unitary fashion. This was disappointing for the Government: farmers' acceptance of its policies now depends on its relationship with the FNSEA, and the entry of MODEF and other *syndicats* to consultative status has proved a hollow victory.

The failure runs deeper than a government having to bend to the force of a powerful pressure group. One of socialism's cumulative aims through its rural policies was to bring farmers out of the 'ghetto' of being special in their relations with the state, to make them feel equal to other citizens with no lesser or greater claim on the nation. Republicanism and Gaullism had both conceded that it was easier to leave farmers in that ghetto than to bring them out of it. At its worst, this meant bowing to the ideology of the sacrosanct and unique nature of the French soil and those who work on it. The banal tendency of all politicians to stress their link with the land and their love of nature and the countryside is part of the ideology (and President Mitterrand is by no means above it). Édith Cresson may not have been a good minister in many respects, but she did express the wish of many Socialists to change the traditional position of agriculture and farmers. Rocard, in marked contrast, went out of his way to pay tribute to the traditional ideology of the French countryside and to recognize the FNSEA as the corporate embodiment of it. This signals a fundamental failure in Socialist policies towards farmers, and it is difficult to see how any land reform can be achieved without a change in ideology.

The Rocard era in agriculture may succeed in raising food production and may even find markets abroad for the surplus products so produced. Agronomists agree that there are still increases in yield to be coaxed out of the land and increases in labour productivity to be coaxed out of farmers, given greater technical aid to agriculture and more education for farmers. These aims will be achieved with least friction by allowing smaller farms to continue their slide out of existence, thus consolidating the medium-sized farms. The Ministry of Agriculture under Socialist command continues to speak of one million viable farms in the mid-1980s, but a more realistic number is 800,000 farms with full-time family labour: the rest will be farms worked by part-time labour to provide a minor addition to the family budget and to provide recreation. Compared with this perspective, the 12,000 farms with young farmers whose establishment was aided by the Government by mid-1983, the policies yet to be begun to aid mountain farmers, and the product marketing offices which are still in the legislative pipeline, are small beer. The Socialist Government's good intentions towards poorer farmers and its desire to maintain farmers' real income cannot detract from the fact that socialism's productivist aim was sufficiently similar to its predecessors' aim to make a minor impact on the agricultural sector. Some worthy reforms have been made but they have made little difference to farming in France and would not have discredited a Giscardian government. Rocard's first major speech after the settlement of the price crisis in the EEC (a settlement which halted farmers' violent protest but left farmers and the FNSEA dissatisfied) was made to the representatives of French farming cooperatives and credit institutions: he appealed for ideas on how to reform the CAP and seemed almost without policies of his own.[51] But the Socialists can justifiably claim, though they are unlikely to do so for fear of showing up their lack of achievement in farming policies, that it is farmers' own intransigence, their near-unified support for the FNSEA, and their instinctive suspicion of anything proffered by the Socialist Government, which has blocked many reforms and pushed structural reform off the agenda. The early years of Gaullist government brought more in the way of change to agriculture than have the first years of Socialist rule.

## NOTES

1. J. Beaujeu-Garnier, *La Population française après le recensement de 1975* (Paris: Armand Colin, 1976), pp. 128–35, 179–85.
2. Detailed figures for 1980 are given by D. Bergmann of INRA, *Le Monde*, 18 January 1983, pp. 17 and 19.
3. M. Gervais, 'L'économie agricole française 1955–1970', in Y. Tavernier, M. Gervais, C. Servolin, eds, *L'Univers politique des paysans dans la France contemporaine* (Paris: Armand Colin, 1972), pp. 16–17 (henceforth referred to as *L'Univers politique des paysans*).
4. Bergmann, op. cit.
5. For a résumé of the Mansholt Plan, see P. Le Roy, *L'Avenir du marché commun agricole* (Paris: Presses Universitaires de France, 1974), pp. 37–60. See also H. Délorme, 'Les paysans et le Plan Mansholt', in *L'Univers politique des paysans*, op. cit., pp. 583–608.
6. J. Klatzmann, *Les Politiques agricoles — idées fausses et illusions* (Paris: Presses Universitaires de France, 19720, pp. 85–7.
7. For more detail and references on the role of cooperatives in moderization, see my 'Rural Change and Farming Politics: a Terminal Peasantry' in P.G. Cerny and M.A. Schain, eds, *French Politics and Public Policy* (London and New York: Frances Pinter, St. Martin's Press and Methuen University Paperbacks, 1980), pp. 218–42.
8. C. Servolin, 'L'absorption de l'agriculture dans le mode de production capitaliste', in *L'Univers politique des paysans*, op. cit., pp. 54–75; C. Servolin, 'Crise de l'agriculture ou crise de l'économie rurale: l'avenir des petites exploitations', in P. Coulomb, M. Gervais, H. Nallet and C. Servolin, *L'Agriculture dans le système social* (Paris: Institut National de la Recherche Agronomique, 1974), pp. 5–15; M. Jollivet, 'Sociétés rurales et capitalisme', in M. Jollivet, ed., *Les Collectivités rurales françaises*, Vol. 2, *Sociétés paysannes ou lutte de classes au village?* (Paris: Armand Colin, 1974), pp. 230–45.
9. P. Hall, ed., *Europe 2000* (London: Duckworth, 1977), pp. 87–92; H. Mendras and M. Jollivet, eds., *Les Collectivités rurales françaises*, Vol. 1 (Paris: Armand Colin, 1971), pp. 21–31 and 187–99.
10. Jollivet, 'Sociétés rurales et capitalisme', op. cit.
11. A.J. Jansen, *Constructing Tomorrow's Agriculture, Report on a Crossnational Research into Alternative Futures for European Agriculture* (Wageningen, Netherlands: Agricultural University, 1975), pp. 14–15.
12. E. Morin, *The Red and the White — Report from a French Village* (New York: Random House, 1970), p. 94.
13. Beaujeu-Garnier, *La Population française après le recensement de 1975*, op. cit., p. 128.
14. S. Berger and M.J. Piore, *Dualism and Discontinuity in Industrial Societies* (Cambridge, Cambridge University Press, 1980), pp. 89 and 88–131.

15. S. Tarrow, *Between Center and Periphery: Grassroots Politicians in Italy and France* (London: Yale University Press, 1977), pp. 74–5.
16. M.S. Lewis-Beck, 'The Electoral Politics of the French Peasantry: 1946–1978', *Political Studies*, 29, No. 4 (December 1981), pp. 517–36.
17. *Le Monde*, Dossiers et documents, *Les Elections législatives de mars 1978*, pp. 53–62; D. Goldey and R. Johnson, 'The French General Election of March 1978: The Redistribution of Support within and between Right and Left', *Parliamentary Affairs*, 31, No. 3 (1978), pp. 307–37.
18. P. Rémy, 'Le gaullisme et les paysans', in *L'Univers politique des paysans*, op. cit., pp. 255–72.
19. H. Wells, *An Ecological Analysis of Communist Voting in France and Britain* (unpublished Ph.D. dissertation, Stanford University, 1975), p. 100.
20. V. Wright, *The Government and Politics of France* (London: Hutchinson, 1978), Appendix 11, 'Voting Behaviour in the March 1978 General Elections'.
21. G. Michelat and M. Simon, *Classe, religion et comportement politique* (Paris: Presses de la Fondation Nationale des Sciences Politiques, 1977), pp. 215–19.
22. Rémy, 'Le gaullisme et les paysans', op. cit.
23. J.T.S. Keeler, 'The Defense of Small Farmers in France: Alternative Strategies for the "Victims of Modernization" ', *Peasant Studies*, 8, No. 4 (Fall 1979), p. 1.
24. V. Wright, *The Government and Politics of France*, op. cit., p. 138.
25. J.M. Denquin, *Le Renversement de la majorité électorale dans le département de la Corrèze, 1958–1973* (Paris: Presses Universitaires de France, 1976), from the preface by G. Burdeau, pp. 6–7. See also J. Lord, A.J. Petrie and L. Whitehead, 'Political Change in Rural France: The 1967 Election in a Communist Stronghold', *Political Studies*, 16, No. 2 (1968), pp. 53–76.
26. *Programme commun de gouvernement: Partie Socialiste, Parti Communiste, mouvement des Radicaux de Gauche* (Paris: Flammarion, 1973). For more details of Communist agricultural policies, see F. Clavaud, J. Flavien, A. Lajoinie and L. Perceval, *Quelle Agriculture pour la France?* (Paris: Éditions Sociales, 1974).
27. Pierre Martin, 'Le basculement électoral de 1981. L'évolution électorale de la droite', *Revue Française de Science Politique*, 31, No. 5–6 (October–December 1981), pp. 999–1014.
28. SOFRES post-election poll, *Le Nouvel Observateur*, 1 June 1981, p. 40.
29. P. Coulomb and H. Nallet, 'Le Syndicalisme agricole', in Coulomb *et al.*, *L'Agriculture dans le système social*, op. cit., pp. 51–5.
30. P. Grémion, *Le Pouvoir périphérique: bureaucrates et notables dans le système politique français* (Paris: Editions du Seuil, 1977), pp. 225–7; see also C. Mora, 'Les Chambres d'Agriculture et l'unité paysanne', in *L'Univers politique des paysans*, op. cit., pp. 507–81.
31. J.T.S. Keeler, 'Corporatism and Official Union Hegemony: The Case of French Agricultural Syndicalism', in S. Berger, A. Hirschman and C. Maier, eds, *Organizing Interests in Western Europe: Pluralism, Corporatism, and the Transformation of Politics* (Cambridge: Cambridge University Press, 1981), pp. 185–208.
32. P. Coulomb and H. Nallet, 'Les Organisations syndicales agricoles a l'épreuve de l'unité', in *L'Univers politique des paysans*, op. cit., pp. 379–413.
33. P. Muller, 'La naissance d'une nouvelle idéologie paysanne en France, 1945–1965', *Revue Française de Science Politique*, 32, No. 1 (February 1982), pp. 90–108.
34. M. Debatisse, 'Trente Ans de combat syndical 1946–1976' (Paris: Supplément Information Agricole 467, FNSEA, 1976); Y. Tavernier, *Le CNJA* (Paris: Presses de la Fondation Nationale des Sciences Politiques, 1966); Y. Tavernier, *Le Syndicalisme paysan* (Paris: Armand Colin, 1969), pp. 135–98; B. Hervieu and A. Vial, 'L'église catholique et les paysans', in *L'Univers politique des paysans*, op. cit., pp. 291–315; G. Duby and A. Wallon, eds, *Histoire de la France rurale*, Vol. 4, *La Fin de la France paysanne* (Paris: Seuil, 1978), pp. 466–92; M. Debatisse, *Le Projet paysan* (Paris: Seuil, 1983).
35. J.T.S. Keeler, 'Corporatism and Official Union Hegemony', op. cit.
36. Y. Tavernier, 'Le mouvement de défense des exploitants familiaux', in *L'Univers politique des paysans*, op. cit., pp. 467–95; G. Duby and A. Wallon, *Histoire de la France rurale*, op. cit., Vol. 4, pp. 492–501.
37. *Le Monde*, 30 and 31 January 1983, pp. 1 and 18, 8 February 1983, p. 22.
38. For a partisan account of the *Paysans Travailleurs* movement, see F. Prévost, *Mutation dans le syndicalisme agricole* (Lyon: Chronique Sociale, 1976).
39. *Le Monde*, 8 February 1983, p. 22.
40. M. François Guillaume combines autobiography with argument against Socialist policies in his recent book *Le Pain de la liberté* (Paris: J.C. Lattès, 1983).

41.   *Le Monde*, 8 January 1983, p. 24.
42.   *Le Monde*, 11 February 1983, p. 28.
43.   *Le Monde*, 13 and 14 February 1983, p. 16.
44.   *Le Monde*, 15 and 16 May 1983, pp. 1 and 17.
45.   F.L. Wilson, 'Les groupes d'intérêt sous la Cinquième République: test de trois modèles théoriques de l'interaction entre groupes et gouvernements', *Revue Française de Science Politique*, 33, No. 2 (April 1983), pp. 220–54.
46.   P. Houée, *Les Étapes de développement rural*, Vol. 2, *La Révolution contemporaine* (1950–1970) (Paris: Les Éditions Ouvrières: 1972), pp. 82–6.
47.   Information on the policies and agencies described below are gleaned from ibid., pp. 170–95, and M. Gervais, H. Tavernier and M. Jollivet, 'La politique agricole' in G. Duby and A. Wallon, eds, *Histoire de la France rurale*, op. cit., Vol. 4.
48.   On the Socialist attitude to the CAP and other aspects of the EEC, see J. Bound and K. Featherstone, 'The French Left and the European Community', in D.S. Bell, ed., *Contemporary French Political Parties*, (London: Croom Helm: 1982), pp. 165–89.
49.   *Le Monde*, 16 November 1982, p. 44.
50.   *Le Monde*, 16 April 1983, pp. 1 and 29.
51.   *Le Monde*, 21 May 1983, p. 40.

# 13 Corporatist Decentralization and Commercial Modernization in France: The Royer Law's Impact on Shopkeepers, Supermarkets and the State*

*John T.S. Keeler*

In recent years a host of studies have examined the evolution of the politico-administrative system in France and have attempted to explain why, during the twenty-three years of center–right rule, widespread 'agreement on the need for decentralization' failed to produce 'serious reforms' of the sort now being implemented by François Mitterrand's Socialist Government.[1] It has been shown that many politicians began to view centralization as counterproductive since 'it block[ed] involvement of new social forces, inhibit[ed] experimentation, and expose[d] the government to taking the blame for anything and everything.'[2] However, the movement toward comprehensive decentralization was hindered by the influence of Debré-style Jacobins within the majority, the resistance of local notables and civil servants, and the political calculation that 'giving more power to all local governments mean[t] giving some power to the left.' As Peter Gourevitch has cogently argued, it was 'fear of the left' which proved to be 'the persistent and recurrent systematic cause of blockage.' 'Despite the clamor for change, despite the endless complaints about centralization, despite the popularity of such general schemes as regionalization, the pressures for reform' were thus 'contained or channeled into safe waters.'[3]

An effort to understand the policies and strategies of the center–right must clearly focus on the 'safe waters' into which such pressures for reform were channeled. A central purpose of this essay is to show that the standard works on the politico-administrative system have failed to do so adequately. For the most part, they have dealt only with the attempts to meet social pressure through creation of modest regional institutions such as those instituted with the 1964 decrees and the Frey Law of 1972. But not all of the 'safe waters' were of the regional type. In response to pressure for policy change and participation from two key socio-economic sectors, commerce and agriculture, the center–right established institutions which circumvented both the traditional and the regional representative–administrative structures by devolving power for the management of specific policy areas into the hands of 'professional representatives' or 'particular interests.' It will be argued here

* The research for this paper, conducted mainly in Paris during the summer of 1980, was made possible by grants from the Graduate School Research Fund and the School of International Studies of the University of Washington. I would like to acknowledge the generous assistance which Suzanne Berger gave me at the initial stages of the project. In addition, I must thank those who provided me with interviews and documents, especially Patrique Jault and J. de Lainsecq of the Ministère du Commerce et de l'Artisanat, Robert Castanet of *Libre service actualités*, Michelle Picard of the Centre d'Étude du Commerce et de la Distribution (CECOD) and Pierre Forestier of CID–UNATI.

that these measures of 'corporatist decentralization' were, in some cases, rather bold innovations and that they played a major role in the effort of the center–right forces to defuse social protest, gain political capital with some of the principal components of their electoral coalition, and overcome some of the administrative problems associated with centralization.

The declining sectors of small commerce and agriculture posed a major political problem for the center–right majority which governed France from the advent of the Fifth Republic until 1981. As Pierre Birnbaum and other analysts have asserted, a 'fundamental contradiction' existed between the majority's desire to pursue a liberal economic policy encouraging a modernization process which threatened these sectors and its need for the electoral support of shopkeepers and farmers.[4] During the 1960s, both the farmers (at the beginning of the decade) and the shopkeepers (at the end of the decade) engaged in violent protests which forced the majority to fashion reforms intended to resolve the contradiction between its economic goals and its political needs. These reforms were strikingly similar in their espoused purposes and their structures. Both the Debré–Pisani Laws (1960, 1962) for agriculture and the Royer Law (1973) for commerce promised to 'humanize' the modernization process not merely through changing policy in favor of weaker sectoral elements, but also through establishing corporatist institutions which would enable sectoral representatives to participate in the formulation and administration of policy, especially at the departmental level.

By establishing systems of corporatist institutions for commerce and agriculture, the center–right majority exercised an option (or options, as will be discussed below) not included in most discussions of politico-administrative reform. Gourevitch, for example, provides the following typology of reform options (presented here in a somewhat revised and simplified form):

*Option A: Hardline Jacobinism.*  The traditional framework of departments and communes is retained and administration remains centrally controlled and tightly coordinated. Bureaucratic dysfunctions are corrected through deconcentration, i.e., the transfer of some decision-making from the capital to agents of the central government in the field (e.g., the prefects) and the lightening of *tutelle* over local governments composed, as in the past, entirely of territorially elected officials.

*Option B: Modernized Jacobinism.*  The traditional framework is deemed inadequate, so a new larger level — the region — is introduced. The regions, which may include functional as well as territorial representatives, are provided with some competence and funds. However, they are essentially instruments of deconcentration; power is delegated to agents of the central government in the field and all decisions are subject to strict central supervision.

*Option C: Participatory Decentralization — Departmental or Communal.*  Power is delegated to local bodies with territorially elected representatives (and perhaps some professional group representatives) and an elected executive. Local units have wide legislative powers, ample means of funding and an ability to organize their own administration in the absence of onerous *tutelle*.

*Option D: Participatory Decentralization — Regional.*  Like option C except that regions replace departments as the basis of local government.[5]

Missing from the Gourevitch typology is the corporatist decentralization option, or rather the two related corporatist options, which the Government exercised in the cases of commerce and agriculture. Logically these options would be situated between options B and C above.

*Option E: Corporatized Jacobinism.* The traditional framework is supplemented by a network of departmental commissions intended to deal with specific areas of sectoral public policy. These commissions include either sectoral representatives alone (delegated by officially recognized interest groups and/or the appropriate professional chambers) or a combination of these and territorially elected officials (delegated, for example, by the general councils). Although these commissions are empowered to deliberate over policy and may exercise a good deal of influence, their official role is limited to providing advice. Decision-making power rests with agents of the central government in the field and the relevant ministry at the center.

*Option F: Corporatist Decentralization.* The commissions of option E are provided with genuine decision-making power within their specific policy area. Agents of the central government in the field supervise their deliberations and the relevant ministry retains the power to reverse their decisions on appeal, but in general they are granted a significant measure of autonomy.

For the governments of the center–right, the exercise of options E and F in combination with options A and later B provided an alternative vastly preferable to either options A and B alone or the implementation of options C and D. Corporatist decentralization, unlike hardline or even modernized Jacobinism, enabled the Government to: (1) *co-opt sectoral elites* by giving them an opportunity to play an important role in policy-making, a role which provided them with a sense of prestige as well as power; (2) *'humanize' the administrative process* for sectoral rank-and-file by implementing some aspects of policy through professional representatives rather than 'faceless and fearsome' state bureaucrats; (3) *shift at least part of the blame* for unpopular decisions to the sectoral representatives involved in the policy-making process. Unlike participatory or 'republican' decentralization, on the other hand, the corporatist form allowed the Government to: (1) *retain ultimate control* over the policy process, preventing 'excesses' or dramatic departures from the orientations desired in the capital; (2) *keep power out of the hands of the left*. Devolving power to sectoral representatives in commerce and agriculture involved minimal political risk, for the left was very weak in each sector and leftist representation within the corporatist institutions could be further reduced through careful control of the delegation/election process.[6]

While corporatist decentralization thus appeared to be both administratively useful and politically profitable, it was not without its disadvantages. First, in *institutional* terms, it involved what Jacobin critics charged to be an illegitimate transfer of state authority from the representatives of the 'general interest' to advocates of particular interests. Second, in *policy* terms, it entailed some sacrifice of economic liberalism and some slackening of the pace of modernization in the traditional sectors. As will be shown, however, proponents were able to argue effectively that these disadvantages were exaggerated and that they were, at any rate, a small price to pay for the maintenance of social peace in potentially disruptive and electorally vital sectors.

Having dealt at length elsewhere[7] with the agricultural case, I will focus in this chapter on the emergence and the impact of corporatist decentralization in the commercial sector. Section 1 will discuss the shopkeepers' protest movement of the late 1960s and early 1970s which compelled the center–right Government to adopt the Royer Law of 1973. Section 2 will analyse the debate over this highly controversial law and describe the corporatist commissions which Jean Royer, the Minister of Commerce, claimed would enable the shopkeepers themselves 'to define, department by department, a sort of *mini-politique du commerce*.' Section 3 will evaluate the performance of these commissions and discuss the degree to which their activity has involved genuine 'corporatist decentralization' rather than mere 'corporatized Jacobinism.' The fourth section will assess the economic and political impact of the Royer reforms. The conclusion will provide a brief summary of findings and discuss the degree to which commercial policy has been altered by the new Socialist Government.

### 1. SHOPKEEPERS VS. SUPERMARKETS: COMMERCIAL MODERNIZATION IN THE 1960s

Commercial modernization developed slowly in post-war France due to the tax advantages enjoyed by small boutiques and the hostility — perceived by politicians and developers alike — of *petits commerçants* toward those who sought to disrupt the traditional system of distribution. The first French supermarkets (defined formally as self-service retail food stores with a surface area of 400-2,500 square meters) opened only in the late 1950s, and these stores received a most inhospitable welcome. The forces of traditional commerce successfully pressured industrialists and distributors to refuse to supply the modern stores, arguing that their low prices constituted a 'source of disorder and disequilibrium.'[8] Indeed they did; while a large grocery store operated on a margin of only 8-12 percent, with a 2-3 percent profit, the prices of the traditional shops were high enough to yield a profit of 10-20 percent.[9]

Frustrated by a boycott which brought the modernization experiment to the brink of collapse, supermarket developers appealed to the Gaullist Government for support soon after the advent of the Fifth Republic. The Government, greatly concerned with the battle against inflation, responded in 1960 by issuing the 'Fontanet circular' expressly forbidding suppliers to refuse to sell to large retailers who undercut the high prices prevalent in small shops. This was the Gaullists' first and most important step in launching a commercial modernization program that 'threatened to undermine and destroy the traditional economic sector.'[10]

Other important measures were also introduced during the 1960s to encourage modernization at the expense of the small shopkeepers. A major fiscal reform bill was pushed through Parliament in 1965 revising the tax system in such a way as to benefit stores operating on a small margin. As of 1968, all retail stores were to pay a TVA (value added tax) geared to profit margin; previously, shops had simply paid a local tax based on 'sales turnover, irrespective of profits.'[11] While the TVA legislation improved the prospects for commercial development, so did the Government's liberal policies in regard to such matters as urban land-use planning, the granting of building permits, the regulation of store hours and terms of employment and the 'despecialization' of commercial licenses.[12] Overall, the commercial policy introduced by the Gaullists during the 1960s made the French politico-economic climate for development almost as favorable as that in West Germany, in some ways more favorable than that in Great Britain and far more favorable than that in Italy.[13] As a result, 'the number of small shops declined by 20,000 from 1966 to 1971 while in the same period 1,887 supermarkets and 143 *hypermarchés*' (defined formally as self-service retail stores, dealing in general merchandise as well as food, with a surface area of more than 2,500 square meters) were opened.[14]

According to opinion polls administered in the late 1960s, French consumers generally welcomed these developments. Fully 75 percent of those queried were favorable to an increase in the number of supermarkets and hypermarkets and 83 percent expressed the opinion that the appearance of *grandes surfaces de vente* was 'a necessity of modern life.' Only 16 percent felt that it would be a 'good thing' to prohibit the opening of *grandes surfaces*.[15]

Needless to say, the majority of small shopkeepers viewed commercial modernization less favorably. A popular argument among the *commerçants* was that supermarkets were a 'social scourge' and that the freedom to develop them should thus be limited by the Government according to the same logic that led to the imposition of limits on the speed permissible for automobiles on the highways.[16] Others stressed the human quality of traditional commerce and portrayed the supermarket promoters as extending their 'gigantic dehumanizing tentacles' all over the country, turning customers into 'robot consumers' brain-washed by 'outrageous' advertising.[17]

Although many small shopkeepers thus viewed commercial modernization as an abomination and a threat, organized protest against government policy encouraging the phenomenon was limited for most of the decade of the 1960s. In large part this was a result of the relatively permissive and, to some, 'progressive' attitudes manifested by the leaders of the shopkeepers' traditional interest groups, especially Léon Gingembre of the long-dominant CGPME (Confédération Générale des Petites et Moyennes Entreprises). Gingembre argued that the CGPME should not 'sentimentally defend the traditional forms' of commerce, but rather 'demonstrate . . . that it is a question for the majority of these enterprises of knowing how to adapt and reconvert, for others of knowing how to profit from the opportunities which this evolution itself provides them for creating and developing new activities responding to the new needs of the consumer'.[18]

In 1969, however, the relative calm which had reigned in the commercial sector — even during the chaos of May–June 1968 — was broken by angry shopkeepers who branded Gingembre and his associates as 'accomplices' of the Government.[19] Both the traditional representatives of small business and the Government were shaken from February onward by the violent protests of shopkeepers and artisans that swept south-eastern France. At the head of these demonstrations was a young café owner named Gérard Nicoud and a group of new organizations which soon merged to form CID–UNATI (Comité d'Information et de Défense-Union Nationale des Travailleurs Indépendants). Shocked by the increasingly threatening policies of the Government, Nicoud condemned the traditional spokesmen of small commerce and proclaimed that the events of May 1968 had revealed a fundamental verity of French politics: violence pays. Acting on this principle, CID–UNATI members not only organized massive street demonstrations but also kidnapped inspectors and sacked tax offices in towns all across France.[20]

Only a few months after Nicoud launched the protest wave, the Government responded in a manner which seemingly supported his analysis of the utility of violence. In July of 1969 it was announced that the new commercial taxation system would be simplified and improved, the health insurance regime for independent workers would be reformed and new advisory commissions (commissions départementales d'urbanisme commercial, or CDUCs) would be established to give small shopkeepers a voice in the process through which building permits were granted for proposed *grandes surfaces* larger than 3,000 square meters.[21] These new commissions obviously represented a governmental effort to channel discontent into the mechanisms of *concertation* and undermine Nicoud's contention that the street was the only *terrain de manoeuvre* available to shopkeepers and artisans.[22]

Over the next few years, however, the promises of the Government were fulfilled too incompletely to calm the angry *petits commerçants* and stifle the development of CID–UNATI. Membership in Nicoud's organization swelled from 23,000 in 1970 to 189,000 in 1971, and surpassed 200,000 early in 1972.[23] At the fourth national CID–UNATI convention held in January of 1973, Nicoud declared that the organization was to be transformed from an association into a union confederation so as to become 'a formidable *machine de guerre* which will make ministers tremble.'[24]

Although CID–UNATI remained formally neutral at the time of the 1973 legislative elections, its mobilization of shopkeepers and artisans against the Government produced results which did cause considerable trembling. Surveys indicated that sectoral support for the Gaullists and their allies declined from 53 percent in 1968 to 36 percent in 1973, while support for the left increased from 23 percent to 34 percent.[25] As Berger has commented, general electoral trends made this result especially troubling for the majority; the increasing polarization of politics and the decline of working-class support for the center–right majority rendered the Government more dependent than ever on its traditional middle-class bases of support.[26] The Government's heightened sense of vulnerability was manifested vividly when, soon after the election, an independent conservative sympathetic to the shopkeepers' cause — Jean Royer, mayor of Tours — was appointed as Minister of Commerce and the Artisanat (a post created in 1972 as a symbol of governmental concern for the sector) and charged with drafting a comprehensive *loi d'orientation pour le commerce et l'artisanat*, now popularly known as the *loi Royer*.

## 2. THE ROYER LAW AND CORPORATIST DECENTRALIZATION

In presenting his reform package to the National Assembly, Royer proclaimed: 'It is fitting to make, in favor of the shopkeepers and artisans, an effort comparable to that made in the past for the farmers.'[27] Several deputies of the majority noted that in both cases the intention was to 'humanize and control the evolution' of the sector so as 'to assure the survival of small family units at the side of industrial enterprises.'[28] For Royer, the orientation law was 'the expression of a passionate search . . . for three complementary equilibriums:' economic equilibrium (between modern and traditional commerce), urban equilibrium (between the center and periphery of cities) and human equilibrium (between the shopkeepers and artisans and other social categories).[29]

Once again the modernization of a traditional sector was to be 'humanized' through a combination of policy changes designed to help *les petits* and institutional reforms intended to increase their participation in the policy-making process. In regard to the former, the Royer Law promised to: improve the health insurance and social security regimes for the self-employed; establish special funds to aid the conversion of independents forced to close their shops and to facilitate the installation of young independents; decrease the competitive advantage of large stores by regulating the terms of their purchases; and replace the *patente*, a local commercial tax, with a lower 'professional' tax.[30]

Along with these alterations of policy, the Royer Law included two institutional reforms viewed by the Minister as a reflection of the Government's desire to encourage 'the spirit of participation' and the development of a 'society of responsibility.'[31] First, the popularly elected *chambres de commerce et d'industrie* and the *chambres de métiers* were to be given more authority (and later more funding) — as had been given to the chambers of agriculture in the early 1960s — so as to 'play an important role in the concrete application' of the orientation law. The chambers were to be empowered to organize technical training programs, participate with local officials in the urban commercial planning process and promote new commercial centers.[32]

The second institutional reform was, as Royer acknowledged, the 'central innovation' of the orientation law and easily its most controversial provision: the commissions (CDUCs) instituted after the protests of 1969 were to be given vastly expanded authority to control commercial development. Previously the CDUCs had been nothing more than a manifestation of timidly *corporatized Jacobinism*: not only were they limited to giving advisory opinions (*avis*), often ignored by the agents of the central Government, they were also restricted in their jurisdiction to proposed projects in the hypermarket range (over 3,000 square meters).[33] What Royer and the Government now proposed was a bold form of *corporatist decentralization*: the composition of the CDUCs was to be altered so as to strengthen the position of sectoral representatives (50 percent of the seats would be given to 'professionals,' 25 percent to locally elected officials and 25 percent to consumer representatives), the jurisdiction of the commissions was to be greatly increased (to projects over 400 square meters in communes of less than 5,000 inhabitants, over 750 square meters in towns with from 5,000-50,000 inhabitants, and over 1,000 square meters in cities with a population above 50,000), and — most importantly — they were to be given a *pouvoir de décision.* Heretofore, noted Royer, 'restrictions on free enterprise [had] been exercised either directly by the state' or 'within the context of extremely precise regulations.' The 'originality' of the CDUCs resided in the fact that 'control [would] be confided to a body external to the administration and disposing, for the exercise of its power, of an extremely large latitude for judgment since the principles to which it must make reference are very broad.' The commissions were indeed to enjoy a great deal of latitude, for they would be empowered to consider not only economic matters such as the strain which new projects might put on local resources, but also the social impact which development might have, i.e., the degree to which it could be expected to disrupt the 'equilibrium between different forms of commerce' and 'provoke the elimination of the weakest.'

The only check on the revamped CDUCs was to be the possibility that their rulings could be overturned through an appeal (by the promoter of a rejected proposal, the CDUC minority or the prefect) to the Minister of Commerce and the Artisanat. Royer made it clear that the Minister could be expected to reverse CDUC decisions only rarely. Indeed, he argued that the very *raison d'être* of the CDUCs was to allow for some control over commercial development without employing a 'formula of *colbertisme*' which would 'tend to reinforce the authority of the state.' The kind of 'transfer of responsibility from the state to departmental bodies representing socio-professional interests' proposed in the orientation law was thus viewed by Royer as necessary, if 'unprecedented.' With this reform, the corporatist commissions would be free 'to define, department by department, a sort of *mini-politique du commerce*.'[34]

Among those with a vested interest in commercial modernization, the reaction to Royer's call for corporatist decentralization ranged from outrage to incredulity. Proponents of development dismissed as absurd Royer's argument that the CDUCs presented less of a threat to the liberal economy than direct state control; to them the corporatist commissions were a nefarious and even bizarre innovation. Fearing that Royer's commissions would 'render the creation of new *grandes surfaces* practically impossible,' the director of a leading supermarket chain (Carrefour) appealed to his customers to oppose the bill and denounced it to the press as an attempt to model the France of 1973 after 'the Italy of 1932 under Mussolini.'[35] Along similar lines, a major journal of the supermarket industry condemned this '*planification corporative*' as '*planification du blocage*' and added that 'we believe that such an attribution or delegation of power by the state would be unconstitutional.'[36]

Many deputies and senators shared this belief and staunchly criticized the bill as an abandonment of state power, a weakening of state authority and even a return to Vichy. In the words of one spokesman: 'this [proposal] violates the principles of our public law according to which the administration, controlled by the elected representatives of the people, must be the only one to make executive decisions.'[37] Responding to such attacks, Royer was forced to stress — in apparent contradiction with statements which, as shown above, were made in other contexts — the degree to which the state would retain ultimate control over the CDUCs. 'The state does not intervene directly,' he asserted, 'but it keeps everywhere, at all levels, its *pouvoir d'arbitrage*.' First, noted Royer, the prefect would preside over CDUC deliberations. Second, the prefect would have the right to appeal CDUC decisions which seemed unacceptable. And third, the minister would have the power to overturn CDUC decisions on appeal.[38] Such arguments, combined with the pressure from small shopkeepers organized by CID-UNATI throughout the parliamentary deliberations, sufficed to convince a majority in the National Assembly and the Senate to support the general principle of corporatist decentralization enunciated by Royer.[39]

It was evident throughout the Royer Law debate, however, that many deputies and senators preferred alternative visions of reform. Hardline Jacobins such as Michel Debré argued that the prefect should be accorded the 'power of decision' regarding development proposals.[40] Advocates of participatory or republican decentralization such as centrist Jean-Jacques Servan-Schreiber opposed the corporatist nature of Royer's commissions and called for a comprehensive devolution of power to local elected officials.[41] Among opposition groups, the Socialists were the most receptive to Royer's proposal; indeed, they contended that his new commissions were quite like those described in the Common Program. However, they demanded that the 'preponderant' role in the CDUCs should be reserved for 'the representatives of all the citizens, that is . . . the elected officials.'[42]

Faced with pressure from both the majority and the opposition, Royer did agree to a compromise regarding the composition of his commissions. In an unusual move, the Government agreed during the initial stages of the Assembly debate to accept an amendment proposed by the Socialists which would grant one-third of the CDUC seats to local elected officials and an equal number to the commercial representatives and to the consumers. Under the pressure of violent demonstrations led by CID–UNATI, however, the Assembly changed course. In the version of the bill which the National Assembly passed along to the Senate, the *commerçants* were granted one-half of the CDUC seats, as in Royer's original proposal, with the local officials receiving the other half; the consumers were now to be excluded from the commissions. While the press and many outside observers condemned the deputies for capitulating out of fear, Nicoud declared that CID–UNATI's 'victory' would be remembered as a historic event. 'Henceforth,' he asserted, 'one knows that a pressure group can intervene directly and impose a decision.'[43]

If CID–UNATI had indeed achieved a victory, it was partially offset by revisions introduced in the Senate: the senators retained the essentials of the bill proposed by Royer but amended two important sections pertaining to the CDUCs.[44] First, the composition of the commissions was altered once again. The principle of parity between commercial representatives and elected officials was respected with each group receiving eight seats, but the consumers were also given two seats. Second, the jurisdiction of the CDUCs was somewhat reduced, much to the relief of developers and others who feared a total blockage of modernization. In the final version of the Royer Law approved by both houses of Parliament, the CDUCs were given the power to rule on all project proposals over 1,000 square meters in towns of less than 40,000 population, and on proposals over 1,500 square meters in cities with more than 40,000 inhabitants.[45]

By the time the Royer Law was finally approved in December of 1973, it had proven to be one of the most exhaustively examined and hotly debated reforms in the history of the Fifth Republic. The National Assembly devoted nineteen sessions to its version of the bill, accepting it by a vote of 302-0 (with 80 abstentions) only after considering 559 amendments.[46] Never before in history, wrote one observer, had a republican parliament 'adopted a law more favorable to . . . the immediate interests' of the small shopkeepers and artisans.[47] A journal of the supermarket industry lamented that 1973 would be remembered as 'a particularly disastrous turning point in the history of French commerce.'[48]

As many deputies and outside observers noted, however, the passage of the Royer Law did not definitively determine the course of commercial development in France. Two major questions remained to be answered in the implementation process. First, how hostile toward commercial modernization would the CDUCs actually prove to be? And second, to what degree would the Minister of Commerce allow the commissions to define their own 'mini-policies of commerce,' respecting what was alleged to be their 'power of decision' rather than using his veto to impose, as in the past, a commercial policy conceived in Paris?

## 3. CDUC PERFORMANCE AND MINISTERIAL *TUTELLE* 1974-1980

Although the orientation law established the basic structure of the CDUCs, the precise distribution of seats was not determined until the issuance of an administrative decree in January of 1974. According to this decree, the composition of each commission was to be as follows: (1) nine representatives of commerce and artisans — eight *commerçants* designated by the Chamber of Commerce and Industry, of which six were to be representatives of independent commerce (i.e., small shopkeepers), and one artisan designated by the *chambre des métiers*; (2) nine local elected officials — the mayor of the commune in which the proposed project was to be developed, a representative of the commune containing the capital (*chef-lieu*) of the department and seven officials designated by the general council (including four mayors, at least two of which were to be representatives of communes with less than 5,000 inhabitants); (3) two representatives of the consumers chosen by the prefect from among nominees presented by departmental consumer associations.[49]

If the proponents of commercial development were dissatisfied with the formal composition given to the CDUCs, they found even more cause for concern when the actual composition of the first commissions was revealed by a survey administered in 1974. What the survey showed was that, while the small shopkeepers and artisans were entitled by law to only 35 percent (7/20) of the total seats, they in fact held 39 percent of the seats nation-wide since 13 percent of the seats allocated to local elected officials had been given to individuals employed in traditional commerce. Moreover, whereas the law required that at least 22 percent (2/9) of the local elected officials be selected from communes with populations under 5,000, fully 56 percent of those allotted seats represented such rural areas.[50] This finding was troubling for the pro-modernization forces because, as Royer had noted in the Assembly debates of 1973, 'the rural mayor ... understands well that a village dies when the small shopkeepers and artisans leave it.'[51] Given this 'scandalous composition' of the CDUCs, commented one commercial journal after reporting the survey results, one could only expect '*immobilisme* and rejection of evolution.'[52]

The implementing decrees for the Royer Law also contained, however, some news which the representatives of traditional commerce found upsetting. The January 1974 decree stipulated that 'the commission can only reject a request for authorization by a majority vote of the members present.'[53] An official government pamphlet explained that this meant, for example, that an authorization would be granted even in a case where — with fourteen members present — seven votes were cast for rejection along with only three votes for authorization and four blank ballots.[54] 'The great battle fought over the [CDUCs],' concluded Nicoud, 'has [thus] produced only one victor, the financial powers [the *grandes surfaces*], while leaving the others [the shopkeepers and artisans] to believe that they have won.'[55]

As Tables 13.1–13.3 illustrate, the worst fears of neither Nicoud nor the pro-modernization forces have been substantiated by the performance of the CDUCs. During their first seven years of operation, the combined commissions approved 48 percent of the projects and 37 percent of the surface area proposed to them by developers. Of proposals in the supermarket range, 47.9 percent of the projects and 41 percent of the surface area were authorized. Hypermarket proposals were not dealt with as generously — only 21.6 percent of the projects and 22.6 percent of the surface area in this category were accepted from 1974 to 1980. On balance, however, the behavior of the CDUCs may be said to have been restrictive without creating a 'systematic blockage' of modernization of the sort feared by many at the time of the Royer Law debates.

**Table 13.1** Total proposals authorized by the CDUCs and by the Ministry (% age) *

| | Proposed projects authorized | | | Proposed surface area authorized | | |
| | By the CDUCs | By the Ministry† | Difference | By the CDUCs | By the Ministry† | Difference |
|---|---|---|---|---|---|---|
| 1974 | 52.4 | 62.7 | +10.3 | 42.0 | 54.0 | +12.0 |
| 1975 | 59.0 | 65.0 | +6.0 | 51.5 | 54.5 | +3.0 |
| 1976 | 55.9 | 58.8 | +3.2 | 45.2 | 44.6 | −0.6 |
| 1977 | 42.6 | 48.0 | +5.4 | 29.9 | 29.5 | −0.4 |
| 1978 | 40.0 | 60.6 | +20.6 | 25.6 | 37.7 | +12.1 |
| 1979 | 44.0 | 63.3 | +22.3 | 30.2 | 43.1 | +12.9 |
| 1980 | 40.1 | 46.1 | +6.0 | 30.9 | 29.3 | −1.6 |
| Total | 48.0 | 58.2 | +10.2 | 37.0 | 42.5 | +5.5 |

\* This table was derived from statistics given in the annual *RELOCA* for 1975–81; each year's report provides statistics for the preceding year (e.g., the 1981 report contains data on 1980 activities), and some reports provide statistics for several preceding years. The figures given are for proposals to create *new stores*; see the *RELOCAs* for figures concerning proposals to expand existing stores.

† The figures in these columns and in the similar ones of Tables 13.2 and 13.3 are, strictly speaking, percentages of proposed projects/surface area *authorized after final consideration of appeals by the Ministry*. Since not all CDUC decisions are appealed, some of the decisions on which these figures are based were not actually made 'by the Ministry' — that shorthand phrase is used in Tables 13.1–13.3 simply to economize on space. The Ministry's official reports refer to such data (somewhat euphemistically) as '*travaux des CDUC après décisions du Ministre*.'

To what degree have the commissions pursued divergent 'mini-policies of commerce' in regard to development? As Map 13.1 shows, the authorization rates of the departmental commissions have varied considerably. The percentage of proposed projects approved by the CDUCs between 1974 and 1980 varied from 0 percent to 100 percent, with a mean of 48 percent and a standard deviation of slightly more than 18 percent.

The map reveals that the CDUCs of some structurally similar, contiguous departments have responded very differently to development proposals. However, the correlation coefficients listed in Table 13.4 reveal some clear patterns of CDUC behavior predicated on socio-economic factors. None of the correlations is very large, but several of them in combination suggest a coherent explanation of divergence from department to department. In general, authorization rates have tended to be relatively low in sparsely populated, rural departments with high densities of small shops and

**Table 13.2** Hypermarket proposals authorized by the CDUCs and by the Ministry (% age) *

| | Proposed projects authorized | | | Proposed surface area authorized | | |
| | By the CDUCs | By the Ministry | Difference | By the CDUCs | By the Ministry | Difference |
|---|---|---|---|---|---|---|
| 1974 | 37.0 | 44.4 | +7.4 | 37.0 | 41.2 | +4.2 |
| 1975 | 31.2 | 39.0 | +7.8 | 33.5 | 37.8 | +4.3 |
| 1976 | 27.7 | 22.9 | −4.8 | 24.7 | 18.7 | −6.0 |
| 1977 | 17.0 | 12.9 | −4.1 | 16.5 | 12.7 | −3.8 |
| 1978 | 12.4 | 20.2 | +7.8 | 11.7 | 18.7 | +7.0 |
| 1979 | 18.4 | 25.5 | +7.1 | 20.3 | 26.1 | +5.8 |
| 1980 | 21.4 | 17.9 | −3.5 | 23.2 | 18.8 | −4.4 |
| Total | 21.6 | 25.0 | +3.4 | 22.6 | 25.6 | +3.0 |

\* The sources for this table are the same as those listed for Table 13.1

**Table 13.3** Supermarket proposals authorized by the CDUCs and by the Ministry (% age) *

| | Proposed projects authorized | | | Proposed surface area authorized | | |
| | By the CDUCs | By the Ministry | Difference | By the CDUCs | By the Ministry | Difference |
|---|---|---|---|---|---|---|
| 1974 | 61.9 | 61.9 | 0.0 | 55.3 | 56.1 | +0.8 |
| 1975 | 57.3 | 55.9 | −1.4 | 53.9 | 52.9 | −1.0 |
| 1976 | 54.3 | 58.6 | +4.3 | 51.2 | 56.1 | +4.9 |
| 1977 | 41.7 | 53.1 | +11.4 | 34.2 | 44.2 | +10.0 |
| 1978 | 40.6 | 75.0 | +34.4 | 32.7 | 73.9 | +41.2 |
| 1979 | 25.7 | 62.9 | +37.2 | 20.5 | 57.2 | +36.7 |
| 1980 | 44.1 | 55.9 | +11.8 | 42.9 | 55.9 | +13.0 |
| Total | 47.9 | 60.5 | +12.6 | 41.0 | 58.0 | +17.0 |

\* The sources for this table are the same as those listed for Table 13.1

proportionately large numbers of small shopkeepers and artisans. Conversely, authorization rates have tended to be relatively high in densely populated, urban departments with fewer small shops and proportionately low numbers of small shopkeepers and artisans.

Collectively, the CDUCs may be said to have pursued a 'policy of equilibrium' between traditional and modern commerce and thus served one of the major purposes of the Royer Law. It should be noted, however, that the CDUCs have generally followed only what could be termed a defensive strategy of equilibrium maintenance. They have not pursued a dynamic strategy of creating an equilibrium among the various forms of commerce by permitting commercial development in departments with low densities of *grandes surfaces*. As Table 13.4 shows, the CDUC authorization rates manifest a small, *positive* correlation with supermarket and hypermarket density as measured in both 1970 and 1980. In general, development proposals have not been warmly received in departments which featured a *dis*equilibrium in favor of traditional commerce before the advent of the Royer Law. Of the CDUCs in the thirteen departments with the lowest densities of *grandes surfaces* as of 1970, 62 percent have compiled authorization rates below the

**Figure 13.1** Percentage of proposed projects authorized by each of the
CDUCs, 1974–80*

* This map was derived from statistics provided in *RELOCAs* for 1977 (which give data
for each department from 1974 to 1976) and 1978–81.

278   *John T.S. Keeler*

**Table 13.4** The correlation between CDUC authorization rates and demographic, economic, organizational and political characteristics of the departments*

| | |
|---|---|
| *Demographic variables* | |
| Size of population | 0.41 |
| Percentage of active population employed as small shopkeepers or artisans | −0.30 |
| *Economic variables* | |
| Density of retail food shops | −0.35 |
| Density of supermarkets and hypermarkets (1 January 1970) | 0.21 |
| Density of supermarkets and hypermarkets (1 July 1980) | 0.07 |
| *Organizational variables* | |
| Percentage of CDUC seats held by small shopkeepers and artisans | −0.24 |
| *Political variables* | |
| Percentage vote for Giscard d'Estaing in 1974 | −0.01 |
| Percentage vote for left parties on first ballot of 1978 | 0.00 |

* The correlation coefficients listed in Table 13.4 are based on the authorization rates for ninety French departments. Figures for Corsica and the Belfort territory are excluded as are those for two departments (Lot and Creuse) which achieved 100 percent authorization rates by voting on only one and three proposals, respectively. Including Lot and Creuse inevitably lowers the correlation coefficients; for example, it decreases the correlation between authorization rates and size of population to 0.29. Lozère was never included because its CDUC reviewed no proposals and thus had no authorization rate.

The 'size of population' statistics are based on departmental population as of 1 January 1979 and are taken from *Libre service actualités*, 11 July 1980, pp. 74-5. The 'percentage of active population employed as small shopkeepers and artisans' statistics are taken from *Recensement général de la population de 1962: résultats du depouillement exhaustif* (Paris: Imprimerie Nationale, 1966), Vols. 01-95. The 'density of retail food shops' statistics (number of retail food shops per 1,000 inhabitants) are taken from *Le Commerce en cent tableaux* (Paris: Ministère de l'Économie et des Finances, 1971), p. 105. The 'density of supermarkets and hypermarkets (1 January 1970)' statistics (number of persons employed in supermarkets and hypermarkets/population) are taken from *Le Commerce en cent tableaux*, p. 123. The 'density of supermarkets and hypermarkets (1 July 1980)' statistics (supermarket-hypermarket surface area/1,000 residents) are taken from *Libre service actualités*, 4 July 1980, pp. 55-61. The 'percentage of CDUC seats held by small shopkeepers and artisans' statistics are taken from *Libre service actualités*, 3 October 1974, pp. 18-19. The 'percentage vote for Giscard d'Estaing in 1974' statistics are taken from Howard Penniman, ed., *France at the Polls: The Presidential Election of 1974* (Washington: American Enterprise Institute, 1975). The 'percentage vote for left parties on first ballot of 1978' statistics are taken from J.R. Frears and Jean-Luc Parodi, *War Will Not Take Place: The French Parliamentary Elections, March 1978* (New York: Holmes and Meier, 1979).

national mean and all thirteen together have compiled an authorization rate of only 38 percent. This is, of course, precisely the sort of 'policy of equilibrium' which developers feared would result from the Royer Law.

An interesting if expected finding reflected in Table 13.4 is the fact that CDUC authorization rates manifest no correlation at all with departmental political behavior. What this statistic underscores is that — as was shown to be true during the debates over the Royer Law — the control of commercial modernization is *not* an issue that clearly sets the left in opposition to the right, but rather one on which there is considerable left–right consensus and some division *within* both camps.

One final fact concerning the performance of the CDUCs from 1974 to 1980 deserves some consideration. As Table 13.4 indicates, the combined departmental commissions began to assume a more restrictive posture toward development in 1977 and continued in this vein with remarkable consistency through 1980; after having authorized from 52.4 percent to 59 percent of proposed projects between 1974 and 1976, the CDUCs approved only from 40 percent to 44 percent of the projects presented between 1977 and 1980. One possible explanation of this phenomenon is that the renewal of CDUC membership in 1977, when the three-year terms of the initial members expired, brought in new members with a tougher anti-development perspective than had been displayed by their predecessors. Given the continuity of CDUC membership (most incumbents were returned) and the nation-wide character of this change, however, another general explanation would seem to be more plausible. As several individuals familiar with the CDUCs and commercial policy asserted in interviews conducted during 1980, the best explanation is probably that the stabilization plan or austerity program introduced by the Barre Government in late 1976 created an economic climate which many CDUC members viewed as both unfavorable to large-scale development and especially threatening to those small shopkeepers who had survived the liberalism of the 1960s and the economic dislocations induced by the oil crisis of 1973-4.[56]

*Ministerial* Tutelle: *The Political Spigot*

As noted in the previous section, Royer was intent on making his CDUC reform a measure of genuine corporatist decentralization. The role which Royer envisioned for the prefects and the minister was thus quite modest. He expected that the former would use their appeal power 'only rarely' and that the latter would overturn very few CDUC decisions.[57] As Royer's successor at the Ministry of Commerce declared in 1974, the law implied that the minister was to play no more than a 'role of correction and regulation,' reversing CDUC decisions only when they seemed to have violated the criteria for judgment spelled out in the 1973 legislation.[58]

During the first year of CDUC operation, it became clear that the provision for an appeal to the minister was sometimes necessary to assure the just treatment of cases. The CDUC members were often burdened with a heavy work-load, especially in urban areas. When many cases were to be considered, the state officials presenting technical reports were forced to be very brief and the project promoter was often forced to present his case in five to ten minutes. Some decisions were thus made in what seemed to be a sloppy and arbitrary manner after brief but heated debate. 'When a decision is made,' commented one CDUC member in 1975, 'it is a little like the end of a battle, there are the victors and the vanquished; it leaves a very disagreeable impression.'[59]

Despite the fact that the nature of the CDUC decision-making process has thus created many opportunities for prefects to justify appeals, they have tended to act in the restrained manner anticipated by Royer. From 1974 to 1980, the prefects appealed to the Minister in only a handful of cases, generally contesting less than 2 percent of the CDUC decisions per year (almost all appeals were submitted by project promoters).[60]

The behavior of the Ministers of Commerce, however, has not been equally restrained. At the end of 1974, the first year of CDUC operation, Minister Vincent Ansquer proclaimed that he had performed his *role régulateur* in the proper fashion: 'a little more than 10% of the decisions of the departmental commissions were modified by the minister. This figure is sufficiently large to show that, in accord with the will of the legislator, the last word rests with the state, and sufficiently modest for the departmental commissions to have a perception of exercising a real power of decision.'[61] What Ansquer failed to note was that, as Table 13.5 shows, he had overturned almost 30 percent of the decisions referred to him on appeal, including 32.6 percent of the rejections appealed. Some CDUC members were 'shocked to see [their decision] treated like a *simple avis.*'[62] One commission member complained that he and his colleagues considered themselves to have been 'treated like minors and irresponsible beings' and concluded that 'the orientation law is a lot more machiavellian than one thought.'[63]

Table 13.5 and Tables 13.1–13.3 illustrate that such protests failed to produce a reduction in the level of ministerial intervention. From 1974 to 1980, the ministers overturned a total of 14 percent of all CDUC decisions and 24 percent of all CDUC rejections, reversing 35 percent of all rejections appealed. In the year of peak ministerial activism (1979), moreover, 44.6 percent of all CDUC rejections and *more than half* of CDUC rejections appealed were overturned. In many such cases, the minister simply ignored an *avis* from the advisory *commission nationale d'urbanisme commercial* (the national-level counterpart of the CDUCs) supporting the decision of the CDUC concerned.

For the representatives of the small shopkeepers and artisans, this development was understandably troubling. In 1980 the national association of *chambres des métiers* (APCM) issued a formal statement charging that 'the multiplication of ministerial decisions overturning rejections pronounced at the department level ... contradicts the spirit of the law.'[64] Stronger language was employed in an APCM report of 1981. Here the association protested vehemently against the 'insidious reinforcement of the *pouvoir central*' and demanded that this 'abusive reinforcement' be curtailed, if necessary, by imposing a limit on the number of cases which could be referred to the minister on appeal each year.[65]

Reviewing the Ministry's treatment of CDUC decisions from 1974 to 1980, one must conclude that the 'spirit of the law' — at least as passionately described by Royer in the debates of 1973 — was indeed violated not only by the degree of ministerial intervention, but also by the kind of motivation behind this intervention. As Figure 13.1 illustrates with striking clarity, the Ministers of Commerce did not exercise their *tutelle* power with the sort of consistency which would reflect a simple desire to 'regulate' or 'correct' CDUC decisions in a technical manner. Instead, the Ministers used their *tutelle* power as a sort of *political spigot*, controlling the flow of commercial development at rates which varied with the electoral season. During politically sensitive pre-electoral periods (1977 and 1980), the spigot was closed tight, so tight in fact that — as Tables 13.1 and 13.2 show — the minister authorized an even *smaller* percentage of total proposed surface area and proposed hypermarkets than the CDUCs were willing to approve! On the other hand, during less sensitive post-electoral periods the spigot was opened wide, many negative CDUC decisions were overturned and commercial modernization was allowed to proceed apace. This was especially true in the period following the 1978 election. As Peter Gourevitch has noted, 'once the left's defeat diminished immediate political pressures, market forces were

Table 13.5 The Ministry's treatment of appealed CDUC decisions*

| | CDUC decisions appealed | | CDUC decisions overturned by Min. | | CDUC decisions appealed | | CDUC decisions overturned by Min. | | Appealed rej./ total appeals |
|---|---|---|---|---|---|---|---|---|---|
| | | | % Total† | % Appealed | | | % Total† | % Appealed | |
| 1974 | 162 | (36.4%) | 10.8% | 29.6% | 141 | (66.5%) | 21.7% | 32.6% | 87.0% |
| 1975 | 92 | (27.7%) | 9.6% | 34.8% | 73 | (62.9%) | 19.1% | 35.6% | 79.3% |
| 1976 | 114 | (28.4%) | 7.7% | 27.4% | 87 | (49.2%) | 14.0% | 28.5% | 77.0% |
| 1977 | 124 | (38.4%) | 11.5% | 29.8% | 104 | (55.6%) | 15.0% | 26.9% | 83.9% |
| 1978 | 136 | (48.7%) | 23.3% | 47.8% | 126 | (75.4%) | 37.1% | 49.2% | 92.6% |
| 1979 | 177 | (53.8%) | 27.7% | 51.4% | 162 | (88.0%) | 44.6% | 50.6% | 91.5% |
| 1980 | 212 | (50.4%) | 11.6% | 23.1% | 181 | (79.7%) | 16.3% | 20.4% | 85.4% |
| Total | 1,017 | (43.9%) | 14.0% | 34.7% | 874 | (67.8%) | 23.7% | 35.0% | 84.0% |

*Source:* Computed from the *RELOCA* of 1975–81.
† These figures are percentages of all CDUC decisions/rejections, including those not appealed to the Ministry.

**Figure 13.2** The political spigot: Ministry decisions from 1974 to 1980*

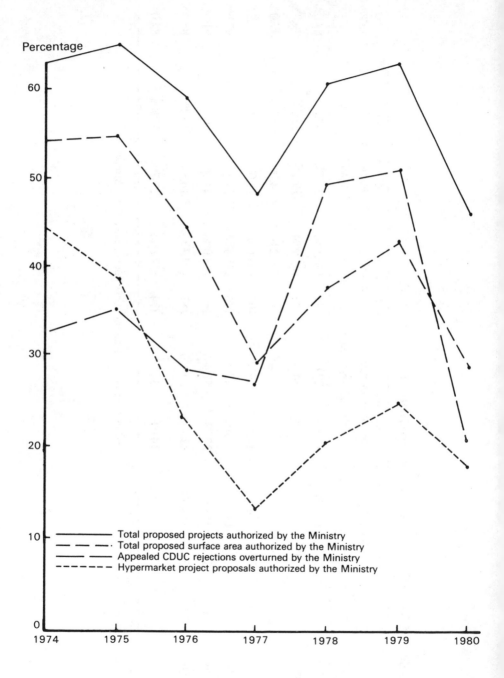

* Derived from Tables 13.1, 13.2 and 13.5

unleashed on French industry, leading to extensive closing of plants and firing of workers.[66] At the same time, the political spigot at the Ministry of Commerce was opened wider than ever before: during 1978 and 1979 the Minister overturned roughly 50 percent of appealed CDUC rejections and authorized far more projects of every dimension than the CDUCs had approved.

It is little wonder that many individuals affected by or involved in the Ministry's decisions gradually became disenchanted with the way in which the Royer Law was being implemented. As the former *Directeur du Commerce Intérieur* confided in an interview not long after the ouster of the center–right Government in 1981, the decision-making process became 'radically politicized' and it was clearly 'the calendar of elections which in fact determined the rhythm of authorizations and rejections.' 'I could only deplore' the fact, he added, that 'commercial urbanism was little by little diverted from its goal and that decisions were rarely predicated on considerations of urbanism, and even less on economic criteria, but rather solely on political concerns.'[67]

## 4. THE ECONOMIC AND POLITICAL IMPACT OF THE ROYER LAW

Despite the Ministry's 'regulation' of CDUC decisions, the mechanisms established by the Royer Law have had a profound impact on commercial development in France. Fewer modern stores have been opened annually since the implementation of the Royer Law, and those which have been allowed to open have generally been smaller in surface area than stores built before 1974. In the supermarket category, the average number of stores opened per year between 1974 and 1980 (262.0) was almost identical to the average for the 1969-73 period (262.8). The miniscule decline here can be largely explained by the fact that not all supermarkets are large enough to require CDUC authorization. Representatives of traditional commerce have complained constantly about this 'loophole' in the Royer legislation and have publicized the increasing number of cases in which developers have obviated the control process by building supermarkets with surface areas just below the limit of CDUC jurisdiction.[68] Nevertheless, the average annual surface area opened by stores in the supermarket range between 1974 and 1980 (180,248 square meters) was *14 percent less* than the average for the 1969-73 period (209,400 square meters). As one would expect from the CDUC statistics discussed earlier, the decline in hypermarket development has been far more dramatic. The average number of hypermarkets opened per year between 1974 and 1980 (24.3) was *47.4 percent less* than the average for the five years before the Royer Law went into effect (46.2), and the average annual surface area opened by hypermarkets from 1974 to 1980 (128,994 square meters) was *52.3 percent less* than the average for 1969-73 (270,240 square meters).[69]

Commercial developers have stridently protested against this 'artificial slowdown' in modernization, a policy which they have charged will inevitably lead to 'sclerosis of the French commercial apparatus.'[70] During the years of center–right rule, representatives of the supermarket/hypermarket industry repeatedly argued that the limits imposed on commercial development were not only unfair, but also in obvious contradiction with the major economic goal proclaimed by the Government: control of inflation.[71] It is doubtful that many of them were surprised by the fact that prices climbed at an annual rate of 9.8 percent during the first three years of the Barre Plan.[72]

It should be stressed, however, that the Royer Law hardly brought commercial development to a halt. From 1975 to 1979, the density of both supermarkets and hypermarkets in France increased at a higher rate than was registered in West Germany, where the economic slowdown and such factors as market saturation contributed to an easing of development. By 1979 French commerce had achieved second rank (behind West Germany) among the four major West European countries in terms of supermarket/hypermarket density.[73]

The small shopkeepers were not oblivious to this fact. Many spokesmen for traditional commerce in France argued that the Royer law had not only come along too late, but had been applied with insufficient rigor.[74] In addition, they stressed that the *petits commerçants* were the ones most severely affected by the general economic slowdown and the Government's austerity program. As the national association of *chambres de commerce et d'industrie* (APCCI) noted in 1981, the Royer Law had brought some improvement, but 'nothing permits one to contend that the reforms which have been implemented are sufficient to maintain the desired equilibriums by assuring the survival of individual enterprise.' In support of this assessment, the APCCI pointed to the fact that the rate of small shop closings had increased steadily over the last five years and that the number of *chefs d'entreprises indépendants* had continued to decline since 1974, the first year of CDUC operation.[75] Clearly, then, the Royer Law did not create the sort of shopkeeper Utopia often depicted in the literature of frustrated proponents of commercial modernization.

Nevertheless, the Royer Law did improve the status of traditional commerce in relative terms and it did bring about a *rapprochement* between the center–right Government and the *petits commerçants*. As the former *Directeur du Commerce Intérieur* confessed in 1981 despite his distaste for the CDUCs, 'one must acknowledge . . . that [the Royer Law] indubitably contributed to appeasing the *malaise* of commerce prevalent during the years 1969-1973.'[76] A good index of this attenuation of shopkeeper hostility is the fate of CID–UNATI since 1974. By 1976 the membership of CID–UNATI had declined to less than half of the 200,000 figure reached in 1972 and Gérard Nicoud was publicly lamenting that 'the Royer Law has demobilized too many shopkeepers and artisans.'[77] Since the mid-1970s, CID–UNATI has continued to suffer from a sharply reduced *raison d'être* and has become plagued by internal dissention.[78] Another useful, if imperfect, measure of the political impact of the Royer Law is the voting behavior of shopkeepers and artisans. A comparison of polls taken in 1978 and 1981 shows that the forces of traditional commerce registered a decline in support for the two major center–right majority parties of only 1 percent (51–50 percent) between the legislative elections of 1978 and those of 1981, a decline lower than that of all other middle-class groups: combined UDF–RPR support fell 2 percent (34–32 percent) in the case of middle management and white-collar workers, 4 percent (64–60 percent) in the case of farmers, and fully 10 percent (57–47 percent) in the case of executives, industrialists, professionals and businessmen (including supermarket promoters!).[79]

During the years of center–right government in France from 1958 to 1981, the movement for comprehensive or republican decentralization made little headway in the face of political fears and serious concerns for the integrity of the state and the traditional policy process. As Gourevitch has written:

Even the most enthusiastic partisans of decentralization acknowledged that it implied more fragmentation of policy formation, the possibility of divergence of policy among different regions of the country, conflict with the central government, and the possibility that partial interests would have their way. No one developed an argument that reconciled the tension between collective and particular interests as applied to local government, that is, an argument able to demonstrate that the common good can emerge from the pursuit of a series of local, hence, inherently partial, interests.[80]

The alternatives to comprehensive decentralization were not, however, limited to the simple maintenance of traditional or even modernized Jacobinism. As this chapter has documented, the violent and disruptive protests within the commercial sector during the late 1960s and early 1970s led to consideration of another option: *corporatist decentralization*. Concerns for the integrity of the state and the policy process remained, but in this case political fears worked not against, but in favor of, reform. Maintaining the electoral support of traditional commerce was a high priority of the center-right Government. Deputies of the majority thus listened sympathetically as Jean Royer developed an argument which — in the face of strong political pressure — seemingly demonstrated that the common good could indeed emerge from the pursuit of a series of local, particular interests. Devolving power for control of commercial development to sectoral representatives would, contended Royer, instil them with a 'spirit of responsibility' and allow for a 'humanized' modernization process which would maintain valued social 'equilibrium.' Moreover, it would permit the control of commercial modernization without reinforcing the power of the state. The other side of this coin was that the state would be at least partially absolved of blame for decisions which might be unpopular in the eyes of developers, shopkeepers or consumers. Royer discreetly refrained from stressing this point in public debate, but opposition leaders were less reluctant. Socialist Jean-Pierre Cot, for example, termed the devolution of power to the CDUCs a 'poisoned gift' (*cadeau empoisonné*). 'When things don't go entirely well after an implantation — or the refusal of an implantation — of a *grande surface*,' he asked, 'who will be responsible? The shopkeepers ... they don't really want to accept this formidable power which should, in fact, be exercised by the state.'[81]

It was Royer and not Cot, however, who correctly assessed the willingness of the shopkeepers to be incorporated into the policy-making process. With very few exceptions, the representatives of traditional commerce have accepted their charge and have been able, as they had hoped in 1973, to play a role in slowing down the commercial modernization process throughout France. An important political result has been, as Royer anticipated, a dramatic reduction of social tensions and a *rapprochement* between the state and the forces of traditional commerce.

The implementation of corporatist decentralization has involved, as the adoption of comprehensive decentralization would have involved, some fragmentation of policy formation, policy divergence from department to department, conflict with the central Government and victories for partial interests (harshly condemned by other partial interests). To some degree, however the center–right Government exploited an advantage of the corporatist form of decentralization — the state's retention of ultimate control — to mitigate the problematic aspects of these consequences, at the expense of some discontent among CDUC members. During politically safe periods, the Minister of Commerce opened his political spigot so as to allow for an increase in the rate of commercial modernization, thus partially resolving the contradiction between the CDUCs' 'mini-policies of commerce' and the Government's primary economic goal: control of inflation. At such times the Government came perilously close to treating the CDUCs' alleged 'power of decision' as a *simple avis* and thus reduced the mechanisms of the Royer Law to little more than a form of corporatized Jacobinism. During politically sensitive periods, however, the Minister and the Government perforce accepted the policy contradictions attendant to CDUC autonomy and enabled the development control system to function as a genuine experiment in corporatist decentralization.

## The Socialist Era

With the ouster of the center–right Government in May of 1981, new questions emerged regarding the fate of corporatist decentralization and commercial modernization in France. It was clear that the Socialist Party was divided on the issue of Royer's legacy. A sizeable faction of the PS had argued, from the time of the 1973 Royer Law debates onward, that the composition of the CDUCs was badly skewed in favor of the shopkeepers and should thus be significantly altered. Socialists such as Michel Rocard favored reform for reasons of principle, policy and politics. They had never been convinced of the legitimacy of Royer's corporatist commissions and preferred, as a matter of principle, to give locally elected officials the predominant role within the CDUCs while increasing consumer representation as well. Instituting this change, they felt, would produce policy benefits for the commercial sector and the economy as a whole; the rate of *grandes surfaces* construction would then be likely to increase, providing a useful contribution to the struggle against inflation. In political terms, this reform would broaden the Socialist Party's appeal by attracting the sort of 'modern middle-class' voters disgruntled with the center–right's capitulation to the neo-Poujadist demands of the small shopkeepers.[82] This modernist–republican approach to commercial policy surfaced in a number of PS documents in the 1970s, but it was not adopted as party policy during the 1981 electoral campaigns.[83] To the contrary, the program officially advocated by François Mitterrand and the PS called for *reinforcing* the obstructionist potential of the CDUCs and was patently designed to win support for the left not from the modernist bourgeoisie, but rather from the 'victims' of modernization.[84]

In line with the Socialists' campaign promises, Mitterrand's Minister of Commerce and the Artisanat, André Delelis, announced soon after taking office that he would not authorize the construction of any new *grandes surfaces* until 'a complete national inventory of [commercial] needs' had been completed.[85] What this meant, in effect, was that the Socialists would continue the center–right's practice of employing ministerial *tutelle* power over the CDUCs as a political spigot. The spigot was closed tighter than ever before during the first six months of Socialist rule, and Delelis left little doubt that this was done primarily to demonstrate the new Government's concern for the plight of the traditional sector. 'It is necessary to protect the weak,' proclaimed the Minister, for 'they have been subjected in the past to a veritable steamroller' of commercial modernization.[86] The 'steamroller' had in fact moved quite slowly from January to May 1981, as the Giscardian Minister of Commerce — with the coming election in mind — reversed only 31 percent (26/84) of appealed CDUC rejections and confirmed only 53 percent (9/17) of appealed CDUC authorizations. Nevertheless, Delelis did his best to bring the 'steamroller' to a halt; from June through December 1981 he overturned none (0/62) of the CDUC rejections submitted to him on appeal and confirmed none (0/14) of the appealed CDUC authorizations.[87] The leading journal of the supermarket industry lambasted Delelis as a man of 'simple ideas' and suggested that his title be changed to *'ministre du commerce . . . immobile.'*[88]

Delelis's image as a new Royer was reinforced when, in September of 1981, he announced that his Ministry was preparing a reform of the 1973 orientation law designed to achieve 'a more just equilibrium between the small shops and the large stores.'[89] Details concerning this reform project were unveiled in the early months of 1982. Among other things, tax laws viewed as advantageous for the *grandes surfaces* were to be revised and commercial competition between large and small units was to be 'moralized' by adding teeth to the 1973 law, certain crucial provisions of which had been 'neither applied, nor applicable, because they were not backed by sanctions.' As had been the case with the Royer Law, the most important and controversial section of the reform package proposed by Delelis concerned the CDUCs. In response to shopkeepers' complaints regarding the *'effets de seuil,'* i.e., the increasingly frequent construction of new supermarkets just barely smaller than the 1,000/1,500-square-meter limits to the CDUCs' jurisdiction, the threshold was to be lowered so as 'to protect small commerce, especially in rural zones.' At a meeting of the Conseil National du Commerce in the spring of 1982, Delelis announced that the new threshold might be set as low as 400 square meters — the level which Royer had originally proposed for the most sparsely populated communes in 1973. To those who protested against such a move, Delelis retorted that 'there is today a parliamentary majority, one far larger than the majority composed of the parties of the Left, which would support a lowering of the thresholds even if the government did not want it.'[90]

Ironically, at just the time that Delelis was portraying a tightening of the Royer Law as inevitable and imminent, a series of negative economic developments began to force the Socialist Government to reconsider its reform plans for all socio-economic sectors, including commerce.[91] Faced with an accelerating inflation rate (particularly troublesome given falling rates in other OECD countries), a swelling budget deficit and a deteriorating balance of payments, the Government shifted to a policy of 'austerity and sacrifice' in May 1982 and then proceeded, in June, to announce a devaluation of the franc (the second in less than a year), accompanied by a temporary freeze on wages and prices.[92] As the Socialists launched their intensive effort to contain inflation and improve the business climate, the visible impact at the Ministry of Commerce was twofold. First, Delelis moved — as his predecessors had done under similar economic and political conditions — to open the political spigot of commercial development. After having authorized the construction of no *grandes surfaces* during the last two quarters of 1981 and only a single project during the first quarter of 1982, from April to June he approved a larger percentage of project proposals than had the Giscardian Minister in the second quarters of 1980 and 1981.[93] Second, Delelis and his associates reluctantly placed their plans for modification of the Royer Law on the back burner.

After months of delay, the Delelis reform package was finally scheduled to be approved for submission to Parliament at the 1 December meeting of the Council of Ministers. Only a few days before that session, however, formal consideration of the Delelis proposals was postponed once again, this time indefinitely. In the context of a continuing economic crisis, Minister of Economy and Finance Jacques Delors — backed by the Minister of Consumer Affairs — convinced Mitterrand and Prime Minister Pierre Mauroy that the Government could not afford to implement a reform which would further impede commercial modernization and hence exacerbate the inflation problem. As *Le Monde* reported, the top officials of the Government began to employ an entirely 'new language' in discussing the proposed reform. Delors allegedly dismissed Delelis's project with the quip that 'one reform of the distribution system every twenty-five years is sufficient.' Meanwhile, one of Delelis's aides at the Ministry of Commerce could do no more than tell the press that the Government saw 'no reason to hurry' in implementing the reform.[94]

By March of 1983, when Delelis was removed from the Ministry of Commerce in a Cabinet shuffle, the Government had still not moved to enact the modification of the Royer Law promised during the 1981 campaign. Indeed, it appeared that the plans to go forward with such a project had been abandoned.[95] Along with many other ambitious Socialist reform proposals, the 'Delelis Law' had become a casualty of the economic downturn and the pragmatic response to it imposed from the Rue de Rivoli. It is likely that revised political calculations simply reinforced the position of the inflation-conscious Delors, for the prospects of attracting small shopkeepers to the left's electoral coalition had worsened considerably since May of 1981. All of the major organizations of shopkeepers and artisans, from CID–UNATI to the CGPME, had been alienated by numerous elements of the Socialist program (e.g., the increase in business taxes and the minimum wage, the shortening of the work week, the imposition of the price freeze) to such an extent that even the 'Delelis Law' now seemed unlikely to produce significant political dividends.[96]

As of mid-1984, therefore, it seems that the traditional CDUC system will remain intact for the foreseeable future. However, some key questions remain to be answered over the next few years. Will Socialist ministers continue to employ their *tutelle* power as a political spigot? Based on the experiences of 1981-3, the best guess is that they will; it will be particularly interesting to observe the impact of the 'political calendar' as the 1986 National Assembly elections loom on the horizon. Will the Socialists, who argued for the predominance of locally elected officials within the CDUCs during the 1973 debate, rest content with the traditional scheme tilted toward the shopkeepers? And most fundamentally, will the integrity of the CDUCs be preserved in the face of the Socialists' commitment to comprehensive, republican decentralization? The Government has already taken some minor steps to increase the involvement of the general councils in the development control process.[97] (See Chapter 8.) It is at least possible that the corporatist decentralization experiment, initiated by a government intent on preserving the Jacobin state in modernized form, will eventually be discarded by a government committed to devolving power in a comprehensive manner not to 'particular interests,' but rather to 'the representatives of all the citizens, that is . . . the elected officials.'[98]

NOTES

1. The citation is from Ezra Suleiman, 'Administrative Reform and the Problem of Decentralization in the Fifth Republic', in William G. Andrews and Stanley Hoffmann, eds., *The Fifth Republic at Twenty* (Albany: State University of New York Press, 1981), p. 79. For a list of recent works on the politico-administrative system in France, see the bibliography (pp. 239-42) in Peter Alexis Gourevitch, *Paris and the Provinces: The Politics of Local Government Reform in France* (Berkeley: University of California Press, 1980).
2. Gourevitch, ibid., p. 228.
3. Ibid., pp. 232 and 228.
4. See Pierre Birnbaum, *Les Sommets de l'État: essai sur l'élite du pouvoir en France* (Paris: Éditions du Seuil, 1977), p. 126; Pierre Birnbaum, 'The State in Contemporary France,' in Richard Scase, ed., *The State in Western Europe* (London: Croom Helm, 1980); Ezra Suleiman, *Elites in French Society: The Politics of Survival* (Princeton: Princeton University Press, 1978), Ch. 9; Suzanne Berger, 'D'une boutique à l'autre: Changes in the Organization of the Traditional Middle Classes from the Fourth to Fifth Republics', *Comparative Politics*, 10 (October 1977).
5. Gourevitch, *Paris and the Provinces . . .*, op. cit., pp. 60-3.
6. The electoral statistics are taken from Howard Penniman, ed., *France at the Polls: The Presidential Election of 1974* (Washington: American Enterprise Institute, 1975).
7. See John T.S. Keeler, 'Corporatism and Official Union Hegemony: The Case of French Agricultural Syndicalism,' in Suzanne Berger, ed., *Organizing Interests in Western Europe: Pluralism, Corporatism and the Transformation of Politics* (Cambridge: Cambridge University Press, 1981), pp. 185-208; 'The Corporatist Dynamic of Agricultural Modernization in the Fifth Republic,' in Andrews and Hoffmann, *The Fifth Republic at Twenty*, op. cit., pp. 271-91.
8. Edouard Leclerc, *Ma Vie pour un combat: stop à l'inflation* (Paris: Pierre Belfond, 1974), p. 65.
9. John Ardagh, *The New French Revolution: A Social and Economic Study of France, 1945-1968* (New York: Harper & Row, 1969), p. 103.
10. Berger, 'D'une boutique à l'autre . . .,' op. cit., p. 128.
11. Ardagh, *The New French Revolution . . .*,' op. cit., pp. 109-10.
12. Berger, 'D'une boutique à l'autre . . .,' op. cit., p. 128; Pierre Cortesse, 'France', in J.J. Boddewyn and Stanley C. Hollander, eds, *Public Policy Toward Retailing: An International Symposium* (Lexington, Mass.: D.C. Heath & Co., 1972).
13. On West Germany, see Helmut Soldner, 'West Germany,' in Boddewyn and Hollander; *Le Commerce de détail en R.F.A.* (Paris: Centre Français du Commerce Extérieur—Direction des Marchés Étrangers, 1980). On Britain, see W.G. McClelland, 'The United Kingdom,' in Boddewyn and Hollander; *Le Commerce de détail en Grande-Bretagne* (Paris: Centre Français du Commerce Extérieur—Direction des Marchés Étrangers, 1980). On Italy, see Aldo Spranzi, 'La Politica commerciale italiana: verso la pianificazione dell'inefficienza,' *Commercio*, 1 (1979); Suzanne Berger, 'Uso politico e sopravvivenza dei ceti in decline,' in Fabio Luca Cavazza and Stephen R. Graubard, eds, *Il caso italiano* (Rome: Garzanti, 1974); *Structures et évolution du commerce de détail en Italie* (Paris: Centre Français du Commerce Extérieur—Direction des Marchés Étrangers, 1980).
14. Berger, 'D'une boutique à l'autre . . .,' op. cit., p. 129.
15. Maurice Roy, *Les Commerçants: entre la révolte et la modernisation* (Paris: Éditions du Seuil, 1971), p. 114.
16. Ibid., pp. 114-15.
17. See CID-UNATI's statement in the annex of the *Rapport sur l'exécution de la loi d'orientation du commerce et de l'artisanat* (Paris: Imprimerie Nationale, 1974), p. 129. Henceforth these reports will be cited simply as *RELOCA*.
18. Roy, *Les Commerçants . . .*, op. cit., p. 157.
19. Gerard Nicoud, *Au Risque de déplaire* (Tours: Gilbert-Clarey, 1977), pp. 40 and 173.
20. Gerard Nicoud, *Les Dernières libertés . . . menottes aux mains* (Paris: Éditions Denoël, 1972), p. 41. Nicoud, *Au Risque . . .*, op. cit., p. 31; Berger, 'D'une boutique à l'autre . . .', op. cit., pp. 130-1.

21. Roy, *Les Commerçants* . . ., op. cit., p. 20; Jean Cluzel, *Les Boutiques en colère* (Paris: Plon, 1975), p. 114.
22. Nicoud, *Au Risque* . . ., op. cit., p. 70.
23. *Le Monde*, 7 March 1972.
24. *France-Soir*, 31 January 1973.
25. Henry W. Ehrmann, *Politics in France*, 3rd edn. (Boston: Little, Brown & Co., 1976), p. 233.
26. Berger, 'D'une boutique à l'autre . . .,' op. cit., pp. 129-30.
27. 'Rapport fait au nom de la commission spéciale chargée d'examiner le projet de loi (no. 493) d'orientation du commerce et de l'artisanat,' Tome I, in *Annexe au procès-verbal de la séance du 2 octobre 1973, Assemblée Nationale*, p. 62.
28. See *Journal officiel*, 1er séance du 2 octobre 1973 (Assemblée Nationale), p. 3974 (M. Pierre Lelong), and 2e séance du 2 octobre 1973 (AN), p. 3980 (M. Loic Bouvard).
29. *Journal officiel*, 1er séance du 2 octobre 1973 (AN), p. 3966; séance du 16 novembre 1973 (Sénat), p. 1745.
30. *Loi d'orientation—commerce et artisanat* (Paris: Ministère de l'Industrie, du Commerce et de l'Artisanat, 1974); Berger, 'D'une boutique à l'autre . . .,' op. cit., p. 131.
31. *Journal officiel*, 1er séance du 2 octobre 1973 (AN), p. 3967.
32. *Loi d'orientation—commerce et artisanat*, pp.33-7.
33. On the commissions created in 1969, see Roy, *Les Commerçants* . . ., op. cit., pp. 121-2; Cluzel, *Les Boutiques en colère*, op. cit., p. 114.
34. 'Rapport fait au nom de la commission spéciale . . .,' op. cit., pp. 57 and 64-5; *Le Monde*, 21-22 October 1973.
35. *Le Monde*, 8 September 1973; for the Carrefour announcement, see *Le Monde*, 4 October 1973.
36. *Libre service actualités*, 24 May 1973.
37. *Journal officiel*, 1er séance du 2 octobre 1973 (AN), p. 3979; see also *Le Monde*, 30 September-1 October 1973.
38. *Journal officiel*, 2e séance du 11 octobre 1973 (AN), p. 4307.
39. For discussions of the pressure organized by CID–UNATI during the deliberations over the Royer Law, see *Le Monde* for October 1973.
40. *Le Monde*, 30 September-1 October 1973.
41. *Le Monde*, 21-22 October 1973.
42. *Journal officiel*, 2e séance du 11 octobre 1973 (AN), pp. 4306 and 4308; see *Programme commun de gouvernement* (Paris: Flammarion, 1973), pp. 58-9.
43. Gérard Vincent, *Les Français 1945-1975: chronologie et structure d'une société* (Paris: Masson, 1977), pp. 235-6.
44. *Le Monde*, 6 December 1973.
45. *Le Monde*, 23 November 1973; *Loi d'orientation—commerce et artisanat*, p. 43.
46. Cluzel, *Les Boutiques en colère*, op. cit., p. 65; *Le Monde*, 21-22 October 1973.
47. *Le Monde*, 21-22 October 1973.
48. *Libre service actualités*, 28 June 1973.
49. *Loi d'orientation–commerce et artisanat*, p. 42.
50. *Libre service actualités*, 3 October 1974, pp. 15-20.
51. *Journal officiel*, 1er séance du 2 octobre 1973 (AN), p. 3977.
52. *Libre service actualités*, 3 October 1974, p. 20.
53. Nicoud, *Au Risque* . . ., op. cit., p. 106.
54. *Loi d'orientation–commerce et artisanat*, p. 45.
55. Nicoud, *Au Risque* . . ., op. cit., p. 106; see also *Cahiers d'information et de documentation* (CID–UNATI), No. 64, 1 May 1977, pp. 10-11.
56. Interviews with Pierre Forestier (CID–UNATI official and member of the *commission nationale d'urbanisme commercial*), Robert Castanet (of *Libre service actualités*) and Patrique Jault (the official at the Ministère du Commerce et de l'Artisanat responsible for compiling CDUC statistics for the *RELOCA*); on Barre's austerity program, see Diana Green with Philip Cerny, 'Economic Policy and the Governing Coalition,' in Philip Cerny and Martin Schain, eds, *French Politics and Public Policy* (London and New York: Frances Pinter, St. Martin's Press and Methuen University Paperbacks, 1980).
57. 'Rapport fait au nom de la commission spéciale . . .,' op. cit., p. 64.
58. *Libre service actualités*, 19-26 December 1974, pp. 74-6.
59. *Libre service actualités*, 27 February 1975, p. 14; see also the *Annexes au RELOCA* of 1976, p. 15, and of 1979, p. 27.
60. See the *RELOCA*, 1975-81.

61. *Libre service actualités*, 5 June 1975, p. 9.
62. *Libre service actualités*, 27 February 1975, p. 15.
63. *Libre service actualités*, 5 June 1975, p. 15.
64. *Annexes au RELOCA* of 1980, p. 20.
65. *Annexes au RELOCA* of 1981, p. 25.
66. Gourevitch, *Paris and the Provinces* . . ., op. cit., p. 152.
67. *Le Monde*, 23 September 1981; the original interview is in *Libre services actualités*, 18 September 1981.
68. See *Le Monde*, 23 September 1981; *Annexes au RELOCA* for 1981, p. 7.
69. The surface area figures given here are taken from the *RELOCA* for 1975-81.
70. *Annexes au RELOCA* for 1979, p. 28, and for 1981, p. 38.
71. *Libre service actualités*, 31 October 1974, p. 19.
72. Green with Cerny, 'Economic Policy . . .,' op. cit., pp. 161-2.
73. See *Self-Service 1980* (Köln: International Self-Service Organization, 1980), pp. 17-18, and the *RELOCA* for 1978, p. 20.
74. Interviews with Castanet and Forestier.
75. *Annexes au RELOCA* for 1981, pp. 5-6.
76. *Le Monde*, 23 September 1981.
77. *Le Monde*, 24 November 1976.
78. Interview with Forestier.
79. Henry W. Ehrmann, *Politics in France*, 4th edn. (Boston: Little, Brown & Co. 1982), p. 255.
80. Gourevitch, *Paris and the Provinces* . . ., op. cit., p. 117.
81. *Journal officiel*, 2ᵉ séance du 11 octobre 1973 (AN), p. 4308.
82. *Libre service actualités*, 7 May 1982; *Le Monde*, 6 April 1982; Volkmar Lauber, *The Politics of Economic Policy: France 1974-1982* (Washington: Praeger, 1983), p. 94.
83. *Libre service actualités*, 7 May 1982.
84. *Le Monde*, 23 September 1981.
85. *Le Monde*, 31 May–1 June 1981.
86. *Libre service actualités*, 20 November 1981.
87. See the *RELOCA* for 1982, pp. 67-8.
88. *Libre service actualités*; 20 November 1981.
89. *Le Monde*, 23 September 1981.
90. *Libre service actualités*, 11 June 1982.
91. For a discussion of the impact of the economic crisis on Socialist policy-making, see my 'Reform, Revolt and Retrenchment in Socialist France: The New Politics of Agricultural Policymaking 1981-1983' and the other chapters in John Ambler, ed., *France Under Socialist Leadership* (Philadelphia: Institute for the Study of Human Issues, forthcoming, 1983).
92. See Lauber, *The Politics of Economic Policy* . . ., op. cit., Ch. 6.
93. *Libre service actualités*, 14 May 1982 and 18 September 1982.
94. *Le Monde*, 1 December 1982.
95. *Le Monde*, 24 March 1983.
96. See *Le Monde*, 10-11 July 1982 ('Revoilà Gérard Nicoud'), 13 and 14 October 1982; *Le Figaro*, 23-24 October 1982 and 4-5 December 1982.
97. See *Le Monde*, 23 April 1981.
98. See note 42.

# INDEX

*Administrations de mission*, 160–1
Afghanistan invasion, 111
  attitude of Mitterrand, 114
  effect on union alliances, 231
Agriculture
  centre-right government policies, 257–9, 266
  decrease in numbers employed, 246, 248
  modernization, 249, 254, 257–9
  political influence, 245, 248
  political orientation of farmers, 248–53
  relationship with state, 253–7
  size of farms, 246–7, 261
  Socialist policies, 259–62
  survival of small farms, 247–8
Agriculture Ministry, 253
Aid to industry, 93, 94–5, 104
Alienation, factor in communist support, 62, 64
Army
  role in defence policy, 120, 123
  restructuring, 112, 120, 122
Atlantic alliance, 110, 124
  renegotiation, 111, 113, 115
Auroux Laws, 1, 9, 99, 182, 220
  offend small business owners, 137
  supported by CFDT, 232
Austerity policies
  adopted by Socialists, 85–9, 96, 217
  criticized by Communists, 51
  economic theory, 203, 205, 216
  effect on decentralization legislation, 197
  effect on economy, 103; commercial development, 287; steel industry, 93
  exacerbate industrial conflict, 9
  trade-union attitudes, 99, 232–3
*Autogestion, see* Workers control

Balance of payments, 82
  affected by austerity policies, 103
  affected by expansionist policies, 85, 101
  affected by rise in dollar, 86
  surplus possible in future, 11, 35
  under Barre government, 83
Banking sector, nationalization of, 91
Broadcasting, bias in appointments, 157
Budget deficits, effect of expansionist programme, 25, 85
Bureaucracy
  becomes more accountable, 29

  control by Gaullists, 22, 27
  control by Socialists, 5
  effect of decentralization, 175, 177
  links with political parties, 22
  natural conservatism, 152-
  politicization, 96
  role in economic planning, 22
  unpopularity, 180
  *see also* Civil service, higher

*Cabinets ministériels*, 132, 139, 150, 151, 158, 159–60
Cable television, 221
Capitalist system, 2–3, 6, 52–3
  and agriculture, 247
  changes in, 44
  Communist attitudes, 56
  condemned by CFDT, 228
  distinguished from state capitalism, 202, 203–11
  nationalized industries, 202
  Socialist attitudes, 135
Centre for Socialist Studies, Research and Education (CERES), 19, 24
  defence policy, 109, 110, 111, 117
Chemical industry, 93
  trade-union membership, 240
Chevènement, Jean-Pierre, 88, 90, 97, 109, 137
Civil service, higher
  attitude towards Socialists, 154–5
  changing role under Socialists, 96, 129–32
  Communists in, 47–8
  guardian of general interest, 144, 152–3
  neutrality, 153–4
  planning role, 188–9, 190–2, 194–8
  policy-making role, 144–6, 147, 148–52
  political control of, 155–61
  position restored, 139–40
  recruitment and training, 146–8, 149, 154
  reform of, 50, 147–8, 170
  relations with changing governments, 143, 144, 149, 152–5, 161
  structure, 149–51
Class structure, 44, 55, 138, 207, 250
  *see also* Middle classes, Working classes
Class struggle in Socialist theory, 137

Coalitions
 local, 67–8, 70, 73
 right-wing, 27, 37; disintegration of, 111
 *see also* Socialist-Communist alliance
Collective bargaining, 9, 98, 204
 effect on inter-union rivalry, 224
Comité d'Information et de Défense–Union
  Nationale des Travailleurs
  Indépendents (CID–UNATI,
  269–70, 273, 284
Commerce
 centre-right policies, 266, 270
 modernization, 268–70, 272; slowdown
  in, 283
 Socialist policies, 286–8
 *see also* Shops
Commerce Ministry
 control over CDUCs, 279–83
 under Socialists, 286–7
*Commissaire de la République*, intervention
  in planning, 192, 193
 *see also* Prefects
Commissions départementales d'urbanisme
  commercial (CDUCs), 270
 authority expanded, 271–2
 composition of, 273–4
 planning authorizations, 275–9
 relations with Ministry of Commerce,
  279–83
 Socialist attitudes to, 286
Common Programme (1972–77), 1, 8, 19, 23
 agriculture policy, 252
 collapse of, 229
 criticized by Communists, 52
 supported by CGT, 228
*Communes*
 Communist strength, 60–1, 65–7
 planning role, 186, 187, 188, 193–4, 195,
  197
 regrouping, 195
 relations with central government, 192, 193
 role and responsibilities, 172, 173, 178
Communists
 influence on Socialist theory, 134, 135
 civil service appointments, 157–8
 *see also* Parti Communiste Français
Confédération Française Démocratique du
  Travail (CFDT)
 austerity programme, 99
 relations with CGT, 23, 224, 225–42; at
  local level, 236–7
Confédération Française des Travailleurs
  Chrétiens (CFTC), 99, 140, 224, 238
Confédération Générale du Travail (CGT)
 attacks government policy, 32, 50
 co-operation with austerity policies, 99,
  217, 233
 links with Communist party, 43, 225,
  226–33
 membership, 236, 237, 238
 relations with CFDT, 23, 224, 225–42; at
  local level, 236–7

Conseil National du Patronat Français
  (CNPF), 8, 98, 227
Consensus politics, 20–1, 22
Conventional defence, 119–22
'Corporatist decentralization', 266
  267, 268, 285
 role of CDUCs, 271, 279
Crédit Agricole Mutuel (CAM), 258–9
Cresson, Édith, 259–60, 261
Currency limits, 137

De Gaulle, Charles, 22, 27, 181, 249
Decentralization, 5, 9, 104
 aims, 192
 background, 166–8, 198
 centre-right policies, 265
 costs, 174
 effect on economic planning, 1, 24
 election programme 1981, 83
 first phase 1982, 169–71
 impact of reforms, 175–9
 motives behind reforms, 179–83
 second phase 1983, 172–5
Defence
 in 1981 presidential campaign, 111–12
 policy dilemmas, 122–4
 Socialist attitudes to, 109–11
 spending cuts, 88–9, 119
 under Mitterrand, 112–22
Defferre, Gaston, 167
Détente, 110
Deficit financing, 204, 206
Deflationary policies, *see* Austerity policies
Delelis, André, 286–7
*Départements*
 benefits from decentralization, 170, 176, 192
 responsibilities changed, 172
Devaluation of franc, 82, 83, 87
 becomes inevitable, 85, 86, 88
 delay in, 102
 effects of, 215
Direction Départementale d'Agriculture
  (DDA), 189, 199
Direction Départmentale de l'Équipement
  (DDE), planning control, 188, 189,
  191, 194, 195–7
Disarmament
 as aim of Socialists, 110
 call for European Conference, 111, 116
 statement to United Nations special
  session, 115
 *see also* Nuclear weapons

Early retirement programme, 86, 220
École Nationale d'Administration (ENA),
  146–7, 151
 emphasis on economic expertise, 145–6
 reform by Socialists, 139–40, 148
 source of government members, 97
École Polytechnique, 145, 146–7
Economic growth, 44, 85
 Communist policy, 53

Economic growth (*cont.*)
  importance for consensual politics, 20–1
  importance for Socialist policies, 5, 6–7, 24, 25, 30
Economic planning
  benefits middle classes, 183
  during Fourth Republic, 22
  role of civil service, 144, 145–6
  under Socialists, 1, 96–8
Economic policies
  of Communists, 51–5
  of Socialists, 34–5; as cause of internal dissension, 5; austerity phase, 85–9; effects of, 100–5; expansionist phase, 83–5
  *see also* Industry, Nationalization
Economic theories, 203–11
Economy
  compared under Giscard and Mitterrand, 101
  compared with Great Britain, 202, 213–14, 215
  control by government, 2–3, 5, 37–8, 203–5, 207
  effect of Socialist policies, 100–5
  European comparisons, 100
  future prospects, 35, 36
  international aspects, 10, 25, 82, 85! 104, 202, 222
  international constraints on defence policy, 108, 113
  policy-making under Socialists, 96–100
  *see also* Industry
Education
  appointments, 157
  government control, 173–4
  reforms, 1, 104
Education Ministry, change of *directeurs*, 156
Elections
  National Assembly 1973 and 1978, 18, 23; 1981, 13, 43, 179
  *see also* European elections, Municipal elections, Presidential elections, Voting behaviour
Electoral system
  effect on Communist support, 42, 45; at local level, 66, 67, 68
  effects on election results, 33
  Municipal Councils, 175, 179
Electronics industry, 94
Elites
  in government, 96
  Socialist and traditional compared, 129–32
Energy, dependence on imports, 82
Environmentalists, 32
Eurocommunism, 18
  Communists' abandonment of 50, 53
  Communists' committment to, 45; effect on CGT relations, 23
European Economic Community (EEC), agricultural policies, 245, 250, 258, 259, 260–1
European elections

1979, Socialist vote, 32
1984, 20, 32, 33, 104; Communist vote, 10, 42; Socialist vote, 10; shift in balance between Communists and Socialists, 52
European Monetary System (EMS)
  dictates economic policies, 102
  French threaten to leave, 88
Exchange rates
  cause of France's economic problems, 82, 100
  effects of change, 215
Exports, encouraged by government subsidies, 93

Fabius, Laurent
  appointment as Prime Minister, 10, 131; Communist reactions, 1, 50
  control over nationalized industries, 91
  performance and reputation, 31, 35
  trade barrier policy, 89
  change in Socialist policies of 1984, 140
Factions, 30–1
  within Socialist Party, 24, 26, 108
Farming, *see* Agriculture
Fédération Nationale des Syndicats d'Exploitants Agricoles (FNSEA), 246, 254, 255–7, 259, 260, 261, 262
Finance Ministry
  Communists in *cabinet*, 158
  control over local fiscal officers, 175
  dispute with Industry Ministry, 149
  dynamic outlook, 146
  orthodox approach, 153
Floating voters, 33–4, 37
  Socialist dependency on, 4, 104
Fonds de Modernisation Industrielle (FMI), 92
Force Ouvrière (FO)
  increase in membership, 238, 239
  opposition to government policies, 99
Foreign policy
  Communist position, 50–1
  *see also* Defence

'Gas pipeline' contracts, 113, 114
Gaullists
  commercial policy, 269
  defence policy, 109
Germany
  French trade with, 213
  importance in Western defence policy, 114, 123–4
  missile deployment, 115
Giscard d'Estaing, Valéry
  defeat in 1981, 34
  opposition to decentralization, 181
  policy on industry, 83
  views on defence policy, 115, 121
'Global deterrence'
  in French defence policy, 120–1
Government
  control of state, 1, 10, 26–32, 35

relations with civil service, 144, 149, 152–5, 161
reshuffles, 13, 25, 30, 36, 104, 260
*see also* Institutional structures, Intergovernmental relations
*Grand corps*, 129, 146, 150, 151
*see also* Civil service, higher
Great Britain
economic comparisons, 202
nationalization policies compared with French, 101, 213–14, 215, 216, 222
*Groupe de travail*, 188–9, 190, 191

Hernu, Charles, defence policy, 109, 111, 112, 120
'Historic compromise', Communist Party, 42–3
'Historic retard' theory, Communist Party, 43–6
Housing construction, control by central government, 173
Hypermarkets
authorizations by CDUCs, 276
decline in developments, 283
*see also* Supermarkets

Immigrants
effect on Communist support, 77
in labour force, 85
*Indemnité viagère de départ* (IVD), 258
Independent nuclear deterrent, 109, 118, 123, 124
Industrial relations, 83, 98
Industry
Keynesian policies, 206
policy under Barre, 25, 83, 91
policy under Giscard, 83, 92
policy under Socialists, 10, 91–6, 103
restructuring, 90, 212–13, 219; effect on trade-union membership, 240
Industry Ministry
planning contracts, 91
control over industrial policy-making, 92
jurisdiction expanded, 94
dispute with Finance Ministry, 149
Inflation
decrease in rate, 35, 103
economic theory, 204, 216
effect of rise in dollar, 86
effect on Socialist government, 24–5, 85
Socialist policies, 87–8
under Barre government, 83
Innovation, places strain on government, 31
Inspection des Finances, 132
Institut d'Études Politiques, 147
Institutional structures, 10, 26–32
control by Communists, 47
economic theory, 208
Socialist reforms, 129, 139–40
used to control civil service, 155–61
Intelligentsia, reduced support for Socialists, 134
Interdepartmental committees, 10, 96–7

Interest payments, 102
Interest rates
economic theory, 204, 206
effect of American rates on French economy, 86, 87
Intergovernmental relations, 168–71, 172, 178
in planning role, 187, 188–92, 193, 194–8
Investment in industry
affected by declining profits, 102
economic theories, 204, 206, 208
promoted by nationalization, 90–1
Socialist policies, 82, 88–9, 95–6
*see also* Aid to industry

Keynesian policies, 5, 82, 83–4, 181, 203, 215
economic theory, 202, 205, 206
in ENA training, 145

Labour force, changes in composition, 240
Land-use, control by municipal governments, 173, 186–7, 188
Left parties
alliance broken, 19
disarray in 1968, 22
future prospects, 57
*see also* Parti Communiste Français, Parti Socialiste Français
Legitimacy of institutions, 27–8
Local government
Communist role in, 60–78
control by Socialists, 5
officials awarded pay and benefits increases, 174
training ground for left politicians, 23
*see also Communes, Départements,* Intergovernmental relations
Local taxes, 168, 172, 174
*Loi Defferre*, 165, 167, 168, 169–71

Machine tool industry, 93–4
Maire, Edmond, 231, 232
Marchais, Georges
style, 20
visit to Moscow, 50–1, 118
Mauroy, Pierre, 25, 129–30
local government background, 167
local government reform, 180
Socialist theory, 134
views on army reform, 119
Mayors
control over planning, 197–8; preparation of plans, 188, 189–92; restrictions in powers, 194, 195; role strengthened, 187; under de Gaulle, 186
modernizing force, 167
role changed by decentralization reforms, 176
Metz Congress 1979, 19, 24
Middle classes
protests against austerity measures, 87
support Socialists, 4, 104
Minimum wage (SMIC), 84

Ministries, changes in directors, 157
Missile deployment, 110, 116
    supported by Mitterrand, 112–13
Mitterrand, François
    acknowledges civil service loyalty, 159
    background, 15, 16, 18
    defence policy, 112–18, 122; meeting with
        Helmut Kohl, 125
    decline in popularity, 33, 88
    domination of Socialists, 15, 16, 18, 19
    independent nuclear capability, 110
    leadership, 35
    personal power, 96
    presidential style, 14, 19, 29–30
    Socialist theory, 134, 135–6
    views on Communist Party, 49
    *see also* Parti Socialiste Français
Mouvement de Défense des Exploitants
    Familiaux (MODEF), 252, 254–5, 256,
    259, 261
Municipal Councils, *see Communes*
Municipal elections
    changes in electoral system, 175, 179
    Communist votes, 61, 67–8, 69–75, 77
    1977, 18, 179
    1983, 20, 33, 61, 66; first round results
        influence government policy, 88;
        growth of right-wing support, 179

National Assembly
    occupations of members, 129–30
    relationship with Prime Minister, 27
National Front
    challenges left and right, 10
    European election results 1979, 32
Nationalization, 1, 3, 9, 83, 89–91, 105, 217
    benefits to middle classes, 183
    CGT support, 226
    Communist policy, 53–4
    Mitterrand's views, 213
Nationalized industries
    costs of, 25
    investment in, 90–1
    local role, 175
    profitability, 11
    state control, 90
    under control of right, 23
Neo-classical economic theory, 202, 203, 206
New technology
    economic theory, 206
    effect on economy, 53, 57
    government aid, 92, 217; compared to
        Great Britain, 220–1
    permeates all industrial sectors, 94, 95
Ninth Plan, 97, 98, 100
North Atlantic Treaty Organization (NATO)
    France hosts Council meeting, 117
    missile deployment, 110
    Mitterrand gives support, 112, 115
    rapid deployment preparations, 122
    relations with France disrupted, 119
    Socialist defence policy, 109, 124

Nuclear diplomacy, 112–14
    France's participation in, 115, 116, 117
Nuclear power programme, 32
Nuclear weapons
    Communist policy, 50–1
    compared to conventional weapons, 111
    costs, 118, 121
    exports, 93
    policy of Socialists, 109
    *see also* Disarmament, Independent
        nuclear deterrent, Missile deployment

Opposition, 28
    natural role for Communists, 63

Paris, base of Communist strength, 69, 74
Parti Communiste Français (PCF)
    attitude to defence policy, 116, 117, 122,
        123
    changes in strategy, 19, 45, 46, 48–55
    decline in national fortunes, 42, 43–52,
        56–8, 78
    historical developments, 42–3
    opposition to *grande école* examinations,
        140
    rejects social democracy, 23
    relations with agricultural sector, 251–2
    relations with CGT, 23, 43, 225, 226–30, 231
    role in local government, 60–77
    supports decentralization, 167
    *see also* Socialist–Communist Alliance
Parti Socialiste Français (PS)
    attacked by Communists, 46–7
    background and development, 13–15, 18
    broadens electoral support, 23
    class system, 134–8, 140
    Communist influences, 42–3, 134, 135
    composition of government elite, 129–32,
        140
    control over civil service, 155–7, 159–61
    control over institutional power structure,
        26–32
    future prospects, 32–8
    internal structure, 24, 29
    implementation of planning laws, 195
    local government base, 179, 198
    local restructuring, 68
    occupations of deputies, 129–30
    relations with farmers, 245, 251, 252–3,
        254, 255
    role in policy-making, 161
    split over defence policy, 109–10
    *see also* Socialist–Communist Alliance
Party system, 18
    and presidential supremacy, 29
    *see also* Political parties
Patronage under Blum government, 158–9
Pau Congress, 18, 24
Peasant society
    special place in nation, 248, 251
    support for political movements, 249
Planning, 186–8, 197–8

preparation of local plans, 188–92
transfer of responsibility to local level,
    188, 192–7
*see also* Economic planning
Plans d'Occupation des Sols (POS), 186, 188–
    92, 193, 194, 197
Policy-making, role of civil servants, 144–6,
    147, 148–52
Political commitment
    factor in Communist support, 64–5, 77
    of *cabinet* members, 132
Political parties
    benefits from decentralization reforms,
        177
    institutionalization, 26
    links with bureaucracy, 22
    relationship with ministers, 161
Popular Defence Force, 119
*Prefects*, 153, 176, 266
    appointment, 156
    control over commerce, 272
    control over planning, 188, 193
    embodiment of state authority, 180
    powers reduced, 169–71, 192
Presidency
    centre of power structure, 10, 14, 19, 28–30
    control of policy-making, 13, 26, 96
    power balance with Prime Minister, 27
Presidential elections, 37–8
    1969, 17, 23
    1974, 44
    1981; Communist campaign, 43, 45, 47,
        74; defence issues, 110–11
Prime Minister
    control of policy-making, 13
    post occupied by former civil servants,
        130
    power balance with President, 27
Privatization, 221–2
Professionals in Socialist government, 129–32
Profitability in industry, 31, 205
Protectionist policies, 87–8, 214–15
    middle classes alarmed by, 137
    supported by CGT, 223
    *see also* Trade barriers
Protest votes
    as basis for Communist support, 64, 72
    directed against Communists, 72–3
Public health, local government control of,
    174
Public interest guarded by civil service, 144–5
Public opinion
    knowledge of defence matters, 121
    on economic policy, 35
    on government performance, 33–4, 77
    on local government, 75–6
Public spending cuts, *see* Austerity policies

Rapid deployment force (FAR), 119, 121–2,
    124
Rassemblement pour la République (RPR),
    27, 32

Rationalization of industry, 90–1, 92–2
Recession, 21
    economic theory, 204, 206, 207, 208;
        development of state capitalism, 211–22
    effects, 6; on working class vote, 4
    *see also* Austerity policies
Reflationary policies, 25, 31, 215
Regional councils
    promoted by Socialists, 105, 167, 170
    role and responsibilities, 171, 172–3, 192
    under centre-right governments, 265, 266
Regional planning, 97, 172, 174
Religion, correlation with voting behaviour,
    250
Research and development, policies
    compared with Great Britain, 220–1
Right-wing parties
    inter-party squabbles, 37
    local politics, 177, 179
Rocard, Michel, 24, 46, 97, 110, 260–1
'Rogers doctrine', 119
Royer Law, 266, 270–4, 283
    Socialist attitudes, 273, 286–8

Savings, source of industrial investment, 93–4
Séguy, Georges, 229–30, 231
Shopkeepers, 269, 284
Shops
    decline in numbers, 269, 283, 284
    effect of Royer Law, 284
    under centre-right governments, 266
    *see also* Supermarkets
Social democracy
    criticized by Mitterrand, 135
    economic theory, 203, 206
    Europe, 20–1, 23
    opposition to communism, 109
    rejected by Communists, 54
Social policy
    of Socialists, 103, 137; Communist
        criticism, 51
    spending cuts, 88
Socialist-Communist Alliance
    breakdown in, 1, 10, 82, 104, 117
    Communist role in, 13, 14, 43, 48, 49–52
    Communist strength in, 83
    created on Mitterrand's terms, 14
    during Eurocommunist period, 23
    effect on trade-union alliances, 228
    effect on American defence policy, 112
    future relations, 36
    *see also* Parti Communiste Français,
        Parti Socialiste Français
Socialists
    attitudes to defence, 108
    background and development, 21
    nature of Socialist parties, 3–4
    opposition role, 22, 23
    *see also* Parti Socialiste Français
Société d'Aménagement Foncier
        et d'Etablissement Rural (SAFERs),
        258

Socio-economic structure
 changes in, 45; effect on Communist
  support, 55, 56; structure plans, 186
Soviet Union
 and French Communists, 55–6
 criticizes Mitterrand's defence policy, 117
 missile deployment, 110, 115
 model for socialism, 44, 47
Special reports, 160
State capitalism
 France and Britain compared, 202
 distinguished from capitalism, 203–11
 and the recession, 211–22
State structure, *see* Institutional structures
Steel industry, 93, 95, 240
Strikes
 agreement on by CGT and CFDT, 231
 encouraged by CGT, 50
 May 1968, 17
 miners 1963, 23
 nature of, 234–6
 trade-union role, 241–2
Supermarkets
 authorized by CDUCs, 276, 278
 increase in, 269, 283, 284
 opposed by traditional shopkeepers, 268

Taxes
 business incentives, 88, 93
 income redistribution, 4
 increases in, 87
 on shops, 268, 270
 reductions promised, 104
 *see also* Local taxes
Teachers in Socialist government elite, 129–32
Textile industry, 93, 240
Third World, 210
Trade barriers, 82
Trade unions
 austerity policies, 5, 32, 96, 98, 104
 decentralization policies, 182
 importance in Communist policy, 54
 industrial reform, 98, 232
 inter-union rivalry, 224–5
 links with left-wing governments, 7
 links with political parties, 225–6
 membership, 237, 239, 240
 role in centre-right governments, 8, 22
 role in Socialist government, 20, 99;
  weakened, 9
 syndicalist traditions, 4
 wage restraint, 220
 *see also* Confédération Française
   Démocratique du Travail,
   Confédération Générale du Travail
Transport planning, 173

Unemployment
 comparison with Great Britain, 219
 decline in trade-union membership, 238
 decline in Communist vote, 77
 economic theory, 206, 208, 216

effect of rise in dollar, 86
European comparisons, 100
increase in, 11, 83, 103
measures to combat, 84–5, 96, 104
public opinion, 35
Union pour la Démocratic Française
 (UDF), 32, 129
United States of America
 defence policy, 119–20
 economic policy, 117
 foreign policy, 114
 importance in Socialist defence policies,
  112–13
 trade balance with France, 213
Urban areas
 Socialist support base, 179
 *see also* Communes
Urban planning, *see* Planning
Urbanization, 186

Valence Congress, 134, 137, 159
Vocational training, 173
Voting behaviour
 agricultural sector, 250
 local patterns, 65–6, 72, 77
 predictions of future trends, 32
 shopkeepers, 284
 shows Communist support base, 65, 73–5

Wage restraint, 7, 20
 compared to Great Britain, 220
 criticized by Communists, 51
 Socialist policy, 88
Welfare state, 5, 6, 20
White-collar workers, support for
  Communists, 73
Williamsburg Summit, 116
Workers control, 24
 casualty of government's economic
  policy, 98–9
 Communist policy, 53
 links with decentralization policies, 182
 nationalization policies, 89–90
 strengthening of trade unions, 9
 supported by CGT, 233
Working classes
 Communist power base, 4, 19, 42, 63, 64,
  69–71, 73–4, 78; decline in support, 57,
  104
 decentralization policies, 182
 Socialist theory, 136
 support for de Gaulle, 22
 wage demands, 203

'Zero option' proposals, 113, 116